Vigilante Justice in Society and Popular Culture

THE FAIRLEIGH DICKINSON UNIVERSITY PRESS SERIES IN LAW, CULTURE, AND THE HUMANITIES

Series Editor: Caroline Joan "Kay" S. Picart, MPhil (Cantab), PhD, JD, Esquire Attorney at Law; Adjunct Professor, FAMU College of Law; former English and HUM professor, FSU

The Fairleigh Dickinson University Press Series in Law, Culture, and the Humanities publishes scholarly works in which the field of Law intersects with, among others, Film, Criminology, Sociology, Communication, Critical/Cultural Studies, Literature, History, Philosophy, and the Humanities.

On the Web at http://www.fdu.edu/fdupress

Publications

Peter Robson and Ferdinando Spina, *Vigilante Justice in Society and Popular Culture: A Global Perspective* (2022)

Joel Silverman, *The Legal Exhibitionist: Morris Ernst, Jewish Identity, and the Modern Celebrity Lawyer* (2022)

Matthew Sorrento and David Ryan, *David Fincher's* Zodiac*: Cinema of Investigation and (Mis)Interpretation* (2021)

T. Patrick Hill, *No Place for Ethics: Judicial Review, Legal Positivism, and the Supreme Court of the United States* (2021)

Caroline Joan "Kay" S. Picart, *Monsters, Law, Crime: Explorations in Gothic Criminology* (2020)

Elaine Wood, *Gender Justice and the Law: Theoretical Practices of Intersectional Identity* (2020)

Orit Kamir, *Betraying Dignity: The Toxic Seduction of Social Media, Shaming, and Radicalization* (2019)

Marouf A. Hasian, Jr., *Lawfare and the Ovaherero and Nama Pursuit of Restorative Justice, 1918–2018* (2019)

George Pate, *Enter the Undead Author: Intellectual Property, the Ideology of Authorship, and Performance Practices since the 1960s* (2019)

Victor Li, *Nixon in New York: How Wall Street Helped Richard Nixon Win the White House* (2017)

Marouf A. Hasian, Jr., *Kafkaesque Laws, Nisour Square, and the Trials of the Former Blackwater Guards* (2017)

Michaela Stockey-Bridge, *The Lure of Hope: On the Transnational Surrogacy Trail from Australia to India* (2017)

Vigilante Justice in Society and Popular Culture

A Global Perspective

Edited by

Peter Robson
Ferdinando Spina

FAIRLEIGH DICKINSON UNIVERSITY PRESS
Vancouver • Madison • Teaneck • Wroxton

Published by Fairleigh Dickinson University Press
Copublished by The Rowman & Littlefield Publishing Group, Inc.
4501 Forbes Boulevard, Suite 200, Lanham, Maryland 20706
www.rowman.com

86-90 Paul Street, London EC2A 4NE, United Kingdom

Copyright © 2022 by The Rowman & Littlefield Publishing Group, Inc.

All rights reserved. No part of this book may be reproduced in any form or by any electronic or mechanical means, including information storage and retrieval systems, without written permission from the publisher, except by a reviewer who may quote passages in a review.

Fairleigh Dickinson University Press gratefully acknowledges the support received for scholarly publishing from the Friends of FDU Press.

British Library Cataloguing in Publication Information Available

Library of Congress Cataloging-in-Publication Data

Names: Robson, Peter, 1947- editor. | Spina, Ferdinando, editor.
Title: Vigilante justice in society and popular culture : a global perspective / edited by Peter Robson and Ferdinando Spina.
Description: Vancouver ; Lanham, Maryland : Fairleigh Dickinson University Press, copublished by The Rowman & Littlefield Publishing Group, Inc., [2022] | Series: Law, culture, and the humanities | Includes index. | Summary: "Vigilante Justice in Society and Popular Culture offers a transnational investigation of vigilantism and its context across a range of eleven different jurisdictions. Focusing on vigilante justice in popular culture, this unique collection enriches the debate by adding the opportunity for comparison which has been lacking in scholarly literature"—Provided by publisher.
Identifiers: LCCN 2022017193 (print) | LCCN 2022017194 (ebook) | ISBN 9781683933540 (cloth) | ISBN 9781683933564 (pbk.) | ISBN 9781683933557 (epub)
Subjects: LCSH: Criminal justice, Administration of—Citizen participation. | Crime prevention—Citizen participation. | Vigilantism. | Vigilantes—Legal status, laws, etc. | Popular culture.
Classification: LCC K5001 .V54 2022 (print) | LCC K5001 (ebook) | DDC 364—dc23/eng/20220624
LC record available at https://lccn.loc.gov/2022017193
LC ebook record available at https://lccn.loc.gov/2022017194

Contents

Acknowledgments   vii

Introduction: Vigilantism—an Overview   1
    Peter Robson and Ferdinando Spina

PART I: THE ANGLOPHONE WORLD   25

Chapter 1: American Vigilantism: Popular Justice and Popular Culture   27
    Michael Asimow

Chapter 2: Vigilantes, the Law and Popular Culture: The British Experience   51
    Peter Robson

Chapter 3: Vigilante Frontier Communities on Australian Screens: Bushrangers, Bikies, and Bogans   79
    Lili Pâquet

Chapter 4: Vigilante Justice In Canada   105
    Rebecca Johnson

PART II: EUROPEAN EXPERIENCES   133

Chapter 5: Vigilante Justice in Germany   135
    Franziska Stürmer

Chapter 6: Vigilantism: The Greek Approach   157
    Nickos Myrtou and Stamatis Poulakidakos

Chapter 7: Vigilantes, the Law and Popular Culture: The Italian Experience   181
    Ferdinando Spina

Chapter 8: The Punishing Hand of Vigilante Justice in Poland 213
Joanna Osiejewicz

Chapter 9: Margins Without Justice: Revenge In João Canijo's
Portuguese Cinema 239
Júlia Garraio

PART III: A SOUTH AMERICAN PERSPECTIVE 265

Chapter 10: "You Said Perpetual!": Approaches to Vigilantism in
Argentine Culture 267
Sebastian Viqueira

Chapter 11: Vigilante Justice and the Rule of Death: The Existential
Threat to the state and its People in Brazil 295
Pedro Fortes

Filmography 323

List of TV Movies and Series 331

Index 335

About the Editors and Contributors 345

Acknowledgments

This book is the result of many years of research, writing, and teaching in the field of law and film and law and popular culture in general. Our mutual interest in vigilantism and revenge has matured over time, primarily because of the massive presence of this theme in popular culture and its undoubted ties to law and justice issues. Moreover, it is also links in with the political and criminological interest which vigilantism inherently entails.

This book has enjoyed the benefit of us presenting our researches in various academic settings including the session organized by the RCSL Working Group in Law and Popular Culture at the conference "Linking Generations for Global Justice" (19–21 June 2019 in Oñati), and a number of guest lectures at the Universities of Plymouth, Warwick, Wuppertal, Örebro, and Coventry.

The ideas and thoughts that have led to this collection have had the opportunity to grow and develop through previous essays in edited books and academic journals. We would therefore like to thank the editors of those books and journals for hosting those contributions and allowing their dissemination and reception.

We would also like to thank colleagues and students at our respective universities who have enriched and enhanced our understanding of the phenomena and sources through their participation in seminars and lectures over the years.

As the book editors, we thank all contributors for their enthusiasm and professionalism in responding to the invitation to participate in this undertaking.

Our sincere thanks go to Caroline Joan "Kay" S. Picart, editor of the Fairleigh Dickinson University Press Series on Law, Culture, and Humanities, for having embraced this project, as well as the editorial and production staff of the Fairleigh Dickinson University Press and Rowman and Littlefield for their helpfulness and support. Furthermore, we would like to mention the anonymous referees for appreciating the book and improving the final result with their punctual and useful comments. We trust that this collection adds to the richness and diversity of the scholarship in this field and may lead to further such enterprises in the future.

Introduction
Vigilantism—an Overview

Peter Robson and Ferdinando Spina

BACKGROUND AND GENESIS OF THE COLLECTION

Vigilantism was in the news during the 2020 US election. With the Proud Boys[1] and various other militia groups[2] the election was conducted under the shadow of alternatives to the quiet and peaceful operation of the rule of law. As events turned out, this, happily, seemed to be more sound and fury than an accurate prediction of post-election events. Following the defeat of Donald Trump and his allegations of massive voter fraud and illegal tampering with the electoral process there were not willful physical attacks on those alleged to be responsible. In the January 2021 Senate elections in the state of Georgia, the complexion of the Senate changed. On January 6, 2021, a mob sought to prevent Congress from formally accepting the decisions of the Electoral College to confirm the election of president-elect Joe Biden. These events and the threatening atmosphere, however, bring the whole notion of vigilantism to the fore and give this examination of "self-help Justice" a sharp focus. It is bolstered by suggestions that there is a spreading "sovereign citizen" movement which also rejects the authority of the law of the state.[3]

The genesis for our interest in vigilantism in popular culture stemmed from a concern with its impact on behavior and the implications for the rule of law. The hegemony of the United States and Hollywood and the problematic politics of its version of vigilantism in film had had a profound impact on British film. In crude terms, British cinema aped America in this subgenre and was a thing of fiction rather than torn from the headlines reflecting day-to-day issues in British society. The Italian cinematic experience, on the other hand, consisted very much of themes drawn from the social and political conflicts and experiences in modern Italy. The themes and concerns are linked to the fragility of the state apparatus and more recently to the dark legacy of the Fascist era. This led the editors to wish to explore across a wider canvas the contrast between the influence of the United States and Hollywood and the vibrancy of local culture. This unique collection documents a transnational investigation into a variety of countries. What emerged was fascinating. We have organized the chapters into three separate sections. We look first at the Anglophone world and the theme of colonialism between Australia, Britain, Canada, and the United States. The European experiences of Germany, Greece, Italy, Poland, and Portugal are linked by strong local narratives reflecting the distinct struggles between local autonomy and the central state with very different issues emerging. The book concludes with a contrast between two South American jurisdictions with their own focus on the local and regional.

On the one hand, we have at the heart of the enterprise American cultural colonialism apparently rampant in the films and overall tone of British popular culture. Colonialism in both Australia and Canada in its more traditional form has shaped the portrayal of vigilantism in these countries. Here the problems identified by the authors of those chapters stem from the particular operation of racial hierarchy which was central to the foundation of those states. The issues which feature stem from the conflicts between the colonial order and the colonized.

What we find, in almost all the various European countries, in contrast to Britain, are quite specific local factors which have determined what kinds of issues drive popular culture representations of vengeance. These are rooted in the local histories of each state and are remarkably diverse. As is noted, not all countries have marked traditions of alternative justice. In their own way, the accounts in the chapters from South America also derive from the local political and social conflicts within these two countries. Again here the American template finds little echo. We have then a fascinating contrast. While it is reasonable to suggest that the American hegemony determines what is likely to be seen across much of the world, it has a limited impact on the actual cultural products from countries other than Britain, and to a very minor extent, Greece and Poland.

Central, then, to our division of the ensuing chapters is the different impact of the colonial experience. The dominant cultural hegemony of Hollywood in the Anglophone world has led to adoption of its vigilante model in British cinema. It is clear from the British chapter that in this respect at least Britain plays the role of the fifty-first state. Elsewhere, the picture is markedly different in terms of popular culture albeit with a significant level of consumption of the products of Hollywood if not their message. We are conscious that our sample of countries is limited, however, and it will be interesting to expand the field of inquiry in due course to see which approach prevails.

REFLECTIONS ON VIGILANTISM

This collection focuses on vigilantism and its context across a range of different countries or jurisdictions. The chapters seek to locate vigilante actions within their historical and legal context as well as illustrate how they appear in local popular culture. Our starting point is the recognition of the proposition that popular culture both reflects social norms as well as shaping them. There is a rich and developing literature on this relationship.[4] For the purposes of this book we take this as clearly established. What is less clear is exactly how the reflection or shaping operates at any one time in any one place. We are hopeful that the chapters in this book should help to shed some further light on the relationship between vigilante action and popular culture. We start our investigations by looking at the distinction between the processes of the legal system and vigilante actions taken by those outside the strict limits of the law.

The relationship between the law's approach to things and that of those operating outside the boundaries of the law comes down to this. The justice system makes possible that there might be acquittal or forgiveness of the accused—the avenger does not but seeks only to punish. Most of the memorable pronouncements on vengeance seem to have stressed these limitations and the attraction of alternatives. From the Talmudic urging to live well as the greatest revenge to Marcus Aurelius' suggestion that the best revenge is to be unlike him who performed the injury a higher plane is reached from avoiding taking revenge.[5] Sir Francis Bacon, for his part, further acknowledged the attractions of revenge but suggested that one achieved more by avoiding this simple response: "In taking revenge, a man is but even with his enemy; but in passing it over, he is superior."[6]

You would probably not guess that this was so from exposure to the representation of revenge themes in popular culture. There has been some coverage of the general theme of revenge, vengeance, and the law in popular culture within recent scholarly and other writing.[7] It has centered on the threat to the notion of the rule of law of justice being enforced by means outside the established democratically agreed-upon codes. Within these broader fields of vengeance and revenge, there is a striking group of individuals whose actions themselves pose the most direct challenge to our notions of due process and legality. These are the vigilantes: those who operate outside the formal structures of the law to alter the course of events. Exactly who has been talked of in terms of taking law into their own hands is not quite standard within different scholarly communities.[8] As these chapters demonstrate, the emphasis has been different with emphases on groups or individuals varying. Although there is no "one size fits all" conception of vigilantism, nonetheless the phenomenon of actions of groups and individuals acting to secure justice irrespective of what the formal justice system has to offer is universal. The forms it takes are what distinguish the jurisdictions which have been examined.

POWER AND JUSTICE VIGILANTISM

There are two principal ways in which "vigilantism" has operated and it is important to note a clear distinction between these uses. One refers to the kinds of actions undertaken to preserve and buttress existing power. Here, in addition to often having influence within the structures of law making and law enforcement, those with money and position have sought to maintain their position against the rest of society by employing informal means of protection. Such "enforcers" discourage, for instance, union organizations of workers as well as nascent political movements. They are well encapsulated in Woody Guthrie's song, "Vigilante Man." In the scenario which Guthrie vividly paints, we hear of the hired thugs discouraging migrants seeking to escape poverty in the 1930s America. Guthrie calls on these "goons" to realize that they are acting against their fellow workers.[9] One could describe such users of force as "power vigilantes." At their most extreme form we find the paramilitaries of Colombia operating to support those in power and with property alongside the established forces of law and order.[10]

On the other hand, we have the more frequently encountered seeker after justice on behalf of the oppressed—the "justice vigilante." While organizing resistance through politics is one way of challenging vested interests this may not always be feasible. It is here that we find resistance to power in the form of extra-legal actions.[11] This is the world of the universal Robin Hood figure of history and myth seeking to defend and advance the cause of the exploited and downtrodden. Within this we find numerous examples of small acts of resistance to specific local acts. There are many examples in different countries of individuals and groups resisting threats to their way of life. These come in the form of resistance to the impact of technology on employment. Hence in Britain there have been clandestine groups such as those in the Rebecca Riots against unfair taxation and individuals going by such names as Ned Ludd or Captain Swing resisting the impact of industrialization.[12] Italy has Carmine Crocco,[13] while Switzerland has William Tell.[14] Other countries have their own local heroes and heroines.[15]

Modern-day vigilantes include individuals and groups who for some reason or another are either resisting the threats posed by change or lack faith in the legal system to deliver justice. Both individuals and groups have rather different motives. One is seeking to effect structural change through challenging the operation of the market or government initiatives. The others are concerned more directly with our principal underlying interest, how the formal justice system operates. It is this latter kind of vigilantism which has tended to capture the attention of filmmakers and producers of other artistic products. This has taken the form of bands protecting those suffering from whatever those locals in power are seeking to do—whether it is extorting money, harsh taxes, or eviction. The tropes common to the film versions of Robin Hood,[16] the *Seven Samurai*[17] and the *Magnificent Seven*[18] are a continuing theme. They are complemented in the Western film with one of Will Wright's Western typologies alongside the classical, transition and professional he writes of vengeance.[19] What is common to these portrayals is that they are all fixed firmly in the past. They thus escape the censure of those restrictions which have pervaded the world of film censorship of allowing "wrongdoers" and breakers of the law not to profit by their actions.[20]

More recently, in the past forty-five years, we have two kinds of filmic representation of the legal system. On the one hand we have the law film in which a lone individual manages to wrestle justice from a legal system which seems hell-bent on convicting the wrong person or denying justice to the victim. In Hollywood, from *Anatomy of a Murder* (1959) and *The Young Philadelphians* (1959) through *To Kill and Mockingbird* (1962), *The Verdict* (1982), and *The Accused* (1988) to *A Civil Action* (1999) and *Erin Brockovich* (2000), brave lawyers risk their reputations and ostracism by taking on the forces of the state or big business to vindicate their clients.[21] This has been the principal focus of much of the Anglo-American and European scholarship of the law and film movement.[22]

Complementing this apparent vindication of the legal system with its demonstration through individual brilliance, that "justice will out," has been a series of lone individuals doing the job of the legal system where it has signally failed to provide any justice. These individuals bring a form of street justice to the individuals responsible. They punish where the law has failed to do. They are the "justice vigilantes." Their names seem more euphonious and direct in Spanish and French—"justicieros" and "justiciers." They include those working within the forces of law and order who are hampered by procedures and protocols and have to challenge the system from within. There has been some writing on the topic covering principally the products of Hollywood and to a lesser extent the films of other jurisdictions. What we have not had, hitherto, has been a detailed look beyond the Anglophone world. Nor has anyone sought to locate the products of popular culture in the context of the specific jurisdictions. There is a world of difference, say, between Canada, the United States, and the United Kingdom in their ownership of firearms, murder rates, and incarceration levels. Is this reflected in the representations of the justice system and its failings in popular culture? What do the laws of individual jurisdictions say about those who do cross the line and do not "back down"?

VIGILANTISM—THE HOLLYWOOD TEMPLATE

The traditional approaches to vigilantism, drawn from Hollywood, suggest we live in a world suffused with random stranger violence. These images and narratives tend not to be reflected in crime surveys and statistics which make clear that those whom we should rationally fear are members of our family, friends, and acquaintances. These themes are allied to media concern with the routine malfunctioning of the justice system. Files are lost. The rules obstruct the way of "true justice" with public prosecutors and judges being obsessed with elaborate rules on what amounts to illegal search and seizure. The narrative conventions of the world of the dominant source of images, Hollywood, are simple. The state has failed an ordinary, identifiable, sympathetic character whose life we know something about. There is a family. Their happiness has been brought to a jarring halt. Justice is denied to them and if the ordinary citizen cannot get justice, what is to be done? The answer from the vigilante cinema of Hollywood is to "seize the time" or "take back the night." The clear implication of these films is that revenge as an option "works." The common final scene in the range of vigilante films is that justice has been effected informally and the world continues. Our *justiciero* has done what had to be done and the world can return to an even keel.[AU: The last 8 sentences are repeated later in the chapter, verbatim.] It is little wonder that the second amendment to the United States Constitution which talks of the "right to bear arms" has so many adherents since not only is there ever-present "stranger danger" but also a strong chance that in order for this to be dealt with individuals will have to take the law into their own hands. Life can then go on but the "evil" will be no more.

It is worth, we think, exploring this American "model" in a little more depth largely because of its pervasive nature. The cultural impact of American cinematic products has been a source of concern since the arrival of the "talkies" in 1927. In some countries, barriers have been erected against market penetration[23] as well as providing financial incentives to encourage films made on local themes with local personnel to protect the local film industry and culture.[24] The Hollywood vigilante model has developed over the past fifty years into a clearly recognized subgenre of the action thriller and enough common recognizable features exist to allow for spoofs and comedic "tributes" as we see in Westerns, disaster movies, and police procedurals with *Blazing Saddles* (1974), *Airplane* (1980), and the *Naked Gun* trilogy (1988,

1991 and 1994). For such examples in the vigilante subgenre we have *Gran Torino* (2009) and *Promising Young Woman* (2020).

The Motion Pictures Producers and Distributors of America (MPPDA), which later became the Motion Picture Association of America (MPAA), adopted a code on March 31, 1930, began enforcing it in 1934, and abandoned it in 1968, in favor of the subsequent MPAA film rating system. In the years between, up until the late 1960s, were the years when the Code (known as the Hays Code) and equivalents elsewhere were in full vigor.[25] Among the issues which the Code frowned on was the belittling of the legal process and any film where the perpetrator of illegal acts did not get their just deserts. Specifically, for our purposes, it was laid down that the "Law shall not be ridiculed nor shall sympathy be created for its violation" and "Revenge in modern times shall not be justified." Hence it is not until the Code has been replaced by a much less intrusive system of film rating in 1968 that we find films with principal protagonists working outside the legal system—people like Pam Grier's eponymous character in *Coffy* (1973) and Charles Bronson's Paul Kersey in *Death Wish* (1974). We are talking about the normal citizen, who if left alone by criminal elements would have no reason to strike back. The simple revenge theme has cropped up in a whole series of films where the original perpetrators are shown as having no redeeming qualities. Their crimes are done almost for sport as in *Sudden Impact* (1983), or *Eye for an Eye* (1996). Here the vigilante seeks to deal directly with a perpetrator whom the legal system has failed to bring to justice. The twenty-first century also has its variants on this theme in the first decade with *Death Sentence* (2007), *The Brave One* (2007), *Gran Torino* (2008), and *Law Abiding Citizen* (2009). Beyond the first decade of the twenty-first century, we have standard lone vigilantes making their appearance in *Seeking Justice* (2011) and *The Equalizer (*2014), *Revenge* (2017), *The Equalizer 2* (2018), *Peppermint* (2018), *A Vigilante* (2018), and *Promising Young Woman* (2020).

The popularity of the vigilante film genre which emerged in the 1970s can also be attributed to the influence of two societal factors that are well summarized by Scottish criminologist David Garland.[26] First there was the growing experience of crime among the middle-class along with the transformation of Western societies (first the U.S., then the UK, and others, like Italy too) into high-crime societies, and at the same time, the acknowledgment of the failure of penal welfarism and consequently the political and cultural consensus for more punitive policies (e.g., critics of Miranda rights, zero tolerance, etc.). With respect to these two social phenomena, media representations and crime films have played, as always, a role in representation of social change but also in the production and conditioning of it. These gave the films a certain contemporary resonance.

There is also the related theme of disaffected legal system personnel who operate in ways that do not meet the expectations of their superiors. One would include within this group "gung ho" police operatives like Axel Foley *Beverly Hills Cop* (1984) and *Beverly Hills Cop 2* (1987) and Martin Riggs in the *Lethal Weapon* series from 1987 to 1998 (1987, 1989; 1992; 1998). Again, the term vigilante has been applied to Harry Callahan of the *Dirty Harry* series with his cavalier attitude to the rights of suspects whose canon of work is discussed in some depth in Michael Asimow's chapter (ch. 1).

There are also elements of individuals operating in ways that are sometimes casually referred to as vigilantism but who are seekers after justice under personal psychological stress. There is then the vigilantism of personal justice which has something to say about the nature of inadequate law and a contrast with those individuals who tip over into mental unbalance and take on the world. People like Joe Curran (Peter Boyle) in *Joe* (1970), Travis Bickle (Robert de Niro) in *Taxi Driver* (1976), or D-Fens (Michael Douglas) in *Falling Down* (1992), whose inner rage explodes against the whole system. In this vein one might mention here the version of the Joker figure featured in Todd Phillips' 2019 film with Joaquin Phoenix as the eponymous protagonist. Arthur Fleck is a miserable, weak, and frustrated man who at one point explodes with rage, killing three attackers on the subway (akin to Bernhard Goetz in the New York subway in 1984). He is not exactly a justice vigilante but his act produces a violent social uprising, an anarchic rebellion against the status quo, the elites, and the police. We would not claim that the film *Joker* fully fits into the genre, but it might be seen as an interesting evolution of it in tune with the zeitgeist of Trump's America. The film has also produced scholarly debate, and is worth noting as it reminds us of the importance of private justice in contemporary cinema and public debate.

The Hollywood model of the vigilante film, then, is principally about what ordinary citizens do when the justice system does not meet their expectations and fails them. There are identifiable generic conventions that can be seen in the most important films in this subgenre of thrillers that center around a question at the heart of the justice system. This is encapsulated in the question posed on the poster advertising the film *The Brave One* (2007)—"What do you do when 'justice' fails?" The vigilante narrative involves the contrast between the normality of family life and the disruption that assails it and a series of events that befall the luckless family, resulting in there being a vigilante response. This vigilante response succeeds, allowing an orderly return to normal life. The opening scene of the modern vigilante film shows the protagonist in their natural environment. This is invariably an ordinary, decent family. We get just enough clues about the lives of the family to infer that this is a happy setting with a bright future beckoning. The family is going about doing ordinary, day-to-day tasks; shopping, for instance. In *Death Wish*

(1974) Paul Kersey's daughter (Kathleen Tolan) and wife (Hope Lange) have returned from getting the groceries and in *Law Abiding Citizen* (2009) father (Gerard Butler) and daughter (Ksenia Hulayev) are both constructing gifts for the mother (Brook Mills). In *Eye for an Eye* (1995), we see the excited preparations for a birthday party. In the most elaborate setup we see the home movies of the family growing up from birth through birthdays to near adulthood in *Death Sentence* (2007). Riley North (Jennifer Garner) is attending a carnival with her daughter and her husband when they are gunned down in *Peppermint* (2018). The vigilante movie introduces this notion of the family in both a traditional form with a wife and children as in *Eye for an Eye* (1995), *Death Sentence* (2007), *Law Abiding Citizen* (2009), and *Peppermint* (2018) as well as a proto-family of vulnerable workplace colleagues in *The Equalizer* (2014) and to a lesser degree in *Equalizer 2* (2018). Into this calm and ordered world there is a sudden and unexpected irruption of stranger violence. The violence is almost always irrational. It is usually unexplained. The perpetrators are evil personified. They have no obvious redeeming social features. They are killing for thrills. In the case of *Death Sentence* (2007) they are doing this as part of a gang initiation rite or they may be laughing "crazies" as we find *Death Wish* (1974) and *Law Abiding Citizen* (2009) or quiet, seemingly normal "loners" as in *Eye for an Eye* (1995). At best they are flagrantly irresponsible taking risks with innocent lives which we see in *The Equalizer* (2014) and *Peppermint* (2018). They are classic examples of "stranger danger" which statistics tell us are far less likely to visit violence upon us than members of our immediate family or people whom we know.[27] In the vigilante film, the essence of the perpetrators is that they should be in some way incompetent at evading the police and be immediately apprehended. They are charged and subjected to the rigors of the law in the apprehension phase of the justice system. This is the core feature of the vigilante film. The legal system is shown to have the potential to apprehend. This aspect of the law's operation appears in vigilante films to be in sound working order as shown in *Death Wish* (1974), *Eye for an Eye* (1985), *Death Sentence* (2007), and *Law Abiding Citizen* (2009). The problem is what has happened to the court system. The law then is shown as operative but also frequently compromised in the adjudicative phase.

The ease with which the malefactor is apprehended is in sharp contrast to the effectiveness of the trial or adjudicative phase. The conviction fails to materialize and the malefactor goes free. Plea bargaining or restrictive rules on the admissibility of evidence conspire together so that the malefactors are subjected to either no penalty or a mockery of what might reasonably have been predicted. Perhaps this is why the perpetrators are so casual about evading capture since they know that the conviction rate is so low and the system a joke. This theme is found in almost all the films in one form or another. It can include the problem of the adequacy of evidence (*Death Sentence* 2007). Other problems range from human foul-ups such as failing to provide the defense with DNA records (*Eye for an Eye* 1995), being unable to use DNA evidence to convict both murderers and having to accept a plea bargain from one of the accused *(Law Abiding Citizen* 2009), or a compromised prosecutor and judge (*Peppermint* 2018).

The initial reaction of the affected individual is to accept the situation and try and get on with life. The victim is not a natural revenger. There is more to life than feuding and revenge. Paul Kersey goes back to designing buildings in *Death Wish* (1974). Karen McCann (Sally Field) attends a self-help group in *Eye for an Eye* (1995) dealing with the loss of loved ones and her first thoughts are not of revenge. Erica Bain (Jody Foster), the radio presenter in *The Brave One* (2007), indeed, gets on with her life and returns to work. There is, however, an event that shakes the victim out of their torpor. There is a realization that something must be done. Unchecked evil raises its ugly head and our protagonist is forced to do something or is put in a situation where action becomes inevitable. Karen McCann seeks counseling for her grief and it is only when she sees the murderer planning and then successfully carrying out another similar crime that she determines to get a gun and avenge her own daughter in *Eye for an Eye* (1995). In *The Brave One* (2007) the victim Erika Bain finds herself in a convenience store that is being robbed and responds to the threat to herself and the storeowner. She does not seek out evil. It comes to her not just once but twice. Spurred by her unexpected confrontations with further evil she determines to put right the original wrongs she has until then borne.

Typically, the amateur victim manages to outwit the perpetrator whether it is nurse Flower Child "Coffy" Coffin (*Coffy* 1973), architect Paul Kersey (*Death Wish* 1974), museum administrator Karen McCann (*Eye for an Eye* 1995), or radio program maker Erika Bain (*The Brave One* 2007). They may turn out to have hidden abilities as a killer or be drawing on their hitherto hidden past. In *Law Abiding Citizen* (2009) Gerard Butler's Clyde Shelton turns out to have been a government operative, and Denzel Washington's Robert McCall has been involved in dark ops for the government in *The Equalizer* (2014). This is the basis for the success of the vigilante film, which allows a true thriller film to be operated within the framework of a moral revenge drama. This spells nemesis for those who appear to have escaped the clutches of the law. The perpetrators are brought down to earth in bloody confrontation. There is no opportunity for them to reflect on their past actions and to repent. Vengeance is exacted in a range of bloody ways.

There is a brief moment for reflection after the elimination of the "evil." This "final scene" is one which seems to valorize the actions of the vigilante.

The vigilante escapes the wrath of the law. There is, in many instances, connivance by the representatives of the forces of law and order to ensure that the vigilante escapes any punishment for their actions—from Paul Kersey, through Karen McCann and Erika Bain to Riley North—so that we are left to cheer the moral actions of the vigilante. Not only have they had their revenge on the perpetrator but also they have been allowed to return to their normal, proper, law-abiding lives. This ranges from simply surviving to live another day (*Eye for an Eye* 1995) or taking up the role of vigilante in a new location (*Death Wish* 1974 and 2018). Vigilantism by part-time amateurs works. The only vigilantes who pay for their actions, and die, are the ones for whom life is already ended—physically with terminal cancer (*Gran Torino* 2009) or where the ending is ambivalent (*Coffy* 1973; *Death Sentence* 2007).

These films have been and continue to be standard mainstream fare available in today's multiplexes. The directors of these vigilante films have also been major figures like John Schlesinger, Steven Soderbergh, Shane Meadows, Michael Winner, and Neil Jordan. These are directors whose work has been recognized both at film festivals and at award ceremonies as well as achieving major box office success.[28] The films had in the past and continue to attract such A-list stars as Kevin Bacon, Gerard Butler, Nicolas Cage, Clint Eastwood, Sally Field, Jodie Foster, Jamie Foxx, Jennifer Garner, Samuel L. Jackson, Carey Mulligan, Liam Neeson, Guy Pearce, and Denzel Washington. There is a consistent roster of Hollywood films over almost fifty years that focus on films which show that the system cannot cope and that the only approach is to settle accounts outside the formal justice system. These films start with *Coffy* (1973) and *Death Wish* (1974)—the original vigilantes—and can be seen in a range of standardized scenarios. This roster covers *An Eye for an Eye* (1981); *Eye for an Eye* (1995); *Red* (2008); *Death Sentence* (2007); *The Brave One* (2007); *Gran Torino* (2009); *Law Abiding Citizen* (2009); *Seeking Justice* (2011); *The Equalizer* (2014); *The Equalizer 2* (2018); *Peppermint* (2018); *A Vigilante* (2018); *Death Wish* (2018); and *Promising Young Woman* (2020).

The narrative conventions largely followed in the films, as we have noted, are simple. The state has failed an ordinary, identifiable, sympathetic character, but our vigilante has done what had to be done to achieve justice, and normality can return. This is in contrast to the distinct subgenre the "rape revenge" film, which has been considered extensively elsewhere[29] as well as in the context of their relationship to vigilante films.[30] The principal distinctions have been the relative obscurity, until very recently, of the rape revenge as well as their lack of engagement with the formal justice system.

VIGILANTISM ACROSS JURISDICTIONS IN THE MEDIA

What we seek to do in this volume is explore how this theme of justice denied but obtained through extra-legal means comes across through the popular media. Film and TV are our principal areas of investigation and we look at what has been produced in each country in the context of how the laws of that country seek to deal with those who take the law into their own hands. This gives us a richer and more nuanced picture of the material which we have asked our contributors to look at in this examination of vigilantes in popular culture. Such has been the dominance of Hollywood in film generally and in this area in particular that the template for analyzing vigilantism in its dominant mode is drawn from the United States, which we have noted above in some detail. What the contributions from other countries seek to do is to use the American model as a marker for comparison. This is complemented by a detailed examination of the actions of members of the forces of American law and order and their contribution to the culture of vigilantism. There are themes and issues which cross borders and are encountered through time which we find in the chapters of this collection. Some of these have extensive coverage such as the fate of the poor, vulnerable, and exploited whose position is often exacerbated by their economic position. This is a common theme through a number of the accounts. More recent developments have been noted in the role of women in relation to revenge, particularly rape-revenge which features in the chapters from Australia, Britain, and Portugal.

This volume is, we hope, the start of a process where the distinct accounts of more countries will be heard. Already in Latin America a project has been started involving Mexico and Argentina. Scholars from the Middle East are also now working in this area. In addition, we are in touch with other scholars working on individual projects in countries not covered in this volume whose schedules prevented them from contributing at this time. We do not have the sense that extra-legal activities are likely to wane in the near future, but as the contributors demonstrate, the nature of vigilantism is varied and the context crucial. Much seems to depend on the effectiveness of democratic institutions and the perceived quality of justice which obtains within jurisdictions. Some of the countries encountered here have significant recent experience of autocratic and undemocratic institutions and the need to seek justice outside the formal legal system and the link to resistance to oppression. On the other hand, others with longer formal democratic traditions are experiencing "democratic deficits" with confidence in the ability of the legal setup to deliver justice in doubt. The traditional myths and legends which are encountered and which resonate in the countries we examine here also seem to offer a key to the vibrancy of extra-legal activities. These are often mirrored in the kind of portrayals found in popular culture. Whether or not such portrayals are reflective or refractive is one way of envisioning the legal system[31] and this is a notion we address after looking at the broad outlines of the various countries' chapters.

VIGILANTISM—A THEMATIC OVERVIEW

The Anglophone World

The extensive variety of vigilantes and their portrayal by Hollywood form the central theme of Michael Asimow's chapter on the United States. He provides the background and a comprehensive overview of the emergence of various organized vigilante groups. The chapter gives prominence to the San Francisco Vigilance Committees of 1851 and 1856 when large numbers of people who were frustrated by crime and corruption took over criminal law enforcement and hanged a number of desperados. The San Francisco's Chinatown Squad of 1879–1920, a group of police assigned the job of law enforcement in Chinatown by any means necessary, is also discussed. Asimow then takes us on a fascinating tour of the many distinct kinds of films with a vigilante element. As he notes there are many different themes within the products of Hollywood with their extraordinary market hegemony. He focuses in particular on one of those identified in the popular imagination as the quintessential "vigilante," Harry Callahan, and how he chimes in with the frustrations of the average citizen. The *Dirty Harry* films were set in San Francisco, which is pictured as a pit of iniquity. The *Dirty Harry* movies glorify a certain kind of police vigilantism and transmit a strong message of political conservatism.

The multi-jurisdictional nature of the United Kingdom means that for Peter Robson's narrative he takes account of the ways in which "outlaws" have traditionally been considered. The notions of resisting injustice and revenge for such injustice are common threads through the history of the British Isles. Individuals who operate beyond the law are part of the myths and folklore. Both at the heroic and mundane level these themes are found in theater and popular literature, whose portrayals over the years have stressed the notion of "revenge." The limited number of films have focused more on the notion of securing justice with both local idiosyncrasies as well nods toward the "Death Wish" Hollywood model. Television has not been a fertile area for "outlaw" characters beyond the children's market. Those small screen "justice" figures encountered are presented principally in historical or comedy/drama contexts. The relatively small amount of actual vigilantism could be connected to the limited recognition of self-defense in the laws of all the jurisdiction in the British Isles and minimal gun ownership. The emergence of pedophilia-centered groups in the twenty-first century is noted as the most recent instance of alternative ways of citizens "dealing with" lawbreakers principally through providing information for the police as well as taking direct enforcement measures. Beyond this, though, there has been no appetite to enshrine "stand your ground" laws into British legislation on the American model. Nor has this apparent surge in vigilante action yet been reflected in popular culture.

The colonial experience of Australia as a prison colony for Britain between 1788 and 1868 means that the subsequent relationship with the formal legal authorities might have been expected to be fractious. In her chapter, Lili Pâquet focuses on vigilantism in Australian film and television by evaluating it through three very different examples, films *Shame* (1988) and *Snowtown* (2011), and the first season of the television series *Cleverman* (2016). Here vigilantism is contextualized through historic examples, mostly by white colonial settlers on Indigenous populations, and contemporary Australian laws around vigilante violence.

Pâquet takes the class division between convicts and guards and shows how it has played out in the cultural life of Australia. Anti-authoritarianism is inscribed in the Australian DNA. Delving a little deeper, we discover, alongside figures like Ned Kelly, "power vigilante" actions taken against Australia's indigenous population. The Australian vigilante is opposed to an ineffectual and prejudiced police force. In terms of film and television these representations have focused on vigilantes working with and empowering disenfranchised communities. These take place within the rural anti-idyll setting of the Australian Gothic. They reveal a very different Australia from the "fair go" egalitarian country of the national self-image. This one is replete with a perversion of "mateship" with car-focused masculine violent hatred against perceived threats such as pedophiles/gays. Most recently in a television series, the links between early and modern vigilante actions against indigenous peoples are made clear in a science fiction series which stresses they are all about negotiating frontiers. These distinctions are then replicated in contemporary Australia's burgeoning urban vigilante scene. The depictions though offer a possibility to reflect on the moral distinctions between criminality and vigilantism.

Quite special issues are raised by Rebecca Johnson in her coverage of Canada. She presents three legal stories—one that springs from the courts, one from the barricades, and one from the movies—that offer a window into the ways that the vigilante can be constructed as both criminal and hero. What one might expect from the civilized, relatively gun-free northern neighbor of the United States would be a contrast. The focus here though is on the struggles of various indigenous peoples in Canada. The conflict goes to the conception of law between indigenous peoples and the colonizers of Canada. Although Canadian society would seem to be firmly rooted in the rule of law and within a long-established and vigorous democratic framework, this is misleading. The clash between the rights and conflict resolution mechanisms of indigenous Canadian citizens and the more recent arrivals is thrown into stark contrast when economic interests are at stake. As Johnson shows, indigenous rights are only allowed to go so far. She illustrates this with accounts of the treatment by the legal system of infractions of the law and retaliation by different people. The impact of this different treatment can be seen most graphically in the range of films which she presents. Reading stories of "getting even" through a nuanced understanding of colonialism will enable us, Johnson argues, to stay with the trouble, open up space for other ways of being and knowing, and more actively question official discourse and legally sanctioned rules.

European Experiences

It is clear that in the countries of Europe which are examined that, again, very specific local factors determine the focus. The German context which Franzisca Stürmer outlines notes the provisions of the law in relation to those who act in self-defense and the role of motive in criminal acts. The German Constitution's recognition of the right of resistance to anyone threatening to abolish the free democratic order provides a rationale for militia actions. Vigilantism at the hands of individuals, however, is not deeply rooted in a German society with modest gun ownership. Reactions to such "self-administered" justice that has occurred suggest a tolerance which may stem from the rarity of this phenomenon and the fact that justice is generally administered under the auspices of the formal legal system. The experience of the S.A. in the 1920s and 1930s and their role in the rise of Hitler mean that such paramilitary activities have been absent until the very recent past. Their reemergence is linked to the rise in right-wing extremism and anti-immigrant politics expressed in street patrols. A distinction is made between these recent developments and the tactics of the RAF (Red Army Fraction) with their targeting of various prominent individuals in the capitalist order. The historical context is explored and the mythology of heroic figures noted. The portrayal of such individuals and actions has centered round myths and legends from the past such as the *Nibelungenlied* and later portrayals of the links between moral right and power in social relations. Self-administered justice continues as a theme in contemporary fiction, cinema, and TV where, among other things, the role of social media is explored, although as noted, it is a minor issue, hitherto in contemporary German society.

Nickos Myrtou and Stamatis Poulakidakos start their chapter on Greece by noting the differences between vigilantism dealing with control of crime, social groups, and regimes. They observe that vigilantism has both a history in Greek society through vendettas as well as finding expression there currently in the context of immigration. They explore the emergence of vigilantism and its relationship to ineffective nascent state power as opposed to the breakdown of established civic norms. They locate the Greek view of vigilantism within the Greek tradition of honor and vengeance. This they link firmly to the patriarchal nature of such concepts in practice. This finds expression in the notion of honor and the respect issues, for example, surrounding the solo dance, *Zeibebekiko*. This has been taken up extensively in Greek cinema along with other issues touching on the reclaiming of honor through violence. Despite the legal framework that controls and prosecutes vigilantism, its representations in the Greek popular culture attempt to "legalize" acts of violence as "manly" and "ethical," acting as mechanisms of social training to promote mainly, but not exclusively, patriarchal values. However, Myrtou and Poulakidakos observe that these concepts also find expression with a female actor in the mold of Antigone. This slight shift is also encountered in their examination of how television has dealt with issues of revenge including for rape.

In the historical and cultural development of modern Italian society, Ferdinando Spina observes a continuous ambivalence over the boundaries between state justice and private justice. In the first part of his chapter, Spina outlines some examples of the different patterns of private justice, whether individual or in groups, which can be traced in Italian history from Unification to the present day. In the second part, he reviews the themes of vendetta and do-it-yourself justice in Italian literature, theater, cinema, and television. For Italian popular culture, the vigilante hero is ultimately a loser, and this is the most striking difference with respect to the American popular culture. Spina notes the link between the "self-help" justice and the fragility of the state, the high level of social conflict and the failure of the legal system. In the past, this ambivalence has favored the emergence of the Fascist "squadrismo," a phenomenon that still raises concern in recent years, since some episodes of vigilantism have occurred against immigrants. Overall, he concludes that in Italian society private justice has been generally condemned and controlled yet sometimes accepted and tolerated.

The long and convoluted history of Poland provides the setting for Joanna Osiejewicz's account of how early state-sanctioned self-help for debts developed. Much more organized extra-legal actions, such as popular uprisings against those who had seized power and were deemed traitors by the mob, are found in Poland's turbulent history in the eighteenth and nineteenth centuries. Examples are encountered in the twentieth century of communal actions against criminals where the courts dealt leniently with the vigilantes. Various recent events of "community justice" are also recorded but they occur on a spasmodic basis. The incidents call to mind the events in Fuenteovejuna.[32] The most frequent recent occurrences have been minor disputes centered around parking of vehicles. After looking at the legal recognition to various extra-legal actions, Osiejewicz focuses on the representations of vigilante actions in Polish cinema noting that they have generally been based on real life both in the past and in the present. There is one example of a fictional lone vigilante on the American model in a rape revenge film. Both individual and group vigilantism is encountered extensively in Polish literature, although it is not a major issue in Polish society. The chapter concludes emphasizing the link between violence and the health of the institutions of society.

The quite distinct development of Portugal is addressed by Julia Garraio who notes, in contrast, the absence of a tradition of vigilante actions in that society. Portugal ranks after Iceland and New Zealand in terms of being a peaceful place. This links to an extent to the official narrative of the pre-1974 image put out by the *Estado Novo* dictatorship following the coup d'état of 1926. This, though, is a paradoxical situation. There are, nonetheless, in Portugal, acts taken by individuals attempting to enact their own rule of law or sense of morality. Garraio outlines the nature of extra-legal actions and their political context in perceptions of insecurity, violence, and crime that exist among large sectors of Portuguese society. They take the law into their own hands. These instances of "self-help" have been the focus of the film-maker João Canijo. Garraio takes us through his films with their focus on the peripheries and margins of Portuguese society. These films demonstrate how the characters in Canijo's films when faced with injustice or crime do not turn to the community or state institutions but take matters into their own hands. They have a lack of trust in the established order and its institutions. The director's camerawork and aesthetics empathize with the characters' loneliness and helplessness, constructing them as bare bodies trying to survive in a violent society marked by deep social and gendered inequalities and pervasive forms of exploitation. The films also reveal female agency, albeit alongside powerlessness. All this in a country which has seen a recent marked decline in political participation and erosion of confidence in democracy.

A South American Perspective

What links the chapters from Argentina and Brazil is not simply their geographical proximity but their common experience of the fragility of the state and its reach. In his account of Argentina, Sebastian Viqueira notes that there have been extensive interruptions in the rule of law in that country as with much of Latin America. There are differences, however, from Mexico and Brazil, with their *autodefensas* and death squads. The specific factors in Argentina have been special crimes and trigger events. He explores the notion of the "pedagogy of cruelty" developed by Segato and its link to gender. This in turn is affected by the specifics of the environment and the generalized feeling of insecurity within Argentina. In the light of this, vigilante actions can be experienced as political. Viqueira illustrates the principal form vigilantism takes by looking at some individual cases, collective actions, and the role of those involved in law enforcement. The response of the Penal Code to these activities can be characterized as benevolent. It is clear that much depends on the specific approaches to the changing judicial role in Argentina with challenges to legalism and the increased role of juries. The chapter concludes with an examination of the critical way in which vigilantism has been presented in the press and popular culture. Negative images of the operation of the rule of law and legal institutions and official tolerance toward certain forms of vigilantism mean that the insecurity engendered by the mass media contributes to the increase in actions taken beyond the law.

The situation in Brazil which Pedro Fortes describes involves a tension between the rule of law and the endorsement of extrajudicial executions. As he explains, there is a range of informal justice providers which are specific to Brazil. Alongside hired killers and criminal gangs there are death squads and militias. These operate where the state rule of law is absent. This is a divided state, in which the central areas of cities and wealthy neighborhoods are shaped by the rule of law, constitutional rights, and political freedoms, but the peripheral areas are subject to the exercise of violent power by hired killers, death squads, organized crime, and militias. In this context, in place of the rule of law, Fortes typifies these areas as dominated by the rule of death. The extensive number of violent deaths along with those carried out by the police provide the context for observing that the formal rules in relation to murder prosecutions involve minimal evidential rules. This allows wide scope for defense arguments in favor of vigilante justice expressed in the phrase "a good bandit is a dead bandit" ("bandido bom é bandido morto"). The corrupted nature of the legal institutions then is key. As Fortes notes, the images which emerge in popular culture are modified in their production and interpretation. Those which concern extra-legal activity in Brazil have been extensive in film, literature, and TV. The threat of real life vigilantism is heightened, Fortes points out, where there is this climate of political polarization.

CONCLUDING REMARKS

What is particularly revealing about these chapters from around the world is the way in which a commonly encountered notion like "vigilante" has very different resonances within the different cultures covered. The powerful influence of the global phenomenon that is Hollywood provides us with a template which we might reasonably imagine as totally representative of the issues and conflicts which give rise to extra-legal actions. The individual legal constraints and historical contexts, however, vary producing distinct local cultural products reflecting these rather than what might be expected under American hegemony. In answer to our initial query about the British and Italian experience it seems clear that the focus of the latter on the locally inspired narrative is the more common experience. Britain, and to a much lesser extent Greece and Poland, are out of step with many of those other countries which engage with vigilantism in its adherence to a fictionalized stranger danger model. That said, the material from Germany and Portugal suggest that vigilantism may not be quite as pervasive as was first assumed.

Finally, the question whether or not any portrayals are reflective or refractive, in the sense that they support the status quo or challenge it, depends not so much on whether the vigilantism is "power" or "justice" but how such actions are framed. The "goons" we see, for instance, in *The Molly Maguires*,[33] may be "power" vigilantes but in the context of the story of the response to attempts to organize and protect workers their actions are seen for what they are. Hence, although we see here "power" vigilantism at work, what is highlighted is the injustice and oppression at work in the economic system. The problem is not just a few bad apples but the whole rotten structure.

As far as support for the status quo is concerned, this depends on whether the identified issue is a systemic one. Hence, it is perfectly possible to see films like *Death Sentence*[34] and *The Brave One*[35] as involving responses to a small group of anti-social individuals within a largely acceptable social environment. This is stressed by the "happy family" context in which the random stranger violence occurs. There is no wide-ranging critique of society although the justice system is almost always flawed. Few of the "justice" vigilante films involve a social critique or imply a broader social malaise. The theme and ending of *Seeking Justice*,[36] with all elements of society suffused with corruption, however, chimes in with modern American notions of conspiracy theories which threaten to pervade society through the expansion of the internet and social media.

Whether being supportive of the status quo, casting a critical light on society or merely critiquing elements of it, the vigilante experience has no standard political meaning across different jurisdictions. As the chapters in this book demonstrate, popular culture and especially the modern media, cinema, and TV, reports on vigilantism and private justice only feature in democratic jurisdictions. We see this explicitly in relation to Italy, Poland, Greece, Portugal, Germany, and Argentina. Under dictatorships there are cases of private justice and there are undoubtedly serious episodes of vigilantism, but they are not part of public discourse.

What these chapters demonstrate is that the language and terminology may be shared but the impact and nature depend on the historical and geographical context. Vigilantism has always been a complex issue. The chapters assembled here enrich the debate by adding the opportunity for comparison which has been largely lacking in scholarly debate hitherto. What people think of as significant when they talk of people taking the law in to their own hands conjures up very different images depending on where one is. The memorable Hollywood image of a lone figure taking to the streets with gun in hand to cleanse society of anti-social elements is but one part of the story which these chapters have shown.

NOTES

1. "Who Are the Proud Boys? A Brit's Guide to the Far-Right Group Trump Refuses to Condemn," HuffPost UK, September 30, 2020, https://www.huffingtonpost.co.uk/entry/trump-proud-boys-presidential-debate-2020_uk_5f7437e6c5b66377b27ad2d7.

2. "Michigan 'Plot': Who Are the US Militia Groups?," *BBC News*, October 9, 2020, sec. US and Canada, https://www.bbc.com/news/world-us-canada-54483973.

3. "What Is the 'Sovereign Citizen' Movement?," *BBC News*, August 5, 2020, sec. US and Canada, https://www.bbc.com/news/world-us-canada-53654318. Anti-government activists who believe they are immune from the law are a worldwide threat, experts say.

4. Julie D'Acci, "Television, Representation and Gender," in *The Television Studies Reader*, ed. Robert Clyde Allen and Annette Hill (London; New York: Routledge, 2004), 373–88; Stefan Machura, "Media Influence on the Perception of the Legal System," in *Understanding Law in Society: Developments in Socio-Legal Studies*, ed. Knut Papendorf, Stefan Machura, and Kristian (Berlin: LIT, 2011), 239–83; Kimberlianne Podlas, "Testing Television: Studying and Understanding the Impact of Television's Depictions of Law and Justice," in *Law and Justice on the Small Screen*, ed. Peter Robson and Jessica Silbey (Oxford; Portland, OR: Hart Pub, 2012), 87–110; Peter Robson, Guy Osborn, and Steve Greenfield, "The Impact of Film and Television on Perceptions of Law and Justice: Towards a Realisable Methodology," in *Law, Culture and Visual Studies*, ed. Anne Wagner and Richard K. Sherwin (Dordrecht: Springer, 2014), 1011–28.

5. Marcus Aurelius, "Meditations on Stoic Philosophy," (170–80) in *Meditations*, ed. Martin Hammond (Uxbridge, Harmondsworth: Penguin, 2006).

6. Francis Bacon, "On Revenge," (1625) in *The Essays*, ed. John Pitcher, Penguin Classics (Uxbridge, Harmondsworth: Penguin, 1985).

7. H. Jon Rosenbaum and Peter C. Sederberg, eds., *Vigilante Politics* (Philadelphia: University of Pennsylvania Press, 1976); Ray Abrahams, *Vigilant Citizens: Vigilantism and the State* (Cambridge: Polity Press, 1998); William E. Burrows, *Vigilante!* (New York: Harcourt Brace Jovanovich, 1976); Les Johnston, "What Is Vigilantism?," *The British Journal of Criminology* 36, no. 2 (1996): 220–36; Peter Robson, "Vengeance in Popular Culture," in *Oxford Encyclopedia of Crime, Media, and Popular Culture*, December 22, 2016, http://criminology.oxfordre.com/view/10.1093/acrefore/9780190264079.001.0001/acrefore-9780190264079-e-45; Peter Robson, "Beyond the Courtroom—Vigilantism, Revenge and Rape-Revenge Films in the Cinema of Justice," in *Framing Law and Crime*, ed. Caroline Joan S. Picart, Michael Hviid Jacobsen, and Cecil Greek (Lanham: Rowman & Littlefield, 2016), 165–202; Kevin Grant, *Vigilantes: Private Justice in Popular Cinema* (Jefferson, NC: McFarland, 2020).

8. For a very wide view see Grant, *Vigilantes*. passim.

9. Why does a vigilante man / Carry that sawed-off shotgun in his hand? / Would he shoot his brother and sister down? (*Vigilante Man*, 1940).

10. So for example, between the acknowledged revolutionary groups like FARC (Revolutionary Armed Forces of Colombia) and the Army there are groups like the Autodefensas Unidas de Colombia—a paramilitary and drug-trafficking group. ("The Rise and Dominance of Colombia's Private Military Contractors," Lima Charlie World, January 4, 2019, https://limacharlienews.com/south-america/colombian-private-military-contractors/.)

11. Grant, *Vigilantes*, chap. 2 on vigilante elements in crime and social problem films.

12. Eric Hobsbawm, *Primitive Rebels: Studies in Archaic Forms of Social Movement in the 19th and 20th Centuries* (New York: Norton, 1965); Eric Hobsbawm and George F. E. Rudé, *Captain Swing* (London: Lawrence and Wishart, 1969).

13. Hobsbawm, *Primitive Rebels*; Hobsbawm and Rudé, *Captain Swing*.

14. Jean-François Bergier, *Wilhelm Tell. Realität und Mythos* (München: Paul List Verlag, 1990).

15. See the individual chapters in this collection.

16. Numerous film versions—the most notable being *Robin Hood* (1922) dir Allan Dwan, *The Adventures of Robin Hood* (1938) dir Michael Curtiz, through *Robin Hood: Prince of Thieves* (1991) dir Kevin Reynolds to *Robin Hood* (2010) dir Ridley Scott and *Robin Hood* (2018) dir Otto Bathurst.

17. *The Seven Samurai* (1954) dir. Kurosawa.

18. *The Magnificent Seven* (1960) dir John Sturges.

19. Wright (1977) Will Wright, *Sixguns and Society: A Structural Study of the Western* (Berkeley: University of California Press, 1977); see also Grant, *Vigilantes*, chap. 1.

20. See below at note 25.

21. Paul Bergman and Michael Asimow, eds., *Reel Justice: The Courtroom Goes to the Movies*, second ed. (Kansas City, MO: Andrews McMeel, 2004); Steve Greenfield, Guy Osborn, and Guy Osborn, *Film and the Law*, second ed. (Oxford: Hart, 2010); Michael Asimow and Paul Bergman, *Real to Reel: Truth and Trickery in Courtroom Movies* (Lake Mary, FL: Vanderplas Publishing, 2021).

22. Stefan Machura, "The Law and Cinema Movement," in *Framing Law and Crime: An Interdisciplinary Anthology*, ed. Caroline Joan "Kay" S. Picart, Michael Hviid Jacobsen, and Cecil Greek (Lanham: Rowman & Littlefield, 2016), 25–58. sub nom "law and cinema movement."

23. Greenfield, Osborn, and Osborn, *Film and the Law*, chap. 5. on the British response with quotas and quota quickie B films.

24. European Commission on support for film culture—Audiovisual | Culture and Creativity (europa.eu).

25. Cass Warner Sperling, Cork Millner, and Jack Warner, *Hollywood Be Thy Name: The Warner Brothers Story* (Rocklin, CA: Prima Pub, 1994); James C. Robertson, *The Hidden Cinema: British Film Censorship in Action, 1913–1972* (London: Routledge, 1989).

26. David Garland, *The Culture of Control: Crime and Social Order in Contemporary Society* (Chicago: University of Chicago Press, 2001).

27. Homicide in England and Wales—Office for National Statistics (ons.gov.uk) (2020) Section 4, *Which groups of people were most likely to be victims of homicide*.

28. *RadioTimes Guide to Films 2015* (London: Immediate Media Company, 2015), 1620–40.

29. Jacinda Read, *The New Avengers: Feminism, Femininity and the Rape-Revenge Cycle* (Manchester: Manchester University Press, 2000); Alexandra Heller-Nicholas, *Rape-Revenge Films: A Critical Study*, second ed. (Jefferson, NC: McFarland, 2021); Claire Henry, *Revisionist Rape-Revenge: Redefining a Film Genre* (New York: Palgrave Macmillan, 2016).

30. Peter Robson, "Developments in Revenge, Justice and Rape in the Cinema," *International Journal for the Semiotics of Law-Revue Internationale de Sémiotique Juridique* 34, no. 1 (2021): 69–88.

31. David A. Black, *Law in Film: Resonance and Representation* (Urbana: University of Illinois Press, 1999).

32. Lope de Vega's play based on incidents in the village of Fuenteovejuna, Castille. Here, in 1476, the local commander of the ruling body, the Order of Calatrava, Fernán Gómez de Guzmán, mistreated the villagers, who banded together and killed him. When a magistrate sent by King Ferdinand II of Aragon arrived at the village to investigate, the villagers, even under the pain of torture, responded only by saying "Fuenteovejuna did it." A modern version is encountered in the 1960 film *Spartacus* where all the slaves in turn claim to be the leader of the slave revolt, Spartacus with the much-imitated line, "I am Spartacus."

33. Paramount, 1970, dir Martin Ritt.

34. 20th Century Fox, 2007, dir James Wan.

35. Warner Bros, 2007, dir Neil Jordan.

36. FilmNation Entertainment Endgame Entertainment, 2011, dir Roger Donaldson (aka *Justice*).

BIBLIOGRAPHY

Abrahams, Ray. *Vigilant Citizens: Vigilantism and the State*. Cambridge: Polity Press, 1998.
Asimow, Michael, and Paul Bergman. *Real to Reel: Truth and Trickery in Courtroom Movies*. Lake Mary, FL: Vanderplas Publishing, 2021.
Bacon, Francis. "On Revenge." (1625) In *The Essays*, edited by John Pitcher. Penguin Classics. Uxbridge, Harmondsworth: Penguin, 1985.
Bergier, Jean-François. *Wilhelm Tell. Realität und Mythos*. München: Paul List Verlag, 1990.
Bergman, Paul, and Michael Asimow, eds. *Reel Justice: The Courtroom Goes to the Movies*. Second ed. Kansas City, MO: Andrews McMeel, 2004.
Black, David A. *Law in Film: Resonance and Representation*. Urbana: University of Illinois Press, 1999.
Burrows, William E. *Vigilante!* New York: Harcourt Brace Jovanovich, 1976.
D'Acci, Julie. "Television, Representation and Gender." In *The Television Studies Reader*, edited by Robert Clyde Allen and Annette Hill, 373–88. London; New York: Routledge, 2004.
Garland, David. *The Culture of Control: Crime and Social Order in Contemporary Society*. Chicago: University of Chicago Press, 2001.
Grant, Kevin. *Vigilantes: Private Justice in Popular Cinema*. Jefferson, NC: McFarland, 2020.
Greenfield, Steve, Guy Osborn, and Peter Robson. *Film and the Law*. Second ed. Oxford: Hart, 2010.
Heller-Nicholas, Alexandra. *Rape-Revenge Films: A Critical Study*. Second ed. Jefferson, NC: McFarland, 2021.
Henry, Claire. *Revisionist Rape-Revenge: Redefining a Film Genre*. New York: Palgrave Macmillan, 2016.
Hobsbawm, Eric. *Primitive Rebels: Studies in Archaic Forms of Social Movement in the 19th and 20th Centuries*. New York: Norton, 1965.
Hobsbawm, Eric, and George F. E. Rudé. *Captain Swing*. London: Lawrence and Wishart, 1969.
Johnston, Les. "What Is Vigilantism?" *The British Journal of Criminology* 36, no. 2 (1996): 220–36.
Machura, Stefan. "Media Influence on the Perception of the Legal System." In *Understanding Law in Society: Developments in Socio-Legal Studies*, edited by Knut Papendorf, Stefan Machura, and KristianAndenaes 239–83. Berlin: LIT, 2011.
———. "The Law and Cinema Movement." In *Framing Law and Crime: An Interdisciplinary Anthology*, edited by Caroline Joan "Kay" S. Picart, Michael Hviid Jacobsen, and Cecil Greek, 25–58. Lanham: Rowman and Littlefield, 2016.

Marcus Aurelius. "Meditations on Stoic Philosophy." (170–80) In *Meditations*, edited by Martin Hammond. Uxbridge, Harmondsworth: Penguin, 2006.
BBC News. "Michigan 'Plot': Who Are the US Militia Groups?," October 9, 2020, sec. US and Canada. https://www.bbc.com/news/world-us-canada-54483973.
Podlas, Kimberlianne. "Testing Television: Studying and Understanding the Impact of Television's Depictions of Law and Justice." In *Law and Justice on the Small Screen*, edited by Peter Robson and Jessica Silbey, 87–110. Oxford; Portland, OR: Hart Pub, 2012.
RadioTimes Guide to Films 2015. London: Immediate Media Company, 2015.
Read, Jacinda. *The New Avengers: Feminism, Femininity and the Rape-Revenge Cycle*. Manchester: Manchester University Press, 2000.
Robertson, James C. *The Hidden Cinema: British Film Censorship in Action, 1913–1972*. London: Routledge, 1989.
Robson, Peter. "Beyond the Courtroom—Vigilantism, Revenge and Rape-Revenge Films in the Cinema of Justice." In *Framing Law and Crime*, edited by Caroline Joan S. Picart, Michael Hviid Jacobsen, and Cecil Greek, 165–202. Lanham: Rowman and Littlefield, 2016.
———. "Developments in Revenge, Justice and Rape in the Cinema." *International Journal for the Semiotics of Law-Revue Internationale de Sémiotique Juridique* 34, no. 1 (2021): 69–88.
———. "Vengeance in Popular Culture." In *Oxford Encyclopedia of Crime, Media, and Popular Culture*, December 22, 2016. http://criminology.oxfordre.com/view/10.1093/acrefore/9780190264079.001.0001/acrefore-9780190264079-e-45.
Robson, Peter, Guy Osborn, and Steve Greenfield. "The Impact of Film and Television on Perceptions of Law and Justice: Towards a Realisable Methodology." In *Law, Culture and Visual Studies*, edited by Anne Wagner and Richard K. Sherwin, 1011–28. Dordrecht: Springer, 2014.
Rosenbaum, H. Jon, and Peter C. Sederberg, eds. *Vigilante Politics*. Philadelphia: University of Pennsylvania Press, 1976.
Sperling, Cass Warner, Cork Millner, and Jack Warner. *Hollywood Be Thy Name: The Warner Brothers Story*. Rocklin, CA: Prima Pub, 1994.
Lima Charlie World. "The Rise and Dominance of Colombia's Private Military Contractors," January 4, 2019. https://limacharlienews.com/south-america/colombian-private-military-contractors/.
BBC News. "What Is the 'Sovereign Citizen' Movement?," August 5, 2020, sec. US and Canada. https://www.bbc.com/news/world-us-canada-53654318.
HuffPost UK. "Who Are the Proud Boys? A Brit's Guide to the Far-Right Group Trump Refuses to Condemn," September 30, 2020. https://www.huffingtonpost.co.uk/entry/trump-proud-boys-presidential-debate-2020_uk_5f7437e6c5b66377b27ad2d7.
Wright, Will. *Sixguns and Society: A Structural Study of the Western*. Berkeley: University of California Press, 1977.

PART I

The Anglophone World

Chapter 1

American Vigilantism
Popular Justice and Popular Culture

Michael Asimow

America has a rich history of vigilantism. Vigilantism refers to a practice by which persons take the law into their own hands because they do not believe that law enforcement institutions can be trusted to capture, convict, and appropriately punish offenders. Vigilantism can be aptly described as "popular justice." The social contract calls for the people to give up the right to exact physical vengeance against those who harm them. Instead, the social contract assigns responsibility to the government to redress such harm and punish offenders, and it confers on government a monopoly on the use of force to do so. Vigilantism occurs when people lose trust in the government to keep its side of the bargain.

    The first part of this chapter discusses the history of American vigilantism, concentrating on the San Francisco Vigilance Committees of 1851 and 1856 and the San Francisco Police Department's Chinatown Squad. The second part of this chapter discusses vigilantism in American movies ("Vigilantism in Pop Culture"), with a particular focus on police vigilantism, especially the iconic Harry Callahan, protagonist of *Dirty Harry* and its sequels. Because *Dirty Harry* is deeply rooted in San Francisco culture, the two halves of this chapter are (perhaps tenuously) connected, and this chapter might aptly be retitled "Vigilantism in San Francisco—Popular Justice and Popular Culture."

AMERICAN VIGILANTISM

The history of American vigilantism is documented in an enormous literature. This is a book-length subject, far too large to be comprehensively discussed in this brief chapter.[1]

Forms of American Vigilantism

A prominent form of U.S. vigilantism were brutal lynch mobs (often organized by the Ku Klux Klan) that functioned from after the Civil War until the 1950s. These mobs murdered African Americans whom, the crowd believed, the legal authorities would not punish quickly or harshly enough or who had committed some perceived offense that the law would not punish at all (such as having sex with a white woman or registering to vote).[2]

But American vigilante history goes far beyond racial violence.[3] Beginning before the American Revolution with the South Carolina Regulator movement in 1767, Americans have often taken the law into their own hands. Vigilantism was particularly prominent on the frontier and in the South, where governmental law enforcement was spotty or nonexistent and the judiciary was suspect. Typically, local property owners formed so-called Regulator groups to capture outlaws or "ne'er do wells," put them on extra-legal trial, and in many cases summarily execute them. Aside from their desire for law and order and suppression of vagrancy, these groups were concerned with the high cost of traditional law enforcement. Vigilantism was much quicker and cheaper, and it provided a stronger deterrent.

Some vigilantes were well-organized groups that functioned for a period of time with broad community support, as in the case of the San Francisco Vigilance Committees, to be discussed in the next subsection, "Organized Vigilantism in San Francisco." In other instances, they were ad hoc lynch mobs that formed spontaneously to deal with a particular perceived outrage. In still other cases, vigilantes were individuals redressing a wrong that had been done to them or their families. Many times, law-enforcement officials quietly supported the vigilantes. Vigilantism was commonplace throughout the 1800s and continues in modified form in the present, in the form of local neighborhood patrols or border patrols. These groups are organized to control and deter crime or illegal border-crossing in areas where police protection is viewed as inadequate, although they usually work with the police and avoid violence.[4] In addition, so-called stand-your-ground laws, adopted in thirty-five states, allow a killer to claim self-defense even if retreat was possible.[5] Florida's law, for example, entitles people to use "deadly force if he or she reasonably believes it is necessary to do so." Such laws obviously encourage people to kill in situations bordering on vigilantism, such as unpleasant and threatening personal encounters.

Organized Vigilantism in San Francisco

San Francisco has a fascinating history of both private and police vigilantism. The vigilance committees of 1851 and 1856 were particularly notorious and often-copied examples of American organized vigilantism.

The 1851 Committee

In the gold rush era of 1851, San Francisco's population swelled rapidly and crime of all kinds was rampant. Much of it was committed by the Sydney "ducks" (sometimes called Sydney "coves") who were immigrants from the penal colonies in Australia. San Francisco's governing institutions, including the judiciary, were corrupt and there was little organized law enforcement. In June 1851, a Committee of Vigilance was formed consisting of about 500 men led by merchants and supported by the working classes.[6]

The 1851 Committee established patrols against fire and theft and deported numerous undesirable persons. It asserted the right to search without a warrant and denied the right of habeas corpus. It was notorious for hanging its captives after brief trials, starting with a "duck" named Jenkins who was caught stealing a safe. Shortly thereafter, a particularly notorious "duck" named Jim Stuart who had committed numerous murders confessed and was summarily hanged. Two more Sydney "ducks" were also dispatched after confessing their crimes. These two were rescued from the Committee by the governor and the sheriff, only to be recaptured from jail and hung seventeen minutes later. The Committee ceased operations by September 1851. Apparently, it was fairly successful in deterring crime during its brief period of operations and for a few months thereafter, but the crime rate soon returned to its previous levels.

The 1856 Committee

By 1856, San Francisco's population had increased greatly and it had a much better organized police and court system. Nevertheless, crime remained a serious problem. Several notorious killings led to the revival of the Vigilance Committee in May 1856.[7] The 1856 Committee consisted of perhaps 8,000 men, again backed by broad popular support. The leader was a respected and able businessman named William T. Coleman who had also been active in the 1851 committee.

The first of the 1856 murders that led to the formation of the 1856 Committee was the killing of a U.S. Marshall named Richardson by a notorious gambler named Charles Cora. The second was the killing of a crusading newspaper editor named James King of William by James P. Casey. Casey was a political crook whom King of William had attacked in print. Cora was prosecuted, but his trial ended in a hung jury; he may well have killed in self-defense. The vigilantes (backed by an impressive show of force) seized the two killers from county jail and hanged them after a secret trial. At that point, the vigilantes controlled the city. They even briefly imprisoned the chief justice of the California Supreme Court, David Terry, and put him on trial for assault. There was little or nothing that the mayor, the governor, the Law and Order Party militia, the state militia which was led by General William Tecumseh Sherman, or even U.S. Navy could do about it. The Committee deported about thirty corrupt public officials and hanged two more murderers. It disbanded in October 1856, following which the crime wave resumed.

Assessment of the 1851 and 1856 Committees

Like vigilantes everywhere in the 1800s, the San Francisco committees of 1851 and 1856 enjoyed substantial public support because of the weakness of law enforcement. They are even referred to respectfully in one of the *Dirty Harry* movies to be discussed below. The San Francisco committees inspired numerous vigilante organizations in other cities and are powerful examples of the profound attraction of vigilante justice in American history.

The verdict of historians on the San Francisco vigilance committees is mixed.[8] The great historian of the West, Hubert Bancroft, interviewed many of the participants for his 1887 book *Popular Tribunals*.[9] Bancroft was a big fan of the vigilantes.[10] To contemporary historians, however, the judgments of the vigilantes in 1856 were grossly unfair and resulted from inaccurate press coverage.[11]

Richard Maxwell Brown suggests that the 1856 Committee should be understood in political and economic terms.[12] He argues that the Committee (or at least its leadership as opposed to the rank-and-file) was more concerned with politics than crime. Brown contends that the police had the crime problem under control. After all, the Committee executed only four people and otherwise cooperated with the police. The two notorious murders by Cora and Casey were a convenient excuse for creating a tightly organized machine that could be converted from crime control to political purposes. The 1856 Committee consisted mostly of Protestants and was controlled by the city's powerful merchants. They were determined to destroy the corrupt Irish-Catholic machine led by David Broderick that was running the city. The Committee also hoped to head off municipal bankruptcy which seemed imminent and to reduce taxes. It wanted to exile the crooks and ballot-stuffers and put the newly organized and merchant-friendly People's Party into power. Indeed, the People's Party won the next election by a 2–1 margin.

San Francisco Police Vigilantism—The Chinatown Squad

Not all San Francisco vigilantism was private. The Chinatown Squad of the San Francisco Police Department (SFPD) consisted of police vigilantes.[13] The Squad was formed in 1879 and was active into the twentieth century. It consisted of police officers determined to suppress murder, gambling, drugs, and prostitution in Chinatown by using vigilante tactics such as raiding gambling and opium dens without bothering to secure warrants. Although anti-Chinese prejudice was certainly involved in the formation and operation of the Squad, it can also be explained by the complete failure of conventional law enforcement methods to halt crime in Chinatown. Although it stopped using vigilante tactics around 1920, the Squad was not disbanded until 1970 (and was later revived as the Gang Task Force).

The Squad's primary responsibility was to stop or at least curtail the murderous Chinatown tong wars, which were battles between rival gangs. The tong wars were often carried out by tong soldiers ("highbinders") using hatchets as well as guns. Because Chinatown was virtually a self-governing and uncooperative island in the middle of San Francisco, the police were unable to halt the tong wars and other criminality. The Squad conducted notorious raids on the tong headquarters where they confiscated weapons and chopped up the furniture. They rounded up and arrested people on the street who looked suspicious or simply beat them up. They drove others out of town or arranged for them to be deported. They tore down dilapidated houses used for crime and displayed tied-up Chinese prisoners from the jail in Portsmouth Square to impress onlookers. They threatened police raids against business people who were paying extortion money to the tongs.

The Chinatown Squad apparently met with strong public and media approval, including from the Chinese Consul General as well as from Chinese and Caucasian private vigilantes who were also fighting the tongs. In 1921, leadership of the Squad passed to the fatherly Inspector Jack Manion, who pioneered community policing and ran the Squad for twenty-five years without using vigilante tactics. During his tenure, the tong wars and wide-open gambling, opium dens, and prostitution finally came to an end.[14]

VIGILANTISM IN POPULAR CULTURE

The media of popular culture reflects what ordinary people think and believe. Given the prominence of vigilantism in American history, and the positive popular response it generally evoked, it is no surprise that vigilantism is a staple theme in American popular culture. Countless movies, novels, and television shows have dealt with various forms of that phenomenon. Many of these media products are discussed in the introduction to this book. Often, these texts treat vigilantes as heroes and evoke warm feelings of satisfaction in audiences. This section begins with a general treatment of vigilantism in American movies before turning to the main focus—police vigilantism. This chapter does not attempt a general discussion on vigilantism in American movies—clearly a book-length subject,[15] nor does it engage with the vast body of police television shows and novels that often include police vigilante themes.[16]

Private Vigilantism in the Movies

Movie vigilantism got off to a strong start in D. W. Griffith's *The Birth of a Nation* (1915) which glorified the Ku Klux Klan. It has been the theme of many, perhaps most, westerns, reflecting the prominence of real vigilantes and the weakness of law enforcement on the American frontier. We might think of western classics like *The Ox-Bow Incident* (1942), which involved a lynch mob punishing cattle rustlers; *Hang 'Em High* (1968), in which an innocent man survives a lynching and returns as a lawman to catch the lynchers; *High Plains Drifter* (1973), involving a town that hires a gunman to protect it; and *The Unforgiven* (1992), in which several prostitutes hire a morally compromised gunslinger to execute the man who cut one of them.[17] Curiously, Clint Eastwood, who played Dirty Harry, starred in all of these westerns other than *Ox-Bow*. Eastwood has become the pop cultural face of vigilantism.[18] Superhero movies are another genre that typically pits the superhero vigilantes against crazed criminals who are beyond the capacity of the police to capture.

Numerous films involve vigilantes who seek personal revenge for wrongs done to them or their families. For example, *In the Bedroom* (2001) concerns a father who murders the killer of his son; *Foxy Brown* (1974) involves a woman seeking revenge for the death of her boyfriend and her own rape (this film also involves a neighborhood vigilante group trying to expel drug dealers). Another group of films concerns private lynch mobs that redress collective injuries that the mob does not trust law enforcement to rectify. These include racial lynch mobs, such as occur in *The Birth of a Nation*, *To*

Kill a Mockingbird (1962),[19] or non-racial mobs who appear in *Fury* (1936), *Young Mr. Lincoln* (1939), *They Won't Forget* (1937),[20] and *The Sun Shines Bright* (1953).[21]

Another group of films concerns individual vigilantes who fight urban crime.[22] The classic urban vigilante movie is *Death Wish* (1974) and its many sequels.[23] Paul Kersey (Charles Bronson), a New York City construction engineer, is a self-described bleeding heart liberal and was a conscientious objector during the Korean War. Three thugs break into his apartment, kill his wife, and rape his daughter who becomes a near-vegetable. On a business trip to Tucson, a client gives Kersey a gun as well as a lecture about the evils of gun control.

On returning to New York, Kersey is mugged but kills the mugger. At first, this nauseates him, but his life acquires meaning as he begins to kill other muggers—but not the criminals who harmed him personally. Indeed, Kersey deliberately tries to attract muggers whom he can kill. These highly publicized vigilante killings immediately cut the rate of New York muggings in half and the media glorifies Kersey. More people start fighting back against muggers (including one elderly lady who uses a hat pin). The police eventually track Kersey down. However, they do not arrest him because of the adverse public reaction this would cause. Indeed, they make a deal—they will toss his gun into the river and forget the case if he leaves town—which he does. The film closes in the Chicago railway station where a bunch of people have arrested a mugger. Kersey turns and makes a mock shooting action with his hand. *The Brave One* (2007) is another worthy member of this subgenre, featuring Erica Bain (Jodie Foster) who kills quite a few bad guys including but not limited to the three who had killed her fiancé and put her into a coma.

Certainly *Taxi Driver* (1976) should not be overlooked in the annals of pop cultural private vigilantes. Travis Bickle (Robert de Niro), a psychotic cab driver, loathes the sleaze he sees every night while driving in New York City. He buys a suitcase full of unlicensed guns and uses them to free a young girl (Jodie Foster) from prostitution by killing her pimp as well as the man who rents her rooms and one of her clients. Media coverage of Bickle's crimes is very positive.

Death Wish, *The Brave One*, and *Taxi Driver* transmit the highly conservative political ideology that will be discussed in the rest of the chapter. Guns are glorified and gun control is mocked. Bleeding-heart liberals become crime-control vigilantes because the police cannot handle the problem or do not even care. Unlike the police, private vigilantes aren't bound by annoying legal constraints. Instead, they can go right out on the street and find and kill criminals. This has a remarkable deterrent effect on the bad guys and it receives a highly positive popular and media response.

Police Vigilantism

The criminal procedure compromise

The rest of the chapter focuses on one small corner of the vigilante pop culture universe: public-sector vigilantism in general and police vigilantism in particular. Public sector vigilantes include frustrated prosecutors who bend the rules to convict offenders who might escape punishment, as occurs in *Night Falls on Manhattan* (1996). Jailers fail to protect their prisoners from lynch mobs as in *Young Mr. Lincoln* (1939). Judges can be pop culture vigilantes when they cover up police misconduct, as also occurs in *Night Falls on Manhattan*. *The Star Chamber* (1983) presents an extreme example of judicial vigilantism—judges hire hit men to seek out and murder former criminal defendants who escaped conviction because of legal technicalities.[24]

Members of the public (and consumers of pop culture) probably feel ambivalent about public sector vigilantism. On the one hand, they want the criminal justice system to protect society by catching, prosecuting, judging, and punishing criminals. This makes them tolerant of vigilantes who take over when conventional law enforcement fails. Plenty of people grudgingly admire rogue judges, police, and prosecutors who find dubious ways to remove dangerous criminals from the streets. On the other hand, many people fear the machinery of law enforcement, since it can be used to suppress dissent, convict and imprison innocent people, or over-punish minor crime. They want officials to follow the rules that were put in place to protect privacy and assure civilized standards of law enforcement, such as avoidance of excessive force, torture, and extra-judicial murder.

Thus we need vigorous law enforcement and we need law enforcement to be checked. We reconcile these goals through what might be called the criminal procedure compromise.[25]

Police violence against suspects is tightly controlled. With many exceptions, police must secure a search warrant before they search for and seize evidence. Probable cause is needed to make an arrest. Arrestees are entitled to warnings that they have the right to remain silent and that anything they say can be used against them. They must be told they are entitled to have a lawyer and one will be supplied for free if needed. Suspects cannot be tortured and their confessions cannot be coerced. They must be treated with basic dignity regardless of the horrible crimes they may have committed. They must be provided with a preliminary hearing or a grand jury indictment to make sure there is probable cause to proceed. At trial, courts exclude relevant evidence that was seized through an illegal search (the so-called exclusionary rule) as well as evidence of prior bad acts. Defendants are entitled to the privilege against self-incrimination, meaning that they cannot be called to testify against their will and that no adverse inference can be drawn from their silence. Prosecutors must establish guilt beyond a reasonable doubt—a very high evidentiary standard. Counsel must be at least basically competent. All these protections of criminal defendants—most of whom are guilty—are part of the criminal procedure compromise.

Public sector vigilantism raises important issues that are different from private vigilantism. Unlike private vigilantes, law enforcement officials have taken an oath to follow the constitution and laws, including the criminal procedure compromise. Law enforcement vigilantes betray that oath. Indeed, public-sector vigilantism threatens the social and political fabric of our society. Nevertheless, the movies come down squarely on the side of letting officials, especially the police, flout the rules that should constrain them. These movies often enjoy rousing commercial success because so many pop culture consumers basically applaud what the rogue police officers are trying to do.

This part concentrates on police vigilante tactics that evade the defendant-protective rules of criminal procedure. These include excessive violence against criminal suspects up to and including extra-judicial murder. Vigilante tactics also include illegal searches, harassing arrests, coerced confessions, ignoring orders from superior officers, perjury, or other forms of cheating. Police vigilantism tends to arise when the resources available to the police are inadequate to deal with the crime problem that the police are expected to control or in situations when the leadership of the police has different priorities from the rank and file.

Police vigilantism is not uncommon in the real world, although the extent to which it occurs is hard to measure. The San Francisco Police Department's Chinatown Squad, discussed earlier in the chapter, is a well-documented example of police vigilantism (as are the more recent Oakland Riders and Los Angeles Rampart police scandals also discussed above).[26] Excessive and unnecessary police violence against African American arrestees triggered the Black Lives Matter movement. Kotecha and Walker report a study in which 105 members of a medium-size police department took in-service training.[27] They were shown clips of the behavior of a fictitious vigilante cop (Bumper Morgan in Wambaugh's *The Blue Knight*) that included summary punishment, harassment, and perjury. The 105 attendees said that such behavior was routine in their department and some even named a particular officer (not in the class) who reminded them of Bumper Morgan.

In police vigilante movies, rogue police officers are fed up with normal police bureaucracy and its insistence on political correctness or satisfying the media. In particular, vigilante police are frustrated by the legal rules of criminal procedure. They disregard these norms as well as the orders of their superior officers in order to gather evidence, catch suspected offenders, torture them into confessing, and murdering them if necessary. Though there have been many such films (a number of them are mentioned in the section below, "The messages in the *Dirty Harry* movies"), I focus here on the figure of Harry Callahan, protagonist of *Dirty Harry* and its four sequels. These movies are a veritable textbook of police vigilantism and sound all of the themes of this genre. I single out them out from all the others because they were so commercially successful and because the Harry Callahan figure has achieved iconic status.

Dirty Harry and its Sequels

Clint Eastwood plays Detective Harry Callahan in all five of the *Dirty Harry* movies, which are among the most famous and familiar American films. They send numerous important messages to the viewer that strongly support police violence and vigilantism. According to these texts, a good policeman ignores the rules of criminal procedure when necessary and should freely disregard the orders of superior officers when the orders seem too cautious or just wrong. These films idolize the police whether they're right or wrong. They mock liberal politicians and the media. As discussed below, the *Dirty Harry* movies preach conservative ideology. The city of San Francisco is an important character in all five films. Despite its many gorgeous views, it is presented as a swamp of depravity and the home of vicious criminals as well as drugged-out hippies.

Dirty Harry (1971)

The first (and undoubtedly the best) of the Harry Callahan films opens by scrolling slowly over a monument to fallen San Francisco police offices. A mournful bell sounds. This shot displays a reverential attitude toward the police, especially the beat cops who were killed in the line of duty. The audience understands that these officers are heroes.

A sniper perched high above the gorgeous city of San Francisco looks down on a rooftop pool where a woman is swimming. He shoots her in the back. Harry Callahan is the homicide investigator. Callahan finds a ransom note signed by Scorpio demanding that the city pay $100,000 or Scorpio will kill a priest or a Black person.

Callahan meets with the chief of police and the mayor. His disrespect for them is obvious. He complains he could be investigating, but instead has been sitting on his ass for forty-five minutes waiting for them. He is astonished that the mayor wants to pay the ransom to avoid bloodshed. The mayor warns him not to repeat what happened last year in the Fillmore where Callahan shot and killed a man to stop an attempted rape. Callahan points out that when you see a naked guy with a butcher knife and a hard-on chasing a woman, he's probably not collecting for the Red Cross. The mayor and the bureaucracy are more concerned that Callahan will cause trouble for the San Francisco Police Department (SFPD) than to encourage him to get out and solve the Scorpio case.

Callahan goes for lunch at the Burger Den. He seems to eat all his meals there, apparently consisting of hot dogs for lunch and dinner. This establishes that Callahan is a regular working class guy like most of the audience. The following scene is repeated in some form in each of the five *Dirty Harry* movies. While eating, Callahan spots a bank robbery in progress and shoots and kills several robbers, while sustaining a leg wound himself. Amid the resulting chaos, he finds one of the wounded robbers on the sidewalk close to his gun. Pointing his beloved .44 Magnum at the guy, Callahan says that he isn't sure if he fired five or six shots in the melee. "Ask yourself," he says to the robber, "do I feel lucky today?" The guy gives up. Callahan pulls the trigger, while still pointing the gun at the robber's head, but the chamber is empty.

Strictly speaking these recurring and very bloody scenes are not vigilantism; they are arguably an appropriate police response to a violent crime in process. Audiences respond positively to these scenes, since they probably feel that the vicious criminals whom Callahan kills had it coming. These criminals would no doubt have taken more innocent lives if Callahan had not shot and killed them first. After annihilating the bank robbers, Callahan is treated by a Black intern for his wound, but feels secure because he and the intern grew up together in the then working-class neighborhood of Potrero Hill. The intern wants to cut his pants but Harry wants to save the $29.50 pants, again establishing his working class credibility.

Back at the police station, Harry says he was up until 3 a.m. working the case. The lieutenant asks why he did not put in for overtime. "That'll be the day," Harry replies, implying contempt for other officers who do the job for the money. He's assigned a new partner, Chico Gonzales. Another cop observes that Harry hates everybody—"micks," "hebes," "niggers" (Irish, Jews, and Blacks). How about Mexicans? "Especially spics," he replies. This dialogue establishes Callahan's dry sense of humor. It is station-house banter but there is implied approval of racism. In any event, it illustrates Callahan's contempt for affirmative action policies. Actually, Harry is more concerned that Gonzales is inexperienced and has a sociology degree from San Jose State. "Just what I need—a college boy. . . . Don't let your law degree get you killed. I'm liable to get killed along with you." This again bonds Callahan with members of the film audience who did not go to college but get along fine without the degree.

Scorpio is a white man with long hair, perhaps a hippie. Throughout the movie, he wears a belt with a peace sign buckle. This and numerous other scenes emphasize the filmmakers' contempt for hippies and others who represent leftist political ideologies and unconventional life styles. Scorpio is staking out a Catholic church from a rooftop, perhaps hoping to bag a priest, but his attention is drawn to a mixed-race gay couple. He lines up a shot on the Black man but is spotted by a police helicopter and flees.

Callahan and Gonzales are cruising the North Beach neighborhood looking for the sniper. This scene takes place amid an array of garish and sleazy strip joints. Harry says, "They ought to throw a net over the whole bunch of them." Here and in many other scenes throughout the five films, the filmmakers express their dislike of the unconstrained sexuality of the hip San Francisco lifestyle of the 1960s and early 1970s.

Callahan has to stop a man from jumping off a building. He ascends with the fire department's cherry picker. The guy tries to take Harry down with him, but Harry manages to subdue him by knocking him out with a blow to the face. He tells his partner that he is called Dirty Harry because he gets all the dirty jobs. Ordinary working people who feel that they get stuck with the dirty jobs will empathize with that message. And they will approve the use of force to save the jumper's life (and to protect Harry as well).

After Scorpio strikes again, killing a Black kid with another rooftop shot, Harry is issued a high-powered rifle for the upcoming stakeout. It could stop an elephant but, the officer tells him, "Remember, Harry, he's not an animal of any kind." Harry's silence in response speaks volumes. Obviously, he thinks Scorpio is indeed a dangerous animal who richly deserves to get shot down and killed by any means necessary.

In the stakeout Harry watches through binoculars a naked prostitute welcome two men to her apartment. Then they spot Scorpio, put a searchlight on him and there is an exchange of gunfire. Scorpio shoots out some Jesus Saves neon lights just for the sheer pleasure of it. Here and in the scenes where Scorpio tries to kill a priest, the message is that Scorpio is loathsome because of his disrespect for organized religion.

The case takes a new turn when Scorpio kidnaps a fourteen-year-old girl, Ann Mary Deacon. Scorpio claims he buried her in a hole where she will run out of oxygen unless the police get him $200,000, delivered by one man with a yellow bag. That man, of course, will be Harry, who tapes a switchblade knife to his leg. His lieutenant says, "It's disgusting that a police officer would know how to use a weapon like that." Harry responds with another eloquent silence.

Scorpio runs Callahan all over the city—he jogs for miles carrying the heavy bag of cash. Violating orders, Gonzales is equipped with a listening device that enables him to overhear Scorpio's phone calls and follow Callahan to each new location. In this sequence, we get interesting pictures of sleazy San Francisco by night. There is an interchange with a transsexual who says, "If you're vice, I'll kill myself." Harry responds, "Do it at home," clearly indicating his dislike for trans people. In phone calls, Scorpio calls him a "pig bastard" and a "rotten oinker," thus disrespecting the police. Finally, they meet up and Scorpio breaks two of Callahan's ribs. When Scorpio announces he is going to kill Harry, Harry goes for his knife and cuts Scorpio badly. Gonzales appears and there is a shootout in which both Scorpio and Gonzales are badly injured.

Back at the police station, Lt. Bressler reprimands Harry (on orders from Chief of Police) for not following orders. Of course, if he had followed them he would be dead and the police would be no closer to Ann Mary. Harry says, "When this is mess is over and he wants my badge, he can have that too." Clearly, the message is that orders from police superiors are often ridiculous and should be disobeyed.

Callahan and his new partner DiGiorgio track Scorpio to an athletics stadium which they break into. They kick down the door of the room Scorpio lives in, all without a search warrant. Harry shoots Scorpio, who begs for mercy and demands a doctor and a lawyer. Then he tortures Scorpio into revealing the location of Ann Mary who turns out to be dead.

Harry expects accolades from District Attorney Rooney. Instead, Rooney tells him he is "lucky I'm not indicting you for assault with intent to commit murder. . . . Where have you been? Does *Escobedo* ring a bell? *Miranda*?[28] I mean you must have heard of the Fourth Amendment.[29] What I'm saying is, that man had rights. . . . As soon as he's well enough to leave the hospital, he walks. I'm not wasting half a million of the taxpayer's dollars on a trial we can't possibly win. It's the law." All Callahan can reply is "the law is crazy." The viewer can only agree.

Callahan's various breaches of criminal procedure law are confirmed by Judge Bannerman, identified as an appellate court justice who also teaches constitutional law at Berkeley Law School (undoubtedly regarded by Eastwood as just another contemptible left-wing bastion). Bannerman states that all the seized evidence (including Scorpio's hunting rifle) is inadmissible. "You should have gotten a search warrant." "Search warrant? There was a girl dying." "The court would have to recognize the police officer's legitimate concern for the girl's life," Bannerman concedes, "but there's no way they can possibly condone police torture. . . . The confession and all physical evidence would have to be excluded . . . I couldn't convict him of spitting on the sidewalk." Harry replies, "And Ann Mary Deacon—what about her rights? She's raped, left in a hole to die. Who speaks for her? . . . Sooner or later he's going to stub his toe and I'll be right there." Rooney replies that "this office won't stand for any harassment." It is not difficult for the viewer to take Callahan's side in this exchange.

Scorpio pays $200 to a Black man to beat him up. As he's hauled into the Emergency Room, Scorpio yells to the reporters that the Callahan did it. Harry admits to the chief that he has been following Scorpio (on his own time). The chief orders him to stop surveilling Scorpio, but it is obvious Harry will not let up.

Harry visits his wounded ex-partner Chico Gonzales in rehab; just about all of Callahan's partners get killed or severely wounded in the line of duty. Gonzales says he is thinking of leaving the force and going into teaching. His wife tells Harry that she is fed up, too, with all the "pig this and pig that" and not knowing if he will be coming home when he leaves for work. Harry concedes that his wife never got used to it either (she was killed by a drunk driver). He supports Chico's decision to quit. "Why do you stay in it?" she asks. Harry replies, "I don't know. I really don't." But we know why. He is there to protect us from horrible criminals, regardless of the physical risks of getting killed or the frustration of dealing with police bureaucracy and the absurd rules of criminal procedure.

Scorpio hijacks a school bus and announces that the kids will be killed unless there is a jet waiting for him along with the $200,000. The mayor gives his word of honor that Scorpio will not be harmed and orders Harry to cooperate. Harry replies that you can just get yourself another delivery boy. Disregarding a direct order to stay out of it, he sets out to intercept the bus. He flushes Scorpio out and shoots him. Harry goes through the same routine he did with the bank robber at the beginning of the film. This time there is one bullet left and he finishes Scorpio off. Callahan hurls his badge into the water as the film ends.

Magnum Force (1973)

This film doubles down on the police vigilante theme. Lt. Briggs organizes a "death squad" of police who kill criminals and gangsters, especially those who avoided conviction on technicalities. Callahan plays it pretty straight in this film and manages to crush the death squad by killing all of them. The *Magnum Force* film raises the obvious question of how to distinguish the death squad's brand of vigilantism from Harry's. Perhaps the difference is Callahan usually kills or tortures evildoers only when it is necessary to apprehend a killer or save innocent lives, not just to administer extra-judicial punishment. Unlike the death squad, Callahan's goal is prevention of crime, rather than retribution against criminals.

The title sequence of *Magnum Force* features a hand holding Callahan's .44 Magnum, which is cocked, pointed at the viewer, and fired. This is part of the gun glorification which takes place in several of the films. We see the death squad assassinate Ricca, a corrupt labor boss who was charged with killing a labor reformer and acquitted on a technicality. Callahan shows up at the crime scene, but Lt. Briggs kicks him off. Harry has been relegated to stakeout duty because the police bureaucrats are worried about his propensity for violence and the bad publicity it might generate. Briggs says he's never taken his gun out of the holster. Callahan remarks, "Well, you're a good man, lieutenant. A good man always knows his limitations," suggesting of course that more gunplay against criminals would be a good idea. Harry eats at a crummy burger joint near the airport. In a scene echoing the bank robbery in the first film, he kills a couple of airplane hijackers at San Francisco Airport by not waiting for orders and by taking the initiative to stop the hijacking.

Harry has a revealing chat with a fellow cop named Charlie. Charlie is frustrated—if you kill a hoodlum you should just dump him on the street because "some snot-nosed young guy down at the DA's office will crucify you one way or the other. . . . A hood can kill a cop, but just let a cop kill a hood . . ." This conversation, of course, is highly resonant in the era of Black Lives Matter. We also see Harry at home, a miserably small and dark apartment with a tiny and empty refrigerator. Again, this helps to establish his working class credibility.

When Harry finally figures out that Lt. Briggs is a member of the death squad, he has a revealing conversation with him. Briggs says, "We're simply ridding society of killers that would be caught and sentenced anyway if our courts worked properly. There simply is no other way, inspector. You, of all people, should understand that." Harry: "I'm afraid you've misjudged me." Briggs: "A hundred years ago in this city people did the same thing.[30] History justified the vigilantes. We're no different. Anyone who threatens the security of the people will be executed. Evil for evil, Harry. Retribution." But Callahan cannot take the step from vigilantism in the service of catching criminals to executing them in cold blood as retribution.

The Enforcer (1976)

An early scene in this film places Harry as a member of an interview board considering which cops should be promoted to homicide inspector. The police bureaucracy insists that at least three women be promoted. Kate Moore (Tyne Daly) is selected even though she has never made an arrest. She then becomes Harry's partner and turns out to be competent and brave, though she ultimately is killed in the line of duty like many of his other partners. In this scene, the filmmakers leave no doubt of their disdain for affirmative action in police promotions or anywhere else.

Meanwhile, a terrorist gang called the People's Revolutionary Strike Force pulls off a burglary to steal guns and explosives. After the Strike Force blows up a police building, the police insist (over Harry's objection) on arresting the wrong man, Big Ed Mustapha (Albert Popwell, a Black actor who appears in almost all of the *Dirty Harry* films). Mustapha runs an organization called

Uhuru and was cooperating with Harry by identifying the actual leader of the Strike Force, Bobby Maxwell. Celebrating Big Ed's arrest, the police bureaucrats heap lavish praise on the incompetent mayor and on Harry and Kate, so the SFPD can get credit for promoting women. But Harry blows the whistle on this phony publicity and earns a suspension.

Harry continues working the case and Mustapha points him to Wanda who is working with Maxwell. The Strike Force kidnaps the mayor and kills a few more people. The cops plan to pay the ransom to get the mayor back—something that Harry always opposes. Looking for Bobby and Wanda, Harry finds his way to a church run by a leftist priest whom he roughs up. Wanda, dressed as a nun, tries to shoot him, but Kate Moore is quicker and shoots Wanda. The movie heaps derision on left-wing churches that shield terrorists. Maxwell and his gang are holed up with the mayor on Alcatraz which Harry and Kate attack on their own, disregarding the normal protocol by not bothering with backup. After the usual chase scene and shootout, Moore is killed, but Harry kills all of the bad guys and rescues the mayor.

Sudden Impact (1983)

The film opens with a female judge dismissing a case because the only evidence was a gun seized by Callahan in an illegal search, again frustrating the viewer who wants to see the bad guys convicted. In the usual scene in which Harry interrupt a robbery in progress by killing the robbers, he bluffs out a gunman holding a waitress as a hostage with the much-quoted line, "Go ahead, make my day." Later, operating on his own, Harry accosts a man at his daughter's wedding, accusing him of killing a prostitute. The man suffers a heart attack. His superiors are furious at this unauthorized intimidation, which destroyed months of surveillance and investigation.

On finding a dead body in a car, Harry describers his job to a reporter: "Wading through the city's scum, being swept away by bigger and bigger waves of corruption, apathy and red tape. . . . Our fingers are in the holes and the whole dyke's crumbling around us." The reporter says, "You're a dinosaur, Callahan—your ideas don't fit today." "What ideas," Harry replies, "that murder's a crime, that it should be punished?"

This film concerns Harry's forgiving attitude toward private vigilantism. Artist Jennifer Spencer (Sondra Locke) survived a gang rape which left her sister in a vegetative state. Spencer kills five men who had taken part in the assault. Ultimately, Harry catches Jennifer who comes up with a stirring tribute to private vigilantism. Harry says, "I guess now I've got to . . ." Jennifer interrupts: "Read me my rights? What exactly are my rights? Where was the concern for my rights when I was being beaten and mauled? What about my sister's rights when she was being brutalized? There is a thing called justice.

Was it justice that they should just walk away? You'd never understand, Callahan." Harry lets her walk free, indicating his reluctant approval of her acts of private vengeance.

The Dead Pool (1988)

This inferior final sequel begins with Harry's superiors ordering him to capitalize on his good PR and cooperate with the press. He has nothing but contempt for the idea. Indeed, he grabs a TV journalist's camera and smashes it as she photographs a grieving friend of a murder victim, thus firmly allying him with murder victims against the press. The theme of this movie (if it can be called that) concerns a "dead pool" of celebrities (including Harry himself). Participants bet on which celebrity will die next, thus providing an incentive to murder list members. The killer is a director of various slasher films. He kills off a critic who trashed the films and a commentator who wants to ban them.

The Messages in the *Dirty Harry* Movies

These five films are highly entertaining (well, perhaps all but the last one). They were financially successful and developed a large following. Many fans still remember them fondly even today, many years after *Dirty Harry* was released in 1971. The messages propagated by these films are clear and consistent. Those messages resonated in the 1970s, a decade of rising crime rates and distrust of all governmental institutions including the police. The films strongly support police and private vigilantism as well as a set of politically conservative ideas.[31]

Harry is obviously a member of the working class. He eats cheap food, wears cheap clothing, lives in a cheap apartment, gets stuck with dirty jobs, suffers with incompetent bosses, and would not dream of putting in for overtime. He did not go to college and is suspicious of those who did. All this endears him to the audience and helps to sell the highly contestable ideas underlying the films.

Police vigilantism

Harry despises the ridiculous rules of criminal procedure (such as exclusion of evidence resulting from an illegal search and seizure) and he feels free to flout these rules. When necessary, he never hesitates to torture bad guys into giving information and he frequently executes them extra-judicially. At one point in *Dirty Harry*, Professor Bannerman, a judge and professor at UC Berkeley, opines on criminal procedure. Obviously, Harry doesn't think much of Bannerman in particular or the famously liberal Berkeley in general.

Harry can't stand the excessive caution displayed by his bosses who are often more concerned with public opinion and political correctness than actually catching criminals. Harry has nothing but contempt for elected officials like the mayor who care only about good publicity and interfere with police work for political purposes. The same goes for the media; he does not care about pleasing reporters and is contemptuous of public relations. He particularly dislikes paying ransom.

Harry frequently disregards the orders of his superior officers and pays no attention to the limitations they impose on him. If he is working on a case, nothing can stop him. If immediate action is called for, he never waits for orders; he just jumps in and starts shooting. Of course, Harry always turns out to be right; his plans for stopping crazed killers work out well and his overly cautious superiors are always wrong. It follows that a good cop should do exactly what he thinks is best (including the use of extreme violence) without seeking authorization and should feel free to disregard inconvenient contrary orders from his superiors.

Harry seems sympathetic to private revenge vigilantism as well. In *Sudden Impact*, he catches but releases Jennifer Spencer, who killed five people in revenge for a sexual assault on herself and her sister. But as much as the *Dirty Harry* films support and praise police vigilantism, there is a line Harry will not cross. In *Magnum Force*, Harry smashes the "death squad," a group of police vigilantes who assassinate criminals who escaped justice. His goal is to prevent crime and protect the public, not to exact retribution from criminals who somehow escaped punishment.

San Francisco[32]

The *Dirty Harry* films are almost completely set in San Francisco, then and now a politically liberal and sexually permissive urban environment. The views are stunning, but the city is portrayed as a pit of depravity, plagued by crime, vicious criminals, and sleaze of every description. The films constantly portray prostitution and pornography. LGBTQ people are treated with contempt. The counter-culture, including hippies and political leftists, is presented in a very negative light. As Harry suggested to his partner in the first film, "They ought to throw a net over the whole bunch of them."

Conservative Ideology[33]

The *Dirty Harry* films reflect Eastwood's strong conservative and individualistic philosophy. Harry disdains affirmative action and political correctness. The rights of victims of crime are much more important than the rights of criminals. Harry's hostility toward sexual permissiveness in San Francisco is unmistakable. The films strongly reflect gun culture which is deeply rooted in America. They romanticize and fetishize Callahan's .44 Magnum. The films also display a reverence for organized religion, as long as it sticks to traditional religion. The repellent Scorpio has only contempt for religion—he wants to kill a priest and he shoots out the "Jesus Saves" lights. And Harry's disdain toward leftist priests and churches that shelter terrorists in *The Enforcer* is very clear.

Other Police Vigilantes

There have been a vast number of police procedural movies and many of them feature cops who walk in the shoes of Harry Callahan. One notable example is Officer Bud White (Russell Crowe) in *L.A. Confidential* (1997). White is the police muscle. He uses brute force to extract information, coerce confessions, and scare mobsters out of moving into Los Angeles to fill the vacuum caused by the conviction of gangster Mickey Cohen. The Los Angeles Police Department is hugely corrupt and White is an honest but extremely violent cop. Viewers probably find him a sympathetic character, since the violence is often in defense of abused women, and because he offers such a contrast to the crooked and sleazy cops in the department.

Gangster Squad (2013) took police vigilantism to the limit—far beyond anything that Harry Callahan ever imagined. LAPD Chief William Parker sets up a secret "gangster squad" to get rid of Mickey Cohen (Sean Penn) by any means necessary. John O'Mara (Josh Brolin) leads a group of cops without badges who bug Cohen's house without a warrant, bust up his various assets and businesses, and kill anyone who gets in the way. Of course, they succeed to vast public acclaim. Parker keeps his job and the public never finds out that O'Mara did the dirty work.

CONCLUSION

Vigilantism is deeply rooted in American culture. From the earliest times, Americans have taken the law into their own hands and administered popular justice. Vigilantism mostly was motivated by crime control, often on the frontier where law enforcement was weak, and it very much included racial lynching. Generally, vigilantes received strong public approval. The San Francisco Vigilance Committees of 1851 and 1856 and the Chinatown Squad were somewhat atypical because they operated in an urban environment, but their brand of popular justice apparently enjoyed massive local support and were widely copied elsewhere.

Given the centrality of popular justice in American history, it is hardly surprising that vigilantism is a familiar theme in popular culture. Much of this cultural product concerns private revenge vigilantism, but a good deal of it represents popular justice. This chapter focused on public-sector vigilantism in the movies, particularly as carried out by the police. The *Dirty Harry* movies strongly support the idea that the police should take the law into their own hands when they believe it is necessary to catch criminals or protect innocent civilians. These films and many others send a powerful message to consumers of pop culture. The message endorses the work of police officers who administer popular justice by acting with extreme violence and disregarding police bureaucracy as well as the rules of criminal procedure.

NOTES

1. Richard Maxwell Brown, "The History of Vigilantism in America," in *Vigilante Politics*, ed. H. Jon Rosenbaum and Peter C. Sederberg (Philadelphia: University of Pennsylvania Press, 1976), 79–109, has a lengthy bibliography.

2. Lawrence M. Friedman, *Crime and Punishment in American History* (New York: BasicBooks, 1993), 187–92.

3. See generally Friedman, chap. 8; Brown, "The History of Vigilantism in America."

4. Gary T. Marx and Dane Archer, "Community Police Patrols and Vigilantism," in *Vigilante Politics*, ed. H. Jon Rosenbaum and Peter C. Sederberg (Philadelphia: University of Pennsylvania Press, 1976), 129–57.

5. "How Stand-Your-Ground Law Works and Where It Applies," The *Independent*, July 23, 2018, https://www.independent.co.uk/news/uk/crime/stand-your-ground-law-explained-self-defence-crime-muggings-burglary-attack-a8460366.html.

6. Friedman, *Crime and Punishment in American History*, 180–81; Frank Soulé, John Gihon, and James Nisbert, *The Annals of San Francisco* (Berkeley: Berkeley Hills Books, 1855); Roger W. Lotchin, *San Francisco, 1846–1856: From Hamlet to City* (New York: Oxford University Press, 1974), 192–94; James A. B. Scherer, *"The Lion of the Vigilantes" William T. Coleman and the Life of Old San Francisco* (Indianapolis: Bobbs-Merrill, 1939), 107–27; Doris Muscatine, *Old San Francisco: The Biography of a City from Early Days to the Earthquake* (New York: Putnam, 1975), 267–71; Kevin J. Mullen, *Let Justice Be Done: Crime and Politics in Early San Francisco* (Reno: University of Nevada Press, 1989).

7. Scherer, *"The Lion of the Vigilantes" William T. Coleman and the Life of Old San Francisco*, 148–221; Muscatine, *Old San Francisco*, 271–82; Friedman, *Crime and Punishment in American History*.

8. Friedman, *Crime and Punishment in American History*, 182.

9. Hubert Howe Bancroft, *Popular Tribunals* (San Francisco: The History company, 1887).

10. Bancroft (*Popular Tribunals*, vol. 1, 10) wrote: "Vigilance recognizes fully the supremacy of law, flies to its rescue, when beaten down by its natural enemy, crime, and lifts it up that it may always be supreme; if the law must be broken to save the

state, then it breaks it soberly, conscientiously, and with the formulas of law, not in a feeling of revenge, or in a manner usual to the disorderly rabble."

11. Lotchin, *San Francisco, 1846–1856*, 194–201.

12. Richard Maxwell Brown, "Pivot of American Vigilantism: The San Francisco Vigilance Committee of 1856," in *Reflections of Western Historians*, ed. John Alexander Carroll (Tucson: University of Arizona Press, 1969), 105–19.

13. See Kevin J. Mullen, *Chinatown Squad: Policing the Dragon: From the Gold Rush to the 21st Century* (Novato, CA: Noir Publications, 2008); Gary Kamiya, "When SF Police Broke the Law to Combat Chinatown's Violent Gangs," *San Francisco Chronicle*, December 13, 2019, https://www.sfchronicle.com/chronicle_vault/article/When-SF-police-broke-the-law-to-combat-14904377.php; Richard H. Dillon, *The Hatchet Men: The Story of the Tong Wars in San Francisco's Chinatown* (New York: Coward-McCann, 1962), chap. 11. The Chinatown Squad fell victim to corruption in 1894 and on numerous later occasions, see Mullen, *Let Justice Be Done*, chap. 7. A more contemporary Bay Area example is the Oakland Riders—four police officers who engaged in racial profiling, false arrests, planting evidence, kidnapping, and other abuses around 2000. Their activities gave rise to criminal prosecution of the officers, federal oversight over the Oakland police, and a large civil settlement. See *"Allen v. City of Oakland,"* in *Wikipedia*, December 27, 2021, https://en.wikipedia.org/w/index.php?title=Allen_v._City_of_Oakland&oldid=1062203517. Just down the coast in Los Angeles, the Rampart police scandal, also around 2000, involved 70 police officers engaged in unlawful shootings and beatings, planting false evidence, and stealing narcotics. See "Rampart Scandal," in *Wikipedia*, January 24, 2022, https://en.wikipedia.org/w/index.php?title=Rampart_scandal&oldid=1067591432.

14. Mullen, *Chinatown Squad*, chap. 14.

15. See WatchMojo.com, "Top 10 Vigilante Justice Movies," October 18, 2016, https://www.youtube.com/watch?v=jF6VvbnfLAE; Kieran Fisher, "18 Great Vigilante Movies," Film School Rejects, March 5, 2018, https://filmschoolrejects.com/18-great-vigilante-movies/.

16. A prominent example of a television series concerned with police vigilante tactics is *The Shield* (2002–2008). It involves the highly extra-legal activities of the Los Angeles Police Department's Strike Team in trying to crush crime in a particularly dangerous precinct and was inspired by the LAPD's Rampart scandal (see note 13).

17. William Ian Miller, "Clint Eastwood and Equity: Popular Culture's Theory of Revenge," in *Law in the Domains of Culture*, ed. Austin Sarat and Thomas R. Kearns (Ann Arbor: University of Michigan Press, 1998), 183–99.

18. Two later Eastwood films carry on the tradition. Eastwood directed *Mystic River* (2003) about revenge gone wrong, and acted in and directed *Gran Torino* (2008) about another scheme to punish a criminal street gang, albeit involving the forces of law and order.

19. Michael Asimow and Jessica Silbey, *Law and Popular Culture: A Course Book* (Lake Mary, FL: Vanderplas Publishing, 2020), chap. 2.

20. These films are discussed in Michael Asimow and Paul Bergman, *Real to Reel: Truth and Trickery in Courtroom Movies* (Lake Mary, FL: Vanderplas Publishing, 2021). The film *They Won't Forget* is based on the real Leo Franks case in Atlanta in

1913; Franks was Jewish, falsely accused of murder, and killed by a lynch mob. The film, however, converted anti-Semitism into anti-Yankee prejudice, probably because the Hollywood Production Code banned any treatment of religious bias (Michael Asimow, "Divorce in the Movies: From the Hays Code to Kramer vs. Kramer," *Legal Stud. F.* 24 [2000]: 221).

21. Director John Ford's favorite of his many films.

22. Miller, "Clint Eastwood and Equity: Popular Culture's Theory of Revenge."

23. Jim Knipfel, "Death Wish and the Golden Age of Vigilante Movies," Den of Geek, March 2, 2018, https://www.denofgeek.com/movies/death-wish-and-the-golden-age-of-vigilante-movies/.

24. These films are discussed in Asimow and Bergman, *Real to Reel*.

25. For treatment of American criminal procedure, see Wayne R. LaFave, *Criminal Law*, Sixth edition (St. Paul, MN: West Academic Publishing, 2017).

26. Brown, "Pivot of American Vigilantism: The San Francisco Vigilance Committee of 1856." See note 13 for discussion of the Oakland Riders and Ramparts Scandal.

27. See Kanti C. Kotecha and James L. Walker, "Vigilantism and the American Police," in *Vigilante Politics*, ed. H. Jon Rosenbaum and Peter C. Sederberg (Philadelphia: University of Pennsylvania Press, 1976), 158–72.

28. *Escobedo v. Illinois*, 378 U.S. 478 (1964); *Miranda v. Arizona*, 384 U.S. 436 (1966). These are well-known Supreme Court decisions that protect a suspect's right to remain silent and to have the assistance of a lawyer.

29. The Fourth Amendment to the U.S. Constitution prohibits unreasonable search and seizure and requires that the police obtain a search warrant in many situations.

30. Briggs is probably referring to the San Francisco Vigilance Committees of 1851 and 1856, discussed in in the first subsection of this chapter. He might also be referring to the SFPD's Chinatown Squad, also discussed in the first subsection, which was active from 1879—around one hundred years before the picture was made.

31. Former U.S. Attorney General William Barr strongly praised the use of torture in *Dirty Harry* and pointed to the positive audience response (Jerry Lambe, "AG Barr: Torture and Vigilantism in Dirty Harry and Death Wish Present 'Interesting Issues' of Justice," Law & Crime, August 8, 2019, https://lawandcrime.com/high-profile/ag-barr-torture-and-vigilantism-in-dirty-harry-and-death-wish-present-interesting-issues-of-justice/. Barr asked: "I say, now, was that an unjust or morally repellent act? Is the reason that the audience applauds when that happens because the audience is morally bankrupt? Or is there something else going on there?" Barr added, "I think these are interesting issues."

32. See Joe Street, *Dirty Harry's America: Clint Eastwood, Harry Callahan, and the Conservative Backlash* (Tallahassee: University Press of Florida, 2016), chap. 3.

33. Street, chap. 2.

BIBLIOGRAPHY

"*Allen v. City of Oakland*." In *Wikipedia*, December 27, 2021. https://en.wikipedia.org/w/index.php?title=Allen_v._City_of_Oakland&oldid=1062203517.

Asimow, Michael. "Divorce in the Movies: From the Hays Code to Kramer vs. Kramer." *Legal Stud. F.* 24 (2000): 221.

Asimow, Michael, and Paul Bergman. *Real to Reel: Truth and Trickery in Courtroom Movies*. Lake Mary, FL: Vanderplas Publishing, 2021.

Asimow, Michael, and Jessica Silbey. *Law and Popular Culture: A Course Book*. Lake Mary, FL: Vanderplas Publishing, 2020.

Bancroft, Hubert Howe. *Popular Tribunals*. San Francisco: The History company, 1887.

Brown, Richard Maxwell. "Pivot of American Vigilantism: The San Francisco Vigilance Committee of 1856." In *Reflections of Western Historians*, edited by John Alexander Carroll, 105–19. Tucson: University of Arizona Press, 1969.

———. "The History of Vigilantism in America." In *Vigilante Politics*, edited by H. Jon Rosenbaum and Peter C. Sederberg, 79–109. Philadelphia: University of Pennsylvania Press, 1976.

Dillon, Richard H. *The Hatchet Men: The Story of the Tong Wars in San Francisco's Chinatown*. New York: Coward-McCann, 1962.

Fisher, Kieran. "18 Great Vigilante Movies." Film School Rejects, March 5, 2018. https://filmschoolrejects.com/18-great-vigilante-movies/.

Friedman, Lawrence M. *Crime and Punishment in American History*. New York: BasicBooks, 1993.

The Independent. "How Stand-Your-Ground Law Works and Where It Applies," July 23, 2018. https://www.independent.co.uk/news/uk/crime/stand-your-ground-law-explained-self-defence-crime-muggings-burglary-attack-a8460366.html.

Kamiya, Gary. "When SF Police Broke the Law to Combat Chinatown's Violent Gangs." *San Francisco Chronicle*, December 13, 2019. https://www.sfchronicle.com/chronicle_vault/article/When-SF-police-broke-the-law-to-combat-14904377.php.

Knipfel, Jim. "Death Wish and the Golden Age of Vigilante Movies." Den of Geek, March 2, 2018. https://www.denofgeek.com/movies/death-wish-and-the-golden-age-of-vigilante-movies/.

Kotecha, Kanti C., and James L. Walker. "Vigilantism and the American Police." In *Vigilante Politics*, edited by H. Jon Rosenbaum and Peter C. Sederberg, 158–72. Philadelphia: University of Pennsylvania Press, 1976.

LaFave, Wayne R. *Criminal Law*. Sixth edition. St. Paul, MN: West Academic Publishing, 2017.

Lambe, Jerry. "AG Barr: Torture and Vigilantism in Dirty Harry and Death Wish Present 'Interesting Issues' of Justice." Law & Crime, August 8, 2019. https://lawandcrime.com/high-profile/ag-barr-torture-and-vigilantism-in-dirty-harry-and-death-wish-present-interesting-issues-of-justice/.

Lotchin, Roger W. *San Francisco, 1846–1856: From Hamlet to City*. New York: Oxford University Press, 1974.

Marx, Gary T., and Dane Archer. "Community Police Patrols and Vigilantism." In *Vigilante Politics*, edited by H. Jon Rosenbaum and Peter C. Sederberg, 129–57. Philadelphia: University of Pennsylvania Press, 1976.

Miller, William Ian. "Clint Eastwood and Equity: Popular Culture's Theory of Revenge." In *Law in the Domains of Culture*, edited by Austin Sarat and Thomas R. Kearns, 161–202. Ann Arbor: University of Michigan Press, 1998.

Mullen, Kevin J. *Chinatown Squad: Policing the Dragon: From the Gold Rush to the 21st Century*. Novato, CA: Noir Publications, 2008.

———. *Let Justice Be Done: Crime and Politics in Early San Francisco*. Reno: University of Nevada Press, 1989.

Muscatine, Doris. *Old San Francisco: The Biography of a City from Early Days to the Earthquake*. New York: Putnam, 1975.

"Rampart Scandal." In *Wikipedia*, January 24, 2022. https://en.wikipedia.org/w/index.php?title=Rampart_scandal&oldid=1067591432.

Scherer, James A. B. *"The Lion of the Vigilantes" William T. Coleman and the Life of Old San Francisco*. Indianapolis: Bobbs-Merrill, 1939.

Soulé, Frank, John Gihon, and James Nisbert. *The Annals of San Francisco*. Berkeley: Berkeley Hills Books, 1855.

Street, Joe. *Dirty Harry's America: Clint Eastwood, Harry Callahan, and the Conservative Backlash*. Tallahassee: University Press of Florida, 2016.

WatchMojo.com. "Top 10 Vigilante Justice Movies," October 18, 2016. https://www.youtube.com/watch?v=jF6VvbnfLAE.

Chapter 2

Vigilantes, the Law and Popular Culture
The British Experience

Peter Robson

BACKGROUND

Resisting injustice and challenging the law has, in the British context, been extensive from the times of recorded history. From the invasion of the Romans and Normans there are groups and individuals who have sought to uphold the rights of the dispossessed against new sources of power seeking to establish "law and order." These range from the resistance to the rule of the Romans by the Queen of the Celtic tribe, the Iceni, Boudicca,[1] and Hereward the Wake.[2] Within Britain there has been a series of groups resisting the hegemony of England over all three of its neighbors. Their goals ranged from total rejection of the invasive English Crown to localized lawlessness and to a resistance to unfair taxes and toll charges. Folk heroes exist in Scotland too at the level of organized resistance to power and rebellion through figures who are known internationally through film such as William Wallace,[3] Robert the Bruce,[4] and Rob Roy.[5] Ireland's subjection to English rule came as a by-product of the Norman invasion of Britain and resistance to this has provided many examples of people acting outside the formal justice system such as the United Irishmen.[6] Figures emerged in Wales after it lost its independence in the thirteenth century from Owen Glendower (Owain Glyn Dŵr) in the fifteenth century[7] through the Red Bandits of Mawddwy (Gwylliaid

Cochion Mawddwy) the following century[8] to the Rebecca Riots between 1839 and 1843.[9]

Those individuals who operate outside the law to achieve justice[10] at the more limited level have also been a feature of the myths and folklore of Britain and are exemplified by the figure of Robin Hood.[11] Whether seen as a historical or rather a mythical figure, the themes of the righter of wrongs and the resister of oppression has been dominated by this image.[12] It has produced many versions in recent popular culture. They also include footpads and highwaymen.[13] These had an element of popular appeal with benefits to the poor by these lawbreakers as seen in the broadsheet ballads in the seventeenth century and in film versions.[14] It is also worth mentioning others breaking the law in defense of their livelihoods threatened by technological change like the Luddites[15] and those agricultural laborers rioting in the name of Captain Swing.[16] Local issues have often led to actions which involve challenging officialdom and how power was being exercised. Examples include the bloody Hexham Riot/Massacre of 1761 and the Battle of Stanhope in 1818. The former involved resistance to new ways of selecting men for the militia in the north of England and led to at least fifty deaths.[17] The latter stemmed from punishment of poaching by starving lead miners and the resulting local resistance to those brought to "justice."[18] In the Irish context there were always strong political elements in localized lawbreaking and the word for bandit (tóraidhe) provided the name by which the British Conservative Party is known.[19]

REPRESENTING VENGEANCE AND VIGILANTISM IN A BRITISH CONTEXT

The universal themes of revenge and justified vengeance which underlie vigilantism have appeared in British cultural products from Marlowe and Shakespeare to the modern day. They come in many forms through the theater and literature to the film and TV material we consume today. While the principal focus of this work is on film and television, it is worthwhile noting the other areas where these themes are found.

Theater

The settings for theatrical revenge are often historic. Just as Greek, Norse, and other myths and sagas were replete with the themes of vengeance, so too classic literature has from its earliest days a deep interest in these issues.[20] Shakespeare in his plays employed the narrative device of revenge to motivate many of his protagonists. These range from those remedying a perceived wrong like *Hamlet* or betrayal like *Othello* to harm to feelings in *The Merchant of Venice* and the playing out of "eye for an eye" in *Titus Andronicus*. Forgiveness is also explored through Prospero in *The Tempest* and in *Coriolanus*.

Although the theme of revenge has proved a generally less compelling subject in modern popular theater, there are some notable exceptions. J. B. Priestley's *An Inspector Calls* (1945) with its notion of bringing to account those responsible for the suicide of a young woman is another version of revenge, albeit of a strange supernatural kind with the Inspector's identity never being made entirely clear. He represents some kind of community conscience and while he does not mete out justice he is its personification.

Related to the justice system, one of the mainstays of popular theater during the twentieth century and into the twenty-first has been the mystery murder or "whodunit." The driving force behind the perpetrator has often been financial gain,[21] jealousy,[22] or true love,[23] but revenge sometimes lies at the back. In the recent professional productions of the Agatha Christie Theatre Company between 2006 and 2019 the theme of revenge crops up. The contrast in terms of the kinds of revenge is marked. One is a cold calculated elaborate ruse in the stage version of the Poirot mystery *Five Little Pigs, Go Back for Murder* (1960). Here the murder is committed out of revenge by the spurned mistress of an artist.[24] By contrast in *Witness for the Prosecution*, the treatment of faithful Christine Helm by the heartless Leonard Vole is the theatrical denouement of the play. Here we see the response of the woman whose cunning artifice has secured the acquittal of her beloved. Betrayed by him for another younger woman, she responds efficiently and effectively with the knife with which he himself had committed the original murder of a wealthy older woman. Christine has her revenge in the most spectacular and public way. It is not only Sir Wilfrid Robarts who is on her side. So too, from my experience, is the mesmerized theater audience. Not all Christie's revenge takers are as emotionally charged.

And Then There Were None features a motley group of people brought together in a remote isthmus, cut off from the outside world by bad weather.[25] The group gradually see their numbers fall as dead bodies become the order of the day. When we are down to only two survivors the motive for the deaths is made clear by the killer—who is in fact one of the "deceased." The judge in the scenario is seeking revenge for reasons which are unusual to say the least[26] but are all part of the desire of the author to provide a "perfect insoluble" murder mystery, with revenge at its heart. One could then describe *And Then There Were None* as operating within the vigilante framework in that the murderer's intention is to visit the death penalty on those whom the judge assesses as actually guilty of murder themselves.[27] Similarly, *The*

Unexpected Guest too involves a murder by a man who turns out to be avenging the death of his son.

The plays based on the work of judge and author Henry Cecil also feature people who have been wronged, gathering together a group of people to subject them to some kind of sophisticated vengeance. *Settled Out of Court*[28] centers on the revenge of an escaped convicted murderer determined to prove he was framed and take revenge on those who had been involved. As with so many of Henry Cecil's better stories there is a twist in the tail. In a later stage collaboration, based on another Cecil book, *Alibi for a Judge*,[29] the plot is convoluted. It revolves around whether the wife of a man accused of bank robbery is trying to extort money from the judge in the case, take her revenge on him or actually trying to clear her husband's name. Again all is revealed at the very last moment. Finally, there is a link between vigilantism and revenge against a serial rapist whom the legal system has exonerated. This is covered, in a slightly bizarre lighthearted stage adaptation of an earlier Cecil novel, in *According to the Evidence*.[30] It is clear, then, that revenge is a theme which theater audiences encounter from these providers of popular stage thrillers and in which vigilantism is encountered. By their nature, though, like their fictional counterparts in novels as these works center on "whodunit" the kinds of endings which we find in vigilante films are absent. The theatrical avenger does not return to a normal life at the end of the play.

Popular Fiction

The mystery, detective, and police genre focused on crime and the justice system now enjoy greater popularity than the rest of fiction in the UK. Crime sales increased by 19 percent between 2015 and 2017 to 18.7m, compared to the 18.1m fiction books sold in 2017.[31] The principal goal, though, as in the theatrical presentations, is on the tracking and apprehension of the perpetrator of a clear crime. Vigilante behavior, by its very nature, goes undetected and unpunished with the perpetrator returning to normal life after having secured "justice." At present it would seem from an examination of the works of writers as varied on law, crime, and justice as Agatha Christie and Henry Cecil that vengeance and the exacting of revenge are popular and ever-present themes. The prodigious murder mystery output of Agatha Christie between 1920 and 1976 almost inevitably lead some of the killers' motivations to have been revenge. Revenge too makes its appearance although as in her plays these motivations range from true love[32] to simple greed for money.[33]

In addition to his plays, Cecil is also known for his light legal fiction. These center on the travails of various lawyers and the machinations of the legal system. A particular mixture of avarice and roguishness motivates most of Cecil's "scallywags."[34] Some of his work is, however, rather more serious in tone and involves people with the motive of revenge. These include a vigilante killing of a murderer of women on whom the police failed to get proper evidence,[35] and a judge killing a man bent on revenge himself.[36] In *According to the Evidence* Alec Morland, an ex-soldier, takes vigilante action against a man accused of being a serial rapist and murderer who has been acquitted for lack of evidence. Alec is, in due course, tried for murder himself but is acquitted in a book with slightly odd elements of humor injected into it. The revenge element in *Portrait of a Judge*, on the other hand, is rather different. It is the judge who commits the murder when threatened by someone resentful of a death sentence passed by the judge years before.

The books of crime writers of recent times have embraced notions of revenge but have for the most part avoided the vigilante theme. When, for instance, one looks at the book on which the revenge film *Straw Dogs* (1971) was apparently based, *The Siege at Trencher's Farm*, by Paisley's Gordon Williams, one discovers that the only things that the book and film have in common are the presence of an American academic, George Magruder, and the West Country setting. The core of the book is the presence at the farm of an escaped convicted pedophile and the desire of the village mob to exact summary justice on him. The conflict arises when Magruder is unwilling to allow this kangaroo court to have its way and defends his home. The film simply has the village mob fueled by an irrational hatred of the outsider and suffused with a desire to mete out justice to someone with a learning difficulty.

An exception to this avoidance of the vigilante and revenge theme can be seen in the works of Helen Zahavi. In two novels she explores the revenge fantasy quite explicitly. In *Dirty Weekend* (1991), the victim of a peeping tom and obscene phone calls complains ineffectively to the police in Brighton. When they do nothing she murders the voyeur and then fate determines that a number of other men who assault her in different ways receive similar treatment. In addition, she defends a "down and out" on the street from being set alight and finally stabs a serial killer who has seen her as easy prey. The novel ends with her free and apparently clear of the long arm of the law.[37] The notion of revenge, though, is found again in *Donna and the Fatman* (1998). Helen Zahavi explained that the original vigilante fantasy came from her own experience working in Brighton and being subject to a voyeuristic obscene phone caller and writing *Dirty Weekend*. Such a theme did not go down well with critics, she noted.

> A year ago, I had the gall to wander off. I wrote a piece of fiction. It went against the grain. It caused offence. Perhaps it even sought to break the mould. It shows an ordinary woman sloughing off docility. She's had enough, and goes out in the

night, and hopes the freaks will find her. She sends the perverts off to perverts' paradise and makes them stiff forever. She treats them like the rabid dogs they are. If they want to batter, rape or murder her, she wipes them out. A reasonable response to unreasonable demands.[38]

The theme emerges in cinema rather more extensively.

Cinema

Sharing a common language with the United States has, since the emergence of talking pictures, proved a mixed blessing in terms of film. While British audiences have never required their films to be dubbed or subtitled, the industry has always been under threat of being swamped by the products of Hollywood. Measures over the years have ranged from quotas on the amount of imports which have been allowed to generous tax arrangements to provide support for the "home grown" product. These have had mixed success.

To access UK film tax relief or be eligible for other public support, such as Lottery funding, a film must be certified as British. To qualify as British, a production must pass the highly mechanistic cultural test for film[39] or be certified as an official co-production under one of the UK's bilateral co-production agreements or the European Convention on Cinematographic Co-production. The cultural test has been in place since 2007, but was revised in 2014 to bring it in line with the more recent creative sector cultural tests. A wide range of films qualified as British under the cultural test in 2018, including *Colette*, *Isle of Dogs*, and *Solo: A Star Wars Story*. To qualify as British under one of the UK's official co-production agreements, films must be jointly certified by the appropriate authorities in each co-producing country. This centers on the creative, technical, artistic, and financial input from each co-producer. Once certified, a film counts as a national film in each of the territories and may qualify for public support in that territory.[40] It is this formula which results in a film like *Kick-Ass* (2010) qualifying as Best British Movie in the Empire Awards of 2011 even though at first glance this would not appear to be much to do with British life or culture.[41] Official UK co-productions can also be certified under the European Convention on Cinematographic Co-production which allows for both bilateral and multilateral film co-productions. In February 2019, the UK became a signatory to the revised Convention which enables European signatories to co-produce with partners outside of Europe without having to use bilateral co-production treaties.[42]

In terms of an industry the British film industry is in the Top 5 of filmed entertainment world markets with a value of between $2.8 and $3.2 billion.[43] Despite the attractions of television and streamed entertainment, film attendances between 2009 and 2019 have been reasonably steady at around 170 million.[44] The British film industry in the second decade of this century produces over 150 films per year. These cover a range of different genres and are dominated by comedies and drama at some 41.9 percent with thrillers comprising 8.5 percent and crime 2.2 percent of releases.[45] In terms of revenue the figures were starker with comedies and drama taking 22.2 percent, thrillers 4.6 percent and crime 0.1 percent.[46] Action films, which were 6.6 percent of production, attracted a disproportionate 21.3 percent of box office takings.[47]

In 2018, 787 films (an average of over 15 per week) were released for a week or more in the UK and Republic of Ireland, 27 more than in 2017, and the second highest figure of the period 2009–2018. The origin of these films was United States 212; UK 197, Europe 152, India 158, and the rest of the world 68.[48]

Twenty-seven percent of all films released in the UK in 2018 were of US origin (excluding UK co-productions) and these films accounted for 51 percent of total box office earnings.[49] UK films, including co-productions, represented 25 percent of releases (up from 21% in 2017) and shared 46 percent of the box office; UK independent films represented 23 percent of releases (up from 18% in 2017) and 13 percent of the box office (up from 10% in 2017), the second highest share since records began. Films originating outside the UK and USA accounted for 48 percent of releases in 2018 (down from 54% in 2017) but just 3 percent of earnings (down from 5% in 2017). Films from non-UK European countries accounted for 1.1 percent of the box office (from 19% of releases), down from 1.5 percent in 2017, while films from India accounted for 1.2 percent of the total box office (from 20% of releases), up marginally from 1.1 percent in 2017.

The most significant trend over the period has been a decline in share for US-only films which has been compensated by an increase in share for UK studio-backed titles. The average combined share of US-only and UK studio-backed films was around 90 percent up to 2010, but fell to around 84 percent for the remainder of the period, with the exception of 2014 when the aggregate share was 76 percent. The main reason for the lower figure in that year was the record share achieved by UK independent releases (16%), which included titles such as *Paddington* and *The Inbetweeners 2*, two of 2014's top five grossing films. The high levels of market share achieved by UK studio-backed films between 2015 and 2018 reflects the number of successful big budget franchise productions making use of the UK's filmmaking infrastructure during those years. The fluctuating pattern of UK market share is dependent on a small number of high grossing titles.[50] The average UK independent market share for the ten-year period was just under 10 percent with a slight upward trend from a low of just over 5 percent in 2010.[51]

The dominance of the United States in terms of box office revenue can be seen in the Top 20 earning films of which nine were US productions and ten were US/UK co-productions—there was one US/Australia co-production of quintessentially British *Peter Rabbit*.[52] The inflation-adjusted box office chart based on the top 20 highest grossing films released in the UK since 1975 (when coverage of leading titles began)[53] is dominated by franchise films. In addition to the four *Star Wars* titles, it includes three *Harry Potter* films, the *Lord of the Rings* trilogy, and two *James Bond* films. The only top 20 films released since 1975 which are neither part of a series or franchise are *Titanic* and *The Full Monty*. Ten are based on stories and characters created by UK writers, such as the authors Ian Fleming and JK Rowling and the playwright Catherine Johnson, which shows the sustained appetite for home-grown material among British audiences.[54]

British films with a vigilante theme are less frequently encountered than their US counterparts but they do share many of the standard themes encountered in Hollywood productions.[55] Those films produced and financed in Britain with a largely British cast and crew also start from a happy family setting and stem from random stranger violence from those with no apparent social worth.[56] Our hitherto model citizen then experiences an ineffective legal system operating and having been driven to take successful vigilante action is able to return to his life once the evil has been expunged. The films with significant vigilante elements emerging from the British film industry include *Get Carter* (1975), *Dirty Weekend* (1993), *The Fourth Angel* (2001), *Dead Man's Shoes* (2004), *Outlaw* (2007), *Harry Brown* (2009), and *Vendetta* (2013).[57]

The very personal nature of revenge covers the actions of Jack Carter in seeking to discover and then deal with the death of his brother in *Get Carter* (1971). Although not principally a vigilante film, it is worth noting for the way in which the motives of the protagonist alter upon finding the circumstances in which his brother died and what has started out as Jack Carter simply doing some "gangland enforcing" changes into a piece of personal vengeance.

The setting for *Dirty Weekend* (1993) is rather more domestic, based on and with a screenwriting credit to author Helen Zahavi. Here the revenge is carried out by a mild-mannered secretary. Advertised as "By the Director of Death Wish," this film is noteworthy for its very clear vigilante theme. As noted above, the protagonist commences her homicidal actions after the law fails to help her deal with a voyeur who has threatened to assault and rape her. It has one unusual aspect which links it to rape-revenge films in that our protagonist ends the film intending to continue to with her crusade against sleazy men after disposing of a further six over the eponymous weekend.

The accidental nature of the justice-seeking vigilante is emphasized in a British-Canadian co-production *The Fourth Angel* (2001) where a journalist loses most of his family in a misguided police attempt to end a terrorist airplane hijacking. Receiving no positive response from the authorities, he takes matters into his own hands. He is able to track down and dispose of all the members of the gang. He ends up lolling on a yacht, his limited task having been achieved.

The hollow nature of revenge is demonstrated in Shane Meadows's *Dead Man's Shoes* (2004). This bleak portrayal of twenty-first-century Britain involves a man returning from service in the army and avenging the abuse meted out to his brother by a gang of drug dealers in his home town. This he achieves in bloody fashion. Having, however, achieved his task of doing away with all but one of the gang who drove his brother to eventual suicide, he then seeks redemption through the ending of his own life.

A variation on the traditional lone vigilante is encountered in an ensemble piece with four men linked by a common thread in *Outlaw* (2007). These men, a disillusioned paratrooper, Bryant; a white-collar worker, Dekker; a barrister, Munroe; and a hotel security guard, Hillier, are thrown together by fate. Bonded through all having suffered at the hands of a local criminal underworld boss, Terry Manning, they set about killing off those associated with Manning, who himself ends up in jail. With Manning released, however, without being charged, there is a final showdown/shootout with the corrupt police involved on the side of Manning. Only one of the gang escapes the bloodbath and in the final scene we see him taunted by Manning that he has not the courage to shoot him. It turns out he does. The credits roll and we can safely assume that perhaps there will be another outing for Dekker.[58]

A slight change of focus is found in another Michael Caine film *Harry Brown* (2009). Here our eponymous hero is a pensioner with emphysema. His life and that of his friend are made difficult by the youth gang who lord it over the low-rent housing complex where they live. His breaking point comes after his friend dies at the hands of the gang after challenging their behavior. Although they are charged by the legal system, they are able to argue that they were acting in self-defense and go scot free. We then discover that Harry has a military background and is able to exact revenge on many of the malfeasants in his area. In the style of Hollywood's *Death Wish*, *The Brave One*, and *A Vigilante* he receives assistance from the local police to avoid the consequences of his various executions. The final scene shows him calmly approaching the previous "no go" area of the pedestrian underpass with the gang now dispersed.

A further interesting aspect of the Harry Brown film is the seriousness of the issue in the eyes of its star, Michael Caine. Writing in his autobiography, *The Elephant to Hollywood* (2010), he analyzes the film and explains how he did not see the film as celebrating violence in the way *Death Wish* was perceived to. "Harry Brown never becomes a willing perpetrator, he always remains the victim." Though he admits it was a fantasy based around the notion of being able to scare those who scare you. He explained that he went "into the film thinking that we should just lock up violent offenders and throw away the key but I completely changed my mind during the course of it." He blames the absence of opportunities in society for young people and lack of goals.[59] The social engineering analysis is a rather different perspective from that of his character. Mostly the contribution of these films to the vigilante roster has been specifically British in relatively muted style and tone.

The film *Vendetta* (2013), however, is very much in the mold of the original New York–based *Death Wish* (1974). A man returns from a spell in the armed forces to discover that someone has brutally immolated his parents. His enquiries lead him to the gang responsible. He takes advantage of his training as a "special ops" interrogation officer in Afghanistan and proceeds to track down and do away with those responsible in a manner that fits the brocard "an eye for eye." The twist at the end is that he has the protection of his old Army unit who allow him to walk away from his final encounter with the corrupt police. This also echoes the endings of *Death Wish* (1974), *The Brave One* (2007), and *A Vigilante* (2018).

There is in the film *Bad Day for the Cut* (2017) an element of vigilantism in the actions of farmer Donal O'Neill, who seeks out those who killed his mother in an apparent home-invasion robbery. He tracks down those responsible, discovering that she was not just a country farmer's wife. His mother was in fact involved with a member of the paramilitaries. The downbeat ending is reminiscent of *Dead Man's Shoes*.[60]

Alongside these various attempts to right wrongs there is also black humor. In *Kind Hearts and Coronets* (1949) the person seeking revenge does so to redress a social slight from an aristocratic family toward his mother.[61] In the process he seeks to dispose of no less than eight members of the D'Ascoyne family who stand between him and his rightful place as the Duke of Chalfont.[62]

What strikes one looking at the British vigilantes is the limited amount of gun violence. What they share with some of the more recent American products, though, is having "amateur" protagonists with an undisclosed and unexpected skill set to allow them to secure justice via retribution. The retribution is generally low key.[63]

British TV in Context

The world of television reception continues to alter at a rapid pace. There have been two quite distinct major developments worth noting. There continues to be an expansion in the number of channels available to license holder viewers free of charge on modern television channels. There are some seventy TV channels available to modern TV sets in Britain, which have Freeview automatically available via antennae.⁶⁴ There are more than 200 channels available to those who have the alternative satellite reception through the BBC/ITV service Freesat.⁶⁵

In addition, the ways of watching the programming has altered. The availability of watching programming via the internet using "catch up" and box sets has altered patterns of media consumption. It now seems likely, that the viewing habits of younger viewers, with their preference for streamed online content over linear viewing, is likely to change the way television is produced in the future just as the same pattern has decimated CD sales with the rise of music streaming.⁶⁶ Viewing of broadcast TV by children (4 to 15 years old) and 16-to 24-year-olds fell 33 percent between 2010 and 2017, and about 9 percent compared with 2015, according to Ofcom's annual Communications Market Report published in August 2017.⁶⁷ The fall in broadcast viewing continued in 2018, with children's viewing falling by 15 percent in 2017 to an average of 1 hour 24 minutes, and 16–24s' viewing fell by 12 percent to an average of 1 hour 40 minutes. Over-54s make up 28 percent of the population of the UK but accounted for 51 percent of television viewing in 2017.⁶⁸

The mixture of license-funded public service television alongside the private advertising model continues to operate in Britain. The politicians of the right who have dominated Parliament since 2010 continue to be against the long-term future of funding the BBC from a flat-rate license fee.⁶⁹ This assessment takes place every ten years or so. One of the principal issues in the most recent process centered around how the BBC should be funded. Due to issues in British politics at the time of writing between the right and left, the license fee was left in place when the December 2016 Royal Charter and Framework Agreement was published.⁷⁰ This runs for a further decade until December 31, 2027,⁷¹ and replaces the 2006 charter.

The emergence of television and the significance of free-to-view public service broadcasting is a notable factor in the kind of programs which have been encountered on British screens over the past sixty years. There have always been skeptics in Britain about the impact of advertising on the fundamental principles which inspired the BBC—namely the goals of education, information, and entertainment. The need to protect the public from crass vulgarity and the lowest common denominator has always featured. Most recently in a discussion of the future of the culture in Britain the emphasis was on the technical rather than the political issue of public service and the goals of education and information.⁷² The BBC in a market-based entertainment world, it has been suggested, would benefit from a democratic input as an alternative to government control and the vagaries of marketization.⁷³ It is in this context that vigilantism features on the British small screen.

Revenge has not been a theme which has dominated British television schedules. Indeed, it is hard to actually find much by way of material in which the issue dominates. It is possible to identify elements of revenge within some of the action programs centered on the oppression of various groups. So in 1950s programs produced in Britain aimed principally at children such as *Robin Hood* and *William Tell* as well as more adult-orientated adventure material of non-state operatives[74] like *The Saint*, *The Four Just Men*, and *The Persuaders*, we have resistance and in due course the oppressors getting their "just deserts." While this involves the oppressors being "paid back" and "scores being settled," there is in these programs little by way of spitefulness and vindictiveness. The "baddies" are crudely drawn and have no redeeming features which might inspire forgiveness. The lawbreakers in the police and detective series between the 1950s and the time of writing were portrayed in a more nuanced way and were driven by various factors including greed and ambition. They were almost never, of course, the police themselves.[75] Vigilantism as a narrative driver, though, is seldom encountered.[76]

A vigilante theme is, however, encountered in a short British mini-series *Gunrush* (2009).[77] In *Gunrush* we have the standard setup found in vigilante films. The happy family's lives are subverted by random stranger violence. The series focuses on the response of a mild-mannered, middle-aged driving instructor to the random shooting of his daughter by a youth in a hoodie. The protagonist's wife objected to the youth and his mate pushing in front of him and his wife in a supermarket queue, resulting in the shooting response. Having later tracked down the murder weapon, our vigilante plans to rescue his other daughter, who has been kidnapped by the rest of the gang, and shoot the perpetrators. Before he is able to do this, the gang themselves are gunned down by a rival gang. The improbable denouement avoids the tricky moral question of whether, having tracked down the killer, the father would have exacted vengeance. There has been no British attempt to replicate the huge success of the *Dexter* series from 2006 to 2013 and its vigilante serial killer core.[78] It may be that the memories of the work of Dr. Harold Shipman and his ending the lives of at least 218 patients in his care are still too raw.[79]

LEGAL CONTEXT

Self-Defense in Britain

England and Wales

The kinds of actions which are covered in the actions of vigilantes in the films, books, plays, and TV programs discussed above are largely criminalized in the law in Britain. The rules go no further than a limited recognition of self-defense. Such self-defense must involve proportionate force. The issue has recently emerged in Britain in the context of whether or not a person is justified in using firearms against someone who is not obviously armed. The portrayal of vigilantes in British films and TV take place in a country where gun ownership is low and where firearms are uncommon in the vast majority of households. The level of authorized gun ownership is estimated to be 4.6 per 100 persons in the United Kingdom compared with 120.5 in the United States, 34.7 in Canada, and 31.7 in Iceland.[80] The most common form of gun ownership is the single or double-barrel shotgun.[81] These are required to be licensed. In order to obtain a Shotgun Certificate a person must provide a referee for such a shotgun certificate and satisfy the police that they have a good reason to have, buy, or acquire a shotgun.[82] When buying a shotgun one is required to show a valid Shotgun Certificate. Homicide deaths per 100,000 of the population by firearms range from 0.07 in Iceland, 0.20 in the United Kingdom, 0.61 in Canada to 12.21 in the United States.[83] There have been three major shooting incidents in mainland Britain in the past forty years—Hungerford 1987, Dunblane school massacre 1996, and the Cumbria shootings in 2010. All involved men with licensed firearms with a total death toll of 44.[84]

To obtain a firearm certificate, the police must be satisfied that a person has "good reason" to own each firearm, and that they can be trusted with it "without danger to the public safety or to the peace." Under Home Office guidelines, Firearm Certificates are only issued if a person has legitimate sporting, collecting, or work-related reasons for ownership. Since 1968, self-defense has not been considered a valid reason to own a firearm. The current licensing procedure involves: positive verification of identity, two referees of verifiable good character who have known the applicant for at least two years (and who may themselves be interviewed and/or investigated as part of the certification), approval of the application by the applicant's own family doctor, an inspection of the premises and cabinet where firearms will be kept and a face-to-face interview by a Firearms Enquiry Officer (FEO), also known as a Firearms Liaison Officer (FLO). A thorough background check of the applicant is then made by Special Branch on behalf of the firearms licensing department. Only when all these stages have been satisfactorily completed will a firearms license be issued, which must be renewed every five years.

The likelihood then of simple recourse to firearms is significantly less in Britain. For anyone who does take action against others and seeks to use the defense of reasonable excuse the law is part of the judge-made common law. Legislation also provides a defense where it can be said someone is preventing a crime when intervening on someone else's behalf.[85] In the Privy Council,[86] it was stated, "The common law has always recognised . . . the right of a person to protect himself from attack and to act in the defence of others and if necessary to inflict violence on another in so doing. If no more force is used than is reasonable to repel the attack such force is not unlawful and no crime is committed."[87] In the Beckford case, the defendant police officer shot dead a suspect, having been told that he was armed and dangerous, because he feared for his own life. The prosecution case was that the victim had been unarmed and thus presented no threat to the defendant. The trial judge directed the jury that the defendant's belief in the need to shoot in self-defense had to be both honest and reasonable. The Privy Council rejected this direction. Lord Griffiths, delivering the single judgment of the court, commented that juries should adopt the guidance of the Judicial Studies Board: "Whether the plea is self-defence or defence of another, if the defendant may have been labouring under a mistake as to facts, he must be judged according to his mistaken belief of the facts: that is so whether the mistake was, on an objective view, a reasonable mistake or not."[88] The defendant therefore, had a defense of self-defense because the killing was not unlawful if, in the circumstances as he perceived them to be, he had used reasonable force to defend himself.

Statutes have elaborated on the standard to be operated. The Criminal Justice and Immigration Act 2008 covers "reasonable force for the purpose of self-defence."[89] Whether the degree of force used by the notional figure D is reasonable in the circumstances is to be decided "in the circumstances as D believed them to be." In deciding that question these cover whether the belief was "genuinely held."[90] If it was mistaken, was the mistake a reasonable one to have made?[91]

There are more generous criteria where one is a "householder." Where one is in a dwelling and one is not a trespasser and the other person is a trespasser then the degree of force is not to be regarded as reasonable if it is "grossly disproportionate" in those circumstances.[92] For other situations the test is somewhat stricter being whether the degree of force is simply "disproportionate."[93] In deciding whether the degree of force was reasonable in the circumstances the legislation specifies that there is no duty to retreat.[94] The possibility that one could have retreated is to be considered as a relevant factor rather than giving rise to a "duty to retreat."

This use of reasonable force then can be based on an honestly held but mistaken belief. In the context of the preemptive strike then Lord Griffith pointed out that, "A man about to be attacked does not have to wait for his assailant to strike the first blow or fire the first shot; circumstances may justify a preemptivee strike."[95] Self-defense must not, however, justify turning into attack as where a man defending himself with a sword against three masked men armed with loaded handguns killed one of them by slashing him repeatedly—for this loss of control shifting from self-defense into an intent to kill he received a sentence of eight years imprisonment for manslaughter due to the element of provocation.[96]

This issue was debated extensively in August 1999, when a farmer, Tony Martin, shot at two young burglars who had been robbing goods at his property. He claimed he had been burgled on ten previous occasions. The burglars were making their way away from him and he killed one of them with his shotgun. He was convicted of murder and was sentenced to life. This was reduced on appeal, as he was found to have a paranoid personality disorder and to have diminished responsibility. He served three years of his five-year sentence for the reduced charge of manslaughter. In 2018 he was interviewed and stated that he had no regrets and would do the same thing again.[97]

Northern Ireland

The Court of Appeal in Northern Ireland, with its separate legal system, indicated that possession of a pistol and ammunition for the purpose of protecting the possessor may be possession for "a lawful object," even though the possession was unlawful, being without a license. This concerned a man in a mixed marriage who had been beaten and attacked on a number of occasions and who acquired a pistol and ammunition which he kept in the home in 1971 a couple of years into the Troubles.

Possession of a firearm for the purpose of protecting the possessor or his wife or family from acts of violence, may be possession for a lawful object. But the lawfulness of such a purpose cannot be founded on a mere fancy, or on some aggressive motive. The threatened danger must be reasonably and genuinely anticipated, must appear reasonably imminent, and must be of a nature which could not reasonably be met by more pacific means.[98]

Scotland

There is also a separate set of Scottish criminal justice rules and the courts for applying these are based wholly in Scotland. Unlike civil law matters there is no appeal beyond the High Court of Justiciary to the Supreme Court in London. The criminal law is a mix of common law and statutes. There is, however, greater weight accorded to commentators on the law known as Institutional writers. In criminal matters the most prominent are Hume and Alison along with a major recent author Gerald Gordon. An accused may use reasonable force in defense of oneself or others is the position at common law. A person may use such force as is reasonable in the circumstances for self-defense, defense of another person, defense of property, prevention of crime, and lawful arrest of an offender. This covers where the victim or another is being attacked and there is imminent danger to life or limb or there is reasonable belief they are going to be attacked. An effort should always be made to retreat or escape from an attack. A person may use force as a last resort if there is no other means whereby they can escape or retreat from an attack. Where, however, a person is acting in self-defense of another person there is no obligation to retreat. Where there is use of force this must be "necessary" in the circumstances; the force used has to be "reasonable in the circumstances"; and the force used must also be "proportionate" to the threat faced.[99]

Ireland

In neighboring Ireland, a new law was enacted to cover this issue of self-defense. The matter arose there in similar circumstances where a farmer who shot dead an intruder was charged with manslaughter. Although he was found not guilty, it provoked debate and led to the passing of the Criminal Law (Defence and the Dwelling) Act 2011. This provides that "it shall not be an offence for a person who is in his or her dwelling or for a person who is a lawful occupant in a dwelling, to use force against another person or the property of another person where they believe the other person is in the dwelling as a trespasser for the purpose of committing a criminal act."[100] The force to be used is only such as is reasonable in the circumstances as the dweller believes. Thus this covers where they protect against injury, assault, detention, or death to themselves or others present. It also covers protection of property against appropriation, destruction, or damage as well as commission of a crime.

It is immaterial in the Irish legislation whether or not the person using the force had a safe and practicable opportunity to retreat from the dwelling before using the force concerned.[101] Nor is there a requirement to retreat from the dwelling.[102] It is also specified that anyone using force in this context shall not be liable for any injury, loss, or damage caused to the intruder.[103] There was a successful use of the defense in a case in June 2016 where a man stabbed another man to death. Two strangers had been found in the family bedroom of his mobile home. The defendant claimed he was attacked and seized the nearest object and hit his assailant with it. The jury asked the judge what the difference between the law before the Act and with it was. The judge replied, "Before that, if you were in a situation, you had to retreat. Now, you have certain rights in your home."[104]

CONCLUSION

It is not suggested that there is a direct cause and effect between the image of the vigilante portrayed in popular culture for British audiences and the changes in the law. Rather, it would seem that the well-established general rules which in the British Isles recognize that not all homicides or assaults are to be punished have been altered by particular circumstances. The issues which have led to legal change seem to resemble moral panics rather than major changes in unlawful behavior.[105]

There is evidence, to some extent, of a resurgence of "new vigilantism" in relation to one specific area of social concern. Actions by residents against those suspected of offenses involving children are not themselves new.[106] Nor is the phenomenon limited to Britain.[107] What is new is the impact of social media. Various anti-pedophile groups have been operating seeking to entrap those using the Internet, such as Letzgo Hunting,[108] Dark Justice,[109] and The Hunted One.[110] One academic has suggested that pedophile hunters might "have the effect of unduly diverting criminal justice resources from sex offenders who pose a considerable risk to the public towards low-risk offenders, the so-called 'low-hanging fruit,'" and that "Paedophile-hunting groups can circumvent procedural safeguards and regulations that exist to moderate state power and protect the human rights of those subject to a criminal process."[111]

Anti-pedophile groups have also extensively been criticized by police for "jeopardizing police work,"[112] and for the propensity of some vigilantes to attack, abuse, and threaten the people they lure. Questions have also been leveled about whether the actions of these vigilante groups constitutes entrapment. In 2017, a sting by the Hunted One involving a team of hunters luring an Indian man to Bluewater Shopping Centre ended with a crowd of men storming the area after watching it on Facebook Live, brutally attacking the man the hunters had lured with punches and kicks before they were restrained by security. Following the sting, two of the hunters involved were arrested by police.[113] The police recognize the impact of such groups.[114] So too do the prosecution authorities. The Crown Prosecution Service acknowledges the existence of these vigilantes. Online child abuse activist groups (OCAGs) are, they note, individuals or groups of individuals who are members of the public using online activity to uncover or "catch" alleged pedophiles involved in online child sexual abuse or interested in meeting children for the purpose of such abuse. They point out that OCAG's activity, "whilst often well intentioned, has the potential to disrupt legitimate covert law enforcement activities." As a result, they have drawn up Legal Guidance on how to work with these vigilantes as well as deal with the possible crimes arising from their work.[115] This is vigilantism in modern-day Britain.

The extent, though, of concern that the law is "out of touch" on these issues would seem to be limited. In order to initiate a discussion in Parliament it is necessary to obtain a minimum of 10,000 signatures. In the past, the issues which have caught the imagination of the public have included petitions to lower the age of bowel cancer screenings (500,000) as well as to free a woman jailed in Iran for allegedly spying—Nazanin Zaghari-Ratcliffe—(2.3 million) and over 6 million to remain the European Union. In July 2018, an online petition to have a U.K. Law enshrining "stand your ground" reportedly attracted only 39 signatures.[116]

NOTES

1. Richard Hingley and Christina Unwin, *Boudica: Iron Age Warrior Queen* (London: Hambledon and London, 2005).
2. Paul Dalton and John C. Appleby, eds., *Outlaws in Medieval and Early Modern England: Crime, Government and Society, c.1066–c.1600* (Farnham: Ashgate, 2009).
3. *Braveheart* (1995).
4. *Robert the Bruce* (2019).
5. *Rob Roy: the Highland Rogue* (1953); *Rob Roy* (1995).
6. John Gibney, ed., *The United Irishmen, Rebellion and the Act of Union, 1791–1803* (Barnsley: Pen & Sword History, 2018).
7. R. R. Davies, *The Revolt of Owain Glyn Dŵr* (Oxford: Oxford University Press, 1995). See also Edward Rees, *Welsh Outlaws and Bandits: Political Rebellion and Lawlessness in Wales, 1400–1603* (Birmingham: Caterwen Press, 2001).
8. J. Gwynfor Jones, *Gwylliaid Cochion Mawddwy* (Bangor: Cymdeithas Addysg y Gweithwyr, 1994).
9. David Howell, "The Rebecca Riots," in *People and Protest: Wales 1815–1880*, ed. Trevor Herbert and Gareth Elwyn Jones (Cardiff: University of Wales Press, 1988), 113–38.
10. Les Johnston, "What Is Vigilantism?," *The British Journal of Criminology* 36, no. 2 (1996): 220–36.
11. Thomas Hahn, ed., *Robin Hood in Popular Culture: Violence, Transgression, and Justice* (Cambridge: D.S. Brewer, 2000).
12. Akin to the "chilling" effect of *12 Angry Men* (1957) on films focusing on the internal debates of juries.
13. Gillian Spraggs, *Outlaws and Highwaymen: The Cult of the Robber in England from the Middle Ages to the Nineteenth Century* (London: Pimlico, 2001).
14. *The Highwayman* (1951); *Dr Syn Alias the Scarecrow* (1963); *Barry Lyndon* (1975); *Plunkett and Macleane* (1999). See also for glamorization of highwaymen *The Wicked Lady* (1945)—albeit concern for others is missing in this account of lawbreaking as a way of fighting off boredom.
15. John E. Archer, *Social Unrest and Popular Protest in England, 1780–1840* (Cambridge: Cambridge University Press, 2000).
16. Eric Hobsbawm and George F. E. Rudé, *Captain Swing* (London: Lawrence and Wishart, 1969).
17. "The Hexham Riot," accessed February 25, 2022, http://ndfhs.org/Articles/HexhamRiot.html.

18. "Revolution in The Weardale," *Weardale UK* (blog), February 27, 2012, https://weardale.uk/revolution-in-the-weardale/.

19. Stephen Dunford, *The Irish Highwaymen* (Dublin: Merlin, 2000).

20. Peter Robson, "Vengeance in Popular Culture," in *Oxford Encyclopedia of Crime, Media, and Popular Culture* (Oxford: Oxford University Press, December 22, 2016), https://doi.org/10.1093/acrefore/9780190264079.013.45.

21. *Spider's Web* (1954); *Black Coffee* (1930); *A Murder Is Announced* (1950).

22. *Towards Zero* (1956).

23. *Murder on the Nile* (1944).

24. A 1942 book in which Poirot solves the mystery sixteen years after the event.

25. It started out as book in 1939. It was adapted for the stage and opened in 1943. It has been filmed three times, in 1965, 1975, and 1989, and a television version was produced in 2015 (Tara Conlan, "BBC's And Then There Were None Puts a Darker Spin on Agatha Christie," *The Guardian*, December 13, 2015, sec. Media, https://www.theguardian.com/media/2015/dec/13/bbc-and-then-there-were-none-agatha-christie).

26. The judge turns out to have a love of seeing people die which his profession as a judge at a time of capital murder in British law gives him full rein along with a desire to make sure that those acquitted by technicalities get their just deserts.

27. In the original book he does this in the knowledge that he is terminally ill and commits suicide. In the theatrical adaptation there are two survivors. In some versions the original ending is maintained.

28. William Saroyan and Henry Cecil, *Settled Out of Court: A Play in Three Acts* (London: S. French, 1962).

29. Felicity Douglas and Henry Cecil with Basil Dawson, *Alibi for a Judge: A Comedy* (London: S. French, 1967).

30. Henry Cecil, *According to the Evidence* (London: Chapman & Hall, 1954).

31. Sophie Hannah, "It's No Mystery That Crime Is the Biggest-Selling Genre in Books," *The Guardian*, April 12, 2018, https://www.theguardian.com/books/booksblog/2018/apr/12/mystery-crime-fiction-bestselling-book-genre-sophie-hannah.

32. *Murder on the Nile* (1944).

33. *Death in the Clouds* (1935).

34. Henry Cecil, *Much in Evidence* (London: M. Joseph, 1957); Henry Cecil, *Unlawful Occasions* (London: M. Joseph, 1962).

35. Cecil, *According to the Evidence*.

36. Henry Cecil, *Portrait of a Judge* (London: M. Joseph, 1964).

37. Subsequently, the scenario is somewhat different in her next novel, *True Romance* (1994) with it being described as "An everyday tale of sado-masochistic troilism" (Harvey Porlock, *Sunday Times* abstracted from "True Romance Reviews," HelenZahavi, accessed February 25, 2022, https://www.helenzahavi.com/true-romance-reviews).

38. Interview at Helen Zahavi, "Answering the Critics," HelenZahavi, accessed February 25, 2022, https://www.helenzahavi.com/answering-the-critics.

39. Films Act 1985 Schedule 1—film passes the cultural test if it is awarded at least 18 points in total. Up to 18 points are awarded in respect of the content of the film as follows:

(a) up to 4 points depending on the percentage of the film that is set in the United Kingdom or another EEA state—points depend on the % (b) up to 4 points depending on the number of the characters depicted in the film that [are qualifying persons] depending on the number of characters depicted in the film, and how many of these are lead characters who are qualifying persons (UK or EEA citizens) (c) 4 points if the film depicts a qualifying story; (d) up to 6 points depending on the percentage of the original dialogue that is recorded in a language recognised for official purposes in the United Kingdom or another EEA state (4) Up to 4 points may be awarded in respect of the contribution of the film to the promotion, development and enhancement of one or more of the following—(a) British creativity; (b) British heritage; (c) diversity. (5) Up to 5 points shall be awarded in respect of work carried out in the making of the film for (i) principal photography; (ii) visual effects; (iii) special effects. Also points for performing and recording the music score created for the film; audio post production and picture post production. (6) Up to 8 points shall be awarded in respect of the personnel involved in the making of the film—director, scriptwriters, producers, composers, actors, heads of department and production crew are qualifying persons.

40. At the end of 2018, the UK had 12 active bilateral treaties in place, with Australia, Brazil, Canada, China, France, India, Israel, Jamaica, Morocco, New Zealand, the Occupied Palestinian Territories, and South Africa.

41. *Kick-Ass* involved a Staten Island teenager who wants to become a superhero and stars Nicolas Cage and Aaron Johnson—the original story is from East Kilbride's Mark Millar and the screenplay was co-written by Jane Goldman from London.

42. BFI, "Screen Sector Certification and Production," 2019, https://www2.bfi.org.uk/sites/bfi.org.uk/files/downloads/bfi-screen-sector-certification-and-production-2019-07-25.pdf.

43. PWC Global Entertainment and Media Outlook 2018–2022, cited in BFI, "The UK Film Market as a Whole," 2019, https://www2.bfi.org.uk/sites/bfi.org.uk/files/downloads/bfi-statistical-yearbook-uk-film-market-2017-2018-12-13.pdf.

44. Of the five major European Union (EU) territories, the UK was the only one that saw an increase in admissions compared with 2017. Attendances were down in France (-4.0%), Germany (-13.9%), Spain (-2.9%), and Italy (-7.0%). According to European Audiovisual Observatory estimates, total admissions in the EU decreased by 3 percent to 955 million. This is 29.4 million less than in 2017, and the fourth lowest level recorded in the EU since 2009. This downward trend in admissions was also seen in the largest European territories outside the EU, with decreases recorded in both Russia (-5.6%) and Turkey (-1.1%). In contrast to the decline in attendances across much of Europe, year-on-year admissions increased in the world's three largest theatrical markets: China (6.0%), India (2.4%), and North America (4.8%). Outside of the three biggest markets, 2018 saw declines in many of the other major global territories, including Mexico (-4.6%), South Korea (-1.8%), Japan (-3.3%), and Brazil

(-10.0%). See BFI, "Film at the Cinema," 2019, https://www2.bfi.org.uk/sites/bfi.org.uk/files/downloads/bfi-film-at-the-cinema-2019-07-25.pdf.

45. BFI, table. 1.
46. Ibid.
47. Ibid.
48. BFI, "Film at the Cinema," 2.
49. BFI, table 7.
50. BFI, table 7.
51. BFI, table 8.
52. BFI, table 9.
53. BFI, table 14.
54. BFI, table 25. A total of 110 feature documentaries (14% of theatrical releases) were shown at the UK and Republic of Ireland box office in 2018, up from 89 in 2017. These films earned £8.3 million which was 0.6 percent of the overall box office gross.
55. For the purposes of tax relief, as noted, films are recognized as British when they satisfy the specific criteria noted above. By these lights a film often included alongside vigilante films—the rape-revenge film—*Straw Dogs* (1971) would have qualified by dint of its cast and financing, although the leading male actor, Dustin Hoffman, and the director, Sam Peckinpah, were both born in California.
56. Although some US-produced films have stars from Britain this is not enough to classify them as British, of course—Terence Stamp in *The Limey* (1999), Liam Neeson in A *Walk among the Tombstones* (2014), and controversially, *Cold Pursuit* (2019). Neeson explained his character's "primal" anger in the latter by recounting an experience some forty years ago. A woman close to him had been raped by a stranger, and Neeson asked what color skin the attacker had; after learning the attacker was black, Neeson said that for about a week, he "went up and down areas with a cosh . . . hoping some 'black bastard' would come out of a pub and have a go" so that Neeson "could kill him." In the interview, Neeson also said he was "ashamed" to recount the experience and that it was "horrible" that he did what he did. "It's awful . . . but I did learn a lesson from it, when I eventually thought, 'What the fuck are you doing?'" ("Liam Neeson: "I Walked the Streets with a Cosh, Hoping I'd Be Approached by a 'Black B******' so That I Could Kill Him,'" *The Independent*, February 4, 2019, https://www.independent.co.uk/arts-entertainment/films/news/liam-neeson-rape-black-man-attack-cosh-cold-pursuit-sexual-assault-interview-a8760866.html.). Born in Ballymena, Northern Ireland, Neeson holds British, Irish, and US Citizenship.
57. There is, in addition a raft of "fan films" which seek to replicate the world of the justified avenger. These are largely confined to the DVD market and are cheaply made with non-professional actors and directors. They feature brutal fight scenes and shootings aplenty and the revenge themes are to the fore. They include *Ten Dead Men* (2007)—ten men stole his life . . . ten men will pay; *Vigilante* (2009)—the hunters have become the hunted. Narrative arcs are simple and the characters are one-dimensional.
58. In fact, the actor, turns up in *Vendetta* some six years later albeit renamed—see below.

59. Michael Caine, *The Elephant to Hollywood: The Autobiography* (London: Hodder & Stoughton, 2011), 349.

60. The influential British film *V for Vendetta* (2005) is set in an authoritarian future. It focuses on a vigilante in a Guy Fawkes mask who spawns a movement against the repressive government of the day. It has been seen as inspirational and libertarian and the V mask has become a common sight at demonstrations and direct action. The plot is elaborate and far-fetched but the final scene of the Houses of Parliament being blown up is memorable.

61. Louis Mazzini's mother was disowned by her family for marrying an Italian opera singer from a lower social station. Louis arranges the demise of all those in the family who stands between him and the Dukedom of Chalfont. See https://www.imdb.com/title/tt0041546/. The original book (*Israel Rank. The Autobiography of a Criminal* by Roy Horniman; 1907) on which the screenplay is based has the hero escaping the attentions of the law and living happily ever after with Sibella.

62. Two die without Louis having to intervene, one due to a naval accident and the other of shock.

63. *Vendetta* (2013)—the revenge carried out by the orphaned Danny Dyer involves him tracking down each gang member and disposing of them brutally—described by film critic Peter Bradshaw as "revenge porn" (Peter Bradshaw, "Vendetta—Review," *The Guardian*, November 21, 2013, https://www.theguardian.com/film/2013/nov/21/vendetta-review).

64. Freeview—https://www.freeview.co.uk/#KXCrcbzFeqqYOCaB.97.

65. Freesat—https://www.freesat.co.uk/.

66. Sam Wolfson, "'We've Got More Money Swirling around': How Streaming Saved the Music Industry," *The Guardian*, April 24, 2018, https://www.theguardian.com/music/2018/apr/24/weve-got-more-money-swirling-around-how-streaming-saved-the-music-industry.

67. "The Communications Market 2017," Ofcom, August 17, 2018, https://www.ofcom.org.uk/research-and-data/multi-sector-research/cmr/cmr-2017.

68. OFCOM, "Communications Market Report," August 2, 2018, 29, https://www.ofcom.org.uk/__data/assets/pdf_file/0022/117256/CMR-2018-narrative-report.pdf.

69. The Committee on Culture Media and Sport concluded that there was no "long term future for the licence fee in its current form"—cited in Peter Robson, "Britain," in *A Transnational Study of Law and Justice on Tv*, ed. Peter Robson and Jennifer L. Schulz (Oxford: Hart, 2016), n. 29.

70. *BROADCASTING: Copy of Royal Charter for the Continuance of the British Broadcasting Corporation*, December 2016 Cm 9365 and *BROADCASTING: An Agreement between Her Majesty's Secretary of State for Culture, Media and Sport and the British Broadcasting Corporation*, December 2016 Cm 9366; see also Philip Ward, "BBC Charter Renewal," Briefing Paper (House of Commons, December 28, 2016), for how these documents went through the process of amendment and discussion.

71. Charter op. cit. at para. 2(3).

72. Department for Digital Media Culture and Sport (June 2019) *Culture Is Digital: June 2019 Progress Report* (available at https://www.gov.uk/government/publications/culture-is-digital/culture-is-digital-june-2019-progress-report).

73. Tom Mills, "The Future of the BBC," IPPR, September 15, 2017, https://www.ippr.org/juncture-item/tom-mills-the-future-of-the-bbc.

74. The work of Bodie and Doyle in *The Professionals* is precisely that. They are working for the secretive but official agency, C5.

75. In only one episode of *Dixon of Dock Green* (1955–1976) (out of 432 episodes) and none of *Gideon's Way* (1964–1966) do we come across "bad apples"—although the 1958 film *Gideon's Day* (aka *Gideon of Scotland Yard*) has this as a minor sub-plot. The miscreant in the film dies in a hit and run.

76. Sue Turnbull, "Border Crossings: The Transnational Career of the Television Crime Drama," in *Cultural Legal Studies*, ed. Cassandra Sharp and Marett Leiboff (Routledge, 2016), 95–112.

77. http://www.imdb.com/title/tt1132157/.

78. In this we have a classic Jekyll and Hyde figure, Dexter Morgan. By day he is a technical expert dealing with blood spatter patterns for the police, while by night he kills those criminals whom the justice system's rules have allowed to go free. See Angus Nurse, "Decoding the Dark Passenger: The Serial Killer as a Force for Justice. Adapting Jeff Lindsay's Dexter for the Small Screen," in *Law and Justice on the Small Screen*, ed. Peter Robson and Jessica Silbey (Oxford: Hart, 2012), 403–23.

79. The Shipman Inquiry (Chair Dame Janet Smith)—6 Reports 2002–2005 (available at https://webarchive.nationalarchives.gov.uk/20090808155110/http://www.the-shipman-inquiry.org.uk/reports.asp).

80. Small Arms Survey 2018 (http://www.smallarmssurvey.org/fileadmin/docs/T-Briefing-Papers/SAS-BP-Civilian-Firearms-Numbers.pdf).

81. https://worldpopulationreview.com/country-rankings/gun-ownership-by-country.

82. There is also since the Hungerford massacre in 1988 a more restricted "firearms licence" for semi-automatic and pump action shotguns.

83. Guns in Iceland, Canada, United States, and U.K. See "Estimated Number of Civilian Guns per Capita by Country," in *Wikipedia*, February 11, 2022, https://en.wikipedia.org/w/index.php?title=Estimated_number_of_civilian_guns_per_capita_by_country&oldid=1071236626.

84. In the United States between 1982 and 2011, a mass shooting occurred roughly once every 200 days. However, between 2011 and 2014, that rate has accelerated greatly with at least one mass shooting occurring every 64 days—i.e., where 4 or more persons are shot. See Amy P. Cohen, Deborah Azrael, and Matthew Miller, "Rate of Mass Shootings Has Tripled since 2011, New Research from Harvard Shows," *Mother Jones*, October 15, 2014, https://www.motherjones.com/politics/2014/10/mass-shootings-increasing-harvard-research/.

85. Criminal Justice and Immigration Act 2008 s 76 (10(b)).

86. The supreme criminal court in England and Wales at the time for such Commonwealth appeals where the law is the same as in England and Wales.

87. Beckford v R [1988] A.C. 130 at 144.

88. loc cit. at 144.
89. section 76.
90. s 76 (4)(a).
91. s 76 (4) (b).
92. s 76 (5A).
93. s 76 (6).
94. s 76 (6A).
95. *Beckford v R* [1988] A.C. 130 at 144.
96. *R v Lindsay* [2005] EWCA 2980 at para 41.
97. *The Interrogation of Tony Martin*, 18/11/18 (Channel 4).
98. *R v Fegan* (1972) NI 80 [reported at (1984) 78 Cr App R 189].
99. *H.M.A. v Doherty* 1954 J.C. 1
100. CLDD Act 2011 s 2 (1).
101. CLDD Act 2011 s 2 (5).
102. CLDD Act 2011 s 3.
103. CLDD Act 2011 s 5.
104. "First Murder Case Defended under Defence and the Dwelling Act Ends in Acquittal," *Irish Legal News*, March 14, 2018, https://www.irishlegal.com/articles/first-murder-case-defended-defence-dwelling-act-ends-acquittal.
105. Stanley Cohen, *Folk Devils and Moral Panics: The Creation of the Mods and Rockers* (London: MacGibbon and Kee, 1972).
106. Jessica Evans, "Containing Communities: A Psychoanalytic Perspective on the Governance of Sexual Offenders," 2007, 2, https://www.kent.ac.uk/scarr/events/papers/EVANS.pdf, where she notes that in August 2000, about 100 adults and children calling themselves "Residents Against Paedophiles," marched through the Paulsgrove estate. They torched cars and firebombed flats and houses where the two suspected sex offenders and pedophiles were thought to live.
107. Laura Huey, Johnny Nhan, and Ryan Broll, "'Uppity Civilians' and 'Cyber-Vigilantes': The Role of the General Public in Policing Cyber-Crime," *Criminology & Criminal Justice* 13, no. 1 (2013): 81–97.
108. "Who Are Vigilante Group Letzgo Hunting?," *BBC News*, September 19, 2013, sec. Magazine, https://www.bbc.com/news/magazine-24143991. Letzgo Hunting is called "Online Child Protection" on their Facebook page - https://www.facebook.com/LetzgoHuntingOfficial/ (last accessed 24 November 2020).
109. Frances Perraudin, "Paedophile Hunters Jeopardising Police Work, Says Senior Officer," *The Guardian*, April 24, 2017, https://www.theguardian.com/society/2017/apr/24/paedophile-hunters-jeopardising-police-work-child-protection; "Police Concerns over Rise of 'Paedophile Hunters,'" *BBC News*, November 6, 2019, sec. England, https://www.bbc.com/news/uk-england-50302912.
110. Perraudin, "Paedophile Hunters Jeopardising Police Work, Says Senior Officer."
111. Joe Purshouse, "'Paedophile Hunters,' Criminal Procedure, and Fundamental Human Rights," *Journal of Law and Society* 47, no. 3 (2020): 384–411.
112. Perraudin, "Paedophile Hunters Jeopardising Police Work, Says Senior Officer."

113. Rozina Sabur, "'Paedophile Hunters' Arrested by Police as Officers Begin Crackdown on Social Media Vigilantes," *The Telegraph*, April 25, 2017, https://www.telegraph.co.uk/news/2017/04/25/paedophile-hunters-arrested-police-officers-begin-crackdown/.

114. Fiona Hamilton, "Paedophiles More Scared of Online Vigilantes than of Us, Say Police," *The Times*, February 8, 2021, sec. news, https://www.thetimes.co.uk/article/paedophiles-more-scared-of-online-vigilantes-than-of-us-say-police-p5jb7pfbj. Pedophiles are more afraid of online vigilante groups than they are of the police and the strategy of arresting sex offenders is failing to stem a tidal wave of abuse, senior officers have warned.

115. "Online Child Abuse Activist Groups on the Internet" (The Crown Prosecution Service, July 23, 2020), https://www.cps.gov.uk/legal-guidance/online-child-abuse-activist-groups-internet.

116. Joe Sommerland, "How Stand-Your-Ground Law Works and Where It Applies," *The Independent*, July 23, 2018, https://www.independent.co.uk/news/uk/crime/stand-your-ground-law-explained-self-defence-crime-muggings-burglary-attack-a8460366.html. the petition actually closed on 3 September 2014—https://petition.parliament.uk/archived/petitions/54402—no other action has been taken in this context. See also Nicole E. Haas, Jan W. de Keijser, and Gerben J. N. Bruinsma, "Public Support for Vigilantism: An Experimental Study," *Journal of Experimental Criminology* 8, no. 4 (December 2012): 387–413, https://doi.org/10.1007/s11292-012-9144-1.

BIBLIOGRAPHY

Archer, John E. *Social Unrest and Popular Protest in England, 1780–1840*. Cambridge: Cambridge University Press, 2000.

BFI. "Film at the Cinema," 2019. https://www2.bfi.org.uk/sites/bfi.org.uk/files/downloads/bfi-film-at-the-cinema-2019-07-25.pdf.

———. "Screen Sector Certification and Production," 2019. https://www2.bfi.org.uk/sites/bfi.org.uk/files/downloads/bfi-screen-sector-certification-and-production-2019-07-25.pdf.

———. "The UK Film Market as a Whole," 2019. https://www2.bfi.org.uk/sites/bfi.org.uk/files/downloads/bfi-statistical-yearbook-uk-film-market-2017-2018-12-13.pdf.

Bradshaw, Peter. "Vendetta—Review." *The Guardian*, November 21, 2013. https://www.theguardian.com/film/2013/nov/21/vendetta-review.

Caine, Michael. *The Elephant to Hollywood: The Autobiography*. London: Hodder & Stoughton, 2011.

Cecil, Henry. *According to the Evidence*. London: Chapman & Hall, 1954.

———. *Portrait of a Judge*. London: M. Joseph, 1964.

Cohen, Amy P., Deborah Azrael, and Matthew Miller. "Rate of Mass Shootings Has Tripled since 2011, New Research from Harvard Shows." *Mother*

Jones, October 15, 2014. https://www.motherjones.com/politics/2014/10/mass-shootings-increasing-harvard-research/.

Cohen, Stanley. *Folk Devils and Moral Panics: The Creation of the Mods and Rockers*. London: MacGibbon and Kee, 1972.

Conlan, Tara. "BBC's And Then There Were None Puts a Darker Spin on Agatha Christie." *The Guardian*, December 13, 2015. https://www.theguardian.com/media/2015/dec/13/bbc-and-then-there-were-none-agatha-christie.

Dalton, Paul, and John C. Appleby, eds. *Outlaws in Medieval and Early Modern England: Crime, Government and Society, c.1066–c.1600*. Farnham: Ashgate, 2009.

Davies, R. R. *The Revolt of Owain Glyn Dŵr*. Oxford: Oxford University Press, 1995.

Douglas, Felicity, and Henry Cecil with Basil Dawson. *Alibi for a Judge: A Comedy*. London: S. French, 1967.

Dunford, Stephen. *The Irish Highwaymen*. Dublin: Merlin, 2000.

"Estimated Number of Civilian Guns per Capita by Country." In *Wikipedia*, February 11, 2022. https://en.wikipedia.org/w/index.php?title=Estimated_number_of_civilian_guns_per_capita_by_country&oldid=1071236626.

Evans, Jessica. "Containing Communities: A Psychoanalytic Perspective on the Governance of Sexual Offenders," 2007. https://www.kent.ac.uk/scarr/events/papers/EVANS.pdf.

Irish Legal News. "First Murder Case Defended under Defence and the Dwelling Act Ends in Acquittal," March 14, 2018. https://www.irishlegal.com/articles/first-murder-case-defended-defence-dwelling-act-ends-acquittal.

Gibney, John, ed. *The United Irishmen, Rebellion and the Act of Union, 1791–1803*. Barnsley: Pen & Sword History, 2018.

Haas, Nicole E., Jan W. de Keijser, and Gerben J. N. Bruinsma. "Public Support for Vigilantism: An Experimental Study." *Journal of Experimental Criminology* 8, no. 4 (December 2012): 387–413. https://doi.org/10.1007/s11292-012-9144-1.

Hahn, Thomas, ed. *Robin Hood in Popular Culture: Violence, Transgression, and Justice*. Cambridge: D.S. Brewer, 2000.

Hamilton, Fiona. "Paedophiles More Scared of Online Vigilantes than of Us, Say Police." *The Times*, February 8, 2021, sec. news. https://www.thetimes.co.uk/article/paedophiles-more-scared-of-online-vigilantes-than-of-us-say-police-p5jb7pfbj.

Hannah, Sophie. "It's No Mystery That Crime Is the Biggest-Selling Genre in Books." *The Guardian*, April 12, 2018. https://www.theguardian.com/books/booksblog/2018/apr/12/mystery-crime-fiction-bestselling-book-genre-sophie-hannah.

Hingley, Richard, and Christina Unwin. *Boudica: Iron Age Warrior Queen*. London: Hambledon and London, 2005.

Hobsbawm, Eric, and George F. E. Rudé. *Captain Swing*. London: Lawrence and Wishart, 1969.

Howell, David. "The Rebecca Riots." In *People and Protest: Wales 1815–1880*, edited by Trevor Herbert and Gareth Elwyn Jones, 113–38. Cardiff: University of Wales Press, 1988.

Huey, Laura, Johnny Nhan, and Ryan Broll. "'Uppity Civilians' and 'Cyber-Vigilantes': The Role of the General Public in Policing Cyber-Crime." *Criminology & Criminal Justice* 13, no. 1 (2013): 81–97.

Johnston, Les. "What Is Vigilantism?" *The British Journal of Criminology* 36, no. 2 (1996): 220–36.

Jones, J. Gwynfor. *Gwylliaid Cochion Mawddwy*. Bangor: Cymdeithas Addysg y Gweithwyr, 1994.

The Independent. "Liam Neeson: "I Walked the Streets with a Cosh, Hoping I'd Be Approached by a 'Black B******' so That I Could Kill Him,"" February 4, 2019. https://www.independent.co.uk/arts-entertainment/films/news/liam-neeson-rape-black-man-attack-cosh-cold-pursuit-sexual-assault-interview-a8760866.html.

Mills, Tom. "The Future of the BBC." IPPR, September 15, 2017. https://www.ippr.org/juncture-item/tom-mills-the-future-of-the-bbc.

Nurse, Angus. "Decoding the Dark Passenger: The Serial Killer as a Force for Justice. Adapting Jeff Lindsay's Dexter for the Small Screen." In *Law and Justice on the Small Screen*, edited by Peter Robson and Jessica Silbey, 403–23. Oxford: Hart, 2012.

OFCOM. "Communications Market Report," August 2, 2018. https://www.ofcom.org.uk/__data/assets/pdf_file/0022/117256/CMR-2018-narrative-report.pdf.

"Online Child Abuse Activist Groups on the Internet." The Crown Prosecution Service, July 23, 2020. https://www.cps.gov.uk/legal-guidance/online-child-abuse-activist-groups-internet.

Perraudin, Frances. "Paedophile Hunters Jeopardising Police Work, Says Senior Officer." *The Guardian*, April 24, 2017. https://www.theguardian.com/society/2017/apr/24/paedophile-hunters-jeopardising-police-work-child-protection.

BBC News. "Police Concerns over Rise of 'Paedophile Hunters,'" November 6, 2019, sec. England. https://www.bbc.com/news/uk-england-50302912.

Purshouse, Joe. "'Paedophile Hunters,' Criminal Procedure, and Fundamental Human Rights." *Journal of Law and Society* 47, no. 3 (2020): 384–411.

Rees, Edward. *Welsh Outlaws and Bandits: Political Rebellion and Lawlessness in Wales, 1400–1603*. Birmingham: Caterwen Press, 2001.

Weardale UK. "Revolution in the Weardale," February 27, 2012. https://weardale.uk/revolution-in-the-weardale/.

Robson, Peter. "Britain." In *A Transnational Study of Law and Justice on TV*, edited by Peter Robson and Jennifer L. Schulz, 37–52. Oxford: Hart, 2016.

———. "Vengeance in Popular Culture." In *Oxford Encyclopedia of Crime, Media, and Popular Culture*. Oxford: Oxford University Press, December 22, 2016. https://doi.org/10.1093/acrefore/9780190264079.013.45.

Sabur, Rozina. "'Paedophile Hunters' Arrested by Police as Officers Begin Crackdown on Social Media Vigilantes." *The Telegraph*, April 25, 2017. https://www.telegraph.co.uk/news/2017/04/25/paedophile-hunters-arrested-police-officers-begin-crackdown/.

Saroyan, William, and Henry Cecil. *Settled out of Court: A Play in Three Acts*. London: S. French, 1962.

Sommerland, Joe. "How Stand-Your-Ground Law Works and Where It Applies." The Independent, July 23, 2018. https://www.independent.co.uk/news/uk/crime/stand-your-ground-law-explained-self-defence-crime-muggings-burglary-attack-a8460366.html.

Spraggs, Gillian. *Outlaws and Highwaymen: The Cult of the Robber in England from the Middle Ages to the Nineteenth Century*. London: Pimlico, 2001.

OFCOM. "The Communications Market 2017," August 17, 2018. https://www.ofcom.org.uk/research-and-data/multi-sector-research/cmr/cmr-2017.

"The Hexham Riot." Accessed February 25, 2022. http://ndfhs.org/Articles/HexhamRiot.html.

Turnbull, Sue. "Border Crossings: The Transnational Career of the Television Crime Drama." In *Cultural Legal Studies*, edited by Cassandra Sharp and Marett Leiboff, 95–112. Routledge, 2016.

Ward, Philip. "BBC Charter Renewal." Briefing Paper. House of Commons, December 28, 2016.

BBC News. "Who Are Vigilante Group Letzgo Hunting?," September 19, 2013, sec. Magazine. https://www.bbc.com/news/magazine-24143991.

Wolfson, Sam. "'We've Got More Money Swirling around': How Streaming Saved the Music Industry." *The Guardian*, April 24, 2018. https://www.theguardian.com/music/2018/apr/24/weve-got-more-money-swirling-around-how-streaming-saved-the-music-industry.

Zahavi, Helen. "Answering the Critics." HelenZahavi. Accessed February 25, 2022. https://www.helenzahavi.com/answering-the-critics.

———. "True Romance Reviews." HelenZahavi. Accessed February 25, 2022. https://www.helenzahavi.com/true-romance-reviews.

Chapter 3

Vigilante Frontier Communities on Australian Screens

Bushrangers, Bikies, and Bogans

Lili Pâquet

Australia's unofficial National Anthem is "Waltzing Matilda," a bush ballad written by legendary poet Banjo Paterson in 1895. The song's jargon-filled lyrics follow a swagman who is waltzing (trekking) with his Matilda (swag). He stops at a billabong (a small watering hole) and makes a billy tea (a billy is a small tea pot), when a jumbuck (a sheep) stops for a drink. He steals the sheep, but is accosted by a squatter (the landowner) and three troopers (police officers). Rather than submit to their authority, the swagman yells, "You'll never catch me alive" and commits suicide in the billabong.[1] For a short ballad, "Waltzing Matilda" manages to capture many Australian national myths. Ideas of Australians as anti-authoritarian, and often criminal, underdogs are translated to contemporary Australians through the creative arts, including film and television. In some of these on-screen narratives, vigilante heroes are given an anti-authoritarian spin, where they rouse a downtrodden community to seek their own legal rights. The Australian vigilante is presented as a galvanizing figure for a community confined to a frontier zone.

Vigilantism has many definitions. This chapter follows a definition of vigilantism by Nicole E. Haas, Jane W. de Keijser, and Gerben J. N. Bruinsma that states:

> Vigilantism can be seen as the result of a so-called injustice gap: a discrepancy between the desired and actual outcome. Taking the law into one's own hands is a way of reducing this perceived injustice gap and restoring one's sense of justice. Vigilantism may occur when people do not want the criminal justice

system authorities to get involved, when the authorities fail to respond, or when the authorities were involved but not to the satisfaction of the affected party.[2]

Further, the vigilantes use violence or the threat of violence,[3] and are motivated by the need for "moral satisfaction."[4]

This chapter argues that Australian vigilantes on screen oppose police and the government, who are represented as not only ineffectual, but also prejudiced. These institutional actors are a barrier to legal rights. Australian on-screen vigilantes are descendants of the Australian Gothic hero, and they work to galvanize oppressed communities in frontier zones. The chapter begins with discussion of cultural myths following British colonization, and then evaluates vigilantism in Australian films *Shame* (1988), and *Snowtown* (2011), and the first season of *Cleverman* (2016).

LITERATURE REVIEW

As a former penal colony, many Australian myths about vigilantism tend to focus on convicts. In *The Fatal Shore*, Robert Hughes argues that the Australian working classes adopted myths based on convicts and bushrangers: "[T]he system inadvertently produced Australia's first folk-heroes, the bushrangers, most of them escaped prisoners. The basic class division of early colonial Australia—guards versus prisoners—lived on as a metaphor of future disputes there."[5] Russell Ward also emphasizes the class divisions that led to bushranging activities during Australia's colonization, and how these divisions epitomized the hatred between the working classes and the police.[6] Babette Smith, on the other hand, disagrees with Ward and Hughes on the idea of bushranging as a classed activity, and points out that George Boxall wrote in 1890 that bushrangers did not perceivably rob from the rich and give to the poor. As she argues, "a wealthy class did not exist in convict times."[7] Further, Smith argues there is little evidence that Australia's egalitarian ethos originated in convict or bushranger experiences.[8]

The many films made about Ned Kelly, Australia's most celebrated bushranger, exhibit the myths of classed frontier disputes. The most well-known films about Kelly are Charles Tait's silent film, *The Story of the Kelly Gang* (1906), the first full-length narrative feature film in the world;[9] Tony Richardson's *Ned Kelly* (1970), controversially starring Mick Jagger; and Gregor Jordan's *Ned Kelly* (2003), starring Heath Ledger. Justin Kurzel (whose debut film, *Snowtown*, is discussed in this chapter) adapted Peter Carey's Booker Prize–winning 2000 novel, *True History of the Kelly Gang*,[10] for release in 2020.[11] Each of these films portray Kelly as a victim of police harassment and economic circumstance, solidifying the myth that bushrangers more generally were Robin Hood figures who stole from the rich to redistribute wealth, with no thought of personal profit. Other films question this myth. *Reckless Kelly* (1993) is a satirical film by Yahoo Serious that depicts Kelly's descendent robbing from banks to give to the poor before "selling out" in Hollywood. More poignantly, Warwick Thornton's *Sweet Country* (2017) follows an Indigenous Australian man named Sam Kelly (Hamilton Morris) in the outback in 1929. In the film, the townspeople cheer for Ned Kelly at a screening of *The Story of the Kelly Gang* (1906), but ironically vilify Sam when he becomes an outlaw for similar reasons as his namesake.

Vigilante literature during the colonial period was written for profit, capitalizing on the prevalent narratives of the time. For example, writing about the sensational autobiography, *Adventures of Martin Cash* (1870), Smith suggests:

> [T]he island colony had always responded to a "gentleman" bushranger whose depredations combined audacity and quick wit with courtesy and honour. Cash embodied this tradition when he took to the bush during the 1840s. Newspapers breathlessly reported hair-raising encounters with his pursuers, a spectacular escape from Port Arthur by swimming across the notorious Eaglehawk Neck, capture while pursuing a faithless wife and the high drama of a death sentence that was commuted to a life imprisonment on Norfolk Island.[12]

Another colonial narrative that received much attention and sensationalism was that of Eliza Fraser, who was stranded on K'gari (now named Fraser Island) with the local Butchulla people until her "rescue," and whose story was subsequently used to prove the supposed danger of Indigenous populations to settlers. As Indigenous law scholar Larissa Behrendt explains, "Stories like Eliza Fraser's sought to reinforce the meta-narrative about Australia."[13] These examples highlight how colonial storytelling was often sensationalized in order to present white men's vigilantism as a positive force for law and order. Cash had chased a "faithless wife" and Fraser became the white heroine of a captivity narrative.

Stories of settler vigilantism on Indigenous Australians and stories of convictism were both suppressed. In 1921, G. A. Wood delivered a paper to the Royal Australian Historical Society, in which he aimed to dispel fears over the morality of Australia's convicts.[14] As Smith suggests, "A collusion of social forces at a public, institutional and at a family level created this national loss of memory. What began as an unspoken agreement to avoid an uncomfortable subject, over time turned into ignorance."[15] Although Hughes and Ward had written about class conflict in the colonial period, Smith and Henry Reynolds argue that there is little evidence to support these claims. In his article, "The Hated Stain: The Aftermath of Transportation in Tasmania," Reynolds writes that he found "no evidence of a feisty working class fired by the resentments of the convict era."[16] In the mid twentieth century, scholarly historians such as Reynolds, Ward, and Hughes began to search for an Australian history. Soon afterward, perhaps inspired by the 1970s American television series *Roots*, family historians overcame their cultural cringe to investigate their own family trees. They found that convicts, their descendants, and government administration had destroyed much historical documentation.[17] In contemporary times, Miriam Dixson suggests that when Australians search for a national identity, they "return to convictism."[18] This identity, however, has been distorted by the destruction of documentation and the colonial storytelling that aimed to cover the convict stain and the massacres of Indigenous Australians. Subsequently, vigilantes in popular culture are often presented as morally righteous citizens, who aim to restore justice to frontier zones. These narratives fill in historical voids using self-affirming national myths.

AUSTRALIAN VIGILANTISM, THEN AND NOW

Historical examples of vigilantism in Australia are more often those of white settlers against Indigenous populations, who were systematically removed from their land or massacred. Indigenous Australians were targeted through arguments that they threatened the well-being of settlers and the burgeoning state,[19] which led to acts of preventative vigilantism. As Chris Cunneen and Sophie Russell argue:

> [T]he notion of "citizen policing" and its overlap with vigilantism have a particular resonance within the colonizing processes of settler colonial states such as Australia. In such states, the concept of citizenship and who were regarded as citizens was built on racialized boundaries of exclusion, through various laws, policies, and practices ... Crime and crime control was deeply embedded in the experiences of colonization and subsequent nation-building.[20]

After the Myall Creek massacre of 1838, several white vigilantes were executed for their crimes, but their trial was atypical.[21] The expansion of the colonial empire from the 1860s into Queensland, South Australia, and Western Australia was accompanied by a rise in vigilantism against Indigenous Australians, who were forced to raid settler supplies of water and cattle when their own sources were curtailed.[22]

In contemporary times, there have been some examples of the kinds of reactive vigilantism the public recognize from screen narratives. For example, a newspaper report on the mob burning of a convicted pedophile's house in Meringur explained that "There was drinking, dancing and cheering. The man had raped a 10-year-old girl, received five years in jail and could be out in 2½. The young victim of the sex attack was reportedly fireside, smiling."[23] This kind of vigilantism is rare, however; most reported cases of contemporary vigilante activity revolve around groups of men patrolling streets or communicating online. These groups are examples of what Richard Hil and Glenn Dawes term transvigilantism: "the 'slippage' of formally constituted groups, such as Neighbourhood Watch, into vigilante-type activity."[24]

In response to media reports of heightened crime in Melbourne by the South Sudanese Apex gang, some of these transvigilante groups were created. Many seem reticent to name these groups vigilantes. The organizer of one such group told reporters, "Vigilante is an American term where you think of people walking around with shotguns shooting people. Nothing I fund would do anything illegal," and that his group was "more like Neighbourhood Watch."[25] Police Association secretary and retired detective Ron Iddles also argued, "I don't call them vigilantes, but concerned residents who patrol and report to the police."[26] A notorious vigilante group who regularly patrol Melbourne are the Soldiers of Odin, whose Facebook page declare that they oppose the right to be "black, Asian, homosexual or transgender."[27] The Alice Springs Volunteer Force (AVF) is a similar group that argues they are responding to a lack of necessary force by local police and justice systems.[28] Their Facebook page, along with those of many other transvigilante groups, indicates that they have a racial agenda against the Indigenous population.[29] Another group with similar aims targets refugees arriving into the country by boat. Frontline Australia advertised for members by writing, "Patrols will be undertaken in international waters without the constraints of political correctness."[30] Much like vigilante activity in the colonial period, contemporary vigilantes appear to focus on the control of immigrants and Indigenous people who they perceive as innately criminal.

AUSTRALIAN LEGAL RESPONSES

Contemporary Australian law does not specifically cover vigilantism. Unlike the US, there are no "stand your ground" laws, and police insist that Australians in danger retreat and call emergency services.[31] Gun violence is very low compared to the US thanks to much tighter weapons restrictions. Although law enforcement have occasionally shown sympathy with some transvigilante groups,[32] joining the Soldiers of Odin, the AVF, or Frontline Australia does not protect members from legal recriminations for their actions. For example, in *Bonnet v R* [2013] NSWCCA 234, Ms. Bonnet appealed her conviction of "robbery with deprivation of liberty" by arguing that she was acting as a vigilante against a pedophile. However, the judge dismissed the appeal. He ruled, "vigilante offences are to be discouraged by general deterrence, and even more so where, as in this case, the perceived crime may be unsavoury to the attackers, but is no crime in law at all."[33] He referred here to the fact that the victim's sexual partner, while young, was legally over the age of consent.

From 2019, the government has increasingly focused on changing federal laws around vigilantism, but not in response to the transvigilante groups described above. So-called vegan vigilantes have an online network around an anti-farming documentary, *Dominion* (2018), which shows covertly filmed footage of animal cruelty on Australian farms. The documentary—narrated by celebrities including Joaquin Phoenix, Rooney Mara, and Sia—is freely available to watch online.[34] In April 2019, the vigilantes coordinated a protest in the Melbourne CBD and raids on farms in the states of New South Wales, Victoria, and Queensland. Reportedly, the protests led to 60,000 views of the documentary in two days.[35] Chris Delforce, the director of *Dominion*, is also responsible for the notorious Aussie Farms interactive map that shows farm locations around the country, which has been criticized as an attack site. Vegans are accused of using the site to trespass on farms, and in some cases to free livestock. For example, vegan activist, James Warden, and others were charged with aggravated burglary, stealing, and trespass after live-streaming conditions from pig farms.[36] John Barilaro, the former NSW Deputy Premier, called these vegan vigilantes "domestic terrorists"[37] and the Australian government led by Scott Morrison passed legislation with harsher penalties for inciting farm trespass.[38] State laws on trespass in New South Wales, Victoria, South Australia, and Western Australia were also amended to create harsher penalties.[39]

Fictional vigilante narratives on screen present the tensions between myths of Australia as an egalitarian place, where everyone gets a "fair go," and realities of contested frontiers. Catriona Elder writes that by viewing on-screen narratives, "Citizens are encouraged to draw on these shared sets of understandings and feelings of what it means to be Australian."[40] Evaluating Australian film and television that deals with vigilantism may thus provide additional insight into how (in)justice is significant to Australians. As Cassandra Sharp argues, "the public is extremely active in the process of consuming stories of law in popular culture that include vigilante narratives as one stimulant to the production, transformation and perpetuation of meaning and desire about law and justice."[41] As such, it is interesting to examine the vigilante stories that Australians consume, and how these narratives portray the application of the law in isolated, frontier communities.

SHAME (1988)

Often, the on-screen vigilante is an outsider who rides into a rural town on his steed, witnesses the corruption or disruption of law and order, and helps the townsfolk by restoring justice. This vigilante figure has a pedigree earned from narratives of the lawless American frontier and Western film genre.[42] In Australian films featuring vigilantes from the 1970s, this solitary male outsider is an important figure. In films such as *Wake in Fright* (1971), *The Cars That Ate Paris* (1974), and *Mad Max* (1979), the stranger rides into town, using modern transport rather than a horse, and is drawn into the struggles of the rural community. The vigilante in these films is someone who lives outside the bounds of the insular community, and acts as a spokesman who challenges the status quo. Each film is set in a rural town and features vehicles as symbolic of masculinity in Australian culture.[43]

Drawing on these earlier masculine examples of the genre, *Shame* (Steve Jodrell, 1988) is a feminist contrast that continues to have cultural relevance. The film follows Asta (Deborra-Lee Furness), whose motorbike breaks down in Ginborak, a fictional rural Australian town. She is trapped there while waiting for mechanical repairs. Asta befriends the mechanic's daughter, Lizzie (Simone Buchanan), who was gang raped by a group of overindulged local youths. The townspeople blame Lizzie and downplay her version of events, even though there are other victims. The rapists proceed to harass Asta, chasing her in their cars one night. She injures one man by smashing his windscreen, the glass slashing his face, which leads the complacent police sergeant to threaten her. At this point, Asta reveals that she is a barrister. Asta's revelation of legal power allows her to build community resistance around Lizzie, other frightened women, and parents, and together they press charges. The legal action is specifically termed "revenge" by one of the rapist's mothers, who tries to buy Lizzie's silence. When the men are immediately released on bail, Asta attempts to implement a restraining order, but the sergeant refuses to take her seriously. The film ends with a violent confrontation between the rapists and Lizzie's family, resulting in Lizzie's death when she falls from their fast-moving car.

Rural settings in films can engender negative or positive connotations. European literature often presents the countryside as an idyll that provides an escape from the industrial urbanization of cities.[44] In more recent horror films, this rural idyll is substituted with what David Bell calls the "anti-idyll."[45] As John Scott and Dean Biron argue:

> While the rural idyll creates rural space as an object of desire because it is not urban, rural space may also be presented as an object of dread for the same reason. There exists in Australian cultural texts a less than Arcadian countryside:

a sick, sordid, malevolent rural underbelly. In this context, the rural needs to be contained, domesticated or avoided outright—the rural is threatening because it is wild. The rural unsettles us by exposing the fragility of civilization.[46]

This Australian anti-idyll is related to American horror films' presentation of rural landscapes peopled by hillbillies and rednecks,[47] who represent a modern generation of "excluded, [and] undignified" peasants.[48]

The Australian Gothic film has a set of recognizable and distinct conventions that differentiate it from other national modes of narrative. It is "typically set in the bush or outback where small, isolated communities are coded as brutal. . . . Aggressive white hetero-normative masculinity is enforced to guard secrets like rape, incest, or lethal racism. These insular communities do not welcome strangers who could learn their secrets or interfere with their way of life."[49] Australian Gothic film is more realist than its continental counterpart, and sets its narrative in the outdoors rather than the interior of the crumbling castle.[50] As Gibson explains, even before colonialization, Europeans envisioned the Australian landscape as mythic, isolated, and wild: "The idea of the intractability of Australian nature is essential to the national ethos."[51] The Gothic mode gives Australian filmmakers a framework for a narrative that articulates colonial experiences of uncertainty in a new landscape.[52] Gerry Turcotte suggests that the Australian Gothic mode is mostly useful to non-Indigenous Australians because of its reliance on the landscape as unfamiliar.[53] In Australian Gothic films, the landscape is vast, sparsely populated, and free from the antiquities that occupy Europe.[54] As Scott and Biron write, the Australian Gothic "plays to a national anxiety of being isolated. The idea of being detached from history and culture is amplified and turned inwards towards an apparently void continent."[55] The rural spaces of this landscape are presented in film as isolated, out-of-touch, and detached from the modern culture found in urban spaces. Cultural norms in these places have not caught up with legal reforms.

Cars often feature in Australian Gothic films, representing the freedom of urban heroes to transgress into the anti-rural setting. As Scott and Biron argue, "the failure of vehicles openly facilitates terror . . . [T]he road itself is positioned as an extension out of urban Australia and into rural danger. The outback is thus perceived of as an ocean of danger lapping up against either side of a narrow bitumen island—an ocean into which the civilized venture at their own peril."[56] Cars also represent the community in the films. The cars are susceptible to damage, which represents the leaking of secrets from an insular community. As Rebecca Johinke argues about the car crashes in *The Cars That Ate Paris*, "A metal carapace shields body parts and contains bodily fluids that could suggest the abject or grotesque. Thus, the car's metal armor (as a denial or refusal of abjection) is ultimately insufficient protection and what should remain inside is penetrated and seeps out."[57] Elsewhere, Johinke notes that Australian Gothic films present motorbikes as challenges to the masculinity of the car. In George Miller's *Mad Max* films, Max Rockatansky represents white, masculine power, while his enemies are homosexual bikies. He is drawn into "forbidden zones" of homosexuality, away from the safety of the "phallic law" of the city.[58] Kieran Tranter also writes that Australians depict their identities and demonstrate their individual power through the cars they drive.[59] These vehicular representations are drawn from the dangerous and culturally learned way that men drive in Australia, which Sarah Redshaw calls "combustion masculinity."[60] While Asta rides a motorbike, the local men perform combustion masculinity by drunk driving in cars and harassing women in public spaces.

Australian identity and culture are often portrayed as masculine in Australian Gothic films.[61] Scott and Biron provide the examples of *Crocodile Dundee*'s Mick Dundee as the manly larrikin archetype of the rural idyll; while his antithesis is Mick Taylor, the bigoted larrikin who lurks in the anti-idyll setting of *Wolf Creek*.[62] *Shame* is one of the few Australian Gothic films that rejects this masculine compulsion. At the film's end, the sergeant appears shocked and distraught when he sees Lizzie's body thrown off the side of the road, but turns to Asta and states, "I hope you're bloody satisfied." The culture of toxic masculinity and victim blaming in the town is clearly not over; however, the townspeople jeer as the young men are arrested for Lizzie's murder, and rally around Asta. Thus, *Shame* portrays a coding of cars as masculine and motorbikes as deviant transgressors, much like in earlier Australian Gothic films, but from a feminist perspective.

Rape-revenge narratives on screen are an oft-reviewed section of vigilante literature. A much-criticized convention for rape-revenge film and television is for the rape to be displayed in sickening detail, before the violent revenge is enacted.[63] However, *Shame* subverts this convention by never showing Lizzie's rape. Similarly, the revenge is ultimately legal rather than violent. Asta almost chokes Lizzie's murderer to death, but other women stop her. The film begins after Lizzie's rape, and the toxic culture that Asta witnesses as soon as she enters the town pub acts as evidence, lending fidelity to Lizzie's account.

Asta's violence is also not premeditated like the conventional vengeance in these kinds of films; she hurts the young man purely in self-defense. She aims to use the legal systems to protect the women of the town. Interestingly, Haas, de Keijser, and Bruinsma find that public support for vigilantism does not necessarily mean less public confidence in legal systems but depends instead on the reasons for the vigilantism. In particular, there is higher support for vigilantism against sex offenders.[64] This finding is replicated in real examples of vigilantism against pedophiles in Australia, such as the Snowtown murders (discussed below), and the earlier example of Meringur, where citizens celebrated outside a pedophile's burning house.[65] *Shame*'s avoidance of purposeful violence presents a legal and, arguably, feminist approach. As Richard Hil writes:

> The connection between vigilantism as a perceived solution to a local crime problem and certain masculine values (toughness, aggressiveness, self-protection) seem to be evident in expressions of autonomous action. The fact that groups tend to be comprised almost exclusively of men, that the dominant "solution" is based on the use of force and that there exists an air of bravado and chest-thumping defiance suggests a particular masculinist undertow to vigilantism.[66]

After the charges are initially laid against the rapists, Lizzie's father is ostracized from the men of the town. A "man-to-man" talk at the pub between him and one of the boy's fathers deteriorates into a bar fight. Asta instead empowers Ginborak's community of women to band together against the apathetic sergeant and to protect themselves as a group. This empowerment of the community is a theme repeated throughout Australian vigilante narratives on screen.

SNOWTOWN (2011)

Snowtown (Justin Kurzel, 2011) is a film based on real vigilante murders that occurred between 1992 and 1999 in an outer suburb of Adelaide. Many of the bodies were disposed of in acid barrels hidden in an abandoned bank in the titular Australian town. John Bunting (Daniel Henshall), the main perpetrator, is notorious as Australia's worst serial killer. Rather than focus constantly on violence, the film spends much of its time highlighting the poverty and lack of opportunities for locals. The film's opening scenes have an ominous blue filter, giving them a stark and detached atmosphere. The camera pans across fibro houses with rubbish piled in their yards, inartistically graffitied shops and fences, and loitering, chain-smoking locals. During the 1990s, unemployment, crime, and sexual abuse were rife in these poverty-stricken suburbs of northern Adelaide.[67] The filming took place in the same area as the murders, where Kurzel, the director, grew up. Interestingly, except for two of the actors (including Henshall), Kurzel hired amateur locals to portray the characters, as he wanted to capture realism in his portrayal of the area's community.[68]

The film follows a single mother, Elizabeth (Louise Harvey), after she discovers that a neighbor has sexually abused her sons. She calls the police to make a statement. Soon afterward, a taxi drops the perpetrator directly across the street from his underage victims. She then meets John Bunting, a charismatic man who riles up a group of locals about the injustice: "It's just not right. If you kids lived in the city, I bet they'd look after you real quick. He wouldn't be out on bail in one fucking day, would he?" The adults hold drunken community watch meetings where they discuss how "the system is fucked." John's character is contradictory; he conflates male gayness with pedophilia and continuously makes homophobic comments; simultaneously, he takes on a fatherly role, especially with Elizabeth's oldest son, Jamie (Lucas Pittaway). He vacillates between the larrikin figure of the rural idyll, and the predatory, damaged villain of the anti-idyll. This ambivalence suits the setting, which borders urban and rural in a frontier characterized by poverty.

The suburbs of northern Adelaide are filled with despair, isolation, and crime, much like the rural anti-idyll setting of Australian Gothic film. However, the characters travel in their cars for one and a half hours with the bodies to dump them in the more isolated Snowtown. The urban murderers use the "narrow bitumen island" to transport unwanted citizens from the outer-urban space into the rural anti-idyll. Further, their placement in the outer suburbs of a city links them to the Australian concept of a bogan, similar to the American redneck. A bogan is defined by the Oxford Australian Dictionary as "uncultured, boorish, and associated with a lower socio-economic class. The *bogan* is usually male."[69] The word's origins are unknown, but have been traced to the 1980s. "Bogan" is often used to describe Australians from "lower socio-economic backgrounds who are car-loving, [and] prone to violence" and who live in outer-urban suburbs, although they can be found elsewhere.[70] Roslyn Rowen argues that bogans approach national identity through convict history and the ANZAC traditions of mateship, and that the term can be used positively, despite its negative connotations.[71] In her *Sydney Morning Herald* article, Mel Campbell argues that bogans are not representative of class, but are "an abstract idea that is expressed through culture. And when we talk about bogans, we're really talking about national identity."[72] She continues to write that bogans are "hyper-Australian" and used to "quarantine ideas of Australianness that alarm or discomfort us. It's a way of erecting imaginary cultural barriers between 'us' and 'them.'"[73] Further, Shannon Harvey writes that contemporary Australian films with low budgets, like *Snowtown*, often depict crime and vigilantism. He calls these films "bogan gothic."[74] The setting of *Snowtown* is a cultural zone inhabited by an insular, overlooked bogan community.

Real-life examples of contemporary vigilantism in Australia tend to circulate around issues of moral contention. Hil writes that Australian vigilantism has increased since the mid-1990s, commonly occurs in rural areas, reflects "tensions in the liberal state" around marginalized people, and is influenced by moral panic.[75] Often, vigilantes are inspired to act not by an actual crime, but by a moral issue.[76] For example, some cases of vigilantism focus on punishing alleged pedophiles who have already served their sentences, whom vigilantes perceive to have escaped adequate punishment. In interviews, Kurzel has suggested that Bunting genuinely believed that the people of the community were victims of injustice.[77] Kurzel uses Jamie as a metaphor for the whole community, and he is depicted as voiceless and helpless, looking for community leaders to fill the void left by police.[78] As Dean Smith writes, "John's energetic confidence and zeal for justice mobilizes the community."[79] In a much darker twist to the vigilante figure who galvanizes the community, Bunting incites hatred and murder.

Over the course of the film, Jamie is drawn into Bunting's vigilante murders of men he considers to be pedophiles, or otherwise morally questionable. At one point early in the film, Jamie's half-brother, Troy, rapes him. It is the only rape shown in the film; consequently, Troy's torture and murder is the only one shown in nauseating detail. Jamie finds the slow torture difficult to watch, and his killing of Troy is depicted as mercy. The film questions whether retaliatory violence is indeed righteous, tapping into the moral conundrum of vigilantism in film and television. As Alison Young suggests, "the violence of wrong-doing is wrong, whereas the violence which responds to wrong-doing is righteous."[80] However, the depiction of violence in *Snowtown*, particularly Troy's murder, has links to Claire Henry's argument that newer revenge narratives ask audiences to question the morality of seeking violent revenge, and whether it satisfies vigilantes.[81]

The film's tension builds slowly, depicting the factors that cause vigilantism, rather than concentrating on gore and violence. Speaking about the filming of the one violent murder scene, actor Daniel Henshall says, "it was the first time all of us had got together and physicalized an actual event, because the film is a lot of intentions and all about relationships so the violence in the film all comes out of that world of relationships."[82] The slow tension and stark grittiness of the film make the occasional acts of explicit violence seem even more disturbing. Unlike Asta in *Shame*, Bunting uses his influence to corrupt a community. The film demonstrates the confluence of circumstances that can lead to vigilantism. The final scene implies the murder of Jamie's stepbrother, Dave (Beau Gosling), and closes the loop of moral questioning. Jamie lures Dave to the bank in *Snowtown* on the false pretense of buying a computer. The film ends with Jamie closing the bank door, leaving a perplexed Dave with Bunting. The murder is senseless rather than retributive, and offers no vigilante satisfaction to viewers.

CLEVERMAN (2016)

While colonial policies have ended, transvigilantism against Indigenous Australians continues. Cunneen and Russell suggest that current issues with structural and institutional racism against Indigenous Australians developed from the legal policies and practices of dispossessing people of their land during the colonial period. These practices were the result of collusion between settlers and the state.[83] Colonial narratives sought to cover up or sanitize vigilante massacres. For example, following the massacre of Indigenous Australians at East Gippsland, Ernest Favenc wrote a novel that suggested aliens were the real first occupiers of Australia, excusing the massacre.[84] In another example, Eliza Fraser's captivity narrative about the Butchulla people of K'gari "unified colonists in what they saw as the rightness of the way they behaved towards Indigenous people."[85]

In her novel, *The Secret River* (2005), Kate Grenville introduced a powerful counter-narrative, adapted in 2015 by the Australian Broadcasting Corporation (ABC) into a two-part mini-series.[86] The narrative follows a convict and his family who settle in the Hawksbury River area (north of Sydney), and experience escalating tensions with a local Indigenous group. At the end, a group of white vigilante squatter-settlers massacre the Indigenous Australians. The settler family then builds a large estate on the now vacant land. As Behrendt writes, Grenville's "symbolism is a striking reminder of the history that lies beneath our modern Australian state and of the ways in which that history has sometimes been deliberately suppressed to give the impression of more noble beginnings."[87] Indeed, Australian narratives and laws were designed to criminalize Indigenous populations for offenses such as drunkenness and vagrancy, but lawmakers turned a blind eye to the criminal conduct of white settlers.[88] This criminalization and the colonial stories told about Indigenous Australians are still evident in contemporary Australia. As Cunneen and Russell argue:

> The [vigilante] narrative feeds into a colonialist view that aboriginal and Torres Strait islander culture is not only primitive but intrinsically criminal. Indigenous Australians are repeatedly spoken of and depicted as "lazy" alcoholics who are unable to look after their children, rather than crime and offending being linked to long-standing social and economic inequalities within Australia.[89]

This colonial narrative of unfair treatment forms the backdrop of the ABC series, *Cleverman*.

Cleverman draws on cultural Dreamtime storytelling with a contemporary science fiction setting. Humans live alongside a slightly different species known as hairypeople or "hairies," noticeable by their profusion of hair, long nails, and super speed and strength. The government has outlawed hairypeople and placed them within "the zone" to live in squalor. Human citizens are fearful of hairypeople, as depicted in the show's opening scene. A young Indigenous woman sits on a public bus minding her own business, when a group of white men begin to harass her. She pulls up her sleeve, exposing an arm covered in thick hair, before scratching the main harasser across the cheek and running from the bus. The other commuters, who ignored the men's harassment of the woman, shrink from her in horror when they realize she is a "hairy." The following scene depicts the immigration minister using the event as a reason to call for tighter control of hairypeople, arguing that they should all be isolated in the zone and should be easily identifiable.[90] As noted by Liam Burke, the use of hairypeople "parallel[s] real world inequalities" in the same ways as the mutants in Marvel's X-Men comic books.[91] Indeed, the writer-producer of *Cleverman*, Ryan Griffen, wrote the series with X-Men in mind.[92] Although comic books by Marvel and DC have attempted to incorporate Indigenous Australian superheroes, they are often hampered by misrepresentation of the Dreamtime and Indigenous cultures, while *Cleverman*, as a "localised interpretation . . . of the superhero idiom" uses Indigenous creators and casts to deepen audiences' understandings of culture, history, and the challenges faced in contemporary Australia.[93]

The series follows Koen (Hunter Page-Lochard), a young Gumbaynggir man who inherits the ancient title of Cleverman when his uncle dies. His half-brother, Waruu (Rob Collins), expected to be named Cleverman, and the rebuke stokes the brothers' feud with each other. Although the brothers are not hairypeople, they are both Indigenous, and these minority groups are shown to have strong connections. In the first episode, Koen helps Djukara (Tysan Towney) and his hairy family escape the zone, and then betrays them to the fictional government Containment Authority (CA) in return for a financial reward. The family is then caught in a confrontation with the CA, and Djukara's young sister is accidentally killed. Across the six episodes of the first season, Koen must come to terms with his new position as Cleverman and make amends for his previous unethical behavior.

Koen's understanding of violence, resilience, and advocacy are important for him as a superhero positioned on the liminal boundary of this world and the Dreamtime. As Cassandra Sharp writes, superhero stories reflect audience dissatisfaction with the law's ability to handle retributive justice and vigilantism.[94] In the fifth episode, Djukara (now in hiding from the CA) sees Koen walking through the zone and recognizes him as the man responsible for his sister's death.[95] He follows Koen and fatally shoots him; however, part of the gift of the Cleverman is Koen's ability to heal very quickly. Koen tells his Aunty Linda (Deborah Mailman) about his role in the family's tragedy: "The CA might have pulled the trigger, but it was my fault she died." Aunty Linda is then called to help a hairy child infected with a spirit. She asks Koen to perform a traditional smoking ceremony to dispel the spirit. Koen sees that it is the spirit of the hairy girl who was shot, and he begs for her forgiveness. She smiles and disappears. Having thus recovered from his past mistakes, Koen accepts his new role. Violence is necessary, according to William E. Burrows, to separate the potential vigilantes (i.e., everyone) from the actual ones.[96] As such, Koen's new physiology as the Cleverman makes him uniquely qualified to enact vengeance—he cannot die nor be permanently maimed and he can see people's futures, which makes him even stronger than the hairypeople.

Vigilantism is often represented as being cultivated in frontier zones. Henry Reynolds claims that pre-colonization, Indigenous Australians used vengeful violence to restore status quo and avoid more widespread warfare.[97] He argues that, following colonization, they:

> [D]ealt with Europeans as though they too were Aborigines. Their violence was judicial rather than martial, seeking revenge rather than military victory. But the settlers were determined upon radical changes. They had no interest in peace and equilibrium until the invasion was fully effected and all resistance crushed . . . Misunderstanding, fear and anxiety merged and simmered in the volatile frontier environment. Violent death and succeeding violent revenge built up brutal momentum as the settlers pushed further into Aboriginal Australia.[98]

Further, as Ray Abrahams suggests, frontiers that foster vigilantism are not always historical colonial frontiers: "Vigilantism is a frontier phenomenon, but the frontiers in question are not always those marked by lines on maps as official, if at times contested, boundaries of states. . . . [T]he term 'frontier' may refer both to a boundary and to a frontier 'zone' . . . The long arm of the law does not stretch everywhere with equal force, and areas where its power is significantly diluted or resisted have a frontier quality."[99] In addition, there can be the so-called no go area which is a "social island that may be spatially quite close to the centers of state power and authority, but which is not easily accessible to state representatives."[100] In these kinds of zones, a superhero vigilante can act in the spaces that lawmakers cannot. As Sharp argues, "The very existence of the superhero . . . presupposes that justice has not and cannot be achieved in the legal systems."[101]

Whenever characters enter the aptly named zone in *Cleverman*, they are subject to intense surveillance by drones. This surveillance alludes to the suspicious treatment of Indigenous Australians by white anti-crime groups such as the Soldiers of Odin and the Alice Springs Volunteer Force.[102] In fact, "Many of the anticrime Facebook groups [in Australia] have an overtly racialized content (in particular, referring to Indigenous young people)."[103] White vigilante groups have incited violence against Indigenous populations in places such as Kalgoorlie (where an Indigenous boy, Elijah Doughty, was run down), South Hedland, and Townsville.[104] As Cunneen and Russell sum up, racist anticrime Facebook groups are not counter-hegemonic, but rather "feed into well-worn tropes concerning populist views of law and order . . . [which, in turn] reproduces a long-running motif of colonial ideology within Australia."[105] The idea that Indigenous youth are somehow "getting away" with crime is also a myth; police intervene with them at a higher rate than they do with non-Indigenous citizens.[106]

In *Cleverman*, the myths, stories, and suspicions about Indigenous people are implicitly depicted through the namorrodor, a creature killing random victims and removing their hearts.[107] After it kills a young white boy, the media and government fuel speculation that vigilante hairypeople are the culprits. Waruu addresses these rumors on a television talk show, urging viewers to trust the judicial system rather than have a trial by media.[108] In the following episode, he inadvertently makes the situation worse by killing a prison guard at a containment facility. The director of the CA (Marcus Graham) then stages the murder as another namorrodor attack by removing the guard's heart and painting symbols on the walls with blood. The murder is linked to the previous murders and also blamed on hairypeople.[109] In the end, Koen must face the namorrodor with his traditional club (a nulla-nulla), before the more difficult task of facing xenophobic police and politicians.[110]

Koen rallies the community, whereas Waruu inserts himself as a self-appointed spokesman. As the season progresses, Koen learns that the role of the Cleverman is not to act as a lone ranger (like Waruu) in the interests of the group, but to act as one of the group. As Gallagher notes in his review, while Western societies prize individualism, Indigenous Australian societies are based around ancient kinship systems, which place "strong emphasis on universal responsibility."[111] According to Gallagher, the hairypeople are similar in that they display strong communal responsibilities and decision-making, and they do not need a vigilante to represent them: "it is not the Cleverman's role to right everybody's wrongs; rather, he serves as a galvanizing figure."[112] Thus, as in earlier Australian on-screen vigilantism, Koen approaches as an outsider and helps the insular community make a stand against institutional oppression.

CONCLUSION

In "Waltzing Matilda" the swagman's only social or legal recourse is suicide because he is an outsider with no legal or political power. In Australian vigilante screen narratives, such as in *Shame* (1988), *Snowtown* (2011), and season one of *Cleverman* (2016), vigilantes instead choose to work with and empower disenfranchised communities. These communities are isolated in frontier zones where they are voiceless and ignorant of their legal rights. When the galvanizing outsider figure appears, he or she can inspire the community to work together to improve their lives. Asta helps the women of Ginborack, John Bunting taps into the unrest of the poor communities in northern Adelaide, and Koen takes on the mantle of Cleverman to help the hairypeople. Despite the differences in the stories, particularly in the moral recourse to violence within *Snowtown*, each of these outsider figures works with an insular community and opposes institutions and police.

Criminals in fictional Australian storytelling are extremely prevalent, yet John Hirst comments that real Australians are generally legally obedient.[113] The vigilante figure allows Australians to consider the morality of criminality in white Australian culture. Protagonists in these films question their use of violence, but ultimately it is used in key moments such as when Asta chokes a rapist-murderer, when Jamie mercifully kills his brother, or when Koen fights the namorrodor. Often, violence is used to depict a loss of innocence; from Koen's causing the death of a young girl, or Bunting's corruption of local youths to commit murder. For the most part, the films and series focus on the social circumstances that can obstruct legal freedoms and lead to vigilantism. *Snowtown* particularly focuses on the conditions that lead to crime, and only shows one of the eleven murders committed by Bunting and his compatriots. In *Cleverman*, viewers see the treatment of a community as criminals, and their own reactive vigilantism.

One of the conditions of crime is the setting within a frontier zone, where a community is disconnected from legal help and subject to misogynistic, racist, and colonialist pressures. Often, the settings are rural, as in *Shame*, linking the vigilante narratives to the Australian Gothic mode, but the frontier zones can also be urban. In *Cleverman*, the zone is bordered off from the rest of the city and subject to preventative surveillance. While there is no such clear border in *Snowtown*, the suburbs around northern Adelaide are places characterized by crime and unemployment, effectively zones for the poor. These frontiers are reminiscent of the myths of the classed colonial frontier, and the struggles that occurred against the British military there. The injustices also have disturbing resemblances to white vigilantism against Indigenous Australians during the colonial period. Contemporary screen narratives draw on these Australian colonial myths and violent realities. Many vigilante narratives reimagine a happier outcome for splintered frontier communities, who are drawn together through a quest for justice.

NOTES

1. "Waltzing Matilda."
2. Nicole E. Haas, Jan W. de Keijser, and Gerben J. N. Bruinsma, "Public Support for Vigilantism: An Experimental Study," *Journal of Experimental Criminology* 8, no. 4 (2012): 389.
3. William E. Burrows, *Vigilante!* (New York: Harcourt Brace Jovanovich, 1976), xiii.
4. Francis Frederick Hawley, "Vigilantism," in *Encyclopedia of Criminal Justice Ethics*, ed. Bruce A. Arrigo (Los Angeles: Sage, 2014).
5. Robert Hughes, *The Fatal Shore* (New York: Knopf, 1986), 158.
6. Russel Braddock Ward, *The Australian Legend* (Melbourne: Oxford University Press, 1958), 136, 144.
7. Babette Smith, *Australia's Birthstain: The Startling Legacy of the Convict Era* (Crows Nest, N.S.W: Allen & Unwin, 2009), 336.
8. Smith, 337.
9. UNESCO, "The Story of the Kelly Gang (1906). UNESCO Memory of the World Register," 2007, http://www.unesco.org/new/en/the-story-of-the-kelly-gang-1906.
10. Peter Carey, *True History of the Kelly Gang* (Brisbane: University of Queensland Press, 2000).
11. Elsa Keslassy, "Memento Films International Boards Justin Kurzel's 'True History of the Kelly Gang' with Russell Crowe," *Variety*, April 30, 2018, https://variety.com/2018/film/news/memento-films-international-true-history-of-the-kelly-gang-russell-crowe-1202791660/.
12. Smith, *Australia's Birthstain*, 318.
13. Larissa Behrendt, *Finding Eliza: Power and Colonial Storytelling* (St. Lucia: University of Queensland Press, 2016), 183.
14. Smith, *Australia's Birthstain*, 56.
15. Smith, 33.
16. Smith, 326.
17. Smith, 4.
18. Miriam Dixson, *The Imaginary Australian: Anglo-Celts and Identity, 1788 to the Present* (Sydney: UNSW Press, 1999), 112.
19. Richard Hil and Glenn Dawes, "The 'Thin White Line': Juvenile Crime, Racialised Narrative And Vigilantism—A North Queensland Study," *Current Issues in Criminal Justice* 11, no. 3 (2000): 310.
20. Chris Cunneen and Sophie Russell, "Social Media, Vigilantism and Indigenous People in Australia," in *The Oxford Encyclopedia of Crime, Media, and Popular Culture*, ed. Nicole Rafter and Michelle Brown (Oxford: Oxford University Press, 2018), 330.
21. Jane Lydon and Lyndall Ryan, eds., *Remembering the Myall Creek Massacre* (Sidney: NewSouth Books, 2018).
22. Hil and Dawes, "The 'Thin White Line,'" 310.

23. John Elder, "Vigilantes Emerge in Time of Fear," *The Age*, January 21, 2007, https://www.theage.com.au/national/vigilantes-emerge-in-time-of-fear-20070121-ge41ce.html.

24. Hil and Dawes, "The 'Thin White Line,'" 314.

25. Andrew Koubaridis, "Street Justice: 'We'll Do it Our Way,'" *News.Com.Au—Australia's Leading News Site*, February 13, 2017, sec. Victoria, https://news.com.au/national/victoria/scared-melbourne-residents-want-new-vigilante-group/news-story/d034c8c4595a3ef3a5110ab2d067abab.

26. Koubaridis.

27. Koubaridis.

28. Ugur Nedim, "Vigilantes Taking the Law into Their Own Hands," Sydney Criminal Lawyers, May 25, 2015, https://www.sydneycriminallawyers.com.au/blog/vigilantes-taking-the-law-into-their-own-hands/.

29. Nedim; Cunneen and Russell, "Social Media, Vigilantism and Indigenous People in Australia," 333.

30. Elder, "Vigilantes Emerge in Time of Fear."

31. Riley Morgan, "Victorian Premier Urges People Not to Become Vigilantes after Teenagers Bring Baseball Bat to Station," SBS News, January 29, 2019, https://www.sbs.com.au/news/article/victorian-premier-urges-people-not-to-become-vigilantes-after-teenagers-bring-baseball-bat-to-station/cfro5do7d.

32. Nedim, "Vigilantes Taking the Law into Their Own Hands."

33. Nedim.

34. "Dominion Movement—Animal Rights Documentary Dominion," accessed March 5, 2022, https://www.dominionmovement.com/.

35. Sean Murphy, "Vegan Activists Vow to Rage against the Farming Machine," *ABC News*, May 30, 2019, https://www.abc.net.au/news/2019-05-30/vegan-activists-vow-to-rage-against-the-farming-machine/11145650.

36. Latika Bourke, "'Offensive': Vegan Vigilantes Warned They Could Lose Charitable Status," The *Sydney Morning Herald*, August 6, 2019, https://www.smh.com.au/politics/federal/offensive-vegan-vigilantes-warned-they-could-lose-charitable-status-20190805-p52e5k.html.

37. Sophie Moore, "Two-Pronged Attack on Vegan Vigilantes," *Newcastle Herald*, July 22, 2019, https://www.newcastleherald.com.au/story/6285312/two-pronged-attack-on-vegan-vigilantes/.

38. "Morrison Government Delivers Farm Trespass Laws." *Attorney General for Australia, and Minister for Industrial Relations*, September 12, 2019, https://www.attorneygeneral.gov.au/media/media-releases/morrison-government-delivers-farm-trespass-laws-12-september-2019.

39. Colin Bettles, "Farm Invasion Laws: Where Is Each State Up To?," *Beef Central* (blog), September 16, 2019, https://www.beefcentral.com/news/farm-invasion-laws-where-is-each-state-up-to/.

40. Catriona Elder, *Being Australian: Narratives of National Identity* (Crows Nest, N.S.W: Allen & Unwin, 2007), 25.

41. Cassandra Sharp, "'Riddle Me This . . . ?'would the World Need Superheroes If the Law Could Actually Deliver 'justice'?," *Law Text Culture* 16 (2012): 370.

42. Ray Abrahams, *Vigilant Citizens: Vigilantism and the State* (Cambridge: Polity Press, 1998), 53–73; Burrows, *Vigilante!*

43. Rebecca Johinke, "Manifestations of Masculinities: Mad Max and the Lure of the Forbidden Zone," *Journal of Australian Studies* 25, no. 67 (2001): 118–25; Rebecca Johinke, "Uncanny Carnage in Peter Weir's 'The Cars That Ate Paris,'" *Sydney Studies in English* 36 (2010): 108–26; Sarah Redshaw, *In the Company of Cars: Driving as a Social and Cultural Practice* (Aldershot, England; Burlington, VT: Ashgate, 2008); Kieran Tranter, "Mad Max: The Car and Australian Governance," *National Identities* 5, no. 1 (2003): 67–81.

44. Raymond Williams, *The Country and the City* (New York: Oxford University Press, 1973); John Scott and Dean Biron, "Wolf Creek, Rurality and the Australian Gothic," *Continuum* 24, no. 2 (2010): 307–22.

45. David Bell, "Anti-Idyll: Rural Horror," in *Contested Countryside Culture*, ed. Paul Cloke and Jo Little (London: Routledge, 1997), 94–108.

46. Scott and Biron, "Wolf Creek, Rurality and the Australian Gothic," 310.

47. Scott and Biron, 310–11.

48. David Bell, "Variations on the Rural Idyll," in *Handbook of Rural Studies*, ed. Paul J. Cloke, Terry Marsden, and Patrick H. Mooney (London: SAGE, 2006), 152.

49. Johinke, "Uncanny Carnage in Peter Weir's 'The Cars That Ate Paris,'" 112.

50. Gerry Turcotte, "Australian Gothic," in *The Handbook of Gothic Literature*, ed. Marie Mulvey-Roberts (Basingstoke: Macmillan, 1998), 10–19, https://ro.uow.edu.au/artspapers/60; Scott and Biron, "Wolf Creek, Rurality and the Australian Gothic," 314–15.

51. Ross Gibson, "Camera Natura: Landscape in Australian Feature Films," in *Australian Cultural Studies: A Reader*, ed. John Frow and Meaghan Morris (Crows Nest, N.S.W: Allen & Unwin, 1993), 211.

52. Turcotte, "Australian Gothic," 10.

53. Turcotte, 18.

54. Scott and Biron, "Wolf Creek, Rurality and the Australian Gothic," 315.

55. Scott and Biron, 316.

56. Scott and Biron, 316.

57. Johinke, "Uncanny Carnage in Peter Weir's' The Cars That Ate Paris,'" 122.

58. Johinke, "Manifestations of Masculinities," 124.

59. Tranter, "Mad Max," 73.

60. Redshaw, *In the Company of Cars*, 80.

61. Amanda Howell, "The Terrible Terrace: Australian Gothic Reimagined and the (Inner) Suburban Horror of The Babadook," in *American-Australian Cinema: Transnational Connections*, ed. Adrian Danks, Stephen Gaunson, and Peter C. Kunze (Cham: Palgrave Macmillan, 2018), 186, https://doi.org/10.1007/978-3-319-66676-1.

62. Scott and Biron, "Wolf Creek, Rurality and the Australian Gothic," 317–18.

63. Lili Pâquet, "The Corporeal Female Body in Literary Rape–Revenge: Shame, Violence, and Scriptotherapy," *Australian Feminist Studies* 33, no. 97 (2018): 384.

64. Haas, de Keijser, and Bruinsma, "Public Support for Vigilantism," 404.

65. Elder, "Vigilantes Emerge in Time of Fear."

66. Richard Hil, "Cautionary Tales: Vigilantism, Crime and Social Order in Australia," *Just Policy: A Journal of Australian Social Policy*, no. 14 (1998): 28.

67. Damon Smith, "Justin Kurzel, The Snowtown Murders | Filmmaker Magazine," *Filmmaker Magazine | Publication with a Focus on Independent Film, Offering Articles, Links, and Resources* (blog), February 29, 2012, https://filmmakermagazine.com/41640-justin-kurzel-snowtown/.

68. Francesca Rudkin, "Interview with the Director & Actors Who Made Australian Film Snowtown," December 13, 2012, https://www.rialtochannel.co.nz/More/Vlogs/ID/146/SNOWTOWN-INTERVIEWS; Matt Barone, "Interview: 'The Snowtown Murders' Director Justin Kurzel Talks His Intensely Disturbing, Real-Life Serial Killer Film," Complex, March 3, 2012, https://www.complex.com/pop-culture/2012/03/interview-the-snowtown-murders-director-justin-kurzel; Smith, "Justin Kurzel, The Snowtown Murders | Filmmaker Magazine."

69. Rachel Ellis, "Bogan," Oxford Australia Word of the Month, November 2008, https://slll.cass.anu.edu.au/sites/default/files/andc/WOTM%20Nov.%202008.pdf.

70. Roslyn Rowen, "Bogan as a Keyword of Contemporary Australia," in *Cultural Keywords in Discourse*, ed. Carsten Levisen and Sophia Waters (Amsterdam: John Benjamins Publishing Company, 2017), 55, 65.

71. Rowen, 78.

72. Mel Campbell, "Perhaps There's a Little Bogan in Everyone," The *Sydney Morning Herald*, June 8, 2006, https://www.smh.com.au/national/perhaps-theres-a-little-bogan-in-everyone-20060608-gdnpim.html.

73. Campbell.

74. Shannon Harvey, "Blame the Bogans," The *West Australian*, June 9, 2011, https://thewest.com.au/entertainment/movies/blame-the-bogans-ng-ya-165570.

75. Hil, "Cautionary Tales," 24–30.

76. Hil, 23.

77. Alexandria Symonds, "Justin Kurzel Finds Hell in Snowtown," *Interview Magazine*, March 2, 2012, https://www.interviewmagazine.com/film/justin-kurzel-finds-hell-in-snowtown.

78. Rudkin, "Interview with the Director & Actors Who Made Australian Film Snowtown."

79. Smith, "Justin Kurzel, The Snowtown Murders | Filmmaker Magazine."

80. Alison Young, *The Scene of Violence: Cinema, Crime, Affect* (Abingdon, Oxon: Routledge, 2009), 24.

81. Claire Henry, *Revisionist Rape-Revenge: Redefining a Film Genre* (New York: Palgrave Macmillan, 2014), 136.

82. Rudkin, "Interview with the Director & Actors Who Made Australian Film Snowtown."

83. Cunneen and Russell, "Social Media, Vigilantism and Indigenous People in Australia," 341.

84. Bruce Pascoe, *Dark Emu: Aboriginal Australia and the Birth of Agriculture* (Perth: Magabala Books, 2014), 223–24.

85. Behrendt, *Finding Eliza*, 195.

86. Kate Grenville, *The Secret River* (Melbourne: Text Publishing, 2005).

87. Behrendt, *Finding Eliza*, 191.
88. Hil and Dawes, "The 'Thin White Line,'" 311.
89. Cunneen and Russell, "Social Media, Vigilantism and Indigenous People in Australia," 341.
90. Purcell "First Contact" *Cleverman* (15/06/2016) Season 1 Episode 1.
91. Liam Burke, "Meet Cleverman: Our First Aboriginal Screen Superhero, with Healing Powers and a Political Edge," The Conversation, para. 8, accessed February 26, 2022, http://theconversation.com/meet-cleverman-our-first-aboriginal-screen-superhero-with-healing-powers-and-a-political-edge-59813.
92. Kevin Patrick, "Dreamtime Mutants and Urban Vigilantes: Aboriginal Superheroes in American Comics—Senses of Cinema," para. 1, accessed February 26, 2022, http://www.sensesofcinema.com/2018/cleverman-australian-superheroes/dreamtime-mutants-and-urban-vigilantes-aboriginal-superheroes-in-american-comics/.
93. Patrick, para. 30.
94. Sharp, "'Riddle Me This . . . ?," 354.
95. Blair, "A Man of Vision" *Cleverman* (29/06/2016) Season 1 Episode 5.
96. Burrows, *Vigilante!*, xiii.
97. Henry Reynolds, *The Other Side of the Frontier* (Ringwood: Penguin, 1995), 72.
98. Reynolds, 78.
99. Abrahams, *Vigilant Citizens*, 24.
100. Abrahams, 25.
101. Sharp, "'Riddle Me This . . . ?," 359.
102. Nedim, "Vigilantes Taking the Law into Their Own Hands."
103. Cunneen and Russell, "Social Media, Vigilantism and Indigenous People in Australia," 333.
104. Cunneen and Russell, 336.
105. Cunneen and Russell, 342.
106. Rob White, "Indigenous Youth and Offensive Spaces," *Social Alternatives* 18, no. 2 (1999): 39.
107. Purcell, "First Contact" *Cleverman*, (15/06/2016) Season 1 Episode 1.
108. Blair, "Containment" *Cleverman* (08/06/2016) Season 1 Episode 2.
109. Blair, "A Free Ranger" *Cleverman* (01/06/2016) Season 1 Episode 3.
110. Blair, "Terra Nullius" *Cleverman* (06/07/2016) Season 1 Episode 6.
111. Cavan Gallagher, "No Spandex Required: 'Cleverman,' Indigenous Stories and the New Superhero," *Metro Magazine: Media & Education Magazine*, no. 190 (2016): para. 11.
112. Gallagher, para. 12.
113. J. B. Hirst, *The Australians: Insiders & Outsiders on the National Character since 1770* (Collingwood, Vic: Black Inc, 2007), 135.

BIBLIOGRAPHY

Abrahams, Ray. *Vigilant Citizens: Vigilantism and the State*. Cambridge: Polity Press, 1998.
Barone, Matt. "Interview: 'The Snowtown Murders' Director Justin Kurzel Talks His Intensely Disturbing, Real-Life Serial Killer Film." Complex, March 3, 2012. https://www.complex.com/pop-culture/2012/03/interview-the-snowtown-murders-director-justin-kurzel.
Behrendt, Larissa. *Finding Eliza: Power and Colonial Storytelling*. St. Lucia: University of Queensland Press, 2016.
Bell, David. "Anti-Idyll: Rural Horror." In *Contested Countryside Culture*, edited by Paul Cloke and Jo Little, 94–108. London: Routledge, 1997.
———. "Variations on the Rural Idyll." In *Handbook of Rural Studies*, edited by Paul J. Cloke, Terry Marsden, and Patrick H. Mooney, 149–60. London: Sage, 2006.
Bettles, Colin. "Farm Invasion Laws: Where Is Each State Up To?" *Beef Central* (blog), September 16, 2019. https://www.beefcentral.com/news/farm-invasion-laws-where-is-each-state-up-to/.
Bourke, Latika. "'Offensive': Vegan Vigilantes Warned They Could Lose Charitable Status." The Sydney Morning Herald, August 6, 2019. https://www.smh.com.au/politics/federal/offensive-vegan-vigilantes-warned-they-could-lose-charitable-status-20190805-p52e5k.html.
Burke, Liam. "Meet Cleverman: Our First Aboriginal Screen Superhero, with Healing Powers and a Political Edge." The Conversation. Accessed February 26, 2022. http://theconversation.com/meet-cleverman-our-first-aboriginal-screen-superhero-with-healing-powers-and-a-political-edge-59813.
Burrows, William E. *Vigilante!* New York: Harcourt Brace Jovanovich, 1976.
Campbell, Mel. "Perhaps There's a Little Bogan in Everyone." The *Sydney Morning Herald*, June 8, 2006. https://www.smh.com.au/national/perhaps-theres-a-little-bogan-in-everyone-20060608-gdnpim.html.
Carey, Peter. *True History of the Kelly Gang*. Brisbane: University of Queensland Press, 2000.
Cunneen, Chris, and Sophie Russell. "Social Media, Vigilantism and Indigenous People in Australia." In *The Oxford Encyclopedia of Crime, Media, and Popular Culture*, edited by Nicole Rafter and Michelle Brown, 3: 329–47. Oxford: Oxford University Press, 2018.
Dixson, Miriam. *The Imaginary Australian: Anglo-Celts and Identity, 1788 to the Present*. Sydney: UNSW Press, 1999.
"Dominion Movement—Animal Rights Documentary Dominion." Accessed March 5, 2022. https://www.dominionmovement.com/.
Elder, Catriona. *Being Australian: Narratives of National Identity*. Crows Nest, N.S.W.: Allen & Unwin, 2007.
Elder, John. "Vigilantes Emerge in Time of Fear." *The Age*, January 21, 2007. https://www.theage.com.au/national/vigilantes-emerge-in-time-of-fear-20070121-ge41ce.html.

Ellis, Rachel. "Bogan." Oxford Australia Word of the Month, November 2008. https://slll.cass.anu.edu.au/sites/default/files/andc/WOTM%20Nov.%202008.pdf.

Gallagher, Cavan. "No Spandex Required: 'Cleverman,' Indigenous Stories and the New Superhero." *Metro Magazine: Media & Education Magazine*, no. 190 (2016): 34–41.

Gibson, Ross. "Camera Natura: Landscape in Australian Feature Films." In *Australian Cultural Studies: A Reader*, edited by John Frow and Meaghan Morris, 209–21. Crows Nest, N.S.W.: Allen & Unwin, 1993.

Grenville, Kate. *The Secret River*. Melbourne: Text Publishing, 2005.

Haas, Nicole E., Jan W. de Keijser, and Gerben J. N. Bruinsma. "Public Support for Vigilantism: An Experimental Study." *Journal of Experimental Criminology* 8, no. 4 (2012): 387–413.

Harvey, Shannon. "Blame the Bogans." The *West Australian*, June 9, 2011. https://thewest.com.au/entertainment/movies/blame-the-bogans-ng-ya-165570.

Hawley, Francis Frederick. "Vigilantism." In *Encyclopedia of Criminal Justice Ethics*, edited by Bruce A. Arrigo, 989–91. Los Angeles: Sage, 2014.

Henry, Claire. *Revisionist Rape-Revenge: Redefining a Film Genre*. New York: Palgrave Macmillan, 2014.

Hil, Richard. "Cautionary Tales: Vigilantism, Crime and Social Order in Australia." *Just Policy: A Journal of Australian Social Policy*, no. 14 (1998): 22–31.

Hil, Richard, and Glenn Dawes. "The 'Thin White Line': Juvenile Crime, Racialised Narrative And Vigilantism—A North Queensland Study." *Current Issues in Criminal Justice* 11, no. 3 (2000): 308–26.

Hirst, J. B. *The Australians: Insiders & Outsiders on the National Character since 1770*. Collingwood, Vic: Black Inc, 2007.

Howell, Amanda. "The Terrible Terrace: Australian Gothic Reimagined and the (Inner) Suburban Horror of The Babadook." In *American-Australian Cinema: Transnational Connections*, edited by Adrian Danks, Stephen Gaunson, and Peter C. Kunze, 183–203. Cham: Palgrave Macmillan, 2018. https://doi.org/10.1007/978-3-319-66676-1.

Hughes, Robert. *The Fatal Shore*. New York: Knopf, 1986.

Johinke, Rebecca. "Manifestations of Masculinities: Mad Max and the Lure of the Forbidden Zone." *Journal of Australian Studies* 25, no. 67 (2001): 118–25.

———. "Uncanny Carnage in Peter Weir's 'The Cars That Ate Paris.'" *Sydney Studies in English* 36 (2010): 108–26.

Keslassy, Elsa. "Memento Films International Boards Justin Kurzel's 'True History of the Kelly Gang' with Russell Crowe." *Variety*, April 30, 2018. https://variety.com/2018/film/news/memento-films-international-true-history-of-the-kelly-gang-russell-crowe-1202791660/.

Koubaridis, Andrew. "Street Justice: 'We'll Do it Our Way.'" *News.Com.Au—Australia's Leading News Site*, February 13, 2017, sec. Victoria. https://news.com.au/national/victoria/scared-melbourne-residents-want-new-vigilante-group/news-story/d034c8c4595a3ef3a5110ab2d067abab.

Lydon, Jane, and Lyndall Ryan, eds. *Remembering the Myall Creek Massacre*. Sidney: NewSouth Books, 2018.

Moore, Sophie. "Two-Pronged Attack on Vegan Vigilantes." *Newcastle Herald*, July 22, 2019. https://www.newcastleherald.com.au/story/6285312/two-pronged-attack-on-vegan-vigilantes/.

Morgan, Riley. "Victorian Premier Urges People Not to Become Vigilantes after Teenagers Bring Baseball Bat to Station." SBS News, January 29, 2019. https://www.sbs.com.au/news/article/victorian-premier-urges-people-not-to-become-vigilantes-after-teenagers-bring-baseball-bat-to-station/cfro5do7d.

Murphy, Sean. "Vegan Activists Vow to Rage against the Farming Machine." *ABC News*, May 30, 2019. https://www.abc.net.au/news/2019-05-30/vegan-activists-vow-to-rage-against-the-farming-machine/11145650.

Nedim, Ugur. "Vigilantes Taking the Law into Their Own Hands." Sydney Criminal Lawyers, May 25, 2015. https://www.sydneycriminallawyers.com.au/blog/vigilantes-taking-the-law-into-their-own-hands/.

Pâquet, Lili. "The Corporeal Female Body in Literary Rape–Revenge: Shame, Violence, and Scriptotherapy." *Australian Feminist Studies* 33, no. 97 (2018): 384–99.

Pascoe, Bruce. *Dark Emu: Aboriginal Australia and the Birth of Agriculture*. Perth: Magabala Books, 2014.

Patrick, Kevin. "Dreamtime Mutants and Urban Vigilantes: Aboriginal Superheroes in American Comics—Senses of Cinema." Accessed February 26, 2022. http://www.sensesofcinema.com/2018/cleverman-australian-superheroes/dreamtime-mutants-and-urban-vigilantes-aboriginal-superheroes-in-american-comics/.

Redshaw, Sarah. *In the Company of Cars: Driving as a Social and Cultural Practice*. Aldershot, England; Burlington, VT: Ashgate, 2008.

Reynolds, Henry. *The Other Side of the Frontier*. Ringwood: Penguin, 1995.

Rowen, Roslyn. "Bogan as a Keyword of Contemporary Australia." In *Cultural Keywords in Discourse*, edited by Carsten Levisen and Sophia Waters, 55–82. Amsterdam: John Benjamins Publishing Company, 2017.

Rudkin, Francesca. "Interview with the Director & Actors Who Made Australian Film Snowtown," December 13, 2012. https://www.rialtochannel.co.nz/More/Vlogs/ID/146/SNOWTOWN-INTERVIEWS.

Scott, John, and Dean Biron. "Wolf Creek, Rurality and the Australian Gothic." *Continuum* 24, no. 2 (2010): 307–22.

Sharp, Cassandra. "'Riddle Me This . . . ?'would the World Need Superheroes If the Law Could Actually Deliver 'justice'?" *Law Text Culture* 16 (2012): 353–78.

Smith, Babette. *Australia's Birthstain: The Startling Legacy of the Convict Era*. Crows Nest, N.S.W.: Allen & Unwin, 2009.

Smith, Damon. "Justin Kurzel, The Snowtown Murders | Filmmaker Magazine." *Filmmaker Magazine | Publication with a Focus on Independent Film, Offering Articles, Links, and Resources.* (blog), February 29, 2012. https://filmmakermagazine.com/41640-justin-kurzel-snowtown/.

Symonds, Alexandria. "Justin Kurzel Finds Hell in Snowtown." Interview Magazine, March 2, 2012. https://www.interviewmagazine.com/film/justin-kurzel-finds-hell-in-snowtown.

Tranter, Kieran. "Mad Max: The Car and Australian Governance." *National Identities* 5, no. 1 (2003): 67–81.
Turcotte, Gerry. "Australian Gothic." In *The Handbook of Gothic Literature*, edited by Marie Mulvey-Roberts, 10–19. Basingstoke: Macmillan, 1998. https://ro.uow.edu.au/artspapers/60.
UNESCO. "The Story of the Kelly Gang (1906). UNESCO Memory of the World Register," 2007. http://www.unesco.org/new/en/the-story-of-the-kelly-gang-1906.
Ward, Russel Braddock. *The Australian Legend*. Melbourne: Oxford University Press, 1958.
White, Rob. "Indigenous Youth and Offensive Spaces." *Social Alternatives* 18, no. 2 (1999): 39–43.
Williams, Raymond. *The Country and the City*. New York: Oxford University Press, 1973.
Young, Alison. *The Scene of Violence: Cinema, Crime, Affect*. Abingdon, Oxon: Routledge, 2009.

Chapter 4
Vigilante Justice In Canada

Rebecca Johnson

In the popular cultural arena, when people think about vigilantism, Canada is not generally the first country that comes to mind. Canada is often suggested to be a kind of counter-story to its American neighbor. If one were to tell the story of the birth of each of these two nations, one might begin by noting that they both have their roots in British Empire, and both emerged through processes of settler colonization, rooted in ideas of the Doctrine of Discovery and terra nullius; the belief that the land was uninhabited in any meaningful way and settlers were entitled to claim it and govern it according to their traditional institutions. The dominant popular culture vigilante stories in the US tradition find roots in story-telling practices in which the West is Wild, and in need of taming, law and order comes to the settler communities after they have been well established. This contrasts with story of the arrival of law and order in Canada—this is a story in which the North West Mounted Police (later renamed the Royal Canadian Mounted Police) arrived first, and then opened the West for settlers, rather than coming in to tame it after the fact. In this Canadian national narrative, there is not a tradition of a recourse to private justice, or to taking "the law" into one's own hands. State law is the primary tool for creating the conditions for peace. Instances of vigilantism are rare, regarded with shock and revulsion, and merit a harsh response from the formal legal system.

But cracks have begun to show in the foundation of this conventional account of both Canada's national narrative, and the place of vigilantism in that story. In part through the highly visible work of both the Royal Commission on Aboriginal Peoples and the Truth and Reconciliation Commission, there is a much richer public conversation about the prior (and continuing) existence of Indigenous legal orders.[1] Increasingly, there is public acknowledgment that Canadian law has been used to criminalize a whole host of Indigenous institutions of governance (like the potlach and the Sundance) and economy (practices of hunting, fishing, agriculture, and trade). While many of the explicitly racist/genocidal laws have been unwound, the impacts are not contained in the past, but persist into the present. The legacy of a 150-year (genocidal) program remains present in the structure of many contemporary institutions (health, education, justice, economy, child welfare), where Indigenous people continue to both encounter barriers and be denied resources. The question of "whose" justice is still on the table. Indigenous law is now something that law schools are expected to teach about and lawyers expected to know about.[2] But there is still a great unevenness in what this means, and many heated and persistent conflicts over paramountcy where there are differences over "the law" that is presumed to be authoritative in different contexts.

In the Canadian context, conversations about "getting even" and "taking the law into one's own hands" cannot be made sense of without an understanding of the ongoing stakes of colonial denial of indigenous legal orders. As the editors of this collection make clear, depending on the lens one takes, the vigilante may be described as a "hero" or "villain." The stories leave us asking what it means to live in accordance with law, to question the laws that we celebrate, and those we ignore.[3] Much is at stake in imagining how we are invited to take the law into our own hands, and about the relationships between upholding and rejecting law, framed not only through the language of vigilantism, but also through the languages of dissent, disobedience, and direct action. In the Canadian context, this also means keeping in the front our minds the question of "which law" is thought to govern our conduct, and about the kinds of action that may be required of us as we consider taking law into our own hands in the context of legal orders that are themselves layered on the territories in which we live our lives.

Questions about the nature of law itself are part of the conversation in the Canadian context. For it makes little sense to speak of taking the law into one's own hands unless one has an idea about what law they believe is being held. How people think about law is shaped by their experiences and history.[4] For many Canadians, the idea of law is mostly clearly associated with ideas of formalized, hierarchically, nation-based, centralized state processes—we could call this a legal *system*. But this is not the only way the law operates in the world. For many Indigenous nations in Canada (and indeed around the world) law derives from what Napoleon identifies as a legal *order*: law is embedded in a configuration of non-state, decentralized and laterally connected institutions (social, political, economic, and spiritual). A crucial challenge has been confronting the ways in which many legal systems in the world have operated (particularly in a colonial context) as if their understandings of law defined the totality of law.

Whether one understands oneself as operating within a vertically organized legal system or a laterally organized legal order, law provides a way for large groups of people to collectively govern themselves. Law is societally informed, has processes for change and movement, includes processes of reasoning and deliberation. It enables people to make decisions, create conditions of safety, maintain and repair relations, and attend to potential abuses of power.[5] The questions raised by both Hart and Fuller in their classic discussion of the nature of law do have application whether one is thinking about legal systems or legal orders. They point us to some central questions that people have of the law:

1. What is the law? How do we come to know what law applies to us, and what law requires of us? I think of this as the authority or legitimacy question. Whether or not we "like" a particular law, what are the processes through which that law is created, and through which we know it publically to take the name of law?
2. How do we know if the law has been broken? I think of this as an evidentiary question. What are the processes by which we know, for example, that a crime has happened, and who it was that committed it?
3. How do we respond to the breaking of the law? I think of this as the "sentencing" question. What is to be done with the law-breaker, or about the results of the law-breaking? This includes the question of "who" has the authority or jurisdiction to make the decision on this point.
4. What is to be done when the law itself needs to be changed? What are the processes for changing the law? (Democratic process? Protest? Civil disobedience?)

These four questions weave themselves through stories of vigilante justice, and I will take them up in our exploration of the Canadian context. In what follows, I will share three stories, each of which gives us a snapshot in Vigilante Justice in Canada. In Story 1, we head "to the Courts." In the linked cases of *R v. Vollrath*, and *R v. Suter* we engage with official judicial discourse as the courts focus their attention on to both the vigilante and the aftermath of vigilantism. In brief, sixty-two–year-old Richard Suter drove his car onto a restaurant patio, killing a two-year-old boy. He was charged with refusing to provide a breath sample in the context of a fatal car accident. Before the trial, he was abducted by a group of vigilantes, including Steven Vollrath, who cut off Suter's thumb with pruning shears. In the courts, judges express concern for the rule of law, and the exclusive jurisdiction of the state to deliver justice. In their sentencing, they affirm the legitimacy of the legal order, of Canadian law, and of the authority of the courts in sustaining the rule of law.

In Story 2, we head "to the barricades" to explore the language of vigilantism in ongoing conflicts flowing from Canada's colonial history, and the encounters of Canadian and Indigenous legal ordering. We will consider a high-profile conflict that occurred in 2020, in response to the proposed building of pipelines through Wet'suwet'en territory in British Columbia. We will look briefly at two locations of protest (in the path of the pipeline, and on the steps of the legislature) to explore the ways different languages of dissent, civil disobedience, and vigilantism point us toward a much more complicated conversation about the politics of struggle over the authority of law, and our fidelity to lawfulness. That is, in this context, the story of vigilantism is intimately bound up with the question of "whose law" applies. This story invites us to consider the ways that both vigilantism and the language of vigilantism are deployed in countries marked by historic and ongoing experiences of colonial legal ordering.

Story 3, we head "to the movies." We move from the world of political action to popular culture, and settle into the space of the imaginary to reexamine themes of revenge and vigilantism in Indigenous film maker Jeff Barnaby's film *Rhymes for Young Ghouls*. In this film, we are invited to inhabit a world in which the Canadian state is described as a space of legally authorized vigilante violence against Indigenous bodies. Here, as in the *Suter* and *Vollrath* cases in our first story, we begin with the death of a child. But we have a very different window into Indigenous imaginings about the ways that the concepts of justice and vigilantism require a massive rethinking in order to truly unsettle the injustices persisting as a contemporary legacy of a colonial vigilante legal order. The invitation here is not simply to describe the problem but to invite reflection on ways to disrupt or emerge from a site of recurring vigilante trauma.

STORY 1: VIGILANTISM IN THE COURTS: *R V. SUTER* AND *R V. VOLLRATH*

This story begins with the death of a child. On May 19, 2013, Sage Morin and George Mounsef were dining with their two small children on a restaurant patio in Edmonton. Without warning, Suter's car, which had pulled into a parking spot beside the patio, lurched forward at high speed and plowed through the glass barricade. It struck a number of people, injuring three, and fatally crushing two-year-old Geo Mounsef against the wall. In the panic of the moment, sixty-two-year old Richard Suter was pulled from the vehicle by bystanders, thrown to the ground and repeatedly hit, kicked, and dragged across the pavement. Another group of onlookers surrounded him to protect him from further attack. When police arrived, Suter was curled in a fetal position on the ground, and needed assistance in walking to the police car.

One might begin by wondering if some of the action at the scene of the accident might be thought of as a kind of spontaneous vigilantism against Suter. Certainly, the actions *of* Richard Suter were of more concern to the police at this point than the actions *against* Richard Suter. There were no charges or investigations arising from the crowd violence against Suter, though there were many witnesses. One might presume that this reflects a sense by the police that the crowd's action against Suter was a kind of "natural" eruption of violence, generated through adrenaline or panic, or that it could be understood as within the reasonable force one might expect in such situations.[6]

At the police station, when Suter spoke with state-funded legal counsel, he was (wrongly) advised to refuse the breath sample.[7] This refusal then played a significant place in the story, since it deprived the public (and the courts) of an objective assessment about the possible role of alcohol in the accident. For many, Suter's refusal was itself evidence of his guilt—a kind of willful disobedience, akin to taking the law into one's own hands.[8] The mother set up a facebook page called "Justice for Geo," focused on reforms to impaired driving laws, and a legacy organization for children whose lives had been harmed by impaired drivers.[9] There was an outpouring of public sympathy and support[10] which flowed in two directions: one of sympathy and love to the parents, the other of rage against impaired drivers in general and against both Mr. and Mrs. Suter in particular.

In the social media feeds, the language of vigilante or mob justice emerged, with calls for increased sentences and penalties.[11] There were statements like "he should be thrown in a cell to miserably rot for the rest of his days & [be] tortured besides." A reporter covering that case said, "I think a lot of people would like him tarred & feathered. Or drawn & quartered. But our courts don't do that." Suter's wife Gayska was also targeted, both for having been in the car, and for standing by her husband. Comments emerged claiming, "they should both be charged." In the two years that passed before the case was finally before a trial judge, the fury did not subside. In addition to social media, threatening notes appeared in the Suter's mailbox, all linked to views about the Suters' role in death of the child. In the summer of 2014, Gayska Suter was assaulted in the parking lot of a strip mall, by a man wearing dark clothes and gloves, with a balaclava covering his head. The man punched her in the face, breaking her nose and teeth, and then fled in a car that was waiting with a getaway driver. She believed that she specifically had been the target of the assault.[12] And then, in January 2015, some twenty months after the death of Geo Mounsef, Mr. Suter was abducted in the middle of the night from his home by three men dressed like police officers. He was blindfolded, bound, and driven to a snowy field. When he asked them why they were abducting him, his captors referred to an incident where Suter had hit a child with his car and the child had died. They then beat him, and cut off his thumb with pruning shears, leaving him unconscious in the snow in his bathrobe and winter boots.

Both the mainstream media and the parents of the dead boy condemned the violence that had been done to Suter. On her facebook page, the mother wrote, "It is utterly heartbreaking to have our Baby Geo's memory associated with this horrible act of violence. Justice For Geo will not come in the form of violence. Our family remains hopeful and entrusting of the legal system to bring Justice For Geo."[13] But social media posts continued to carry far more unsettling messages. One encountered statements like, "I wish they would have pulled out his heart instead of a thumb," or, "I would have dumped his body in a lake after breaking his arms and legs," or "he deserves a good prison rape," and "I would like to shake the hands of each and everyone of the people that did what the rest of society didn't have the courage or guts to do!!! Hats off to you all."[14] Again, the language of vigilantism was very much present in social media.

Sentencing Suter

When the case finally went to trial, the Crown dropped all the charges except the offense of refusing to provide a breath sample following a fatal collision. Suter pled guilty, and so the matter was set over for a five-day sentencing hearing, at which the judge listened to all the evidence, and over twenty-five victim impact statements. The judge concluded that the evidence did not support the widely held public belief that Richard Suter had been impaired at the time. Rather, the judge concluded that the crash was a non-impaired accident, and that Suter's post-crash appearance (unsteady and confused) was the result of shock and trauma of both the accident, and the crowd violence he had been subjected to. The judge noted the significant mismatch between Suter's actual guilt (for refusing to provide a breath sample), and the sentence executed against him by the vigilantes. Part of the problem, it seemed, was a kind of mistargeted rage/sorrow that attached itself to both of the Suters, amplified by the strength of the social media condemnations. The judge was left struggling with the question of how (or whether) the vigilante violence Suter had suffered should impact his sentence. In the end, the trial judge sentenced Suter to four months.

The case was appealed, and again there was a flurry of social media commentary. The Alberta Court of Appeal increased Suter's sentence to twenty-nine months, concluding that the extra-legal violence Suter had suffered should not influence the sentencing process. From there, the case went to the Supreme Court of Canada. The court began by noting that vigilantism was so rare, that it was hard to find a comparator case: "The facts in Suter's case are entirely unique. There are no similar offenders in similar circumstances against which his sentence can be reasonably measured."[15] In the context of this case, for example, had Suter provided a breath sample, and had that sample shown no evidence of intoxication, one might be left to conclude that Geo's death was a tragedy, but not a crime. In such situations, the Supreme Court concluded that a sentence in the range of fifteen to eighteen months would generally be appropriate for the refusal to provide a breath sample. They also concluded that the ten and a half months Suter had already served was adequate in this specific case, and there would be no benefit to sending him back to jail to serve further time. On the "vigilantism" question in general, they concluded that a sentencing judge could take vigilantism into account, at least to a limited extent:

> Violent actions against an offender for his or her role in the commission of an offence necessarily form part of the personal circumstances of that offender, and should therefore be taken into account when determining an appropriate sentence. . . . However, vigilante violence should only be considered to a limited extent, as giving it too much weight at sentencing allows these kinds of criminal conduct to gain undue legitimacy in the judicial process.[16]

Sentencing Vollrath

That vigilantism is understood as a particularly reprehensible kind of criminal conduct is clear in judicial commentary in the trial of Steven Vollrath, a thirty-year old man implicated in the attack on Suter. Vollrath was charged with kidnapping, aggravated assault, possession of a weapon for a dangerous purpose, and personating a police officer. He was sentenced to twelve years in jail. Here a note on the Canadian prison system is in order. There is a well-documented literature on the systemic over-incarceration of Indigenous peoples.[17] In 2020, in January, Indigenous people comprise more than 30 percent of the federal inmate population; Indigenous women make up 42 percent.[18] One response to this is s. 718.2(e) of the Criminal Code, which says that in sentencing Indigenous offenders the courts are to consider their unique circumstances.[19] In *R v. Gladue* and *R v. Ipellee*, the Supreme Court directed that judges should have access to information about Indigenous offenders, in order to find a sentence that responds both to these histories and to the resulting systemic over-incarceration of Indigenous offenders. This information appears in the form of what is referred to as a Gladue Report. Because Mr. Vollrath had a Métis parent (a father who was unknown to him), a Gladue report was prepared for the sentencing judge, exploring the connections between his criminality and the deprivations he had experienced as an Indigenous person. This report showed that Mr. Vollrath had undergone a life of exceptional hardship, violence, and neglect. By the age of eight, he was homeless, and using cocaine, was in gangs by the age of ten and was incarcerated from the age of thirteen on. The sentencing judge noted this history, but concluded that "It is not clear how Mr. Vollrath's unfortunate background bore on his commission of these particular offences. His constrained circumstances do not diminish his moral culpability for these offenses."[20] Further, the judge added, there was no evidence about "the kind of intergenerational dislocation and trauma that often characterizes aboriginal offenders coming before the Court."[21] That is, the judge did not see how the dysfunction in Mr. Vollrath's life was connected to any aboriginal history. Thus, the most important thing in this case, said the judge, was to denounce the vigilantism and deter others.[22]

Again, the Alberta Court of Appeal was asked to reexamine the sentence. The defense argued that the court had paid insufficient attention to the Gladue Report before it. The majority judges disagreed. They found no error in the trial judge's reasoning. This was a case of "pure vengeance," they argued, which was perhaps an even more aggravating factor.[23] In such a case, background factors related to the offender had to be minimized—deterrence and denunciation had to take priority. The appeal court quoted from the Supreme Court of Canada in *Suter*, saying: "Vigilantism undermines the rule of law and interferes with the administration of justice. It takes justice out of the hands of the police and the courts, and puts in into the hands of criminals. As a general rule, those who engage in it should expect to be treated severely."[24] If social media commentators had suggested they wanted to shake the hands of the Vollraths of the world, the majority of the Court had quite a different view. They upheld the twelve-year sentence. I note here that one of the appeal judges had a dissenting view. Taking the Gladue Report into account, he argued that it was an error to focus so strongly on deterrence and denunciation to the neglect of the principle of restraint, and the importance of acknowledging the context of violence, abandonment, dislocation, deprivation that shaped Mr. Vollrath's life, whether or not attributable to his aboriginal heritage. He would have substituted a sentence of nine years.[25]

I pause here to reflect on the substance of the Vollrath Gladue sentencing report. It raises some heartbreaking questions. Without entering into the debate about the appropriate sentence, the report speaks to an absence of the rule of law. Certainly, it is hard to find justice in the story of an eight-year-old beaten and on the streets. It is a painful story of disconnection from family and roots. It is a small story that invites questions about what it means to have an Indigenous identity in the first place (since Mr. Vollrath's Métis father was never known to him). It raises questions about blood and identity and uncertainty, and lack of community or resources. It echoes with story after story that can be heard in the Truth and Reconciliation Commission's Report documenting the impacts of Canadian campaigns of genocide against Indigenous peoples. The TRC report makes visible of histories of gross injustice. It raises questions about the social media commentary with its rage about the (accidental) death of a two–year-old. One is left wondering about the seeming societal (certainly judicial) lack of interest in the "constrained circumstances" of the young Vollrath, and on the impact of those circumstances on his adult decision-making.

If one were to take this case as a whole, both Suter and Vollrath and the ways their stories wind their way through to the Supreme Court of Canada, there are a number of themes that can be seen. In the *Suter* case, a child dies, the charge is failure to provide a breath sample, and the sentence served is ten months. In the *Vollrath* case, a thumb is lost, the charges are of kidnapping, impersonation, and assault, and the sentence is twelve years. Both cases are tied together through the death of a child, but much shifts depending on how one understands that death (as accident or because of impairment), as well as how one understands what it means to pay for one's crimes. The case points us in the direction of another problem, which is the problem of who dispenses justice, and what it means to think about vigilantism and the rule of law.

To sum up, in this official story of the state response to vigilantism, we have the space to identify the various moments of vigilantism that emerge. First, there is the spontaneous sort as bystanders intervene and assault Suter at the scene of the accident. There were no charges arising against any of the bystanders involved the rough handling of Suter at the scene of the accident. Second, when one follows social media around the case, one can trace a significant body of calls for vigilante justice. These, one might note, were framed in inflammatory terms, targeting Suter, his wife, and indeed the judge involved in the case. Third, there was the movement of these energies from the spoken to the physical, in the form of threatening notes, the attack on Mrs. Suter in a mall parking lot, the violence against Mr. Suter. Though the courts identify the *Suter* and *Vollrath* cases as being unique, they make visible some of the ways that vigilante energies, and the language of vigilantism emerged in the context of the operation of the conventional justice within the Canadian state system as well as in the spaces of silence.

STORY 2: VIGILANTISM, CIVIL DISOBEDIENCE OR COUNTER PROTEST: THE WET'SUWET'EN PROTESTS

As noted earlier, through the 150 years of Canada's existence, Indigenous peoples have continued to challenge Canadian assertions of exclusive sovereignty over the land, and over Indigenous peoples. These challenges have engaged with legislatures, courts, and the public imagination. In the legal realm, working within the framework of Canadian law, Indigenous peoples have shifted the colonial terrain, such that even the courts have acknowledged the continuing existence of Indigenous title to land. By 1997, in *Delgamuukw*, the Supreme Court recognized Aboriginal Title; the territory of the Wet'suwet'en people (in northern British Columbia) had never been ceded and was still governed by the Wet'suwet'en.[26] The courts understood that Canada had yet to negotiate with the Wet'suwet'en to develop a framework under which their governance of the territory would be acknowledged. But this direction to negotiate languished. In the meantime, business as usual in a country running its economy largely through extractive industries, meant that pipeline developments continued.[27]

In 2010, public protest in Western Canada was mobilized around three proposed pipelines, each of which would cut across Northern BC, to transport liquefied natural gas and diluted bitumen to the coastal town of Kitimat for tanker transport to Asian markets.[28] One these was the LNG (liquefied natural gas) pipeline proposed by Coastal GasLink. The pipeline would pass through twenty First Nations territories along its way. Both the province and the company had signed benefit sharing agreements with the elected councils of all twenty First Nations bands along the route, despite the legality that each band's jurisdiction is limited to within its reserve boundaries. The pipeline would not pass through any Wet'suwet'en reserves.

But the Unist'ot'en,[29] a group within one of the thirteen Houses of the Wet'suwet'en nation, challenged the authority of these band councils (constituted under the provisions of the *Indian Act*) to make decisions about Unist'ot'en territory. Such decisions, they said, did not lie in the hands of the band chiefs, but required the involvement of the hereditary chiefs, and needed to be made in accordance with Wet'suwet'en governance systems.[30] As noted above, the Supreme Court had recognized the existence of Aboriginal title in the *Delgamuukw* case, affirming that the Wet'suwet'en continued to exercise governance on their lands. In this case, some identified a kind of divide and conquer approach by both government and industry, in terms of which governance bodies were or were not consulted.

A number of the Wet'suwet'en hereditary chiefs opposed work on their territories, while many of the elected chiefs and band councils supported the project. Over the next eight years, groups within the Unist'ot'en began building camps in the location of the proposed pipeline, reestablishing traditional trap lines, and occupying the territory with their physical presence (and the support of allies [both Indigenous and non-Indigenous] who joined in the work). This included the establishment of blockades and checkpoints along roads which led into the territory.

In late 2018, Coastal GasLink went to court to seek an injunction targeting theses blockades, claiming that these interfered with their (contractual) right to build the pipeline. In the court documents submitted, the Unist'ot'en responded that their actions were fully in accordance with Wet'suwet'en law and the Wet'suwet'en legal process. The actions of Coastal GasLink, they asserted, were not.[31] In January 2020 the court granted the injunction to Coastal GasLink, an injunction which authorized the RCMP to conduct a raid on a second camp set up by the Gidimt'en (another of the clans of the Wet'suwet'en Nation), a raid which resulted in the violent arrest of fourteen people. This raid captured attention both in Canada and internationally. It also generated a further amplification of the legal dispute, with the Gidimt'en suing Coastal GasLink for damages.

How was one to describe the conflict between Coastal GasLink and the Wet'suwet'en? At the heart of these debates were conflicts over law itself. This means that it becomes difficult to identify who is the vigilante in this story. On Wet'suwet'en territory, who has the authority to make decisions about whether or not a pipeline will proceed? Is this a question for contract law within the common law? Is this a matter of private economic decision-making? Are those at the barricades simply vigilantes taking the law into their own hands? Are they protesting against a law they deem unjust (civil disobedience), or are they following their own law? How are outsiders, in this context, to understand the actions of Coastal GasLink in going to the courts? And further, how are we to understand the action of the courts in authorizing the RCMP to intervene? One could argue that this a situation where neither the courts nor the RCMP have authority. In effect, in this account, they are acting in unceded territory, where they do not have authority, and have become, in effect, a vigilante mob enforcing a form of colonial vigilante law.[32]

In the wake of the RCMP invasion of the camp, protests sprung up across Canada as other First Nations and allies created protests and blockades in solidarity; from west coast to east coast, protestors created significant disruption to important trade corridors with demonstrations and blockades at key rail and port locations across Canada.[33] One of the most visible demonstrations was set up on the steps of the BC legislature. This protest, begun by "Indigenous Youth for Wet'suwet'en" had groups of young people camped on the ceremonial stairs of the legislature.[34] They were joined by university students (who walked out from classes in support), and others, expressing their demand that the BC government acknowledge Indigenous law and Indigenous jurisdiction, that they acknowledge the legal authority of the Wet'suwet'en hereditary leaders.[35] They set up camp, and maintained a twenty-four-hour vigil for more than eleven days. In the fraught politics of the moment, the government for the most part did not intervene to take action against the youth. The protesters also worked hard to maintain peaceful protest (to minimize the risk of violence). Many people trained as observers to ensure the safety of those protesting, and lawyers prepared to work with those willing to be arrested. One could see, in some ways, a kind of "pause" or "breath" in this space of encounter.

This détente was broken finally when students were invited inside the building to speak to Scott Fraser, the Minister of Indigenous Relations; when they were unwilling to leave after ninety minutes, the government used trespass law to justify arresting the students. The government presented themselves as firmly on the side of law. Alan Mullen, chief of staff to the Speaker of the Legislative Assembly said, "It was an incredible show of good faith on behalf of Minister Scott Fraser to invite these folks in to sit down to talk, and you know it was very disheartening to see how that turned out."[36] Mullen also claimed that the government had been very lenient with the youth, despite policies prohibiting overnight camping and open flame in the legislature precinct. Refusing to leave when asked to was, in his words, crossing the line: "We will never allow the rule of law to be disrespected or broken."[37]

As lawyer Richard Overstall later pointed out, there was a certain historical irony and amnesia here. A century earlier, the settler community had disrespected and broke their own laws to dispossess Wet'suwet'en families from their homes and farms in the Bulkley Valley. It was a time when the Grand Trunk Pacific Railway (now the Canadian National Railway) was about to be built and real estate speculators were grabbing the newly surveyed agricultural land in anticipation of an influx of European settlers. At that time, Governor Douglas' *Proclamation No. 15* and its successor provincial legislation forbade the preemption of lands on which there were "Indian" houses and other buildings. In response, the speculators and their agents burnt the homes while the families were away trapping or fishing and staked out the land. When the families returned, they were told they were trespassing and were evicted by the speculators aided by the priest, the police, and the Indian Agent. One of the most active speculators was Francis Mawson Rattenbury, the architect of the Legislative Building that the Speaker's staff was attempting to defend against the youthful Wet'suwet'en supporters in early 2020.[38]

In any event, the students, for their part, continued to remind the public that the legislature itself stood on unceded lands.[39] They too were acting to affirm the rule of law. And their protest, in spite of the later arrests, seemed to achieve some of its aims. One result of the highly public protest (including the arrests) was the decision of both provincial and federal ministers to finally meet with the Wet'suwet'en to discuss the recognition by the Canadian governments of the authority of the Wet'suwet'en. One is then left to ask a question about how to best describe both the actions of the Wet'suwet'en, and of the students in support. Were the actions best described as protest or civil disobedience? Is it best described as a form of vigilante action, denying the jurisdiction of the BC government? In refusing to leave the legislature, were the students defying law, or affirming law?

There is much at stake in how we describe the problem. One aspect of Wet'suwet'en protest is precisely over this question. Who needs to be involved in a decision about the pipeline? The Canadian law identifies elected bands as the decision makers. Wet'suwet'en law has its own rules of procedure for approaching these questions. The question for an outsider is perhaps less, which one is correct, but is rather, what are the resources within Wet'suwet'en law to address these differences? But what I want to make visible here is the productive slippage in the words we use to describe the conflict in this situation. At stake are questions both about authority and questions about justice. Who is defending law and who is acting outside of law? Within conventional vigilante discourses there are always questions about both the substance of law and its enforcement. Whether one understands the vigilante as criminal or as hero depends on how one understands the legal problem one faces. Is the law in need of reform or should it be resisted altogether?[40]

The challenge here is that this is not simply a matter of two perspectives on the current state of Canadian law. At stake is another view which foregrounds Indigenous legal orders and which would place the state clearly on the side of unlawful vigilante action. This latter viewpoint is particularly unappealing to many as it would require a fundamental unthinking of the underlying premise that Canada is a nation built on law and order and the rule of law. In short, if one stops to interrogate the language we use around vigilantism, revenge, civil disobedience, and the rule of law, a space opens up to think about our commitments to the rule of law and the very real challenges of the rule ahead, for settler societies as they take up the challenges of working around multiple legal orders in ways that respect the impulses toward justice of those embedded in both societies. What forms of imagination might be necessary to help us construct different pathways through the impasse that seems to be before us, as we think about the rule of law in a context where legality and justice are still ongoing projects. The contemporary language of vigilantism can only address a small sliver of this problem.[41]

In the third intervention, I turn to popular culture, to show how these two questions (about both "whose law" and about "justice for the dead" weave themselves together). How do the currents we have seen above swirl around in the realm of the imaginary, where we can put our finger on the pulse of not just "authority," but also the ways that the questions around vigilante justice might open space for thinking toward the future?

STORY 3: *RHYMES FOR YOUNG GHOULS*

I want to turn finally to *Rhymes for Young Ghouls* (2013).[42] This picture is a powerful contemporary contribution to the revenge genre, written and directed by Mi'kmaq filmmaker Jeff Barnaby. The Press Kit package gives this synopsis:

> Red Crow Mi'gMaq reservation, 1976: By government decree, every Indian child under the age of 16 must attend residential school. In the kingdom of the crow, that means imprisonment at St. Dymphna's. That means being at the mercy of "Popper," the sadistic Indian agent who runs the school. At 15, Aila is the weed princess of Red Crow. Hustling with her uncle Burner, she sells enough dope to pay her "truancy tax," keeping her out of St. Ds. But when Aila's drug money is stolen and her father Joseph returns from prison, the precarious balance of Aila's world is destroyed. Her only options are to run or fight . . . and Mi'gMaq don't run.[43]

The DVD cover clearly announces the film's place within the revenge genre: "Growing up Means Getting Even." But the question is, what does "getting even" look like in the context of the colonial legal order?[44] The film is very explicit in situating all that follows against a backdrop of law. Indeed, we are drenched with legal orders: the law of the colonial state, the law of the residential school, the law of the reservation. The first of these is the colonial law that constructs a system of Indian reservations and Indian residential schools.[45] The open shot of the film lays the text of this law on the screen before us:

> The law in the Kingdom decreed that every child between the age of 5 and 16 who is physically able must attend residential school.
>
> Her Majesty's attendants, to be called truant officers, will take into custody a child whom they believe to be absent from school using as much force as the circumstance requires.
>
> A person caring for an Indian child who fails to cause such a child to attend school shall immediately be imprisoned, and such person arrested without warrant and said child conveyed to school by the truant officer.
>
> *Indian Act*, by will of her Majesty the Queen in Right of Canada

The film thus opens with a stark summary of the *Indian Act*.[46] We are invited to imagine ourselves in a space where we are governed by such law, a law authorizing the removal of children from their families, and the use of force against parents who resist. It invites us to imagine living under one hundred years of such a legal order, one that ruptures connections between parents and children, one that places children into the hands of strangers.

It also invites us to imagine living under a second set of rules: those constructed by the truant officers into whose care an Indian child will be placed. Twenty minutes into the film, we listen to Popper (the truant officer/Indian agent) articulate a second set of rules: those that govern the Indian children who come within the walls of the residential school.[47] The children are told:

> For you new boys, the rules are simple: You get caught out of your beds, you catch a beating, you mend in isolation; you get caught talking to each other you get beat; you get caught coughing, crying, sneezing, pissing, breathing too fucking loud, you get beat and put in isolation. Now, habitually fuck with these rules, and you'll wind up on the hill [*in the graveyard*]. And from here on in, it's the Queen's fucking English. Relish it.

These rules are delivered to us not through a textual overlay, but through the voice of the person claiming and exercising law making authority. The rules are clear, and it is equally clear to whom these rules apply, and that there are mechanisms for implementation. Also clear is the invitation for the viewer to feel the affective gut punch of the violence and injustice of such rules.

There is yet a third set of rules, this time spoken in the voice of Aila, through whose eyes we will experience all that follows. These are the laws that govern life on the reservation in the shadow of the first two layers of colonial law: these are the rules of survival for living in what she names "the Kingdom of the Crow."

> Rule #1: Never befriend an Indian Agent—it'll get your ass kicked, or killed, by other Indians. Rule #2: Stay out of debt to Indian Agents—they don't speak Indian, they only speak money, and not paying will only get you beat up. Rule #3: Take care of your family. Rule #4: Don't act like a badass if you can't fight—ain't nobody above an ass-kicking. Rule #5: Don't show weakness, or let your emotional barrier down.

These rules come to us not "at once," but are shared with us one by one, scattered through voiceover throughout the film, as Aila conveys to us her mastery of these rules of "Customary Law," built up through lived experience. Each rule is shared as we are placed in contexts which allow us to see these rules in application (largely through moments when the reason for the rule becomes evident, or where we see what follows from a violation of the rule).

We are situated as viewers to see these three competing sites of law: lawfulness, authority, and conflict. We are invited to see and to judge these legal orders, and to see the impasses and violence they create in their wakes. In this space of fiction, the film invites us to share a world where generations of residential school experience have produced a legacy of trauma, alcoholism, drug abuse, and violence. It is a world of violence from both from within and without. And so the question of vigilantism, of "getting even," occurs against this backdrop. It is in this context that we are invited to identify a number of crimes/harms that may require redress.

The first of these happens in the opening moments of the film. Immediately following our introduction to the formal *Indian Act* laws that structure life for those in the Kingdom of the Crow, we have a flashback to 1969, where Aila's parents Joe and Anna (Glen Gould and Roseanne Supernault) work late into the night in a kitchen full of empty beer bottles, smoking pot while they bag and tag product from the local grow-op for the resale market. An eight-year-old Aila sits outside on the hood of the car, drawing pictures of warriors and protectors for her five-year-old friend Tyler (Louis Beauvais), also up and unattended late at night. At the end of the evening, Uncle Burner and Anna load a drunken Joe into the backseat of the car. When Anna backs out of the driveway, she accidentally runs over and kills Tyler. In her grief, Anna hangs herself. Joe then turns himself into the police, claiming that he is the one that killed Tyler. Aila is left in the care of her uncle Burner.

And so, as with the *Suter* and *Vollrath* cases, the story is put in motion through the death of a child. And from the outset, even before we encounter the vicious Indian Agent, we see what it is to be living in the ruins of a world structured through a policy of genocide. For it is the law which takes them all to the residential school, and which returns them, if at all (that is, if they do not end up in the graveyard "on the hill"), as broken bodies, to continue forward in a kind of half-life. We see that the laws of the Kingdom have produced a set of characters who are carrying the wounds of this world, are deeply flawed, and embedded in structures of repetitive and recurrent violence. They are skilled in what Aila refers to as the "arts of forgetfulness," drawing heavily on a world of drugs and alcohol to survive their experience of colonial legality. But this forgetfulness also plays a part in Tyler's death, Anna's death, Joe's incarceration, and Aila's place within the drug economy. It is also her skills in that economy that enable her to earn the money she needs to remain outside the rules that govern the inside of the residential school.

All this is context for the film's exploration of "getting even." The film's action ostensibly circles around Popper's theft of Aila's drug money (the "tax" she must pay him), and the efforts of Aila and her young friends to steal that money back. And in response to the question of whether such a restoration is "enough," they also fill the school water tank with sewage so that when he takes his nightly shower, Popper is shown (literally) as the shit he is. As expected, such interventions only amplify the cycle of violence. In the end, it is Aila's young friend Jujijj (one of the youngest children at the school) who shoots Popper, saving Aila from a brutal beating and rape. In some ways, such an ending fits within the revenge film genre: Popper dies, and Aila gets even. But the fit is not easy, because the questions are not easy, and the film presses us to see deeper.

There are two techniques in the film that support this deepening. One is the use of animation which pushes us actively into the world of the imagination. The second is a kind of visual afterlife that draws characters who are dead into the film as interlocutors. It is this moving between the space of the dead and the space of the imaginary that stalls the rush of forward movement that might lead us too quickly to conclusions about the vigilante, whether as criminal or hero. This particular film asks us to pause, particularly at this moment of supposed reconciliation to think through the deeper lessons that the discourse of vigilantism might hide.

Certainly, the violence in this film does not quite manage to be regenerative. The violence of the film carries an element of truthfulness that in many ways leaves the story feeling a bit "too close" to provide some of the pleasures that one could expect of the vengeance genre.[48] But what is useful for our purposes is to consider the ways the film both delivers and refuses to deliver on the fantasy of vigilante justice. It does this in part by saturating us in multiple and overlapping layers of law, lawlessness, death, and grief. In the context of the collision of legal orders, and the multitude of zombie lives, it seems clear that the death of Popper can only touch the surface of that which demands justice.

The pathway to simple judgment is blocked, because the injuries do not only come from the outside. As Aila says of her own father, who returns to the reservation after seven years in jail after confessing to a crime he did not commit, "no one would call him a good man." She notes instead that he is a man who did bad things for good reasons, and good things for bad reasons. This is also true of her uncle and her mother.

These complications are captured in two moments where elders tell stories to Aila. In the first of these, Ceres, the old woman who runs the greenhouse where the drugs are grown, tells Aila the story of "The Wolf and the Mushroom." As she speaks, the story spills out in an animated sequence occurring with a visual apocalyptic field. It is a story in which the Wolf, broken and starving, in a world of destruction, mistakes children for mushrooms, and eats them. When he realizes what he has done, in grief, he continues to eat, starting at his tail, and continuing until he has consumed his own heart.[49] The images that animate the story begin and end on the pages of Aila's book, emerging into our visual field, now with a story to hold them together in narration. We are invited to begin thinking about how to break this cycle of grief, disruption, and injustice.

Rhymes for Young Ghouls asks us to rethink what a commitment to the rule of law means in the context of a history so saturated with violence that it is hard to imagine a pathway forward. The visual field of the film pushes us actively toward a kind of dreamscape, one which refuses any easy answer; it makes visible the horror of the current situation, while blocking avenues which would offer too quick a move toward judgment. That which haunts might productively demand more of our attention. The dead continue to be present in the film, and continue to ask questions about justice. In one dream scene, Aila is in the forest graveyard, and her mother emerges from the ground like a zombie. Anna places something in Aila's hand, and speaks only one word: "Vengeance." We know that Anna took her own life. So it unclear precisely who that vengeance would be directed against. And a zombie version of the young boy Tyler also appears to Aila, as she draws in her book. But from whom does Tyler seek justice? Neither ghostly appearance seems to unsettle Aila. She seems to accept the dead as regular presences in her life. The woods are full of crosses signaling the dead. But if they continue to haunt, they do not terrorize. They come with a reminder of connections to those loved and lost. Lack of release for the many ghosts, we are told, comes from the way that they were buried without names, without truths to enable them to move along. And so we are left wondering what it is the Anna seeks, or Tyler seeks. What is it that they ask from Aila? And would the killing of Popper be enough? As Aila's friends ask here, as they plan to steal back their drug money, is this form of "getting even" enough?

I said above that the film contains two moments of storytelling, moments where the forward action is suspended as an elder tells a story to Aila. The second of these is brief. Joe, drunk and distraught, is on the cusp of breaking the law (by taking his boat out on the water). An elder referred to as the Old Man drives Aila to where Joe is down by the water. As they drive, the Old Man tells Aila that her grandfather had saved the Old Man's life during the War. He tells a story of young men sent to take an impossible beach, hopelessly trudging forward through an increasing mass of bodies piled upon bodies. When she asks what she is to take from the somewhat cryptic story, the Old Man tells her: "Sometimes courage, Aila, means gritting your teeth and moving forward. Not paying attention to the consequences." And move forward she does, standing up for her father, and taking a beating from Popper and his friends which results in both Aila and Joe finding themselves locked up in the space of the residential school. With Joe unable to help, it is the youth who create plans to find a way out. And though they escape from the school with Aila's money, there is nowhere to run, and the violence against them escalates until the final moments of "cleansing violence" that are expected with the revenge genre.

What is interesting about *Rhymes for Young Ghouls* is that it both delivers and refuses to deliver on the fantasy of vengeance. We do have the satisfaction of seeing the Indian Agent come to his deserved end: that is the promised deliverance. Certainly, Popper is constructed as so monstrous a person that his end could not come soon enough. But his end simply does not deliver full satisfaction. A story must still be constructed to explain the trail of bodies and drugs. Joe once again claims to have been responsible for the deaths, and returns to prison. Aila will not be sentenced for her part in these crimes, and is again left in the care of her uncle Burner (whose name captures the way that he too "burns"/betrays those around him). The film has made visible throughout that Popper, the Indian Agent, is just one cog in the colonial system that has legally constructed a regime of genocide and cruelty. Popper's demise does not give us an end to the pattern of residential schools, nor does it give us an end to the damage that the community carries forward with it from the past.

In the final scene of the film, Aila and Jujijj sit alone outside, much like Aila and Tyler did in the opening scenes. The Old Man approaches them. He tells Aila that he will not allow her to continue with the grow-op. She returns his gaze, and says, "Good." He leaves, and again we are left alone with the youth. "Boss," Jujijj says to Aila, "what's next?" The viewer is invited, with Aila, to reflect on that question. Yes, what is next? The film pulls into a close-up, with a tight focus on Aila's eyes. There is the smallest suggestion of a smile, and then the screen cuts to black.

And so we are left with the big question. Revenge? Vengence? Courage? What is to be next? *Rhymes with Young Ghouls* takes up the question of vigilante justice. It offers us the satisfaction of solving the small problem, while leaving us with the big problem. What would revenge look like, where it is a situation of war? And of law. What laws will be carried forward? What are the arts of forgetfulness and remembering? What is to have the courage to slog through, to stay with the trouble? While the DVD cover tells us "growing up means getting even," the film itself has pinned to its center the story of the Wolf and the Mushroom, to our practices of consuming our own hearts. It invites us to imagine how, in Settler states such as Canada, one might harness this "hunger for justice" and ask instead, "What's next?"

CONCLUSION

What then can be said of vigilante justice in Canada? Story 1, captured in the *Suter* and *Vollrath* cases, makes visible that, in the "official discourses," though there are very few cases in which private justice emerges into the public realm, the power of the demand for blood remains present, particularly in cases involving the death of children. The courts affirm the power of the state's demand that it has the exclusive power to identify, prosecute, and sentence wrongdoers. In some ways, what we see in this case is the ways that the aroma of vigilantism brings out the belief that society is held together through an affirmation of the power of public justice. There is a big difference in how the courts talk about the histories that brought each of these offenders before them. In this story, Indigeneity plays a minor role at best. It is not linked in any meaningful way to the story before the court. What takes center stage is the importance of deterring non-state interventions in the delivery of justice.

Story 2 suggests that there is much to learn about the power of the discourse of vigilantism to take attention off questions about the underlying legitimacy of the rules that are being invoked or challenged. In the Wet'suwet'en case, we have protestors on both sides, intervening in support of one understanding of Wet'suwet'en law, or intervening to protest one understanding of Canadian law. One question is, within the Wet'suwet'en legal authority, what are the processes for making decisions about pipelines? What are the processes of disagreement or dissent within Wet'suwet'en law? How do we know the difference between "protest" and "refusal"? On the Canadian side we have the same question. What is the difference between vigilantism and civil disobedience? How do we think about the actions of corporations in deciding which legal orders to work within or against? Is the question one of primacy? Which order trumps the other? And how can these questions help us understand action as either lawful or unlawful?

Story 3 invites us to step back from the battle, or the contest between legal orders. We are invited to accept the entanglement of the situation in which we find ourselves. The Canadian context, as represented in *Rhymes for Young Ghouls*, is indeed one in which the bloodiness of a colonial history is increasingly visibilised. The languages and practices of vigilantism, as explored in the film, exert a powerful pull, but blind us to the ways that this hunger can lead us to consume our own hearts. The movie is an invitation to Canadian audiences (and others) to "stay with the trouble," to keep open a space for dreaming, and to consider how attention to vigilante energies might open space to consider the kinds of courage that it will take to collectively begin to ask not "who is guilty," but "what is next?"

ACKNOWLEDGMENTS

I am grateful to have access to a community of generous and thoughtful colleagues, friends, and family. I am grateful to those who have helped me think through the ways our hungers for justice require some rethinking. In particular, I am grateful for the interventions of Jess Asch, Ruth Buchanan, Gillian Calder, Deb Curran, Irina Ceric, Arta Johnson, Bonnie Johnson, Mary Johnson, Ria Meronek, Val Napoleon, Richard Overstall, Kate Plyley, and Mark Zion. Jeevan Ahuja provided valuable research assistance in the strange COVID-19 times we occupy, and Dino Bottos (lawyer for Richard Suter) was generous in his willingness to both talk about the case, and to share materials. I am also grateful to the editors of this volume for the opportunity to articulate a set of connections that had been, to that point, still rather inchoate.

NOTES

1. The foundational resources here are the multivolume *Report of the Royal Commission on Aboriginal Peoples* (Canada, 1996) and the *Report of the Truth and Reconciliation Commission on Canada's Residential Schools* (Canada, 2015). For a telling of the history of Canada in graphic novel form from multiple Indigenous perspectives, see Kateri Akiwenzie-Damm et al., *This Place: 150 Years Retold* (Winnipeg: Highwater Press, 2019).

2. See for example the Truth and Reconciliation Commission's Calls to Action#28 directed to Law Schools, and #27 directed to Law Societies. http://www.trc.ca/assets/pdf/Calls_to_Action_English2.pdf. Task forces across the country have been set up to do this work, new research centres for Indigenous law have taken root, and there is a new joint law degree program in Canadian Common Law and Indigenous Legal Orders at the University of Victoria. https://www.uvic.ca/law/about/indigenous/jid/index.php.

3. For a detailed discussion of this challenge, see Kathryn Plyley, "Tolerated Illegality and Intolerable Legality: From Legal Philosophy to Critique" (PhD in law, University of Victoria, 2018).

4. Val Napoleon, "Thinking About Indigenous Legal Orders," in *Dialogues on Human Rights and Legal Pluralism*, ed. René Provost and Colleen Sheppard, Ius Gentium, v. 17 (Dordrecht; New York: Springer, 2013), 249–45.

5. For a helpful graphic to provide an introduction for thinking about the broad categories through which Indigenous laws find expression, see "Indigenous Law 101," available from the Indigenous Law Research Unit at the University of Victoria, accessible at: http://ilru.ca/wp-content/uploads/2020/08/Indigenous-Law-101-With-Resources.pdf.

6. For a discussion of the differences between spontaneous and planned vigilantism, see J. Paul Grayson, "Vigilantism in Canada and the United States," *Legal Stud. F.* 16 (1992): 21.

7. The lawyer gave evidence of this at the trial, and was disciplined by the Law Society for his negligent advice. This was one of the other central issues before the Supreme Court in Suter's case.

8. Slav Kornik, "Man Accused of Killing Toddler Appears in Court; Mother Demands Justice | Globalnews.Ca," Global News, May 21, 2013, https://globalnews.ca/news/578370/mother-of-boy-killed-in-patio-crash-calls-for-justice/.

9. Patricia Kozicka, "Grieving Mother behind 'Justice for Geo' Speaks to Global News—Edmonton | Globalnews.Ca," Global News, February 7, 2013, https://globalnews.ca/news/688631/grieving-mother-behind-justice-for-geo-speaks-to-global-news/.

10. This included a children's party, and a fundraising event held by Monster Pro Wrestling. See Kozicka.

11. Several pages of examples were gathered by Dino Bottos, the lawyer for the Suters, and put before the Sentencing judge. See *Her Majesty the Queen v. Richard Alan Suter—Proceedings*, Provincial Court of Alberta, June 5, 2015; October 19, 2015 to October 23, 2015; December 17, 2015 Sess. 431, particularly at pp. 59–61. I am grateful for the assistance of Jeevan Ahuja in gathering together comments from across a number of social media platforms. A memo detailing these sources is on file with the author.

12. No one was apprehended or charged in the assault. She gave evidence about the event, and her belief that she had been targeted because of social media commentary about her and her husband during the sentencing hearing. See *Her Majesty the Queen v. Richard Alan Suter—Proceedings*, Provincial Court of Alberta, June 5, 2015; October 19, 2015 to October 23, 2015; December 17, 2015 Sess. 431, Testimony of Gayska Suter at 301–2.

13. "Mother Condemns Assault of Driver Accused of Killing Toddler," CBC News, January 24, 2015, https://www.cbc.ca/news/canada/edmonton/geo-mounsef-s-mother-condemns-assault-of-accused-drunk-driver-richard-suter-1.2930734.

14. See pp. 59–61 in *Suter—Proceedings*, above.

15. *R v. Suter* [2018] 2 SCR 496, 503.

16. loc. cit. at 522.

17. Marie Henein, "Opinion: Breaking the Law: How the State Weaponizes an Unjust Criminal Justice System," *The Globe and Mail*, June 13, 2020, https://www.theglobeandmail.com/opinion/article-the-state-is-kneeling-on-the-job/.

18. The data on over-incarceration in federal prisons can be found on the website of the office of Canada's Correctional Investigator: https://www.oci-bec.gc.ca/cnt/priorities-priorites/aboriginals-autochtones-eng.aspx The provincial data shows even higher patterns of Indigenous over-representation.

19. Section 718(2)(e) of the *Criminal Code of Canada* says, "all available sanctions, other than imprisonment, that are reasonable in the circumstances and consistent with the harm done to victims or to the community should be considered for all offenders, with particular attention to the circumstances of Aboriginal offenders."

Following the interpretation of this section by the Supreme Court of Canada in *R v. Gladue* [1999] 1 SCR 688, judges are required to take into account the unique cultural conditions that have led to the well-documented over-incarceration of Indigenous Inuit and Metis people in Canada. This has meant the preparation of "Gladue reports": narrative texts the aim at providing a judge with a better picture of the specific conditions and life experiences that have brought the offender before the court. There is a significant literature about the impact of these reforms, most of it noting that non-Indigenous offenders have benefited from sentencing reforms and the over-incarceration of Indigenous offenders has only increased. For a discussion of the most recent data, see Marie-Eve Sylvestre and Marie-Andrée Denis-Boileau, "Les rapports Gladue, une expérience concluante?," *Relations*, no. 801 (2019): 24–25.

20. *R v. Vollrath*, 2016 ABPC 258 (at para 144).

21. loc. cit. (at para 140).

22. loc. cit. (at para 152).

23. *R v. Vollrath*, 2018 ABCA 351 (at para 19).

24. loc. cit. (at para 17), citing the Supreme Court in *R v. Suter* 2018 SCC 34 at para 58.

25. loc. cit., paras 27–46.

26. *Delgamuukw v. British Columbia* [1997] 3 SCR 1010. See also *Tsilhqot'in Nation v. British Columbia* [2014] 2 SCR 256.

27. For an exploration of the contrast and contest between colonial and indigenous infrastructure, as well as a helpful introduction to the pipeline conflicts in Northern BC, see Anne Spice, "Fighting Invasive Infrastructures: Indigenous Relations against Pipelines," *Environment and Society* 9, no. 1 (2018): 40–56.

28. The Enbridge Northern gateway tar sands oil pipeline was cancelled in 2016. Debates continue about the expansion of the Trans Mountain Pipeline System. For more on the place of Injunctions and contempt proceedings arising from public protest, see Irina Ceric, "Beyond Contempt: Injunctions, Land Defense, and the Criminalization of Indigenous Resistance," *South Atlantic Quarterly* 119, no. 2 (2020): 353–69.

29. "Unist'ot'en" means "the far-out people"—those Wet'suwet'en who did not regularly return to Witset to fish for salmon each summer. In this case, the Unist'ot'en are members of the Yikh Tsawilhggis (Dark House) of the C'ilhts'ekhyu (Big Frog Clan).

30. For a primer on the conflict, see Chantelle Bellrichard and Jorge Barrera, "What You Need to Know about the Coastal GasLink Pipeline Conflict," CBC News, February 5, 2020, https://www.cbc.ca/news/indigenous/wet-suwet-en-coastal-gaslink-pipeline-1.5448363. For an extensive reading list and links to articles, books, blogs, and more, see Bruce McIvor, "Wet'suwet'en Reading List," First Peoples Law, June 5, 2020, https://www.firstpeopleslaw.com/public-education/blog/wetsuweten-reading-list.

31. *Coastal Gaslink Pipeline Ltd. V. Huson*, 2018 BCSC 2343, para 28. See Ceric, "Beyond Contempt" for a robust exploration of the legalities involved. As she notes, many drew attention to the disconnect, as the very people who had done the work to establish Aboriginal title in the *Delgamuukw* case, were subject to raids and arrests in their own territory.

32. In the popular cultural realm, this scenario is played out in the HBO TV series *Deadwood*. In that series, we are asked to consider a history where an outsider legal order seeks to establish itself over another legal order. See Rebecca Johnson, "Television, Pleasure and the Empire of Force: Interrogating Law and Affect in Deadwood," in *Law and Justice on the Small Screen*, ed. Peter Robson and Jessica Silbey (Oxford: Hart, 2012), 33–61.

33. Alleen Brown and Amber Bracken, "No Surrender: After Police Defend a Gas Pipeline Over Indigenous Land Rights, Protesters Shut Down Railways Across Canada," *The Intercept* (blog), February 23, 2020, https://theintercept.com/2020/02/23/wetsuweten-protest-coastal-gaslink-pipeline/.

34. Roxanne Egan-Elliott, "Lieutenant-Governor Arrives at Legislature as Protesters Block Entrances," Coast Reporter, November 2, 2020, https://www.coastreporter

.net/local-news/lieutenant-governor-arrives-at-legislature-as-protesters-block-entrances-3116742; Mike Hall and Liza Yudza, "Indigenous Youth Protest at Legislature in Support of Wet'suwet'en Hereditary Chiefs," CityNews Vancouver, February 26, 2020, https://vancouver.citynews.ca/2020/02/26/indigenous-youth-protest-at-legislature-in-support-of-wetsuweten-hereditary-chiefs/. See also "Indigenous Youth Camped at B.C. Legislature Call for RCMP, Pipeline Workers to Leave Wet'suwet'en Territory," CBC News, February 26, 2020, https://www.cbc.ca/news/canada/british-columbia/bc-legislature-victoria-demonstration-wetsuweten-solidarity-1.5476822. The ceremonial entrance is used only for the arrival of the Queen's representative, the Lieutenant-Governor, for event like the opening of the legislature, and the throne speech. In the face of the protest, the LG simply used another entrance, rather than breaking the blockade.

35. William Gaetz, "UVic Students to Sleep at B.C. Legislature alongside Wet'suwet'en Supporters," Vancouver Island, March 4, 2020, https://vancouverisland.ctvnews.ca/uvic-students-to-sleep-at-b-c-legislature-alongside-wet-suwet-en-supporters-1.4839043.

36. Other government officials, however, called the minister's judgment into question, noting that his decision to meet the students inside the building was against the advice of security officials. It also meant that the discussions did not occur in public, and the students' unwillingness to leave after ninety minutes resulted in what the students described as violent arrest, an arrest that couldn't be monitored by all those trained as independent observers who were at the protests. See Harnett, Cindy E. "Protesters Pack up Camp at Legislature; Five Arrested after Refusing to Leave Building." *Times Colonist*, March 5, 2020. https://www.timescolonist.com/news/local/protesters-pack-up-camp-at-legislature-five-arrested-after-refusing-to-leave-building-1.24090931.

37. Cindy E. Harnett, "Protesters Pack Up Camp at Legislature; Five Arrested after Refusing to Leave Building," *Victoria Times Colonist*, May 3, 2020, https://www.timescolonist.com/local-news/protesters-pack-up-camp-at-legislature-five-arrested-after-refusing-to-leave-building-4679578.

38. See Tyler McCreary, *Shared Histories* (Smithers, BC: Creekstone Press, 2018), 18–22, 42. I am grateful to Richard Overstall (lawyer for several of the Wet'suwet'en hereditary chiefs) for his close reading of this paper, and drawing this story to my attention.

39. For a clear articulation of the lack of foundation for a claim of Canadian sovereignty over British Columbia, see Nicholas Xemtoltw Claxton and John Price, "Whose Land Is It? Rethinking Sovereignty in British Columbia," *BC Studies*, no. 204 (2019): 125–48.

40. Kent Roach, "Reforming and Resisting Criminal Law: Criminal Justice and the Tragically Hip," *Manitoba Law Journal* 40, no. 3 (2017): 1–52. He explores this difference using two classic Canadian songs "38 years old" and "Wheat Kings." It is the difference between understanding the vigilante as "hero" or "bully." The point gets at the differences between resistance aimed at reform, and resistance aimed at refusal. In people's protests at the barricades, there is likely to be a healthy measure of variance in people's responses to the law, and identification of what is needed.

41. I acknowledge here that one silence in this chapter relates to the many violences done to Indigenous people by Settler-Canadians making claims of self-defense or justification. The challenge is not only the failure of the state to protect, but is also the colonial imaginary which underpins such act of violence. Though I did not pick up that thread for this discussion, I hope that Canadian readers will feel the echos of Colton Boushie, Tina Fontaine, Cindy Gladue, Chantel Moore, and Joyce Echaquan in this discussion. The power of story to structure who is or is not understood to be occupying the role of the vigilante is explored in Dallas Hunt and Gina Starblanket, *Storying Violence: Unravelling Colonial Narratives in the Stanley Trial* (Winnipeg: ARP Books, 2020). Tasha Hubbard's 2017 film, *Nîpawistamâsowin: We Will Stand Up* is a powerful witness to this form of deep structurally vigilante violence.

42. See the trailer here https://www.youtube.com/watch?v=AhgztjlLye0. Also interesting is an interview with director Jeff Barnaby on "George Stroumboulopoulos Tonight," CBC Television, January 31, 2014. https://www.youtube.com/watch?v=7cT_U8n8Cm4.

43. http://rhymesforyoungghouls.com/RFYG-PRESS-KIT.pdf, Prospector Films Press Kit.

44. In his appearance on "George Stromboulopoulos Tonight," Barnaby speaks about Alanis Obamsawin's important film *Incident at Restigouche* (National Film Board, 1984), a cinematic capture of protests that occurred in Barnaby's own community when he was a four year old, and the echos of which continued in the struggles that continue to Elsipogtog. https://www.youtube.com/watch?v=7cT_U8n8Cm4.

45. *The Indian Act* was first passed in 1876, and continues to this day. It is a piece of legislation that purports to govern nearly all aspects of Indigenous life, from birth, through marriage, and into death (including the question of who or who does not qualify as "an Indian"). While the film does not point to specific language from the act, it accurately captures elements of the law that have been in place. More on the Indian Act can be found here: https://indigenousfoundations.arts.ubc.ca/the_indian_act/.

46. For an introduction to its asserted jurisdiction over Indigenous lives in Canada, see Robert P. C. Joseph, *21 Things You May Not Know about the Indian Act: Helping Canadians Make Reconciliation with Indigenous Peoples a Reality* (Port Coquitlam, BC: Indigenous Relations Press, 2018).

47. This occurs at around minute twenty-two in the film.

48. Chelsea Vowel, "Why Every Canadian Should Watch Rhymes for Young Ghouls," CBC News, July 23, 2014, https://www.cbc.ca/news/indigenous/why-every-canadian-should-watch-rhymes-for-young-ghouls-1.2687357. See also Sean Carleton, "On Violence and Vengeance: Rhymes for Young Ghouls and the Horrific History of Canada's Indian Residential Schools," *Decolonization* (blog), October 24, 2014, https://decolonization.wordpress.com/2014/10/24/on-violence-and-vengeance-rhymes-for-young-ghouls-and-the-horrific-history-of-canadas-indian-residential-schools/; Caitlyn P. Doyle, "Truth Unreconciled: Counter-Dreaming in Jeff Barnaby's Rhymes for Young Ghouls," *Film Criticism* 44, no. 1 (2020); Taylor Sanchez Guzman, "'Moving with the Dead' in Rhymes for Young Ghouls," *Cléo: A Journal of Film and Feminism* 6, no. 2 (December 14, 2018), http://cleojournal.com/2018/12/14/moving-wih-dead-rhymes-young-ghouls/; Chris Knight, "Rhymes for Young Ghouls,

Reviewed: A Powerful Condemnation of Abuse That Also Manages to Entertain—No Small Feat," *National Post*, January 30, 2014, https://nationalpost.com/entertainment/movies/rhymes-for-young-ghouls-reviewed-a-powerful-condemnation-of-abuse-that-also-manages-to-entertain-no-small-feat.

49. A clip containing this scene can be found here: https://www.youtube.com/watch?v=4MZn3MEkd74 [accessed May 11, 2020]. This scene draws here, and extends a number of stories of Windigo, Wetiko, cannibal sicknesses. These stories are elaborated in Louise Erdrich, *The Round House* (New York: Harper Collins, 2017); Hadley Louise Friedland, *The Wetiko Legal Principles: Cree and Anishinabek Responses to Violence and Victimization* (Toronto: University of Toronto Press, 2018); Robin Wall Kimmerer, *Braiding Sweetgrass* (Minneapolis: Milkweed Editions, 2013). Here is the text of the story as told to Aila in the film:

Now I am going to tell you a story about what happened with the wolf and the mushroom. Once upon a time, the weather was rough. The sky was full of smoke and stunk like the smell of sulphur and all the animals had starved and fled. The wolf was all alone. Sick and alone. He leaves and goes to the forest. As he's walking around, he sees a tree. He begins to hallucinate. Mi'gmaq children are hanging from the tree. The wolf, so hungry, blacks out and shakes the tree really hard until the children begin to fall. He sees them as though their heads have become mushroom caps and their bones as stalks. He begins to eat, and eat. Until finally, he's eaten all the children. When he comes back to reality, he looks around at the world. He feels so sorry for what he has done. Not knowing what to do, he continues to eat. As he sits there, he begins to eat his tail, he gets to his stomach, and begins to eat his stomach. He finishes his stomach, then gets to his heart and eats his heart. He has finished his heart completely, and then he has finished eating himself.

BIBLIOGRAPHY

Akiwenzie-Damm, Kateri, Sonny Assu, Brandon Mitchell, Rachel Qitsualik-Tinsley, Sean Qitsualik-Tinsley, David Alexander Robertson, Niigaanwewidam James Sinclair Storm, Jennifer, et al. *This Place: 150 Years Retold.* Winnipeg: Highwater Press, 2019.

Bellrichard, Chantelle, and Jorge Barrera. "What You Need to Know about the Coastal GasLink Pipeline Conflict." CBC News, February 5, 2020. https://www.cbc.ca/news/indigenous/wet-suwet-en-coastal-gaslink-pipeline-1.5448363.

Brown, Alleen, and Amber Bracken. "No Surrender: After Police Defend a Gas Pipeline Over Indigenous Land Rights, Protesters Shut Down Railways Across Canada." *The Intercept* (blog), February 23, 2020. https://theintercept.com/2020/02/23/wetsuweten-protest-coastal-gaslink-pipeline/.

Carleton, Sean. "On Violence and Vengeance: Rhymes for Young Ghouls and the Horrific History of Canada's Indian Residential Schools." *Decolonization* (blog), October 24, 2014. https://decolonization.wordpress.com/2014/10/24/on-violence-and-vengeance-rhymes-for-young-ghouls-and-the-horrific-history-of-canadas-indian-residential-schools/.

Ceric, Irina. "Beyond Contempt: Injunctions, Land Defense, and the Criminalization of Indigenous Resistance." *South Atlantic Quarterly* 119, no. 2 (2020): 353–69.

Claxton, Nicholas Xemtoltw, and John Price. "Whose Land Is It? Rethinking Sovereignty in British Columbia." *BC Studies*, no. 204 (2019): 125–48.

Doyle, Caitlyn P. "Truth Unreconciled: Counter-Dreaming in Jeff Barnaby's Rhymes for Young Ghouls." *Film Criticism* 44, no. 1 (2020).

Egan-Elliott, Roxanne. "Lieutenant-Governor Arrives at Legislature as Protesters Block Entrances." Coast Reporter, November 2, 2020. https://www.coastreporter.net/local-news/lieutenant-governor-arrives-at-legislature-as-protesters-block-entrances-3116742.

Erdrich, Louise. *The Round House*. New York: Harper Collins, 2017.

Friedland, Hadley Louise. *The Wetiko Legal Principles: Cree and Anishinabek Responses to Violence and Victimization*. Toronto: University of Toronto Press, 2018.

Gaetz, William. "UVic Students to Sleep at B.C. Legislature alongside Wet'suwet'en Supporters." Vancouver Island, March 4, 2020. https://vancouverisland.ctvnews.ca/uvic-students-to-sleep-at-b-c-legislature-alongside-wet-suwet-en-supporters-1.4839043.

Grayson, J. Paul. "Vigilantism in Canada and the United States." *Legal Stud. F.* 16 (1992): 21.

Guzman, Taylor Sanchez. "'Moving with the Dead' in Rhymes for Young Ghouls." *Cléo: A Journal of Film and Feminism* 6, no. 2 (December 14, 2018). http://cleojournal.com/2018/12/14/moving-wih-dead-rhymes-young-ghouls/.

Hall, Mike, and Liza Yudza. "Indigenous Youth Protest at Legislature in Support of Wet'suwet'en Hereditary Chiefs." CityNews Vancouver, February 26, 2020. https://vancouver.citynews.ca/2020/02/26/indigenous-youth-protest-at-legislature-in-support-of-wetsuweten-hereditary-chiefs/.

Harnett, Cindy E. "Protesters Pack up Camp at Legislature; Five Arrested after Refusing to Leave Building." *Victoria Times Colonist*, May 3, 2020. https://www.timescolonist.com/local-news/protesters-pack-up-camp-at-legislature-five-arrested-after-refusing-to-leave-building-4679578.

Henein, Marie. "Opinion: Breaking the Law: How the State Weaponizes an Unjust Criminal Justice System." *The Globe and Mail*, June 13, 2020. https://www.theglobeandmail.com/opinion/article-the-state-is-kneeling-on-the-job/.

Hunt, Dallas, and Gina Starblanket. *Storying Violence: Unravelling Colonial Narratives in the Stanley Trial*. Winnipeg: ARP Books, 2020.

CBC News. "Indigenous Youth Camped at B.C. Legislature Call for RCMP, Pipeline Workers to Leave Wet'suwet'en Territory," February 26, 2020. https://www.cbc.ca/news/canada/british-columbia/bc-legislature-victoria-demonstration-wetsuweten-solidarity-1.5476822.

Johnson, Rebecca. "Television, Pleasure and the Empire of Force: Interrogating Law and Affect in Deadwood." In *Law and Justice on the Small Screen*, edited by Peter Robson and Jessica Silbey, 33–61. Oxford: Hart, 2012.

Joseph, Robert P. C. *21 Things You May Not Know about the Indian Act: Helping Canadians Make Reconciliation with Indigenous Peoples a Reality*. Port Coquitlam, BC: Indigenous Relations Press, 2018.

Kimmerer, Robin Wall. *Braiding Sweetgrass*. Minneapolis: Milkweed Editions, 2013.

Knight, Chris. "Rhymes for Young Ghouls, Reviewed: A Powerful Condemnation of Abuse That Also Manages to Entertain—No Small Feat." *National Post*, January 30, 2014. https://nationalpost.com/entertainment/movies/rhymes-for-young-ghouls-reviewed-a-powerful-condemnation-of-abuse-that-also-manages-to-entertain-no-small-feat.

Kornik, Slav. "Man Accused of Killing Toddler Appears in Court; Mother Demands Justice | Globalnews.Ca." Global News, May 21, 2013. https://globalnews.ca/news/578370/mother-of-boy-killed-in-patio-crash-calls-for-justice/.

Kozicka, Patricia. "Grieving Mother behind 'Justice for Geo' Speaks to Global News—Edmonton | Globalnews.Ca." Global News, February 7, 2013. https://globalnews.ca/news/688631/grieving-mother-behind-justice-for-geo-speaks-to-global-news/.

McCreary, Tyler. *Shared Histories*. Smithers, BC: Creekstone Press, 2018.

McIvor, Bruce. "Wet'suwet'en Reading List." First Peoples Law, June 5, 2020. https://www.firstpeopleslaw.com/public-education/blog/wetsuweten-reading-list.

CBC News. "Mother Condemns Assault of Driver Accused of Killing Toddler," January 24, 2015. https://www.cbc.ca/news/canada/edmonton/geo-mounsef-s-mother-condemns-assault-of-accused-drunk-driver-richard-suter-1.2930734.

Napoleon, Val. "Thinking About Indigenous Legal Orders." In *Dialogues on Human Rights and Legal Pluralism*, edited by René Provost and Colleen Sheppard, 249–45. Ius Gentium, v. 17. Dordrecht; New York: Springer, 2013.

Plyley, Kathryn. "Tolerated Illegality and Intolerable Legality: From Legal Philosophy to Critique." PhD in Law, University of Victoria, 2018.

Roach, Kent. "Reforming and Resisting Criminal Law: Criminal Justice and the Tragically Hip." *Manitoba Law Journal* 40, no. 3 (2017): 1–52.

Spice, Anne. "Fighting Invasive Infrastructures: Indigenous Relations against Pipelines." *Environment and Society* 9, no. 1 (2018): 40–56.

Sylvestre, Marie-Eve, and Marie-Andrée Denis-Boileau. "Les rapports Gladue, une expérience concluante?" *Relations*, no. 801 (2019): 24–25.

Vowel, Chelsea. "Why Every Canadian Should Watch Rhymes for Young Ghouls." CBC News, July 23, 2014. https://www.cbc.ca/news/indigenous/why-every-canadian-should-watch-rhymes-for-young-ghouls-1.2687357.

PART II
European Experiences

Chapter 5

Vigilante Justice in Germany

Franziska Stürmer

LEGAL CONTEXT—GENERAL OBSERVATIONS AND CURRENT JURISDICTION

Vigilantism is a generic term which comprises things like "Selbstjustiz" (self-administered justice)—the actions of one individual against another individual, and the collaborative actions of a group of individuals like in "Bürgerwehren" (militia). One common denominator of all forms of vigilantism—which is also crucial for defining it as a phenomenon—is that violence is exercised by private persons, not by the state or a public body.[1] That characteristic makes it strictly illegal in Germany as it violates the state's unconditional monopoly on violence: only the state is allowed to judge, condemn, and punish. Nevertheless, both phenomena (self-administered justice and militia actions) do of course exist. However, there is a big difference between the two in German public opinion and, to some degree, also in terms of jurisdiction. Therefore, it makes sense to treat both phenomena separately during the course of this chapter. But regardless of their differences, all forms of vigilantism in their various appearances need to be distinguished from moral courage,[2] self-defense, and the legal right to resistance.[3]

Self-Administered Justice

"Selbstjustiz" (self-administered justice) means legally unapproved retaliation carried out by an individual immediately affected by (real or felt) injustice. Self-administered justice has to be distinguished both from self-defense and from the right to resistance. For an action to be regarded as self-defense, there has to be an emergency entailing an immediate threat. The conditions for self-defense are strictly laid down in § 32 of the criminal code ("Strafgesetzbuch," StGB) and § 227 of the civil code ("Bürgerliches Gesetzbuch," BGB): "(2) Notwehr ist die Verteidigung, die erforderlich ist, um einen gegenwärtigen rechtswidrigen Angriff von sich oder einem anderen abzuwenden."[4] According to this paragraph, self-defense is any kind of defense which is necessary to fend off or resist an immediate assault on someone's individual rights ("gegenwärtigen rechtswidrigen Angriff"). The person assaulted does not necessarily have to be the one acting in self-defense; it might also be a helpful bystander ("von sich oder einem anderen")—e.g., a husband is allowed to protect his wife who is threatened by force.

The important point of this "legally licensed form of violence" anchored in the "Notwehr-Paragraph" cited above is that any assault has to be still in the process of happening; as soon as the assault is completed and the perpetrator has stopped his unlawful actions, it is no longer a case of self-defense but self-administered justice, and therefore illegal. In practice, however, there is some argument as to whether an attack on the former perpetrator immediately after he stopped his initial assault might still be regarded as self-defense ("extensiver Notwehrexzess," extensive excess of self-defense). The majority view holds that §33 StGB (ensuring that an excess of self-defense due to confusion, fear, or terror will not be punished) is not applicable to this extensive form of excess (only to the intensive form, related to the amount of force or violence used in self-defense). However, some argue that immediately after the end of an assault, the psychological situation of the victim is the same as while under attack and any action taken immediately afterward might therefore still be regarded as self-defense.[5]

This problematic category of a deed being "psychologically comprehensible" is particularly relevant when dealing with homicides. § 211 Abs. 2 StGB defines the conditions for murder: "(2) Mörder ist, wer aus Mordlust, zur Befriedigung des Geschlechtstriebs, aus Habgier oder sonst aus niedrigen Beweggründen, heimtückisch oder grausam oder mit gemeingefährlichen Mitteln oder um eine andere Straftat zu ermöglichen oder zu verdecken, einen Menschen tötet." According to this paragraph, a murderer is a person who kills someone out of lust to kill, sexual appetite, avarice, or other base motives, perfidiously or cruelly or in a way dangerous to public safety or in order to enable or conceal another crime act. The important criterion here is the mention of "other base motives." Regularly or systematically, killing out of revenge as an act of self-administered justice would be regarded as showing such a "base motive" as it not only denies the state's monopoly on violence and puts individual sensitivities above the legal order, but it also hands out a punishment which is ostracized in Germany, and therefore is highly antisocial.[6] "Tötungen aus Rache [. . .] sind prinzipiell höchstverwerflich"[7]—killing out of revenge is, as a matter of principle, highly objectionable (the term "höchstverwerflich" meaning that it should automatically lead to the penalty for murder—a life sentence—without mitigating circumstances). In practice, however, this view is not taken by the Bundesgerichtshof (Germany's highest court). In 2006, there was a leading judgment. The judges decided that killing out of revenge does not automatically make it a murder (rather than manslaughter) because it might be psychologically understandable. If such a homicide was psychologically understandable, the judges argued, it would not have been done out of a base motive ("niederer Beweggrund," §211 Abs. 2 StGB) required for murder,[8] and might therefore be treated as manslaughter, for which the penalty is five to fifteen years.[9] Of course, just like with the question of an extensive excess in self-defense, problems arise just the same as soon as the criterion of psychological understanding is taken into account: for instance, how long after an initial attack would a (deadly) counterattack still be acceptable, and how gruesome would the initial deed have to be to instigate such a desire for revenge?[10] Nevertheless, the High Court's decision, contentious as it may be, is highly relevant because it mirrors judicial practice and conforms with public opinion. This will become clear from the prominent cases of self-administered justice in German history of the law noted below.

Vigilantism and Militias

It is debatable whether the self-defense paragraph also covers the right to resistance found in the German Constitution ("Grundgesetz"; GG): "(4) Gegen jeden, der es unternimmt, diese Ordnung zu beseitigen, haben alle Deutschen das Recht zum Widerstand, wenn andere Abhilfe nicht möglich ist"[11]—according to this paragraph, all Germans have the right to resistance against anybody seeking to abolish the free democratic basic order in Germany, should all other means to stop that fail. The majority view is that the self-defense paragraph of the StGB is equally applicable to enforce the legal order in case of an emergency;[12] other views hold that it is only applicable as far as individual rights are concerned.[13] Self-defense there crosses the boundary into moral actions: in those cases where, strictly speaking, no individual rights are violated, but people are through their attitude or behavior indeed threatening or violating the legal order (acts of rioting, vandalism, illegal propaganda, etc.). This will become relevant in one of the fictional examples of vigilantism discussed below.

Moreover, vigilantes in militias often invoke this legitimate right to resistance enshrined in the German Constitution. In Germany, this is done mostly by right-wing factions who claim that the state is not or no longer able to fully protect the people ("das Volk"; a term which is much more nationalistically tainted than "the people"). However, as Germany does not really have a tradition of vigilantism, militia activity is generally frowned upon by the public and the media, especially so because of the right-wing ideology usually associated with it. Opinions are not as unanimous when it comes to individual actions; here, both public opinion and, as has been outlined above, legal practice do not fully represent the official position but show some sympathy and understanding for perpetrators carrying out acts of self-administered justice.

PROMINENT CASES OF VIGILANTISM AND SELF-ADMINISTERED JUSTICE IN GERMAN HISTORY OF LAW

Self-Administered Justice

In many cases, the public seems to show understanding for vigilantism and self-administered justice: This is reflected in the (social) media and news coverage of the more spectacular vigilante acts; they often display a mixture of (official) contempt for the illegality and fascination with the courage and determination of these violent conflict solutions.[14] One of the most spectacular (and also one of the first) cases of self-administered justice in German legal history is the case of Marianne Bachmeier, who in 1981 shot the alleged rapist and murderer of her seven-year-old daughter in court on the third day of the trial and was after twenty-eight days of trial finally sentenced to six years for manslaughter (released on license after three years). Her story has been made into three films so far[15] and was widely (and controversially) discussed in public at that time. As is always the case with sexual assaults on children, there was a huge wave of sympathy and sometimes even outright approval for Bachmeier's deed; it also led to a new awareness in court both regarding safety issues and the treatment of sexual perpetrators.[16] Moreover, this same sympathy and understanding for Bachmeier's deed shows the disjunction discussed above between the official position regarding revenge murders—and actual judicial practice, as can be seen from Bachmeier's very low sanction and the fact that her deed was not treated as a case of self-administered justice at all.[17]

A less spectacular but more recent case—if only because it did not involve a homicide—is the case of André Bamberski, who sought to finally seek justice for the death of his fourteen-year-old daughter Kalinka. The background history of Bamberski's case is much more complex and involves several complications both in the German and French parts of the previous prosecution of Dieter Krombach, Kalinka's stepfather. Krombach had been convicted of bodily harm with fatal consequences in France in 1995, but Germany then denied extradition. Later, that judgment was repealed due to a procedural error. To exact a final judgment, Bamberski had Krombach kidnapped and carried off to France in 2009. He was deposited close to a court house, badly roughed up, tied and gagged. After his identity had been confirmed, France indeed put him to trial again and finally convicted and sentenced him to fifteen years. Bamberski, in turn, was sentenced to one year on license (in Germany). Bamberski's case has likewise been made into several films; two documentaries and one movie.[18] His case shows the enduring demand for justice and the failures of both the German and the French legal system. Bamberski's story has been covered in the media throughout the years and his attempts to achieve justice have been extensively covered, almost always showing sympathy to Bamberski.[19]

Both examples show the spectacular effect self-administered justice has had with the German public and in the media; it is far from a common occurrence for someone to take the law into their own hands in Germany. However, both the press reactions and the legal response to both vigilantes—their very low penalties—show a huge amount of understanding and sympathy for acts which are officially strictly outlawed. It might just be possible that their penalties were that low exactly because self-administered justice so rarely happens in Germany; were it a more commonplace behavior, or the trust in the legal system lower, maybe penalties would be a lot higher to discourage imitators.

Vigilantism and Militias

André Bamberski did not set out to have Krombach kidnapped at the beginning. Instead, he started with several vigilante actions such as harassing Krombach and his family and handing out flyers denouncing Krombach as a rapist; he also repeatedly made serious complaints about the German legal system.[20] Those actions resemble typical militia behavior. Members of militias often feel that they act in lieu of the state, which is not able or willing to provide the degree of security necessary for their citizens to feel safe (that desired feeling of safety in a modern state includes the need for legal certainty, not only protection from assaults).

Historically, a militia tradition in Germany is close to nonexistent. Before the revolution in 1848 (a failed attempt at founding a republic), "Bürgerwehren" (militia) were quite common in Germany; after hopes for a self-determined Republic were shattered in 1848, however, militias rapidly lost their former relevance and proliferation, and security and law enforcement tasks were increasingly handled by the military with its increased strength. They experienced a short-term revival during the interim period between the First and Second World Wars; most prominently, the SA ("Sturmabteilung"; storm troopers, a paramilitary division of the Nazi Party—the NSDAP) gained ground after its formation 1921 and in 1933, after Hitler's nomination as Reichskanzler (Chancellor), had more than four million members.[21] After the end of the Second World War, however, paramilitary and vigilante groups and organizations were as good as gone in Germany.[22]

This remained so until in 2015/2016, when militia activity saw another wave of revival instigated by fears and prejudices in the wake of the European refugee crisis of 2015. This short-term rise in militias across Germany was provoked by events which took place in Cologne during the celebrations on New Year's Eve 2015. On that night, several women were sexually assaulted by large groups of (mostly) migrant men; the police proved unable to deal with this situation initially and regrettably even tried to hush it up at first to prevent panic reactions and acts of retaliation. Social media thoroughly frustrated those plans, however, and as a spontaneous response, militias did indeed form not only in Cologne, where the assaults had taken place, but also in Austrian cities like Vienna and Graz and on social media.[23] This is central to the image of militia and vigilantism in Germany; vigilante groups and their supporters talked of the need for protection (of "our women," "the people" etc.) from alleged dangers threatening from within (that is, migrants and their supporters).[24] This rhetoric of protection, however, is generally closely associated with right-wing ideology, often bordering on terrorism, especially so since all dangers to "the people" seem to emanate from persons not belonging to this people (i.e., migrants).[25] According to their own declarations, vigilantism of this kind wishes to be seen as "systemstabilisierende[] Selbstjustiz nichtstaatlicher Akteure mit vorgeblich protektiven Motiven"[26]—self-administered justice by non-government actors intended to stabilize the system out of protective motives. This stresses the self-perception of vigilantes acting in lieu of the state; with their allegedly protective, supportive, and complementary actions, they can be said to form the "dark side" of civil society.[27] In the media, those vigilantes are sometimes described as "besorgte Bürger" (concerned citizens)—a term Juli Zeh implies in her novel *Leere Herzen* (*Empty Hearts*, 2017), which can be said to touch on this issue (if not vigilantism as such). It describes the rise of anti-democratic forces in the wake of the European Refugee Crisis since 2015 and the various profiteers of this decline of democracy, law and order toward a reign of those said concerned citizens.[28] One prominent real-life example would be the "Bürgerwehr Freital"—Freital Civil Defense. They existed from 2015 to 2018 and were responsible for several bomb attacks and attempted assassinations from a right-wing background. They started out, however, with a claim to protect public transport after an alleged assault on pupils in one bus line to Freital. On their Facebook page, they claimed: "Widerstand ist Notwehr & Verpflichtung—Deutsche wehrt euch"[29] (resistance [against migrants and refugees] is an act of self-defense and a matter of duty—Germans, defend yourselves!). Not all vigilantes become terrorists, of course; most view their actions as a form of protest and do not do anything more than utter threats to take matters into their own hands in due course. Moreover, the majority only ever act digitally on social media; here, modern vigilantism in Germany finds its most pertinent platform.[30] Here, discontent is expressed and real-life acts of vigilantism and militia activity are discussed (sometimes approvingly, sometimes controversially).[31] These platforms and discussions can eventually cross into internet vigilantism; a phenomenon which was treated artistically in the exhibition "Whistleblower & Vigilanten." This exhibition was shown 2016 in Dortmund and endeavored to draw attention to the ambiguities of the various forms of digital and real-life activism between moral actions and terrorism. Thus, the Norwegian racist terrorist Breivik is also a part of the exhibition, alongside famous whistleblowers like Assange and Snowden. A whole section of this exhibition was devoted to internet vigilantism and the growing phenomenon of denunciations and hate posts on social media.[32] Sebastian Fitzek's crime story *AchtNacht* touches on this issue, too; for further discussion, see below.

Talking about terrorism, there must, for the sake of completeness, of course, be a mention of left-wing terrorism as well. Left-wing terrorism experienced its heyday in Germany in the 1970s, when terror attacks by the RAF ("Rote Armee Fraktion," Red Army Fraction) were in full swing and the whole Republic was in constant fear of further assassinations and bomb attacks. However, there is a difference between the left-wing terrorism of the RAF and current right-wing vigilantism. The RAF always claimed responsibility for their assassinations, often with explicit political statements and explanations, because they wanted to rouse the public from its apathy by their activities. Moreover, there is no left-wing tradition of militia activity, of patrolling the streets or acting as supplementary controlling bodies for the state. Right-wing vigilantes usually do not declare themselves as such or try to explain their assaults on migrants, unpopular politicians and volunteers in refugee centers—allegedly, they only carry out "the will of the people" and generally do not feel any need for further comment.[33] Of course, this cannot and should not provide an excuse for any kind of terrorist activity; however, it serves to highlight the particular danger lying in the alleged "normality" of right-wing vigilantism. Finally, yet another variety would be religiously motivated vigilantism, which rarely but quite spectacularly has occurred in Germany: for instance, in 2014 a self-declared police force calling themselves the "Sharia Police" patrolled the streets in Wuppertal. This vigilante group attracted some media attention throughout Germany. They set out to walk the streets of Wuppertal at night to stop young Muslims entering discos, bars, and brothels.[34] After several legal complications, fines of various levels were finally imposed on the members in 2019.[35] Honor killing sometimes is an issue in this context, too; there are some cinematic responses to this topic, as will be dealt with more extensively below.

Weapons—Numbers, Laws, Opinions

The use of firearms is not very common in Germany; German weapons law is very restrictive and requires anybody who wants to own a weapon legally to fulfill several preconditions. Among others, this person has to be of full age (that is, eighteen years or older), he or she has to show detailed knowledge of the weapons law, prove him-or herself trustworthy and to document the personal need for possession and handling of a weapon.[36] There is a National Firearms Register (established in 2013) documenting and tracking the circulation of legal firearms in Germany. In 2019, there were around 250,000 registered hunters and all in all about 2.3 million owners of legal weapons (that includes hunting and shooting for sport, but also professions with the use and possession of guns involved, like policemen and soldiers).[37] There is a small weapons lobby in Germany, too; the GRA. It propagates "Förderung des Schießsports, der Jagd und des legalen Waffenbesitzes in Deutschland!"[38] (advancement of competitive shooting [as a sport], hunting and legal possession of weapons in Germany). This last claim—advancement of legal possession—is the most hotly debated issue, as it sometimes touches on vigilante ideals of freedom and self-protection. Often, it goes together with concepts of an idealized masculinity and traditional forms of heroism.[39]

FICTIONAL REPRESENTATIONS

Historical

One prime example of such traditional heroism can be found in the oldest and most prominent instance of revenge in German literature: the *Nibelungenlied* (early thirteenth century), a medieval heroic epic poem in two parts dealing with Kriemhild's revenge on her brothers. Brünhild, Queen of Iceland, is tricked into marrying Gunther, King of Burgundy. His ally in treachery is Siegfried, King of Xanten, who marries Gunter's sister Kriemhild after their joint betrayal of Brünhild. To conceal the decisive part Siegfried played in Gunter's courtship of Brünhild, Gunter finally is persuaded to support Siegfried's murder. At the end of the first part of the epic, Kriemhild returns to her brother's court after Siegfried's death. There, she is robbed of the treasure Siegfried had given her as a morning gift.[40] The second part entirely deals with Kriemhild's revenge. She marries Etzel, King of the Huns, and persuades him to invite her brothers. In the course of several calculated provocations and escalations, Kriemhild's brutal revenge finally leads to a huge bloodbath and the death of almost every character (apart from Etzel, who survives the massacre in his court, and Dietrich and Hildebrand, two other well-known heroes of medieval heroic literature). Revenge in this text is not a matter of mere bloodlust; different worldviews collide, both concerning social structures and gender roles.[41] Especially Kriemhild's treatment by her brothers appears unjust, though legally legitimate. Her revenge, however, is explicitly condemned by the characters, and she is beheaded in the end as a punishment. Consequently, the *Nibelungenlied* has continued to inspire writers throughout the centuries; up until today, adaptations, parodies, and popular versions continue to be published every few years.[42]

During the seventeenth century, justice and retribution are not dealt out by humans but are generally limited to divine forces—any other forms of revenge or punishment are usually depicted as unjust. This becomes especially evident in the Martyr plays such as *Catharina von Georgien* (1657) by Andreas Gryphius. In those plays, one morally impeccable character stoically (and devoutly) suffers all threats, assaults, torture, and death imposed on her or him by tyrants and their cronies; in the end, however, justice will be done by God, who inevitably will judge and condemn the tyrants and reward the martyr with eternal bliss in heaven.

With the rise of the bourgeoisie in the course of the eighteenth century, justice and the means to achieve it became an issue for the people, too. No longer were decisions about right and wrong limited to God and the afterlife, but became a matter of worldly relevance as well. For instance, questions of the right and just behavior of aristocrats toward their subjects implicitly underlie famous "bürgerliche Trauerspiele" (bourgeois tragedies) like Gotthold Ephraim Lessing's *Emilia Galotti* (1772)—although more from a moral than a legal standpoint (as the legal standpoint was pretty clear—the aristocrat had all, the citizens close to no rights). The most prominent example of the tightrope walk between a legitimate desire to achieve justice from aristocrats and a crusade of revenge and self-administered justice is Heinrich von Kleist's *Michael Kohlhaas* (1808). Kohlhaas, out to sell two fine horses, is harassed on his way by Squire Wenzel von Tronka with requests for a particular permit which, as it turns out, never existed in the first place. Kohlhaas's horses, which he left as a security, have in the meantime been treated badly and used for heavy work as farm horses, so that they are now worthless for sale. Kohlhaas hereupon demands compensation at the Elector of Saxony's court but is turned down repeatedly. After all attempts at achieving justice by legal means fail, Kohlhaas starts a personal vendetta. He gathers a bunch of outlaws, attacks von Tronka's castle, and murders everybody inside. After several more complications and escalations, Kohlhaas finally is granted a fair trial, in the course of which von Tronka is ordered to pay damages;

Kohlhaas, however, is sentenced to death because of his breach of the public peace. Michael Kohlhaas displays typical vigilante behavior and motivation: his main aim is to achieve justice within the legal and formal boundaries of his state. Only after this legal framework lets him down repeatedly and proves itself to be unable to fulfill its purpose—to deal out justice when needed—only then, does he decide to take matters into his own hands. His vengeance then escalates hugely, of course; murdering a whole castle full of people and marauding through the land is way out of proportion to a loss in value of two horses. However, at this point Kohlhaas's desire for justice turns into personal aggression and thirst for revenge.[43] Those two motivations for self-administered justice are often closely intertwined; so much so that in most cases it is impossible to say which of the two dominates. Rarely do vigilantes restrict themselves to proportionate actions—like, one could argue, André Bamberski did: he only had Krombach kidnapped and carried off to France in order to have him put to trial there; he did not endeavor to execute the punishment himself (at least not to the degree Kohlhaas or, in real life, Bachmeier did). *Michael Kohlhaas* is one of the few examples in German literature which deals solely with this ambiguity of justice and revenge, and, even more outstanding, it does so without referring to religious judgment. Instead, it is more inspired by enlightenment legal theory and philosophy.[44] *Kohlhaas*, like the *Nibelungenlied*, continues to inspire literary and cinematic adaptations until today.[45]

This is the case in ballads of the late eighteenth and early nineteenth century as well; ballads are particularly inclined toward stories of crime, punishment, and revenge as they partly evolved out of the "Bänkelsang"—travelling singers who recounted tales of particularly gruesome crimes and public trials standing on a bench ("Bänkel," little bench) and often showing pictures to go with the story. Ballads therefore often dealt with historical or supernatural events and thus were especially suitable for revenge on both sides of the grave. However, justice here is likewise restricted to divine forces, mostly—in Conrad Ferdinand Meyer's *Die Füße im Feuer* (*The Feet in the Fire*, 1882), a lone rider seeks hospitality in the castle of a squire whose wife, as it turns out, he tortured to death a few years ago in this very same castle. After an uncanny night, where memories of the torture (especially the image of two feet twitching in the fire, thus the title of the ballad) and murder are intertwined with the rider's growing fear and nervousness, the squire bids him an icy farewell with the verdict: "Gemordet hast du teuflisch mir / mein Weib! Und lebst! . . . Mein ist die Rache, redet Gott."[46] Hereby he both declares his identity and refrains from vigilante action at the same time, stating that revenge can only be taken rightfully by God. Another spectacular case of (divine?) revenge is found in Heinrich Heine's ballad *Belsatzar* (1820). This ballad narrates the story of Belsatzar, king of Babylon, who blasphemes Jehovah. Immediately after his blasphemy, flaming letters appear on the wall as if written by an invisible hand. Unlike in the original story from the Bible (Dan 5), however, the flaming words written on the wall cannot be deciphered by anybody and Belsatzar is killed by his minions the same night. This small change Heine makes gives a completely new emphasis; in his version, Belsatzar's death is not obviously a divine judgment, but he is killed by the anonymous mob of his minions, which places retribution and the administration of justice in the hands of the people, ultimately—supposedly with implicit divine approval, even (through the writing).

Another very prominent example of the people carrying out an act of retribution, although instigated by one single person, is Friedrich Dürrenmatt's *Der Besuch der alten Dame* (*The Visit of the Old Lady*, 1956). Dürrenmatt is from Switzerland, however, so it is not a national German text (although written in German). But there are modern treatments of the power of the community and the part the society plays in vigilante activities. Such examples can be found in Juli Zeh's novel *Unterleuten* (2016)[47] and, in popular literature, in Sebastian Fitzek's crime story *AchtNacht* (2017) (see below for discussion of both).

Contemporary Works

Nowadays, fictional representations of revenge often intertwine issues of self-administered justice or other forms of vigilantism with German history, namely the crimes committed during the Nazi regime. Well-known examples are Ferdinand von Schirach's short novel *Der Fall Collini* (*The Collini Case*, 2011). An old man is murdered in his hotel room; his murderer (Collini) willingly lets the police arrest him, but remains completely silent. There is no apparent connection between the killer and his victim; the main character, a young lawyer taking on his first big case with Collini's defense, is almost desperate when he finally stumbles upon information about Collini's past which then unveils the victim's deep involvement in crimes committed in Italy during the early 1940s. Those revelations are, of course, meant to shed a different light on the murderer's deed, providing explanations, if not excuses, for his murder. The story ends with Collini committing suicide before a judgment can be made, thus avoiding an official legal statement and leaving the reader to make his or her own judgment, as it were. As has been outlined above, this is in accord with current judicial practice, if not theory, in connection with revenge killings; psychological understanding and sympathy for revenge murders feature largely in the court of public opinion, as became clear in both the Bachmeier and Bamberski cases. Moreover, their modest sentences and the statement of the BGH show the high significance attributed to the individual motivations for revenge murders. Von Schirach's story has recently been made into a movie (2019).

Talking of movies, there is very little material at all which can be found in German films. They do not generally address legal issues or crime and revenge stories; they are mostly comedies or dramas centering on personal problems and conflicts. The one issue of interest for this study which is most commonly found in German films is honor killing. Sometimes films touch on the issue implicitly, like Fatih Akın's *Gegen die Wand* (*Against the Wall*, 2004)—Sibel, the female protagonist, strives for independence and repeatedly collides with the more restrictive views and stances of her male family members. She finally migrates to Istanbul, where she finds a fragile kind of peace. Honor killing is not extensively debated in this film, but her brother, for instance, on one occasion chases her along the street and shouts threats at her. There are films, however, which explicitly address honor killings; most recently, the story of a real case from 2005 in Berlin has been turned into a documentary movie: Sherry Horman's *Nur eine Frau* (*Just a Woman*, 2019).

Although there is a huge market for legal series on TV, they are mostly courtroom series (often scripted reality formats), crime series like *Tatort* or police series like *Alarm für Cobra 11*.[48] Vigilantism and self-administered justice, if addressed at all in those series, are always sharply condemned. The legal system, although it might be questioned by some of the characters, is never challenged as such. The overall message is always affirmative, and any unlawful action outside the boundaries of the law is punished. However, there are some comical renditions of vigilante topics. In *Der Bulle von Tölz* (*The Tölz Cop*) for instance, a Bavarian crime series heavily relying on local color for its success, one of the main characters on one occasion tries to organize a militia to find out who stole her garden furniture.[49] The theme is handled lightly in the series and the character's call for revenge and self-protection is ridiculed; justice is achieved by the authorities, not by individuals acting singlehandedly. This is in line with the general treatment of vigilantism throughout German films and series. In *Der Tatortreiniger* (*The Crime Scene Cleaner*), a series centering around the eponymous crime scene cleaner and the various crime scenes he encounters, the main character once stumbles into a sort of shrine for Adolf Hitler, guarded by a bunch of rather stupid neo-Nazis. He tricks them and disposes of their whole collection of Third Reich memorabilia before they have a chance to object. Although likewise treated comically, this episode is really one of the very few examples where vigilante action is approved of. One might ask whether the behavior of the cleaner in this episode is indeed a case of vigilantism at all—or not in fact a case of protection of the free democratic basic order of the state and an act of legitimate resistance. As noted, this right to resistance is enshrined in the German Constitution and states that all Germans have the right to resist anybody endeavoring to abolish the free democratic basic order in Germany, should all other means to stop that fail (Grundgesetz [Constitution], Art. 20(4)). On the other hand, the main character does not try to stop the illegal activities (possession of Nazi devotional objects is illegal in Germany) by, for instance, calling in the police or informing the Federal Office for the Protection of the Constitution, but takes matters into his own hands without stopping to inform or consult anybody, which makes it a genuine classic case of system-affirmative justice vigilantism.

The entanglement of vigilantism and social media is investigated in a thriller by Sebastian Fitzek, a prominent German writer of crime stories and (psycho-) thrillers. In his novel *AchtNacht* (2017),[50] somebody starts a sort of lottery where every German is invited to suggest a person who, in his or her opinion, deserves to die. On the eighth of August (hence the one meaning of "Acht"), two names are allegedly arbitrarily drawn from this lottery, and for one night—starting at 20:08 and ending at 08:08 the next morning—these two people, Ben and Arezu, are ostracized; the operators of the lottery claim that everybody is free to kill them without fear of legal consequences. Furthermore they promise to pay a bounty of ten million for the "hunter" who succeeds in killing the ostracized. Immediately after Ben and Arezu are drawn from the lottery, AchtNacht is being discussed on every radio and TV broadcast and there is an argument at first about the possible legality of the experiment. As the night wears on, however, things soon get out of hand: Ben's and Arezu's personal data—telephone numbers, home addresses, etc.—are published online, and quickly mobs of "hunters" form and begin to track their movements by their mobile phones. As the night wears on, the hunt gains momentum; private information, both true and false, about the two victims is published on the internet and they are among other things denounced as psychotic (Arezu) or pedophile (Ben). Aggression escalates due to that information, and soon the mob starts to seriously go for the throat. After several close escapes, during the course of which Arezu kills one of the hunters by accident and then is herself seriously injured, in the end the representatives of the rule of law prevail and a policeman manages to overwhelm Oz, the operator of AchtNacht, who was confronting Ben on the edge of a rooftop.[51]

With shockingly convincing developments Fitzek deals with the mass media hysteria stirred up by this lottery and the novel closely resembles real cases of digital (and non-digital) manhunts which took place after the publication of the data of, for instance, alleged child-murderers or rapists.[52] For various examples of such real cases of this form of denunciation and internet vigilantism, see #vigilantismus on twitter;[53] instances of internet vigilantism are collected and displayed there.

In Juli Zeh's novel *Unterleuten* (2016), the dynamics of social control within a small and remote village take on the characteristics of vigilante activity, as frequently violent conflict solutions are presented as "what is done," whereas calling in the police is viewed as a crass breach of etiquette among the villagers: if there is any trouble, you do not call in officials, you take matters into your own hands. As the story unravels and conflicts intensify, various violent assaults, even with deadly outcomes, are integrated into the villagers' doctrine of arranging things among themselves. The narrative changes focus from chapter to chapter and thus manages to minutely sketch the psychological processes taking place among the new villagers, who slowly get drawn into the dreadful business of this miniature surveillance society and their vigilante ideology, until one of them—a retired professor of sociology, of all things—regards it as absolutely normal and appropriate behavior to sneak into his neighbor's yard and beat him up severely in order to "teach him a lesson" and protect his wife from possible threats. The novel has recently been made into a TV film and was highly successful; all three parts achieved the highest audience ratings during prime time and held market shares of about 20 percent.[54] It closely follows Zeh's original text.[55]

CONCLUSION

All in all, Germany displays a very high degree of trust in its legal system. Vigilantism does not have any distinct recent tradition in the country, and this is mirrored in all three aspects covered here: jurisdiction, coverage of real cases and fictional representations. There is, however, a difference between the various kinds of vigilantism. As far as self-administered justice is concerned, there is a hiatus between law and legal practice. While the law sharply condemns all forms of self-administered justice, particularly acts committed out of revenge, both public opinion and legal practice show a lot more compassion and understanding for the psychological background and motivation of these revenge crimes. This appeal to human empathy and psychological understanding for revenge murders is employed in fictional representations as well, as can typically be seen in Kleist's *Michael Kohlhaas* or, in contemporary literature, in von Schirach's *Der Fall Collini*.

A similar discrepancy can be seen in relation to militia actions, but here it is not a hiatus between the people and the text of the law, but a strictly political/ideological one between right-wing supporters of vigilante actions and the democratic and law-abiding majority condemning such actions. As is shown in Sebastian Fitzek's *AchtNacht* or Juli Zeh's *Unterleuten*, however, mass phenomena, especially in cases of internet vigilantism, are capable of instigating widespread reactions from an otherwise probably quite peaceful and not explicitly right-wing or militant population.

Finally, the legal reactions to real cases of self-administered justice—the often very modest sentence—show a huge amount of understanding and sympathy. A surmise would be that sentences are that limited exactly because self-administered justice is such a relatively rare occurrence in Germany. As trust in the legal system is generally very high, matters rarely have to be taken into one's own hands, and therefore punishment is not needed to discourage further perpetrators. This high amount of trust in the legal system is also reflected in fictional representations, as in the overwhelming majority of all films, series, and texts, justice is done in the end by the authorities.

NOTES

1. Thomas Schmidt-Lux, "Vigilantismus. Ein Phänomen Der Grenze," *Kriminologisches Journal* 44, no. 2 (2012): 121.

2. For research on vigilantism as a sociological phenomenon, see Schmidt-Lux, 122–23. The ambivalence between the two is the topic of the exhibition "Whistleblower & Vigilanten"; for a description, see https://www.hmkv.de/ausstellungen/ausstellungen-detail/whistleblower-vigilanten-figuren-des-digitalen-widerstands.html. More about this exhibition below.

3. I would like to thank Patrick Meier for advice and inspiration for the following (legal) part of this chapter.

4. Strafgesetzbuch (StGB) [Criminal Code], §32(2).

5. Jürgen Sauren, "Zur Überschreitung Des Notwehrrechts," *Jura*, 1988, 567–73; Urs Kindhäuser, "§ 33, Rn 11," in *Strafgesetzbuch*, ed. Urs Kindhäuser, Ulfrid Neumann, and Hans-Ullrich Paeffgen, fifth ed. (Baden-Baden: Nomos, 2017).

6. Hartmut Schneider, "§ 211 Rn. 95–99," in *Münchener Kommentar Zum Strafgesetzbuch*, ed. Bernd von Heintschel-Heinegg, third ed., vol. 5. §§ 263–358 StGB (Munich: C.H. Beck, 2017), sec. 95.

7. Ibid.

8. Schneider, "§ 211 Rn. 95–99," sec. 96.

9. Strafgesetzbuch (StGB) [Criminal Code], §213.

10. See Schneider, "§ 211 Rn. 95–99," sec. 97.; also see ibid. sec. 98: "Allein die psychologische Erklärbarkeit eines Tötungsdelikts besagt grundsätzlich nichts über dessen rechtliche Bewertung anhand der insoweit allein ausschlaggebenden normativen Kriterien"—the fact alone that a homicide might be psychologically explicable cannot lead to differences in its legal assessment.

11. Grundgesetz (GG) [Constitution], Art. 20(4).

12. Georg Freund, *Strafrecht Allgemeiner Teil: Personale Straftatlehre* (Berlin: Springer, 2009), para. 3. sec. 85–86; Christian Jäger, "Das Dualistische Notwehrverstiindnis Und Seine Folgen Für Das Recht Auf Verteidigung: Zugleich Eine Untersuchung Zum Verhältnis Der Garantenlehre Zu Den Sozialethischen Einschränkungen Des Notwehrrechts," *Goltdammer's Archiv Für Strafrecht* 163, no. 5 (2016): 258.

13. Volker Erb, "§ 32 Rn. 18," in *Münchener Kommentar Zum Strafgesetzbuch*, ed. Bernd von Heintschel-Heinegg, third ed., vol. 1. §§ 1–37 StGB (Munich: C.H. Beck, 2017), sec. 18.

14. Schmidt-Lux 2012, S. 119 (FN 5). Schmidt-Lux, "Vigilantismus. Ein Phänomen Der Grenze," 119, n. 5.

15. Bohm, Hark: *Der Fall Bachmeier—keine Zeit für Tränen* (1984); Driest, Burkhard: *Annas Mutter* (1984); Gramberg, Michael: *Die Rache der Marianne Bachmeier* (2006).

16. Monika Köpcke, "Rache im Gerichtssaal," Deutschlandfunk, June 3, 2006, https://www.deutschlandfunk.de/rache-im-gerichtssaal-100.html.

17. Ibid.

18. Hilka Sinnig: *Kalinkas Letzte Reise* (2006); Hilka Sinnig: *Das tote Mädchen vom Bodensee* (2010); Vincent Garenq: *Im Namen meiner Tochter—der Fall Kalinka* (*Kalinka*, 2016).

19. Trying to see both sides: Stefan Simons, "Kalinka-Fall: Prozess wegen Entführung gegen Bamberski in Mulhouse," *Der Spiegel*, May 22, 2014, sec. Panorama, https://www.spiegel.de/panorama/justiz/kalinka-fall-prozess-wegen-entfuehrung-gegen-bamberski-in-mulhouse-a-970670.html; all in favor of Bamberski: "Der Fall Kalinka. Selbstjustiz - ein Akt der Verzweiflung," *Süddeutsche Zeitung*, March 3, 2011, https://www.sueddeutsche.de/panorama/der-fall-kalinka-30-jahre-durch-die-hoelle-1.1079171; Andrew Anthony, "Thirty Years in Search of Justice," *The Guardian*, October 23, 2010, https://www.theguardian.com/world/2010/oct/24/thirty-year-search-justice; Tanja Kuchenbecker and Albert Link, "Entführer vom Horror-Arzt," bild.de, October 25, 2009, https://www.bild.de/news/2009/kalinkas-raecher-spricht-10211710.bild.html.; with literary ambition: Joshua Hammer, "The Kalinka Affair," The *Atavist Magazine*, March 6, 2012, http://magazine.atavist.com/the-kalinka-affair/.

20. Isabel Meixner, "Fall Kalinka - 'Die deutsche Justiz war blind,'" Süddeutsche.de, October 11, 2016, https://www.sueddeutsche.de/bayern/fall-kalinka-die-deutsche-justiz-war-blind-1.3241845.

21. The SA might best be described as what Robson and Spina call "power vigilantes" (see the introduction to this volume)—thugs supporting those already in power by threatening politically dissident or ethnically unfavored population groups.

22. See Matthias Quent, "Selbstjustiz im Namen des Volkes: Vigilantistischer Terrorismus," bpb.de, October 6, 2016, https://www.bpb.de/shop/zeitschriften/apuz/228868/selbstjustiz-im-namen-des-volkes-vigilantistischer-terrorismus/.

23. "Vigilantismus," in *Wikipedia*, January 8, 2022, nn. 10–12, https://de.wikipedia.org/w/index.php?title=Vigilantismus&oldid=218925406. Such mass phenomena, especially the role of the (social) media and internet vigilantism, are fictionally investigated in Sebastian Fitzek's novel *AchtNacht* (see below).

24. Quent, "Selbstjustiz im Namen des Volkes."

25. For research on vigilantism and right-wing terrorism see Matthias Quendt, *Rassismus, Radikalisierung, Rechtsterrorismus: Wie Der NSU Entstand Und Was Er Über Die Gesellschaft Verrät* (Weinheim: Beltz Juventa, 2019), 135–62.

26. Quent, "Selbstjustiz im Namen des Volkes."

27. Roland Roth, "Die Dunklen Seiten Der Zivilgesellschaft. Grenzen Einer Zivilgesellschaftlichen Fundierung von Demokratie," in *Zivilgesellschaft Und Sozialkapital: Herausforderungen Politischer Und Sozialer Integration*, ed. Ansgar Klein (Wiesbaden: VS Verlag für Sozialwissenschaften, 2004), 41–64. Also see Peter Waldmann, *Terrorismus: Provokation der Macht.* (Hamburg: Murmann Publishers GmbH, 2011), for discussion of this system-supportive sort of (vigilante) terrorism.

28. Zeh, Juli: *Leere Herzen* (2017). Juli Zeh clearly alludes to the relatively new right-wing party AfD (Alternative für Deutschland, alternative for Germany) with the layout of the "Besorgte Bürger Bewegung" (concerned citizens movement) in her novel. For discussion of concerned citizens vs. Neonazis, see the works of Matthias Quent.

29. Vgl. Freies Tal—Freital ist und bleibt deutsch, 30.3.2016, http://www.facebook.com/Freiheitfuerdeutschland/posts/540266182811549«; quote from Quent, "Selbstjustiz im Namen des Volkes."

30. Quent.

31. For an analysis of online discussions about the legitimacy of militia acitivity, see Thomas Schmidt-Lux, *Gerechte Strafe Legitimationskonflikte um vigilante Gewalt* (Weinheim: Beltz Juventa, 2017). He carves out several cognitive, normative, and emotional strategies which are displayed in online discussions to legitimate vigilante violence.

32. For descriptions of the exhibition see, for instance: "Held oder Verbrecher: Whistleblower im Dortmunder U," https://www.ruhr24.de, June 16, 2016, https://www.ruhr24.de/dortmund/held-oder-verbrecher-whistleblower-dortmunder-13085573.html; Marcus Meier, "Von Pentagon bis Panama (nd-aktuell.de)," April 13, 2016, https://www.nd-aktuell.de/artikel/1008301.von-pentagon-bis-panama.html.

33. Maximilian Pichl, "Rechtsterrorismus und Staat," *Verfassungsblog* (blog), June 19, 2019, https://verfassungsblog.de/rechtsterrorismus-und-staat/.

34. "'Scharia-Polizei' in Wuppertal: Salafisten als 'Sharia Police' in NRW," *Der Spiegel*, September 5, 2014, https://www.spiegel.de/politik/deutschland/scharia-polizei-in-wuppertal-salafisten-als-sharia-police-in-nrw-a-990152.html.

35. "Wuppertal: Gericht spricht 'Scharia Polizei' schuldig," *Der Spiegel*, May 27, 2019, https://www.spiegel.de/politik/deutschland/wuppertal-gericht-spricht-scharia-polizei-schuldig-a-1269527.html.

36. Bundesministerium des Innern, für Bau und Heimat.

37. Lucius Teidelbaum, "Waffen-Lobby," *Der Rechte Rand*, March 2019, https://www.der-rechte-rand.de/archive/4840/waffen-lobby-afd/.

38. https://german-rifle-association.de/.

39. See Teidelbaum, "Waffen-Lobby."

40. The term for a gift to the bride from the husband on the morning of their marriage.

41. Out of the huge body of literature on the *Nibelungenlied*, see for instance: Jan-Dirk Müller, *Spielregeln Für Den Untergang: Die Welt Des Nibelungenliedes* (Tübingen: Niemeyer, 1998); Tilo Renz, *Um Leib Und Leben: Das Wissen von Geschlecht, Korper Und Recht Im Nibelungenlied* (Berlin; Boston: De Gruyter, 2012); Walter Seitter, *Das Politische Wissen Im Nibelungenlied: Vorlesungen* (Berlin:

Merve, 1987); Walter Seitter, *Versprechen, Versagen: Frauenmacht Und Frauenästhetik in Der Kriemhild-Diskussion Des 13. Jahrhunderts* (Berlin: Merve, 1990).

42. To name a few very prominent (or very popular) ones: Wolfgang Hohlbein: *Hagen von Tronje* (1986) (fantasy novel for young adults); Helmut Krausser: *Unser Lied. Gesang vom Untergang Burgunds—Nibelungendestillat* (2003) (stage version); John von Düffel: *Best of Nibelungen (Die Out-Takes). Die Abenteuer von Gernot und Giselher. In drei Reinfällen* (2007) (stage version); Ulrike Draesner: *Nibelungen. Heimsuchung* (2016) (poetry).

43. On this issue, see Johannes Friedrich Lehmann, *Im Abgrund Der Wut: Zur Kultur-Und Literaturgeschichte Des Zorns* (Freiburg: Rombach Verlag, 2012), 266–96.

44. Of course, *Kohlhaas* has been analyzed by jurists many times; see, for instance: Andreas Voßkuhle and Johannes Gerberding, "Michael Kohlhaas Und Der Kampf Ums Recht," *Juristenzeitung*, no. 19 (2012): 917–25.

45. Again, to name a few recent examples: Aron Lehmann: *Kohlhaas oder die Verhältnismäßigkeit der Mittel* (2012) (film); Arnaud Des Pallières: *Michael Kohlhaas* (2013) (film); Christoph Hein: *Der neuere (glücklichere) Kohlhaas. Bericht über einen Rechtshandel aus den Jahren 1972/73* (1994) (story); Corinna Bethke: *Bis vor den Richterstuhl Gottes. Die Fehde des Hans Kohlhase* (2007) (historical novel).

46. "Fiendishly, you murdered / my wife! And still you live! . . . vengeance is mine, says the Lord."

47. The title is ambiguous; "unter Leuten" meaning among people, but written like this, as one noun, it also suggests an allusion to "Untermenschen," subhuman beings. It also is the name of the village where the story takes place.

48. Stefan Machura and Michael Böhnke, "Germany," in *A Transnational Study of Law and Justice on Tv*, ed. Peter Robson and Jennifer L. Schulz (Oxford: Hart, 2016), 99–112; Franziska Stürmer, "Germany: Diversity on Its Way," in *Ethnicity, Gender, and Diversity: Law and Justice on TV*, ed. Peter Robson and Jennifer L. Schulz (Lanham, MD: Lexington Books, 2018), 87–100.

49. A case which is, after all, not as far-fetched or humoristic as it may seem, as there are cases of real militia in Germany which were called into existence to stop a growing amount of burglaries; see Schmidt-Lux, "Vigilantismus. Ein Phänomen Der Grenze."

50. A pun which is quite hard to translate; "Acht" being both the number eight and the state of being ostracized. The novel has been inspired by *The Purge* (2013).

51. There are many more twists and complications to the story than recounted here; however, they mostly deal with the personal problems of Ben and Arezu. They add nothing to the topic of internet vigilantism and lynch law and therefore are omitted.

52. See, for real instances of this internet vigilantism, for example the above mentioned exhibition Whistleblower & Vigilanten 2016; see also Robert Booth, "Vigilante Paedophile Hunters Ruining Lives with Internet Stings," *The Guardian*, October 25, 2013, https://www.theguardian.com/uk-news/2013/oct/25/vigilante-paedophile-hunters-online-police; Celia Hatton, "China's Internet Vigilantes and the 'Human Flesh Search Engine,'" *BBC News*, January 28, 2014, https://www.bbc.com/news/magazine-25913472.

53. https://twitter.com/hashtag/vigilantismus?src=hash&lang=de.
54. See quotenmeter.de: a website broadcasting figures about TV consumer behavior.
55. Matti Geschonneck: *Unterleuten. Das zerrissene Dorf* (2020).

BIBLIOGRAPHY

Anthony, Andrew. "Thirty Years in Search of Justice." *The Guardian*, October 23, 2010. https://www.theguardian.com/world/2010/oct/24/thirty-year-search-justice.

Booth, Robert. "Vigilante Paedophile Hunters Ruining Lives with Internet Stings." *The Guardian*, October 25, 2013. https://www.theguardian.com/uk-news/2013/oct/25/vigilante-paedophile-hunters-online-police.

Süddeutsche Zeitung. "Der Fall Kalinka. Selbstjustiz - ein Akt der Verzweiflung," March 3, 2011. https://www.sueddeutsche.de/panorama/der-fall-kalinka-30-jahre-durch-die-hoelle-1.1079171.

Erb, Volker. "§ 32 Rn. 18." In *Münchener Kommentar Zum Strafgesetzbuch*, edited by Bernd von Heintschel-Heinegg, third ed. Vol. 1. §§ 1–37 StGB. Munich: C.H. Beck, 2017.

Freund, Georg. *Strafrecht Allgemeiner Teil: Personale Straftatlehre*. Berlin: Springer, 2009.

Hammer, Joshua. "The Kalinka Affair." The *Atavist Magazine*, March 6, 2012. http://magazine.atavist.com/the-kalinka-affair/.

Hatton, Celia. "China's Internet Vigilantes and the 'Human Flesh Search Engine.'" *BBC News*, January 28, 2014. https://www.bbc.com/news/magazine-25913472.

https://www.ruhr24.de. "Held oder Verbrecher: Whistleblower im Dortmunder U," June 16, 2016. https://www.ruhr24.de/dortmund/held-oder-verbrecher-whistleblower-dortmunder-13085573.html.

Jäger, Christian. "Das Dualistische Notwehrverstiindnis Und Seine Folgen Für Das Recht Auf Verteidigung: Zugleich Eine Untersuchung Zum Verhältnis Der Garantenlehre Zu Den Sozialethischen Einschränkungen Des Notwehrrechts." *Goltdammer's Archiv Für Strafrecht* 163, no. 5 (2016): 258–65.

Kindhäuser, Urs. "§ 33, Rn 11." In *Strafgesetzbuch*, edited by Urs Kindhäuser, Ulfrid Neumann, and Hans-Ullrich Paeffgen, fifth ed. Baden-Baden: Nomos, 2017.

Köpcke, Monika. "Rache im Gerichtssaal." Deutschlandfunk, June 3, 2006. https://www.deutschlandfunk.de/rache-im-gerichtssaal-100.html.

Kuchenbecker, Tanja, and Albert Link. "Entführer vom Horror-Arzt." bild.de, October 25, 2009. https://www.bild.de/news/2009/kalinkas-raecher-spricht-10211710.bild.html.

Lehmann, Johannes Friedrich. *Im Abgrund Der Wut: Zur Kultur-Und Literaturgeschichte Des Zorns*. Freiburg: Rombach Verlag, 2012.

Machura, Stefan, and Michael Böhnke. "Germany." In *A Transnational Study of Law and Justice on TV*, edited by Peter Robson and Jennifer L. Schulz, 99–112. Oxford: Hart, 2016.

Meier, Marcus. "Von Pentagon bis Panama (nd-aktuell.de)," April 13, 2016. https://www.nd-aktuell.de/artikel/1008301.von-pentagon-bis-panama.html.

Meixner, Isabel. "Fall Kalinka - 'Die deutsche Justiz war blind.'" Süddeutsche.de, October 11, 2016. https://www.sueddeutsche.de/bayern/fall-kalinka-die-deutsche-justiz-war-blind-1.3241845.

Müller, Jan-Dirk. *Spielregeln Für Den Untergang: Die Welt Des Nibelungenliedes*. Tübingen: Niemeyer, 1998.

Pichl, Maximilian. "Rechtsterrorismus und Staat." *Verfassungsblog* (blog), June 19, 2019. https://verfassungsblog.de/rechtsterrorismus-und-staat/.

Quendt, Matthias. *Rassismus, Radikalisierung, Rechtsterrorismus: Wie Der NSU Entstand Und Was Er Über Die Gesellschaft Verrät*. Weinheim: Beltz Juventa, 2019.

Quent, Matthias. "Selbstjustiz im Namen des Volkes: Vigilantistischer Terrorismus." bpb.de, October 6, 2016. https://www.bpb.de/shop/zeitschriften/apuz/228868/selbstjustiz-im-namen-des-volkes-vigilantistischer-terrorismus/.

Renz, Tilo. *Um Leib Und Leben: Das Wissen von Geschlecht, Korper Und Recht Im Nibelungenlied*. Berlin; Boston: De Gruyter, 2012.

Roth, Roland. "Die Dunklen Seiten Der Zivilgesellschaft. Grenzen Einer Zivilgesellschaftlichen Fundierung von Demokratie." In *Zivilgesellschaft Und Sozialkapital: Herausforderungen Politischer Und Sozialer Integration*, edited by Ansgar Klein, 41–64. Wiesbaden: VS Verlag für Sozialwissenschaften, 2004.

Sauren, Jürgen. "Zur Überschreitung Des Notwehrrechts." *Jura*, 1988, 567–73.

Der Spiegel. "'Scharia-Polizei' in Wuppertal: Salafisten als 'Sharia Police' in NRW," September 5, 2014. https://www.spiegel.de/politik/deutschland/scharia-polizei-in-wuppertal-salafisten-als-sharia-police-in-nrw-a-990152.html.

Schmidt-Lux, Thomas. *Gerechte Strafe Legitimationskonflikte um vigilante Gewalt*. Weinheim: Beltz Juventa, 2017.

———. "Vigilantismus. Ein Phänomen Der Grenze." *Kriminologisches Journal* 44, no. 2 (2012): 118–32.

Schneider, Hartmut. "§ 211 Rn. 95–99." In *Münchener Kommentar Zum Strafgesetzbuch*, edited by Bernd von Heintschel-Heinegg, third ed. Vol. 5. §§ 263–358 StGB. Munich: C.H. Beck, 2017.

Seitter, Walter. *Das Politische Wissen Im Nibelungenlied: Vorlesungen*. Berlin: Merve, 1987.

———. *Versprechen, Versagen: Frauenmacht Und Frauenästhetik in Der Kriemhild-Diskussion Des 13. Jahrhunderts*. Berlin: Merve, 1990.

Simons, Stefan. "Kalinka-Fall: Prozess wegen Entführung gegen Bamberski in Mulhouse." *Der Spiegel*, May 22, 2014. https://www.spiegel.de/panorama/justiz/kalinka-fall-prozess-wegen-entfuehrung-gegen-bamberski-in-mulhouse-a-970670.html.

Stürmer, Franziska. "Germany: Diversity on Its Way." In *Ethnicity, Gender, and Diversity: Law and Justice on TV*, edited by Peter Robson and Jennifer L. Schulz, 87–100. Lanham, MD: Lexington Books, 2018.

Teidelbaum, Lucius. "Waffen-Lobby." *Der Rechte Rand*, March 2019. https://www.der-rechte-rand.de/archive/4840/waffen-lobby-afd/.

"Vigilantismus." In *Wikipedia*, January 8, 2022. https://de.wikipedia.org/w/index.php?title=Vigilantismus&oldid=218925406.

Voßkuhle, Andreas, and Johannes Gerberding. "Michael Kohlhaas Und Der Kampf Ums Recht." *Juristenzeitung*, no. 19 (2012): 917–25.

Waldmann, Peter. *Terrorismus: Provokation der Macht.* Hamburg: Murmann, 2011.

Der Spiegel. "Wuppertal: Gericht spricht 'Scharia Polizei' schuldig," May 27, 2019. https://www.spiegel.de/politik/deutschland/wuppertal-gericht-spricht-scharia-polizei-schuldig-a-1269527.html.

Chapter 6

Vigilantism
The Greek Approach

Nickos Myrtou and Stamatis Poulakidakos

APPROACHES TO VIGILANTISM

The rule of law and respect for the judicial functions of the state are generally considered to be essential components of contemporary democratic societies.[1] Within this context, vigilantism represents a situation in which (an) individual(s) harm(s) (an)other individual(s) in an attempt to punish that individual(s) for wrongdoing.[2] Etymologically, the term originates from the Latin *vigilare* ("to keep awake") and the Spanish *vigilante* ("watchman" or "guard") and means some form of protection from danger.[3] Based on its etymological roots, vigilantism is associated with an attempt of a single person or a group to achieve some "improvement" or "refinement" in the social order.

Although continuing theoretical debates perpetuate the conceptual ambiguity of the term,[4] vigilantism can be described as the actions of self-organized, autonomous, and voluntary individuals or groups of individuals, who act independently from the state and use actual or threatened violence to reinstate what they view as the rule of law, public order, and justice.[5] In any case, when someone seeks to scrutinize case studies of vigilantism, s/he has to take into consideration the code of ethics of the perpetrator(s), as well as other factors that might influence or even cause the exercise of vigilante acts, such as disappointment at the hands of the official judicial system, along with social and psychological factors.[6]

The existence of "multiple" codes of ethics underlines the ambivalent dimension of vigilantism. Acts of vigilantism are reported across the world and reactions to vigilantes differ both between countries and among individuals. Vigilantes have both been publicly decried as criminals and publicly celebrated as heroes.[7] On one hand, at least in theory, vigilantes aim to be models of good citizenship and are thus conceptually distinct from organized crime groups (OCGs), mobs, and criminal gangs.[8] On the other hand, though it is beyond the scope and purpose of this chapter to define and make evaluative propositions on all different forms and cases of vigilantism, one should note possible biases emerging from the subjective codes of ethics that accompany any kind of vigilante activity. First, it is rather likely that the victim (or the relative of a victim) will assign more blame to the offender than more distant third parties would agree that the offender deserves. Second, such biases and over-ascribed blame are what make revenge such a sloppy form of justice. A procedurally fair, formalized adjudication of offenses is a superior form of justice restoration rather than vigilantism. This process minimizes and counter-balances individual biases of victims, thus usually leading to fairer verdicts and punishments.[9]

Focusing on the objectives of vigilante actors and admitting that a certain overlap may exist, one can approach the phenomenon according to a threefold typology of vigilantism: (a) crime control; (b) control of social groups; and (c) regime control.[10] In the crime-control type, vigilantes act as an informal police force, taking action against individuals they believe committed or may commit crime, according to their interpretation of deviance.[11] Protesting against government inaction, inefficiency, corruption, and/or simply a lenient sentence, vigilantes perform street patrols, apprehend real or perceived offenders or transgressors, and deliver what they think is a "just" punishment for them.[12] Within this category falls the so-called vendetta, the vengeance of an alleged crime—even murder—in the same or even more strict way by the victims or the relatives of the victims, which can still be encountered in modern-day Greece.[13]

In social-group-control vigilantism, self-organized groups of vigilantes shift their attention from street patrols to the social environment.[14] They attack distinct social groups, aiming to neutralize the danger to the social or public order they consider these groups to be posing. This form of vigilantism is often driven by racial and/or ethnic considerations (e.g., attacks on immigrants and their settlements).[15] A typical example of this form of vigilantism is lynching, which has its roots in the United States and has been encountered in various countries all over the world.[16]

Finally, regime-control vigilantes attempt to "alter" the government and its agencies when they fail or are perceived as "failed." They intend "to alter the regime, in order to make the 'superstructure' into a more effective guardian of the 'base.'"[17] This is one of the most violent and organized forms of vigilantism. It should be noted here, however, that vigilantism is different from rebel or revolutionary movements. The latter seek to overthrow the established order, whereas vigilantism seeks to "correct" state failures in specific domains.[18]

With regard to force, it is generally agreed that vigilante groups employ some form of violence. Otherwise, vigilantism would be no different from political and social movements. Some scholars acknowledge that vigilantes do not "necessarily engage in forceful action but . . . their operational philosophy permits such engagement."[19] Therefore, the use of violence should be understood broadly, encompassing both actual and threatened force.[20]

Nowadays, theorists have pinpointed the emergence of new forms of vigilantism falling under the umbrella term "cyber-vigilantism" due to their implementation digitally. Cyber vigilantism is defined as a mediated search process whereby people take initiatives to collaboratively track down some individuals and disclose information about them. The process usually starts when there is a public outrage at certain corrupting or socially undesirable behavior that has been captured and circulated online.[21]

THE SOCIAL AND MEDIA CONTEXT OF VIGILANTISM

As evident from the attempt to define it and the different forms it can take, vigilantism can be characterized as a multifaceted and multifactorial phenomenon, in need of careful scrutiny for each case study. Generally speaking, vigilantism involves perpetrating a wrong in order to punish a perceived wrongdoing, which creates a morally ambiguous situation.[22]

In a socio-historical context, forms of communal justice can be found in all societies and have a long history. Throughout most of human history, the punishment of crime was presumably a matter of retribution by the wronged victims and their kinfolk. Repeated episodes of violence, going far back into our past, have imprinted upon the citizenry a propensity to violence. Human history has produced and reinforced a strain of violence.[23]

Until the late Middle Ages, European legal codes and customs recognized blood feuds, with the killing of the slayer or members of his family, as a legitimate way to avenge a slain family member. The advance of formal law and court procedures was slow and uneven. As societies started becoming organized into states, hence entering modernity (mainly from the thirteenth century onward), the newly established state structures sought to intervene in personal disputes and conflicts in order to resolve them through the implementation of law. However, as rivalries and hatreds between clans were not easy to resolve, conflict resolution often remained a predominantly private issue.[24]

Among the rural populations of Western Europe, rituals of punishment and shaming, known as *rough music* in English, *Katzenmusik* in German, *charivari* in French, and *samosud* in Russian, persisted well into the late nineteenth century and often included severe physical abuse. Although these rituals were mostly exercised to enforce community values and limited to ridicule and corporal castigation, communal punishment sometimes included deadly violence.[25]

However, it would be misleading to see vigilantism just as the continuation of premodern traditions and mentalities that were somehow carried over into the modern world, since several contextual factors—for example financial, political, or social conditions—may influence in an at least "dualistic" way the occurrence of violent incidents. The first concerns the role of these factors in shaping an individual's personality at all stages of her/his development, through the social patterns and values s/he adopts when socializing. The second is through the external situations that a person experiences during his or her lifetime, such as professional success or failure, social exclusion or social inclusion, lawlessness or order.[26]

The social context-oriented arguments about the sources of vigilantism can be separated into two broad categories: state centric and civic centric explanations.[27] On one hand, state-centric accounts can be further divided in two subcategories, namely (state) evolution and devolution. While the evolutionist perspective suggests that vigilantism occurs because the state has not yet successfully established a monopoly of force, the devolutionist view sees popular justice as a response to the breakdown of government institutions—the state no longer being capable of effectively enforcing its claim to a monopoly of violence.[28] The evolutionist approach explains vigilantism as a response to the state's failure to police, prosecute, or imprison,[29] a problem that is magnified by processes of political transition when institutional routines are in flux.[30] Others explain vigilantism as a response to the state's failure to provide meaningful access to social rights, probably due to incompetence or even corruption[31]—a problem that is most acute in states that fail to transform authoritarian institutions.[32] Under a similar rationale, others see vigilantism as a response to "State withdrawal," where states, under conditions of neoliberalism, "outsource" the state's security functions in poor areas to vigilante groups who provide "a cheap form of law enforcement."[33] The American frontier ideology epitomizes the evolutionary model, whereas the devolutionist approach is closely linked to state failure in postcolonial settings, for example in Africa.[34]

On the other hand, some scholars see vigilantism as a response to collapsing civic and communal trust and the state legitimacy often associated with them.[35] Other scholars highlight the challenges of integrating indigenous or rural populations that have their own justice traditions into modernist legal institutions.[36] Still others look to political competition that frays connections between citizens and states, a problem made most acute when politicians use security concerns to mobilize voters.[37] A final group, often focusing on the American context, connects vigilantism to racial or ethnic violence where extrajudicial punishment serves as an informal means for ensuring racial dominance in a divided society.[38]

Bourdieu has developed a rather interesting approach linking vigilantism with patriarchy. In his ethnographic study he paints a really clear picture of the significance of honor in a patriarchal society, and therefore the need to protect or avenge it.[39] The socially imposed separation of male and female social roles, as well as the use of a symbolic violence to train boys to become men that ultimately turns into the use of actual violence, set the males for a life of domination.

The study of Bourdieu clarifies the norms on Mediterranean and Balkan cultures whilst also providing an understanding of Western societies in general. Masculinity is measured via expectations of strength, power, and sexual competence.[40] Those values are enforced on the individual and are used as scoreboards of both not having enough and having too much masculinity. Vigilantism as an act is traditionally assigned to males and therefore incorporates all the values imposed on masculinity via patriarchy, and at the same time by being a good storytelling module assists in promoting those values.[41] Central in enforcing those values is popular culture especially after the domination of television in the 1980s.[42]

As we have seen, in academic literature the conceptual boundaries of vigilantism remain rather blurred, inviting further analytical and case study–oriented exploration. Similarly, the media representations of vigilantism range from the usually "heroic" framing of fictional content, to the ethical approaches of the information content.

The world of medieval Icelandic saga is typical of a "noble" culture based on honor. In such a culture of honor, vigilantism is an integral part of the social and moral order, which further regulates interpersonal relationships.[43] In addition, contemporary popular culture has produced a rather static image of vigilantism, where super heroes are often portrayed as archetypal "vigilantes"—heroes courageously helping their communities on the margins of the law under conditions of disorder.[44]

In terms of news coverage, due to the dramatized way that media choose to frame the news, there is a possibility of a rather one-sided approach in the act of vigilantism, which, by usually emphasizing the tragedy of the murder, results in the mere description of (a chain of) crimes.[45] This approach exaggerates the spectacle and relies on an ethical and simplistic rhetoric. In addition, there are cases when the act of revenge is viewed as a "primitive" form of custom-based law, while compared to other societies and cultures it is cut off from the specific social context in which it takes place. Approaches of this kind usually come from the media, legal and judicial circles.[46]

VIGILANTISM IN GREECE

Greece is a country that in both historical and contemporary terms is replete with instances of vigilantism. Revenge was very common in ancient Greece, and Homer describes several instances of war heroes fleeing and seeking protection near a king or city in order to be saved from the revenge of their victims' dead relatives. The religious feeling about the onslaught created by the murder, which endangered not only everyone who accepted the killer, but also the city where he had fled, as well as the irreparable act, made the state's intervention in personal conflicts necessary.[47]

In several local societies of Greece (with the most typical examples being Crete and Mani),[48] one can still encounter the phenomenon of "vendetta." The vendetta is the subject of a "dialogue" between customary law, which it constantly invokes, and constitutional law that attempts to reject it and "punish" it under the Common Penal Code.[49] The term "vendetta" refers to "symbolic debt repayment." It signifies relationships between social groups who fight each other on the basis of kinship relationships. It marks the vengeance of a closed society that consciously takes the law into its own hands in order to restore order and justice. The avengers, though they already know the consequences that they and their families will suffer by exacting retribution, choose to deliberately ignore them in order to fulfill the necessary moral retribution.[50] Notions of honor and shame that are tied up with a family are at the root of this kind of retaliation. Intense quarrels, disputes, political and property issues trigger reactions and provoke self-determined "justice." In a vendetta, one's life is usually not immediately threatened, and the vengeance is usually much more severe than the original act that caused it.[51]

VIGILANTISM IN THE GREEK POPULAR CULTURE

Literature, Myths, and Songs

In Greek tradition, issues of honor and vengeance are recurring themes. It is our view that in those repeated motifs we see the footprints of the patriarchal culture that is still dominant in modern Greece. If we go back in history, and start with the two major epics of Homer (*The Iliad* and *The Odyssey*) we can distinguish some different aspects of honor and the actions one would take in order to avenge the trauma to his honor and reputation. In *The Iliad*, the war against Troy is an act to restore the honor of Menelaus for the loss of his wife Helen. It is apparent that the woman is considered a part of the man's property, the woman has no autonomy (Helen is being manipulated by Aphrodite and is her gift to Paris) and the man seeks restoration. Since the disrespect was due to the actions of a foreigner the whole of Greece comes to the aid of Menelaus, disregarding other disputes. In the same text we see the disrespect of Agamemnon toward Achilles on the division of loot (the loot in question is actually a woman captured who after her captivity would serve as a slave) and his refusal to fight for the restoration of Menelaus' honor. The death of Patroclus, Achilles' companion (friend and lover), who took his place to inspire fear in the Trojan army, leads to Achilles' revenge on Hector. In addition, the end of *The Odyssey* describes the bloody vengeance of Odysseus on the forty suitors of his wife who all have aspirations to his throne.

Similarly, in the great tragedies, the wrongdoing is always being avenged either by man or by the Gods. Special mention is required for *Antigone* in Sophocles' tragedy. Antigone sets the tone for the distinction between the law of men (legal) and the law of gods (ethical). Antigone refuses to uphold a law that disrespects the divine will of the treatment of the dead. Thus, she could be considered an archetypical vigilante, as she points out the errors of those in power and takes upon herself the task of doing what is in accordance with a higher power, even though she does not use violence and faces the violence of the king's retribution.

Before going on with our analysis, we must note that in some parts of Greece, specifically Crete, the traditional laws of revenge are very strong. Vendettas are a family issue; it has to do with protecting the family honor and wealth. According to Aristotle, vigilantism was a well set and accepted means of justice with its roots in the Minoan Era.[52] This tradition is still strong and appears in contemporary Greek popular culture. Vigilante justice appears in Greek literature, music, and theater but we choose to focus on audiovisual texts (films and TV series) that were in some form acclaimed (critically or via public opinion) and depict acts of vengeance and/or the need to "do the right thing."

These motifs of doing the right thing, even in the face of death, and of avenging the loss of a companion and property can be found in many places. For instance, there is a traditional song, "Pote tha Kanei Ksasteria," which describes a vendetta between two families, even though with the passing of time the true meaning was lost and has been transformed into a political song about the civil war. The lyrics clearly describe the wait for a night with no moon to allow for the mountain to be left and the rival men to be killed as dictated by the vendetta. It is important to note that the song recognizes the pain caused by the killing to the surviving relatives but disregards it, as it is a man's job to be tough and unforgiving in matters of honor. In this notion of *machismo*, we can identify the roots of violence against women. The men are the victims, but the real punishment is intended against "the mothers with no sons and wives with no husbands." This violence easily turns into abuse. The significance of the patriarchal notion of honor is shown in the refusal of the media to use the term "femicide" instead of the misleading "crime of passion" or "crime of honor" that we regularly come across.

In the following section of our chapter, we conduct a qualitative content analysis, a method for systematically describing the meaning of qualitative material,[53] of specific cinematic and television content of contemporary Greek popular culture, which depict instances of vigilantism, focusing mainly on its gender aspect as already underlined in our theoretical background.

Representations of Vigilantism in Contemporary Greek Cinema

Greek music has many distinct periods and forms, but the Rebetiko subculture is very dominant in various forms.[54] The Rebetiko came to Greece after the evacuation of Smyrna. The displaced population of Greeks residing in Asia Minor was received with hostility and racism and as a result many of them were forced into poverty and/or criminal actions. Rebetiko is considered the music of pain, injustice, broken dreams, and is the music of fringes. Within Rebetiko music we find the Zeibekiko, a male dance that is perhaps the only accepted way of males to show their pain and despair. The Zeibekiko is a solo dance in mainstream culture. The ordering of a Zeibekiko signifies the request for an empty space to be danced in by the man who ordered it. The disrespect of a special order is a direct attack on the honor of the dancer and the one who ordered the song (usually the same person, but there are cases where a friend orders a song for his friend).

This introduction of the Zeibekiko is important in examining the first movie of this chapter. *Paraggelia (A Special Order)* is a Greek film directed by Pavlos Tassios and shot in 1980 which takes place in 1973 and is based on true events. The hero of the film is Nikos who goes out with his brother and friends and ends up killing three people with his knife. Nikos Koemtzis is the actual person the movie portrays. In 1973 Koemtzis murdered three police officers who disrespected his brother's Zeibekiko. He was apprehended and convicted as a common criminal. Nikos Koemtzis was born in a family persecuted for their communist beliefs. This made his life very difficult and eventually he became a small-time criminal. In 1973 Greece was still under the military Junta Regime and the police were feared. Koemtzis himself did not associate his actions with his political beliefs, but for many his actions represented a political action against the Junta Regime. The movie, however, interprets the events from a clear political standpoint.

The film has an interesting form as the action is interrupted by poems of and narrated by Katerina Gogou. Gogou's poems are very political and talk about inequalities urging social resistance. Her strong words juxtaposed by images of a Tsifteteli belly dance and men drinking and smoking create a powerful context. In *Paraggelia* we see Nikos angry and frustrated. It is clear that he is in a bad mood and he turns to violence when a bouncer tries to stop him from entering the nightclub. Alcohol is also a component of the macho culture; the man silently drinks a lot and thinks about his situation. The night takes a bad turn when police officers enter the nightclub and look at Koemtzis' table and his girlfriend. In an argument outside the nightclub, Koemtzis finds out that his fiancée knows one of them. He takes that as a betrayal and his temper turns to violence. He strikes his girlfriend repeatedly while shouting "I say I love and you want to call the police?," making very clear that violence against women is considered an act of love. In the same scene, the bouncer observes the fight while smiling and not interfering. After the fight, Nikos is left alone in the club with his brother and orders more alcohol. The third male friend takes the women to their home and in a monologue, he explains how the woman is at fault for not supporting her man. He will not betray his friends like a woman and goes on to give a description of Koemtzis as a decent fellow—a "standup guy." Nikos is a man who speaks the truth and does not compromise. It is apparent that in the film Koemtzis is a hero of the people being crushed by the unjust regime. Koemtzis seems to believe that the police officers are there for him and describes how he was asked to become an informant, an offer he turned down. With images of men dancing and plates being broken on the dance floor, we reach the climax of the film. Koemtzis asks his brother to dance for him a *Paraggelia*. In a previous scene the announcer of the band has made clear that they accept orders and she instructed the rest of the patrons not to dance as the next song is an "order." Again, the singer announces the special order that was made by Koemtzis' younger brother and the song starts. In slow motion and again with the narration of Gogou (a poem about the harsh life on the fringes) the policemen stand up and dance during the special order. The slow-motion filming with selected freeze frames gives a very dramatic tone to the dishonor that is being committed. Combined with the powerful lyrics about the oppressed standing tall we are ready for what is being portrayed as fully justified violence. The film returns to normal speed and the singer repeats that this is a special order. A fight starts and the three policemen attack the young man. What we witness as the reason for the attack by Koemtzis are multiple attacks on his honor. The policemen have been disrespecting him all night long with their gazes and presence. They disrespected the "sacred" Zeibekiko and they unfairly attacked three on one. While we understand that Koemtzis is drunk, his vigilante response is not considered a mistake. His actions are well within the bounds of protecting one's honor. The end of the film is a final testament as to how popular culture interprets the patriarchy. In the courtroom Koemtzis fights his father and reprimands his brother. With lines like "I did what I did and as a man I will face the consequences" to his father and "Men don't cry" to his brother the final stand of this fictional Koemtzis is a testament to the macho culture of upholding your honor with no regard for your life.

The next film in our analysis is one by Pantelis Voulgaris, *Ola einai Dromos* (*Everything Is a Road*, 1998). This is an anthology film consisting of three short stories interconnected by the scenery of northern Greece and the portrayal of maleness. There is a clear connection between the two films. On the one hand, both take place in Northern Greece (Thessaloniki and the surrounding areas) and both use Rebetiko music. *Ola einai Dromos* is not in its entirety a vigilante film. The vigilantism portrayed in the second part (*The Last Dwarf Geese*) is quite different. However, the way Greek males are portrayed has similarities to the rest of the films we selected.

In the first story we meet a man (an archaeologist) whose son has committed suicide during his army service, in the second the main character is an everyday man, a guide in the protected wetland of the river Evros delta, and the last one a wealthy merchant who spends his money drinking and breaking plates in a nightclub. The common thread is that all three men are alone and have an inner pain that they cannot communicate. Also, for all of them alcohol is an important part of their lives (e.g., in the second story, alcohol is called the "foundation of everything"). All three are without their wives. We know that the wife of the archaeologist works in Brussels, the guide's wife for some reason is still in Hamburg, and the last man cheated on his wife and she left him.

It is interesting to note that women are very rare in the film. Even in the second part, where we have two female characters, their part is of minor importance. Women in the film are silent participants or sex objects. The film criticizes the way women from Bulgaria were brought to northern Greece as sex workers and the mistreatment they all faced. That is, however, secondary as the main focus is on how men grieve, drink, and act.

Our main focus is on the second story. A team of scientists is following the last geese. There were only five left but four had been killed, so this dwarf goose is the last chance to observe their migratory patterns. This setup exists to allow us to meet the guide, a man who was a hunter himself, but slowly explains how he quit hunting and how much he despises hunters now. He has a very strong distaste for non-licensed hunters who disrespect animals and nature. We see that this man in his solitude has replaced human contact with his love for nature. The realization that he is witnessing the end of a species takes a toll on him.

The character is brought to life through the amazing acting of Thanassis Veggos, a widely loved and very expressive comedic actor. His well-known facial expressions make us connect deeply with his pain that is still silent and numbed by alcohol and trivial stories. He seems to be unable to remain silent when in company, but his words are stories of limited or no importance for the rest. And then it happens, a hunter shoots down the last goose before she[55] can complete her journey. Our hero hears the shots of a gun prohibited for licensed hunters and exclaims, "Poachers, I have warned you not to mess with me." He sails alone to look for the goose and witnesses her end. He meets the poacher and poses as an old hunter; he is very friendly and, after having gained the poacher's trust, he shoots him with his own gun. There is no explanation, no elegant speech of why the poacher is being punished. A lonely man has taken upon himself to avenge, at least symbolically, the destruction of a species. There is no heroic speech, no celebration of the act. Our hero in a terrifyingly simple way takes a life and feels justified. His act is not a crime of passion. He is not under stress. It is not his "honor" that he reclaims through violence. It is pure vigilante justice, as for him nature and even more so the goose, Maria, is a friend murdered and subsequently avenged.

In a chronological order, the next movie is *Omiros* (*The Hostage*) directed by Konstantinos Giannaris in 2005, takes place again in northern Greece, and is inspired by true events that took place in Athens in 1998 and Thessaloniki in 1999. The main character of the film is an Albanian immigrant who hijacks a bus full of people. This film is very important as it tries to tackle a lot of issues in Greek society like racism, abuse, homophobia, and the abuse of power. Also, it is a comment on the common grounds of Albanian and Greek notions of honor and vendetta. Although it does not fall under the remit of this chapter, it should be noted that Cretans and Albanians have very similar notions of vigilantism.[56] The film's timeline is truncated and we see flashbacks and memories that slowly reveal the true reasons for what happens. In the film we have a series of actions that have to do with the notion of honor and payback. The main hero has been victimized in a number of ways by the Greek police, but this victimization is actually a punishment. Giannaris does an excellent job in portraying the racism against Albanians in the 1990s. His hero commits the "crime" of sleeping with a Greek man's wife. This man is also a police officer. The policeman's vengeance consists of setting up a "sting" operation to buy illegal guns. As viewers, we come to know that he is a corrupt cop who steals the weapons, destroys the papers of the protagonist, and beats him up. But that is not punishment enough. Our hero is a foreigner so, as in *The Iliad*, the dishonor of a Greek man has to be heavily punished. When he is arrested for being in the country with no papers, he is an "illegal," as the authorities like to term refugees and immigrants with no papers. The policemen punish him for the crime they really care about. They sexually abuse him and rape him with a bottle to punish him for bedding a Greek policeman's wife. The patriarchal norms are very clear in the film. The language consists of sexist slurs degrading women, gays, and of course the threat of sex as a means of punishment. The protagonist is so traumatized that when he remembers the abuse, he has a lisp. We have a vortex of crimes of honor. The outsider is punished for bedding a married woman. Again, the woman is considered property and thus an act of punishment is justified for the man. The Greek policeman also dishonors the protagonist by stealing from him and attacking him, but as a foreigner he gets crushed by the system and faces the further dishonor of sexual abuse.

However, our protagonist would not seek revenge, if his ordeal did not have an effect on his life in Albania. As a patriarchal society his homeland treats him as a lesser man because of the rape and he loses his fiancée. That is why he tries to get revenge. His plan is to punish the thief, expose the abuse, and reclaim his lost honor. His hostages align with him, they recognize the injustice and wish to help him by staying on the bus and talking to the police to stop the persecution of the man, but they ultimately fail. Since two patriarchal societies consider the protagonist a lesser man, he has no way of reclaiming his "honor" and in the end he is executed. His execution is again an act of vigilantism, despite being carried out by law enforcement agents. There is no real will to arrest him by the authorities and the policeman acts as judge and executioner just as family members do in a vendetta. Thus in the case of *Omiros*, we encounter a narrative that exposes the porous borders between vigilantism and official justice, under the "oppression" of the social norms of two patriarchal social structures.

The next film in our analysis is *O ehthros mou* (*The Enemy Within*) by Yorgos Tsemperopoulos. The "Enemy Within" is somewhat revealing about the internal struggle the protagonist goes through, while the original Greek title keeps that as a surprise for the viewer. The film reminds us a lot of the 1974 film "*Death Wish*"—an iconic movie about vigilantism. The protagonist is a peaceful, educated, liberal, middle to upper class man, whose life changes after a burglary in his house, for which he seeks to get revenge. An interesting similarity between the two movies is that both protagonists are seen in social situations taking a stand against guns and vigilantism and eventually become vigilantes themselves, making a statement for the disagreement about justice and punishment between liberals and conservatives. Before moving on to our analysis of the film, we should note that in both films—as well as in other titles—there is an apparent failure of the police force to stop both criminals and vigilantes.

The protagonist of the movie is Kostas, the father of the family. His life and especially his beliefs change after his home is invaded by a gang. The father tries to resist and gets beaten up and the younger child, the daughter, is raped. The rape is not portrayed but is heavily suggested and later admitted. The filming shows the inability of the father to deal with it. During the whole film the father does not speak about it with his daughter despite being tormented by it. Tsemperopoulos manages to present all the internal struggles of the Greek middle class. The peaceful father feels very guilty for his inability to protect his family, fortune, and especially his daughter, getting called on that by his racist father. As a patriarchal society, Greece still values the "honor" of women in regard to their sexual activity and virginity. Thus, the rape of a young girl is not judged on the severity of the crime but as a "loss of value." Women are still considered property and the majority of crimes of honor are based on this belief system.

The way Tsemperopoulos addresses this issue is impressive. We see a number of awkward silences, family arguments, and explosive fights. The family does not talk about the incident, especially about the rape, so the victims are unable to heal their trauma. Of course, the father figure has the major responsibility for that. Immediately after the home invasion he is angry and blames himself for his failure to protect the family—"his" family. In order to sleep he holds an old rifle to feel like a guard or sentinel.[57] The father is not alone in deciding to become a vigilante and execute the rapist. His descent into madness is suggested by a neighbor. The neighbor who claims to have also been a victim has installed an elaborate security system that provides information on the home invasion. The neighbor is clearly of a right-wing ideology and very elaborately explains his distrust of the authorities. He refuses to give information to the police but is strongly hints that the father should become a vigilante. The father tormented by his guilt eventually executes the man he believes is the rapist.

Completely unlike the protagonist in *Death Wish*, Tsemperopoulos' protagonist is now in fear of retribution from the gang of his victim. In the film the act of vengeance is one part of the hero's internal struggle. We witness how a victimized liberal, peaceful man is unable to handle fear, guilt, and his perception of societal values. Despite his liberalism he feels ashamed; he needs to keep the rape a secret and his family calls him on that. The film is a testament on how fragile masculinity really is and how misplaced are the patriarchal values.

The last film is the most recent one, a 2016 production titled *Eteros Ego* (*My Other Self*) directed by Sotiris Tsafoulias. The film is a crime/mystery drama, in which the police request the help of a brilliant criminologist to track down a serial killer. The murders follow a pattern based on Pythagorean ideas.[58] The reason we include this film is because the serial killer acts in order to avenge the death of a close friend and to punish all those who assisted in the cover-up. The serial killer is a woman, and even though that is quite original it does not affect the plot, but is a nice surprise to see on screen a female friendship strong enough to lead to vengeance, since the mainstream pattern—as we have seen up to now—is that the vigilantes portrayed are male.

The criminologist and the killer share a common experience—both of them have a loved one who was killed in a car accident. That connection makes the protagonist reluctant to pursue the serial killer. In a dialogue that brings memories of Antigone's decision to bury her brother in the tragedy by Sophocles, the hero states, "I know what my job is, what I wonder is what my obligation is." The disagreement with his mentor is on the subject of vigilantism and our hero brings forth the old question of law and ethics. At the end of the movie, the criminologist does not share all the information with the police, thus he is able to meet the killer and talk to her himself.

The end of the film clarifies the underlying question of the film and the protagonist. "If the law was just, there would be no room for interpretation," says the vigilante killer, and when asked about forgiveness she states that "it is God's job, not mine." The metaphysical dialogue about God is the attempt of our hero to find answers through the interpretation of the killer's actions. Instead, he is faced with an aphorism expressed by the killer: "I did what I had to do, now I do not care what happens to me; so now do what you have to." In a cyclical way, the end of this film is the same as of our first one (*Paraggelia*), only that the primarily male obligation to avenge, is now in the hands of a woman, who, as Antigone did, asks the question of legal versus ethical.

Representations of Vigilantism in Contemporary Greek Television

In 1999, a production of Mega Channel with the title *Vendetta* aired.[59] The action took place in the mountains of Mani, a part of southern Peloponnese also known for family feuds and vendettas. In this series a murder for reasons of honor revives an old vendetta on the village. It is very interesting to note the similarities, with aforementioned characters, in the portrayal of the protagonist (Sarantos) who murders his ex-business partner and friend (Elias) in order to protect his honor. In the first episode we see Sarantos portrayed as a psychologically and emotionally exhausted man, financially frustrated who drinks and does not share his pain, not even with his old mother. His financial issues can be arranged, if he asks for the help of his brother who lives abroad, but he is too proud to do that. We watch him as he goes to his ex-partner and they argue about whether he is owed money or not. Later on, Sarantos receives a message that he should meet his ex-partner and he will receive the support he needs. He then visits the house of his ex-friend Elias and we understand that he is secretly in love with Elias' wife. The friend is not there but out drinking with his mistress. Sarantos sees that and while both of them are drunk they fight. In the next scene the protagonist is waiting for his ex-friend and shoots him at point blank range and flees the village. In his eyes the murder is justified as it corrected the damage to his honor. The ex-friend disrespected him, did not act in what he considered a manly way, and was executed. After the murder the families recollect an older vendetta that they now consider active again and older people talk to the younger members of the family in order to take on the vendetta as a "real" man should. The traces of patriarchal mentality are very clear. A "real" man is strong, silent, and violent. The protection of what is considered honor is above all, above life and law. We must note that even though family values seem important and families stick together during a vendetta the acts of the men contradict those values. The protagonist does not care for his mother or for the widow and orphan child of his victim. They all must pay a price for his right to reclaim an elusive sense of honor. Again, we are faced with the same motifs in the song "Pote tha kanei ksasteria"; men decide and act, women and children pay the price.

The last show in this chapter is titled *Ti Psihi Tha Paradoseis Mori?* This strange title belongs to an interesting albeit canceled Greek TV series. In 2000 it aired six one-hour episodes and a seventh half hour one that tried to put an end to the canceled show. The title literally translates to "What soul will you deliver?" and the last word (mori) means stupid woman and is both an insult and a term of endearment depending on the context. The actual meaning is "in what shape will your soul be?" and is a commonly used phrase to criticize actions and thoughts that do not comply with social morality. The phrase is used of course for minor sins and the specific title adds comedic value.

The series seems to wish to make some political statements as it begins in the past during the military Junta regime period and cuts to our heroines. The writers make a very clear reference to a well-known economic scandal of that period (rotten meat supplies to the army). Also, the first episode closes with the line "on earth a woman is sexually or physically abused or harmed in other ways every 30 seconds." The story line is about four different women who as twelve-year-olds were in an orphanage and all of them were raped and abused by the villain of the series named Mantas. We see them live completely different lifestyles, but all of them are still in different kinds of abusive relationships. When they learn that their tormentor has come back to the country and is considered a philanthropist who cares for abused children, they decide to kill him. The show is a situation comedy where four different frightened women try to become killers to avenge their past and protect society from this monster.

Despite the show being a comedy and the plot evolving around failed attempts to execute their plan, they merit worthwhile comments. First, it is one of rare cases that women are the vigilantes. Traditionally, in Greek culture the man is responsible for avenging the wrongdoings against him and his family. Vendettas only include male members of the family. On the same note, the heroines are not consumed by the idea of revenge, they are living their lives and what drives them to their decision is the shock of their tormentor's return. It is a clear statement of the show of how women are still not believed and sexual abuse goes unpunished. Interestingly enough, their decision to take revenge seems to give them strength to act against the everyday abuse from their families. Their lives can be described as being in a state of learned helplessness and their trauma keeps messing up their lives, but their decision gradually converts them to autonomous persons—or it would, had the series not been canceled.[60] As a comment on how sexual abuse is handled, our heroines know that they cannot go to the police. They know that no one will believe them. It is a clear statement of women with no voice in a patriarchal society. On the other hand, when they are at a turning point where they may fail and die, one of them uses a tape recorder to explain all. In her actions we see that women feel they have more chance to be heard after their death.

A second interesting point is that in this show the women do not address their rape as a loss of honor as it happens in texts that promote the patriarchal line of thought. They want to punish their abuser in order to reclaim their right to not be afraid and to be respected. Once they call it a crime of honor, "It is not a crime of revenge, it is a crime of honor and you know what honor I mean." Their honor has not been lost by the acts of the abuser (like the hero of *Hostage* feels). Their lost honor is the fear and shame they live with. For the four women their trauma is a source of fear and insecurity, it is the reason they cannot break free from other abusers. When one of them asks their leader, "What will change if we kill him?" the answer sets the tone: "Everything will be different, we will not be afraid anymore and they will respect us."

CONCLUSION

In the current chapter we have sought to depict characteristic instances of vigilantism in the audiovisual production of contemporary Greek popular culture. We started off by discussing different approaches to the notion of vigilantism and socio-political causes for its existence, especially in contemporary societies. Among them, Greece stands as a prominent example in terms of its long tradition in vigilante practices under customary law (e.g., the vendetta in Crete and Mani[61]). Notions of honor and shame that are tied up with a family are at the root of this kind of retaliation. Intense quarrels, disputes, political and property issues trigger reactions and provoke self-determined "justice." This social condition is diachronically depicted over time in various genres of Greece's cultural production (e.g., ancient tragedies, poems, folk songs, and more recently audiovisual products). The cases of vigilantism depicted in the Greek cultural production, fall mainly under the rationale of perpetrating a wrong in order to preserve the personal/family honor and to punish a perceived wrongdoing, creating a morally ambiguous situation,[62] predominantly aiming at "punishing" an accomplished crime.[63]

After our qualitative content analysis on selected audiovisual content of the contemporary Greek pop culture (both in cinema and television), we have shown that representations of vigilantism in popular culture incorporate mainly the basic values of patriarchal societies and masculinity. Representations of strong, silent men who take the law into their own hands or who avenge an injustice are dominant. The vigilante action is tied with the notion of honor, making it almost a male prerogative and obligation.

At the same time, those representations of masculinity also support the patriarchal ideas of male superiority. By portraying vigilantism as an ethical obligation, primarily of men, popular culture exemplifies the use of male attributes as the norm. Vigilantism and masculinity are communicating vessels that both promote the hegemonic model of masculine domination. The justification of violence as well as the separation of male and females in the social space appears to be dominant in popular culture despite some exceptions to the rule (e.g., *Eteros Ego, Ti Psihi Tha Paradoseis Mori?*). We can identify that in those mechanisms of social training that Bourdieu identified, we need to add popular culture as an important structural support of the patriarchic values.

As to the future, the current research can and should be expanded to other contemporary content genres (poetry, literature, music) in order to depict in a more systematic way the major tendencies, in terms of vigilantism, appearing in the Greek popular culture. This would allow the establishment of more robust links between contemporary cultural production and the socio-political structure and tradition. It would enhance the connection between the attribution of specific gender roles and consequent "obligations" in the implementation of acts of vigilante justice.

NOTES

1. Jim Handy, "Chicken Thieves, Witches, and Judges: Vigilante Justice and Customary Law in Guatemala," *Journal of Latin American Studies* 36, no. 3 (2004): 533.

2. Christine M. McDermott and Monica K. Miller, "Individual Differences Impact Support for Vigilante Justice," *Journal of Aggression, Conflict and Peace Research* 8, no. 3 (2016): 194.

3. Yuliya Zabyelina, "Vigilante Justice and Informal Policing in Post-Euromaidan Ukraine," *Post-Soviet Affairs* 35, no. 4 (2019): 2.

4. Varvara Vagianou and Despoina Tzani, "The Multiple Faces of Vigilantism," *Crime Times*, January 24, 2019, https://www.crimetimes.gr/τα-πολλά-πρόσωπα-της-αυτοδικίας/.

5. Zabyelina, "Vigilante Justice and Informal Policing in Post-Euromaidan Ukraine," 6; Vagianou and Tzani, "The Multiple Faces of Vigilantism"; Aristides Tsantiropoulos, "Vendetta in Central-Northern Crete: Family Conflicts and Social Organisation" (PhD thesis, University of the Aegean, Department of Social Anthropology, 2000).

6. Tsantiropoulos, "Vendetta in Central-Northern Crete: Family Conflicts and Social Organisation"; Manfred Berg and Simon Wendt, "Lynching from an International Perspective," in *Globalizing Lynching History: Vigilantism and Extralegal Punishment from an International Perspective*, ed. Manfred Berg and Simon Wendt (New York: Palgrave Macmillan, 2011), 1–18; Justice Tankebe and Muhammad Asif, "Police Legitimacy and Support for Vigilante Violence in Pakistan," *International Journal of Comparative and Applied Criminal Justice* 40, no. 4 (2016): 343–62; Vagianou and Tzani, "The Multiple Faces of Vigilantism."

7. Berg and Wendt, "Lynching from an International Perspective," 5–6.

8. Zabyelina, "Vigilante Justice and Informal Policing in Post-Euromaidan Ukraine," 3.

9. Thomas M. Tripp, Robert J. Bies, and Karl Aquino, "A Vigilante Model of Justice: Revenge, Reconciliation, Forgiveness, and Avoidance," *Social Justice Research* 20, no. 1 (2007): 19.

10. Zabyelina, "Vigilante Justice and Informal Policing in Post-Euromaidan Ukraine," 2.

11. Mark Button, *Private Policing* (Cullompton, Devon, UK: Willan Publishing, 2002).

12. Berg and Wendt, "Lynching from an International Perspective," 8; Zabyelina, "Vigilante Justice and Informal Policing in Post-Euromaidan Ukraine," 2–3.

13. Tsantiropoulos, "Vendetta in Central-Northern Crete: Family Conflicts and Social Organisation."

14. Ami Pedahzur and Arie Perliger, "The Causes of Vigilante Political Violence: The Case of Jewish Settlers," *Civil Wars* 6, no. 3 (2003): 9–30.

15. Christos Vrakopoulos and Daphne Halikiopoulou, "Vigilantism in Greece: The Case of the Golden Dawn," in *Vigilantism against Migrants and Minorities*, ed. Tore Bjørgo and Miroslav Mareš (Abingdon, Oxon: Routledge, 2019), 183–98.

16. Walter T. Howard, "Vigilante Justice and National Reaction: The 1937 Tallahassee Double Lynching," *The Florida Historical Quarterly* 67, no. 1 (1988): 32–51; Tripp, Bies, and Aquino, "A Vigilante Model of Justice"; McDermott and Miller, "Individual Differences Impact Support for Vigilante Justice."

17. Rosenbaum and Sederberg (1974) 556.H. Jon Rosenbaum and Peter C. Sederberg, eds., *Vigilante Politics* (Philadelphia: University of Pennsylvania Press, 1976), 556.

18. Zabyelina, "Vigilante Justice and Informal Policing in Post-Euromaidan Ukraine," 2–3.

19. Les Johnston, "What Is Vigilantism?," *The British Journal of Criminology* 36, no. 2 (1996): 228.

20. Zabyelina, "Vigilante Justice and Informal Policing in Post-Euromaidan Ukraine," 3.

21. Stella C. Chia, "Seeking Justice on the Web: How News Media and Social Norms Drive the Practice of Cyber Vigilantism," *Social Science Computer Review* 38, no. 6 (2019): 655–72.

22. McDermott and Miller, "Individual Differences Impact Support for Vigilante Justice," 188.

23. Richard M. Brown, *Strain of Violence: Historical Studies of American Violence and Vigilantism* (New York: Oxford University Press, 1975), vii; Tsantiropoulos, "Vendetta in Central-Northern Crete: Family Conflicts and Social Organisation," 18.

24. Tsantiropoulos, "Vendetta in Central-Northern Crete: Family Conflicts and Social Organisation," 22.

25. Berg and Wendt, "Lynching from an International Perspective," 5–6; McDermott and Miller, "Individual Differences Impact Support for Vigilante Justice," 187.

26. Vagianou and Tzani, "The Multiple Faces of Vigilantism."

27. Nicholas Rush Smith, *Contradictions of Democracy: Vigilantism and Rights in Post-Apartheid South Africa* (Oxford: Oxford University Press, 2019), 6.

28. Berg and Wendt, "Lynching from an International Perspective," 5–6.

29. Smith, *Contradictions of Democracy*, 6.

30. Zabyelina, "Vigilante Justice and Informal Policing in Post-Euromaidan Ukraine," 5.

31. Zabyelina, 5.

32. Smith, *Contradictions of Democracy*, 6.

33. Handy, "Chicken Thieves, Witches, and Judges," 533; Judith Matloff and Katie Orlinsky, "Mexico: Vigilante Justice," *World Policy Journal* 31, no. 1 (March 1, 2014): 58–69, https://doi.org/10.1177/0740277514529718; Smith, *Contradictions of Democracy*, 6.

34. Berg and Wendt, "Lynching from an International Perspective," 5–6.

35. Danielle Carter Kushner, "Nonstate Security and Political Participation: Reinforcing Ruling Party Support in South Africa," *Africa Today* 62, no. 1 (2015): 107–35, https://doi.org/10.2979/africatoday.62.1.107.

36. Jason Hickel, *Democracy as Death: The Moral Order of Anti-Liberal Politics in South Africa* (Oakland: University of California Press, 2015).

37. Laurent Fourchard, "The Politics of Mobilization for Security in South African Townships," *African Affairs* 110, no. 441 (August 16, 2011): 607–27, https://doi.org/10.1093/afraf/adr046; Laurent Fourchard, "Security and Party Politics in Cape Town," *Geoforum*, SI - Party Politics, the Poor and the City: Reflections from South

Africa, 43, no. 2 (March 1, 2012): 199–206, https://doi.org/10.1016/j.geoforum.2011.12.002.

38. Smångs (2016), Smith (2019) 7. Mattias Smångs, "Doing Violence, Making Race: Southern Lynching and White Racial Group Formation," *American Journal of Sociology* 121, no. 5 (March 2016): 1329–74, https://doi.org/10.1086/684438; Smith, *Contradictions of Democracy*, 7.

39. Pierre Bourdieu, *Masculine Domination*, trans. Richard Nice (Stanford: Stanford University Press, 2001).

40. Chris Haywood and Máirtín Mac an Ghaill, *Men and Masculinities: Theory, Research, and Social Practice* (Buckingham: Open University Press, 2003).

41. Dimitris A. Xiritakis, *An Affair of Honor: Cretan Vendetta Stories* (Athens: Melani, 2011).

42. Neil Postman, *Amusing Ourselves to Death: Public Discourse in the Age of Show Business*, twentieth ed. (New York: Penguin Books, 2006).

43. Tsantiropoulos, "Vendetta in Central-Northern Crete: Family Conflicts and Social Organisation," 21.

44. Zabyelina, "Vigilante Justice and Informal Policing in Post-Euromaidan Ukraine," 2.

45. John Fiske, *Television Culture*, second ed. (London; New York: Routledge, 2011); Postman, *Amusing Ourselves to Death*.

46. Tsantiropoulos, "Vendetta in Central-Northern Crete: Family Conflicts and Social Organisation," 4.

47. Tsantiropoulos, 18.

48. Vagianou and Tzani, "The Multiple Faces of Vigilantism."

49. Tsantiropoulos, "Vendetta in Central-Northern Crete: Family Conflicts and Social Organisation," 10.

According to Article 331 of the Greek Common Penal Code, which defines the concept of vigilantism: "Anyone who arbitrarily claims a right which (s)he actually possesses or believes (s)he possesses shall be punished with imprisonment of up to six months or with a fine. Prosecution is exercised only after charges have been pressed. The punishment scheme may change in the cases of the co-existence of another crime along with the one of vigilantism, e.g., homicide. On top of that, Greece has a rather strict legal framework regarding gun ownership and use. Law 4678/2020 that introduces several changes to law 2168/1993-in order to align the Greek national law with the relevant EU directive-, expands the meaning of what constitutes a weapon, including objects that do not belong to the 'standard' concept of a weapon, i.e., an object that fires bullets at high speed, causing death. The concept of a weapon therefore includes, in addition to the classic items such as revolvers, pistols, semi-automatic and automatic weapons, rifles, shotguns and air-guns, all items that are suitable for attack or defense. A weapon according to the law is anything that is capable of harming the human body and causing serious injury or even death (e.g. knives of all kinds, swords, spears, weapons with taser type electricity, bows, swords, bats, folding knives, spear guns, pepper sprays etc.). Knives that are justified for educational use, fishing, hunting, or home use are not considered weapons. Prohibition of possession of firearms includes not only weapons (as previously defined), but also the necessary components for their use, as well as explosives and relevant mechanisms. Mufflers, replicas that can be turned into real weapons, telescopic sights, grenades, ammunition cartridges and any essential part of a weapon or its spare part are prohibited. Weapons components that are not necessary for their operation are not considered weapons, such as a rifle harness.

The import of weapons is allowed only for special purposes and for special types of weapons and with permission from the authorities. Weapons allowed under strict conditions are, for example, the weapon used by the starter in races, the sword of the swordsman, the special devices that drive the birds out of the airports, the revolver that fires flares for SOS signal etc. The export of weapons is also prohibited.

The trade of firearms is strictly prohibited, revolvers and pistols are sold with special permission and to persons who either serve in positions where guns are allowed, e.g., police officers or are under serious threat, such as owners of jewelry stores who have repeatedly received firearms. These firearms licenses are issued sparingly, after very strict scrutiny of the applicants. The final decision is taken by the Prosecutor. Air guns are freely sold to people over 18 years of age and shotguns to those who have a hunting license. It is generally illegal to possess a weapon, unless the holder holds a special permit from the relevant police authority. The person who legally possesses a weapon must keep it in a safe and inaccessible place, have the ammunition kept separate from the weapon, always have the weapon empty, disassembled and not give it to third parties. In addition, anyone who finds a weapon must hand it over immediately to the nearest police station. The owner of a shotgun is obliged to have a relevant permit from the police and to have undergone a physical and mental medical examination.

Unintentional shootings are not allowed and are an independent crime. Illegal carrying, possession and use of firearms are misdemeanors (punishable by imprisonment of up to 5 years) independent of the crime committed through them e.g., attempted murder, homicide, robbery, grievous bodily harm, etc. That is, in the indictment of a robbery, in addition to article 380 of the Penal Code on robbery, there will also be illegal carrying, possession and use of weapons" (https://www.e-nomothesia.gr/kat-opla-ekrektika-puromakhika/nomos-4678-2020-phek-70a-20-3-2020.html-last accessed 4 August 2020, https://www.kamouzis.gr/nomos-peri-oplwn-oploforia-oplokatoxi-oploxrhsia/-last accessed 4 August 2020).

50. Vagianou and Tzani, "The Multiple Faces of Vigilantism."

51. Vagianou and Tzani. The Greek Penal system discriminates between vendetta (vigilantism) and self-defense. For self-defense, the provision of the law is quite clear. We quote Article 22 of the Penal Code, which refers to the case of Defense:

1. The act performed in case of defense is not unfair.

2. Defense is the necessary action against the attacker which an individual undertakes, in order to defend himself or any other from an unjust and present attack directed against them.

3. The necessity of defense is judged by the threat rate of the attack, by the type of the threatened damage, by the manner and intensity of the attack and by the other circumstances.

In each case under scrutiny, the one who invokes the state of defense must prove that he is under attack and "responds" to an attack that is in progress. The ex-post attack falls rather within the context of vigilantism, as it is conducted for revenge (https://www.alfavita.gr/koinonia/268684_pote-mia-biaii-energeia-entassetai-sto-plaisio-tis-aytoamynas-symfona-me-ton-nomo-last accessed 4 August 2020).

52. Xiritakis, *An Affair of Honor: Cretan Vendetta Stories*.

53. Margrit Schreier, *Qualitative Content Analysis in Practice* (Los Angeles: Sage, 2012).

54. During the Greek Junta, Greek folk music labeled "traditional" coexisted with classical music as a sign of culture. In 1981 the year that PASOK took power a choice was made to support the culture of Bouzoukia and Rebetiko in order to distinguish the new socialist era from the past. As a result, the music of the fringes became mainstream. For more on that both on the history of Greek TV and the presence of bouzoukia on mainstream TV and cinema, please see Nickos Myrtou, Stamatis Poulakidakos, and Panagiota Nakou, "Greece," in *A Transnational Study of Law and Justice on TV*, ed. Peter Robson and Jennifer L. Schulz (Oxford: Hart, 2016), 113–30.

55. We do not really know the sex of the bird but we know the team named the bird Maria to honor the scientist's mother, a common practice in Greece to give to the offspring the name of a grandparent especially if the grandparent is not alive.

56. If Bourdieu's analysis of the masculine hegemony is not enough to notice the similarities in Balkan and Mediterranean countries, then for a deeper understanding of the similarities of the Greek and Albanian vigilante traditions and practices one should read: Margaret Hasluck, *The Unwritten Law in Albania* (Cambridge: Cambridge University Press, 2015); Tsantiropoulos, "Vendetta in Central-Northern Crete: Family Conflicts and Social Organisation"; Aristides Tsantiropoulos, *The Vendetta in the Contemporary Mountainous Central Crete* (Athens: Plethron, 2004); Efi Avdela, *For Reasons of Honour: Violence, Emotions and Values in Post-Civil War Greece* (Athens: Nefeli, 2002); Xiritakis, *An Affair of Honor: Cretan Vendetta Stories*.

57. It worth noting that the gun he embraces is not functional so the scene consists of an excellent metaphor on feelings of impotence and guns as phallic symbols.

58. The title is a Pythagorean expression for a friend being considered your other self.

59. Note that in 1986 the public channel ERT also premiered a show called "Vendetta," later titled as "Revenge" in a replay, since the series aired also in mid 1990s. It is a murder mystery that examines if the murder of a Greek American took place because of an old Cretan vendetta. Despite the title, vendetta was just a red herring and the crime had nothing to do with it.

60. Aristotelis Rigas the screenwriter/director has disclosed his complete plan of the women taking revenge and then driven by guilt they confess and finally in the court the truth comes out and the society treats them as heroines and not criminals. The plot was firstly revealed in an interview in the newspaper *Ta Nea* and since then has been partially reproduced in various website. See for example: https://menshouse.gr/sires-tenies/48965/ti-psychi-tha-paradosis-mori-afto-itan-anatreptiko-finale-tis-siras-pou-den-idame-pote accessed on June 2021.

61. Vagianou and Tzani, "The Multiple Faces of Vigilantism."

62. McDermott and Miller, "Individual Differences Impact Support for Vigilante Justice," 188.
63. Zabyelina, "Vigilante Justice and Informal Policing in Post-Euromaidan Ukraine."

BIBLIOGRAPHY

Avdela, Efi. *For Reasons of Honour: Violence, Emotions and Values in Post-Civil War Greece*. Athens: Nefeli, 2002.

Berg, Manfred, and Simon Wendt. "Lynching from an International Perspective." In *Globalizing Lynching History: Vigilantism and Extralegal Punishment from an International Perspective*, edited by Manfred Berg and Simon Wendt, 1–18. New York: Palgrave Macmillan, 2011.

Bourdieu, Pierre. *Masculine Domination*. Translated by Richard Nice. Stanford: Stanford University Press, 2001.

Brown, Richard M. *Strain of Violence: Historical Studies of American Violence and Vigilantism*. New York: Oxford University Press, 1975.

Button, Mark. *Private Policing*. Cullompton, Devon, UK: Willan Publishing, 2002.

Chia, Stella C. "Seeking Justice on the Web: How News Media and Social Norms Drive the Practice of Cyber Vigilantism." *Social Science Computer Review* 38, no. 6 (2019): 655–72.

Fiske, John. *Television Culture*. Second ed. London; New York: Routledge, 2011.

Fourchard, Laurent. "Security and Party Politics in Cape Town." *Geoforum*, SI - Party Politics, the Poor and the City: Reflections from South Africa, 43, no. 2 (March 1, 2012): 199–206. https://doi.org/10.1016/j.geoforum.2011.12.002.

———. "The Politics of Mobilization for Security in South African Townships." *African Affairs* 110, no. 441 (August 16, 2011): 607–27. https://doi.org/10.1093/afraf/adr046.

Handy, Jim. "Chicken Thieves, Witches, and Judges: Vigilante Justice and Customary Law in Guatemala." *Journal of Latin American Studies* 36, no. 3 (2004): 533–61.

Hasluck, Margaret. *The Unwritten Law in Albania*. Cambridge: Cambridge University Press, 2015.

Haywood, Chris, and Máirtín Mac an Ghaill. *Men and Masculinities: Theory, Research, and Social Practice*. Buckingham: Open University Press, 2003.

Hickel, Jason. *Democracy as Death: The Moral Order of Anti-Liberal Politics in South Africa*. Oakland: University of California Press, 2015.

Howard, Walter T. "Vigilante Justice and National Reaction: The 1937 Tallahassee Double Lynching." *The Florida Historical Quarterly* 67, no. 1 (1988): 32–51.

Johnston, Les. "What Is Vigilantism?" *The British Journal of Criminology* 36, no. 2 (1996): 220–36.

Kushner, Danielle Carter. "Nonstate Security and Political Participation: Reinforcing Ruling Party Support in South Africa." *Africa Today* 62, no. 1 (2015): 107–35. https://doi.org/10.2979/africatoday.62.1.107.

Matloff, Judith, and Katie Orlinsky. "Mexico: Vigilante Justice." *World Policy Journal* 31, no. 1 (March 1, 2014): 58–69. https://doi.org/10.1177/0740277514529718.

McDermott, Christine M., and Monica K. Miller. "Individual Differences Impact Support for Vigilante Justice." *Journal of Aggression, Conflict and Peace Research* 8, no. 3 (2016): 186–96.

Myrtou, Nickos, Stamatis Poulakidakos, and Panagiota Nakou. "Greece." In *A Transnational Study of Law and Justice on TV*, edited by Peter Robson and Jennifer L. Schulz, 113–30. Oxford: Hart, 2016.

Pedahzur, Ami, and Arie Perliger. "The Causes of Vigilante Political Violence: The Case of Jewish Settlers." *Civil Wars* 6, no. 3 (2003): 9–30.

Postman, Neil. *Amusing Ourselves to Death: Public Discourse in the Age of Show Business*. Twentieth ed. New York: Penguin Books, 2006.

Rosenbaum, H. Jon, and Peter C. Sederberg, eds. *Vigilante Politics*. Philadelphia: University of Pennsylvania Press, 1976.

Schreier, Margrit. *Qualitative Content Analysis in Practice*. Los Angeles: Sage, 2012.

Smångs, Mattias. "Doing Violence, Making Race: Southern Lynching and White Racial Group Formation." *American Journal of Sociology* 121, no. 5 (March 2016): 1329–74. https://doi.org/10.1086/684438.

Smith, Nicholas Rush. *Contradictions of Democracy: Vigilantism and Rights in Post-Apartheid South Africa*. Oxford: Oxford University Press, 2019.

Tankebe, Justice, and Muhammad Asif. "Police Legitimacy and Support for Vigilante Violence in Pakistan." *International Journal of Comparative and Applied Criminal Justice* 40, no. 4 (2016): 343–62.

Tripp, Thomas M., Robert J. Bies, and Karl Aquino. "A Vigilante Model of Justice: Revenge, Reconciliation, Forgiveness, and Avoidance." *Social Justice Research* 20, no. 1 (2007): 10–34.

Tsantiropoulos, Aristides. *The Vendetta in the Contemporary Mountainous Central Crete*. Athens: Plethron, 2004.

———. "Vendetta in Central-Northern Crete: Family Conflicts and Social Organisation." PhD thesis, University of the Aegean, Department of Social Anthropology, 2000.

Vagianou, Varvara, and Despoina Tzani. "The Multiple Faces of Vigilantism." *Crime Times*, January 24, 2019. https://www.crimetimes.gr/τα-πολλά-πρόσωπα-της-αυτοδικίας/.

Vrakopoulos, Christos, and Daphne Halikiopoulou. "Vigilantism in Greece: The Case of the Golden Dawn." In *Vigilantism against Migrants and Minorities*, edited by Tore Bjørgo and Miroslav Mareš, 183–98. Abingdon, Oxon: Routledge, 2019.

Xiritakis, Dimitris A. *An Affair of Honor: Cretan Vendetta Stories*. Athens: Melani, 2011.

Zabyelina, Yuliya. "Vigilante Justice and Informal Policing in Post-Euromaidan Ukraine." *Post-Soviet Affairs* 35, no. 4 (2019): 277–92.

Chapter 7

Vigilantes, the Law and Popular Culture
The Italian Experience

Ferdinando Spina

The objective of this chapter is to provide a historical and cultural understanding of the Italian tradition of private justice and vigilantism. The concerns that form the background to this analysis, on a broader socio-legal and criminological level, are linked to the rise of certain troubling phenomena, specifically certain opinions on private justice that are becoming increasingly frequent in public and legal discourse and social practices in Italy.

As Zimring[1] points out, "the vigilante content of policies or behavior is a matter of interpretation, and such interpretations can always be contested. In that important sense, vigilantism, like beauty, is always in the eye of the beholder." This fine simile confirms the utility of studying narratives of private revenge and more generally law and criminal justice in popular culture.[2] This is also aimed at avoiding that the analysis is conditioned only by current political events and recent trends in media representation.

In the first part, I will outline some examples of the different patterns of private justice, whether individual or in groups, which can be traced in Italian history from Unification to the present day. I will also try to link these tendencies with the wider political, social, and legal context in which actual vigilante justice occurs. In the second part, I will review the themes of vendetta and do-it-yourself justice in Italian popular culture. The starting point will be literature and theater, after which I will focus on mass culture as exemplified by cinema and television.

VIGILANTE JUSTICE IN ITALY: HISTORY, EXAMPLES, AND LAW

In Italy, the earliest example of a group of private citizens formally recognized by the public authorities to maintain public order is the Citizens Patrols Corps, established in Bologna in 1828.[3] Originally, the corps consisted mainly of nobility and professions, not "a civic guard but rather a loose collection of Bologna's better citizens out to protect their property."[4] Over the years, the Citizens Patrols obtained free weapons' licenses and supported the police in some crime-fighting activities until 1986.

The creation of the Kingdom of Italy in 1861 marked the beginning of the gradual process of the establishment of a modern state. According to the classic definition of Max Weber, a state is an organization that has a monopoly on the legitimate use of violence within a specific territory.[5] One of the areas of greatest conflict between the state and social groups is criminal law and, as far as we are concerned, the punishment of homicide, even in cases of private or collective revenge. The control of the state takes place typically in a centrifugal process, from the urban areas to the most remote rural areas of the country.[6] In Italy, in the inland areas of Sardinia, Calabria, or Apulia, forms of private justice such as vendettas and feuds have been practiced, in increasingly less frequent cases, up to the present day.

In the absence of dedicated statistical data, the incidence of state control over violence and private justice can be deduced from the homicide rate. In the nineteenth century, the homicide rate in Italy was higher than the average of European countries: between 1850 and 1874, it was 12 per 100,000 of the population. With the establishment of the national state, between 1875 and 1899, the rate dropped to 5.5 per 100,000.[7] For Eisner, the drop appears to be related to the decline of private revenge and the vendetta. The homicide rate progressively decreased in the following decades until the 1970s, except in some periods of serious social tension, such as the beginning of the century and the years immediately following the two World Wars.[8]

Between the end of the nineteenth and the beginning of the twentieth century, class conflict was very acute. In this context of social unrest, the action of the state seemed ineffective in maintaining public order and protecting the conflicting interests according to the guarantees of the rule of law. A wide-ranging legal debate was therefore opened, especially by positivist jurists, on the need to extend the constraints that the liberal penal code in force, the so-called Zanardelli Code, provided for the use of arms by private citizens, self-defense, and the formation of armed corps.[9] Several legislative changes and court decisions recognized an ever-increasing space for the action of private groups of armed guards, night watchmen, and rural guards. As a result, a profound political, legal and cultural ambivalence developed over the boundaries between state justice and private justice. This allowed armed groups of citizens born to defend the interests of local elites to start daily actions of intimidation against workers and to repress strikes directly by force of arms.[10]

The postwar phase was even more dramatically turbulent. The "Red Biennium" of 1919 and 1920 saw continuous strikes in the cities and the countryside, and the electoral growth, both nationally and locally, of the Socialist Party. Workers' demands increased the middle class apprehension of imminent revolution. The level of private violence escalated dramatically, while public authorities were unable to maintain order and security. In these years, the vigilante squads already operating in rural areas of some regions in defense of the agrarian elites constituted the basis on which fascist "squadrismo" was formed.[11] This can be seen with the Association for Social Defense case in Bologna, which in 1920 merged into the "Bolognese fascio."[12]

The shift from vigilantism to violent political para-military squads constitutes a peculiar trait of the historical configuration of social, institutional, and cultural factors that Italy experienced in that period. According to Clark,[13] "squadrismo" is an indigenous Italian tradition closely linked to vigilantism. "Squadrismo" was crucial to the political rise of Fascism but, with the establishment of the dictatorship in 1925, it was gradually regimented while public order was controlled by the police and prefectures.[14] The Criminal Code introduced under the fascist regime, the so-called Rocco Code, although amended several times, is still in force in Italy.[15] Compared to the previous liberal penal statutes, it extended the right of defense for those attacked as far as killing the aggressor, provided it was proportionate as between the offense and the defense.

Between 1943 and 1948, in the transition from the collapse of the fascist regime to the establishment of the new Republican State, numerous episodes of private justice, such as lynching, extrajudicial trials, and private vendettas, were carried out against fascists or collaborationists.[16] These acts were a reaction to the brutal violence that many individuals and communities had suffered during the years of the regime and the Nazi occupation. Emblematic in this respect was the lynching in Rome of Donato Carretta, the prison warden, during the trial of the fascist police chief in 1944.[17] The incident was filmed by Luchino Visconti for the documentary *Giorni di gloria* (*Days of Glory*, 1945) on the Italian Resistance. In the end, the lynching scenes were cut since such furious collective revenge against a scapegoat was not acceptable for the new democracy that was intended to be established after the war.[18]

In the postwar period, Italy embarked on a path of steady decline in crime and violence.[19] Between 1950 and the mid-1970s, the homicide rate was 1.3 per 100,000 population, becoming after centuries comparable to that of other Western European countries.[20] Although the southern regions still experienced, in addition to serious organized crime and banditry, cases of feuding and blood revenge, Eisner points out that by 1950 their occurrence had become massively reduced.[21] However, still in 1960, a brutal lynching of a vagrant took place in a small town in the Po Valley.[22]

The 1970s saw a sudden upsurge in crime rates, including an increase in homicides, due to political violence and terrorism.[23] A strong distrust of state institutions and their representatives emerged in public opinion. The emergence of the Italian vigilante films, to which we will return in the next section, is a vivid consequence of the anxieties of Italians at that juncture. The increase in criminality and political violence provoked the reaction of vigilante citizen groups. In Bologna, the Citizens Patrols carried out controversial actions patrolling the city in place of the police.[24] Projects to set up citizens' patrols were initiated in other large Italian cities such as Rome or Milan, although they were never formally approved.[25]

In the early 1980s, when the dramatic phase of terrorism was over, a new crime emergency arose with the Mafia and the Camorra. Faced with the serious threat of these powerful and violent criminal organizations, Italian public opinion turned to the police and especially the judiciary to uphold legality and justice. In those years, cinema and television offered very popular figures of policeman or magistrate vigilante.

In the 1990s, fear of crime became an increasingly political issue. In the main cities of northern Italy, neighborhood committees were set up whose activities ranged, to this day, between forms of neighborhood watch and vigilantism against immigrants, prostitution, drug dealing, and urban decay.[26] Local councils signed agreements with voluntary associations such as the City Angels.[27] The "green shirts" of the right-wing and secessionist party *Lega Nord* militants also appeared in those years. Since then, neighborhood watch patrols' activities have been generally politically framed and improperly designate in the public debate with the term "ronde," reminiscent of the dreadful antecedent of "squadrismo." Furthermore, it has become one of the flagships of the electoral propaganda and government program of right-wing parties.

Two controversial legislative measures were introduced in response to the social demand for tackling crime: they are paradigmatic examples of Jonathan Simon's concept of "governing through crime."[28] The first one was Law 59/2006 reforming self-defense. It introduced a presumption of proportionality in cases of unlawful entry into domestic premises but only in the case of an actual danger of physical attack. The second one was Law 94/2009, which, as part of a broad symbolic response to the crime issue, provided the cooperation between unarmed groups of volunteer observers and mayors or law enforcement agencies in order to report damage to urban security and situations of social unease. Despite the bitter controversy, the two laws were not a legalization of vigilantism.[29] The much-feared "ronde" replacing or flanking police as vigilante groups have never taken off. Rather, hundreds of civic agreements between citizens committees and local administrations have been signed seeming to reduce the level of anti-social behavior and the fear of crime.[30]

However, in recent years, there have been few but significant incidents of aggressive vigilantism and downright violence with predominantly ethnic and racial motivations. Especially between 2007 and 2008, there were reprisals against crimes committed or blamed on foreigners and Roma.[31] In some large cities, groups of Italians carried out some beatings, attempted lynchings, assaults with Molotov cocktails, and fires in Roma camps.[32] In the suburbs, groups of citizens, lamenting the negligence of institutions in contrasting perceived criminality of the Roma, organize night watch patrols.[33] Riding the wave of fear of crime and foreigners, right-wing extremists try to legitimize themselves by vigilante actions such as the "security walks," also relying on the symbolic legacy of fascist "squadrismo."[34] More generally, hate crimes recorded by police motivated by racism and xenophobia are increasing.[35] Nevertheless, this increase reflects positive changes in police recording practices and a greater public awareness of racist incidents. Vigilantism against foreigners is currently an alarming event but, in my opinion, it is under control by the police and the judiciary.

In Italy nowadays, we see contradictory trends. On the one hand, the homicide rate is 0.57 per 100,000 inhabitants, among the lowest in the EU Member States, while predatory crimes have been steadily decreasing since 2014.[36] On the other hand, the level of trust in Parliament, in the judicial system, and in political parties remains very low, while trust in police is higher.[37] There is a more favorable attitude toward the possession and use of weapons by private citizens.[38] Moreover, according to a 2018 poll carried out by the *Corriere della Sera*, the leading national newspaper, more than half of Italians seem to believe that recourse to personal defense is always legitimate.[39]

However, in Italian courts between 2013 and 2016, there were ten trials for self-defense (and five for negligent excess of self-defense),[40] a negligible number out of the total number of over 1.3 million pending criminal proceedings.[41] Yet again, Law 36/2019 amends the Criminal Code expanding the right to legitimate self-defense by declaring unpunishable any excess in domestic self-defense taking place under severe emotional distress and including provisions for crime victims' compensation.

At present, the principle of self-defense is set forth in article 52 of the Criminal Code, according to which "the person who is forced to commit an act due to the necessity to defend his own rights or those of another against the existing danger of an unfair offense is not subject to punishment, provided the defense is proportionate to the gravity of the offense." As the doctrine and court cases have underlined, for the justification of self-defense, three requirements must be fulfilled in a case: the actual danger of an unlawful crime; the "necessity" of defense (i.e., no possible means of escaping without danger); finally, the defense must also be proportionate to the attack.

As regards the use of firearms, this is allowed by a license that can be easily obtained: it is sufficient to be eighteen years of age or older, have no criminal record, and not be suffering from nervous or psychiatric illness. In Italy, in 2017 there were 1.398.920 licenses that authorized the possession of firearms.[42] Unfortunately, there is no official data on the actual number of legally owned weapons. On the contrary, we only have some estimates according to which in Italy there were 8,600,000 civilian-held legal and illicit firearms in 2017.[43] These figures are currently not so much a concern for possible vigilantism incidents as for the number of women killed by firearms. Here there is a strong link to the level of firearms availability.

VIGILANTE JUSTICE IN ITALIAN POPULAR CULTURE: LITERATURE AND THEATRE, FILMS, TELEVISION

From a long-term perspective, how much space has been dedicated to the themes of vendetta and do-it-yourself justice in Italian popular culture? To what extent has popular culture covered the institutional and legal developments we have briefly outlined above? The following review does not claim to be exhaustive, but I believe I have included the most significant authors and works in terms of interest and popularity in the context of vigilantism.

Literature and Theater

The theme of revenge has accompanied the development of Italian literature since its origins. It is a frequent narrative theme although not to the extent that it characterizes a narrative genre or a precise historic period, as is the case for example with the revenge tragedy in English literature.[44]

Well-known, highly expressive, and constantly recycled in print and other media is the episode in Dante Alighieri's *Divina Commedia* (*The Divine Comedy*, ca. 1304–1321) involving Count Ugolino (*Inferno*, cantos 32–33): in the circle of the *Inferno* (*Hell*) reserved for traitors to their country, Dante meets the nobleman from Pisa who avenges the tragic death by starvation of himself and his children by gnawing the skull of his enemy.

The *novella* writers of the fourteenth and fifteenth centuries, including Boccaccio and Matteo Bandello, often tell stories of revenge, in moralistic or comic terms. From the sixteenth to the eighteenth centuries, in some tragedies that had wide circulation, revenge is a cruel instrument adopted by the tyrant against the desire for freedom and justice.[45] In other cases, it represents a way to restore justice against the arbitrary power of the tyrant himself.[46]

With the Age of Enlightenment and the reformist approach to crime promoted in Italy by Cesare Beccaria, the law was seen as superseding all forms of vendetta. These principles were popularized by two of the great figures of Italian literature: Carlo Goldoni and Alessandro Manzoni.[47] What emerges in their works is a powerful critique of retribution, vendetta, and private justice. For Goldoni, who was a lawyer, "revenge is an odious thing."[48] His comedies excoriate vengeful characters, who fail to achieve their goals, admit their guilt and receive a salutary punishment. In contrast, the characters who spurn revenge, such as the merchant Pantalone in *L'uomo prudente* (*The Prudent Man*, 1748), are moving but realistic. In the criminal trial of his wife and son, who attempt to poison him in order to obtain his wealth, he hides the evidence of the crime, has his guilty family members acquitted, and thus avoids inflicting a "public vendetta" at the hands of the judge.

Alessandro Manzoni is one of the key cultural and civil reference points of Italians in the period of the Risorgimento and the struggle for national unity. The novel *I promessi sposi* (*The Betrothed*, 1827 and 1842) marked a new beginning for Italian culture: even today it is taught in all the schools, it has been made into at least three feature films and three television series.[49] The main characters in the novel are two young people of humble origin, Renzo and Lucia, whose marriage is unjustifiably obstructed by the arrogant local noble Don Rodrigo. The latter character imposes his will through violence, with no interference from political and religious institutions, who are in fact frequently complicit in his evil deeds. At many points of the novel, Manzoni dwells on the constant injustice and oppression suffered by the lower classes and the weakest individuals ("It's a sad thing to be born poor, dear lad," Renzo is told). At times with powerful irony, the author condemns the total inadequacy and indeed the corruption of the officers and institutions of the law. The figure of the pettifogging and quibbling lawyer known as Azzecagarbugli (Dr. Quibbler) is memorable in this sense. Renzo discovers to his cost that justice is completely subjugated to power, unable to defend the oppressed and even complicit in their oppression.

Thus, throughout the novel, the young protagonist is prompted to conduct a personal vendetta against his tormentor Don Rodrigo.[50] However, Renzo does not become an avenger, a hero of the people against their oppressors. Nothing could be further from the moral standpoint of the novel. Indeed, whenever Renzo expresses any desire for vengeance he is obliged to change course in the face of reproach on the part of other key characters in the novel, such as his beloved Lucia and above all the friar who protects the two young people, Fra Cristoforo. The latter renounced all earthly comforts and became a monk after he himself killed a man in a duel out of pride and his "thirst for justice." Fra Cristoforo is thus familiar with the tragedy of private justice and explains to Renzo (and the reader) that true justice is obtained by means of forgiveness, patience, and trust in Divine Providence.

For our purposes, it is clear that in *The Betrothed* the alternative to private hatred and vendetta is to be found in Catholic morality rather than the law. Indeed, in this novel as in other works such as *Storia della colonna infame* (*The Column of Infamy*, 1842), Manzoni expresses a constant and tragic pessimism regarding the possibility of justice ever being achieved via the institutions of society. Renzo is the archetype of a character that would be seen on many subsequent occasions in higher and popular culture: the "anti-avenger," who initially seeks revenge but ultimately renounces or regrets the act of vengeance or fails in the attempt. The difference between Renzo and the would-be avengers that came after him is the paramount role of religion. Whereas in *The Betrothed*, at the end of the story justice is done by and in the name of Providence, in many other stories told in literature, cinema, and television, the just man cannot count on the comfort of this divine vindication and must act without the guarantee of justice that it implies.

In the period that saw the formation of the new nation-state in the nineteenth and twentieth centuries, other works condemned private vengeance in all its forms, without however promoting the law as a valid alternative. Private vengeance is the cause of the desperate plight of the pageboy Rigoletto in the opera of the same name by Giuseppe Verdi (1851), and of the death of the young Turiddu in *Cavalleria Rusticana* (*Rustic Chivalry*, 1890) by Pietro Mascagni, based on a short story by Giovanni Verga.[51] Collective vengeance leads to irrational and futile violence, including lynchings and disorder, and is categorically condemned by writers from Manzoni in *The Betrothed*[52] to Verga in the short story *Libertà* (*Liberty*, 1883), Gabriele D'Annunzio in *La morte del duca d'Ofena* (*The Death of the Duke of Ofena*, 1902), and Luigi Pirandello in *I Vecchi e i Giovani* (*The Old and the Young*, 1913).

However, the Italian masses of that era saw the vendetta as the only available response to a situation of pronounced inequality, restricted social mobility, widespread injustice, and the inadequacy of the public administration. For Gramsci, it was precisely the "inferiority complex" of the poorer classes that lay behind the "fantasies about revenge, punishing those responsible for their adversities, etc."[53] This explains the great success of serialized stories in the nineteenth century: the clearest example is the vendetta of the Count of Monte Cristo by the French writer Alexandre Dumas. Highly successful in Italy were the serial novels ("*romanzi di appendice*") by Carolina Invernizio, such as *Il bacio della morta* (*The Kiss of a Dead Woman*, 1886). The basic narrative schemes of these novels involved a heroine (since the main character was usually a woman) who succeeds in taking revenge on her enemies, who are typically driven to suicide or madness. Then there is the historic novel, also popular at that time, by the Sicilian writer Luigi Natoli, *I Beati Paoli* (1909), which is of interest to us here since it is one of the rare examples in Italian popular culture of glorification of a secret society of avengers that was founded in order to fight injustice and the abuses of the Sicilian nobility, but in reality seeks to impose its own justice, beyond the limits of the law and the expectations of the oppressed.[54] With its secret rituals, code of silence, and justice not based on class distinctions, *I Beati Paoli* served to legitimize and mystify organized crime, in other words—the Mafia.[55] From the same period are the writings of the Nobel Prize–winner Grazia Deledda, who described the culture of revenge that characterized the community of Barbagia, an inland region of Sardinia. This island has been considered in literature and broadly in popular culture to be wild and pastoral, reflecting the traits of a premodern society.

The theater of the early twentieth century includes interesting works centered on the thirst for vengeance. These include the *Cena delle Beffe* (*The Jest*, 1909) by Sem Benelli, with a Renaissance setting, one of the biggest successes of the Italian stage in the twentieth century; *Liolà* (1916) and *Il Giuoco delle parti* (*The Rules of the Game*, 1918), two comedies by Pirandello which highlight the betrayals and vendettas inherent in personal relations and social conventions; *Notte in casa del ricco* (*Night in the Rich Man's House*, 1938), by Ugo Betti, in which the thirst for vendetta of one of the protagonists is linked to the need to reestablish order in the face of the betrayals and injustices committed by human beings. In the plots of these works, the act of revenge becomes the nemesis not just of those who seek it but also of everybody involved in the story: none of them get what they desire.

A different approach is seen in the novel by Dino Buzzati, *Bàrnabo delle montagne* (*Bàrnabo of the Mountains*, 1933). Here, the main character's determination to restore his honor and avenge himself on his enemies—brigands and murderers—fades when he perceives the humanity of his adversaries, the passage of time, and the futility of death. This preference for peace is also partly the result of the spell cast by the mountains and an awareness of the eternity of nature.

In the postwar period, the search for justice by means of vendetta was a theme in literary genres. A common feature seems to be the reference to contemporary cases and issues, abandoning the evocation of past epochs and the existential dimension. A good example of this is the oeuvre of Leonardo Sciascia, whose work, perhaps more than that of any other Italian writer or intellectual, has focused on the problem of justice and the need to fight violence, crime, and the abuse of political power by upholding the law. It is thus no surprise that Sciascia's oeuvre contains numerous references to private justice and its relationship to its official counterpart. In the meaningfully titled short story *Western di cose nostre* (*Mafia Western*, 1973), we find the classic figure of the avenger. Above suspicion and acting alone, a normal citizen carries on a personal vendetta against the local Mafia, on which the police seem to make little impression. But it is also a vendetta against an anti-modern social organization that stifles individual liberty and social mobility. In the end, the avenger is killed by the Mafia, but his act of rebellion represents a rare case in which the "habitual arrogance" of the gangs is momentarily shattered, it is the Mafiosi who terrorize the town who feel fear, and justice is done despite the failure of the police and the judiciary.

Sciascia then wrote *Il contesto* (*Equal Danger*, 1971), which is based on a simple idea: a vendetta stemming from a judicial error. A pharmacist begins killing the judges who unjustly convicted him of the attempted poisoning of his wife in a trial that was affected by prejudice and faulty procedures. While the police chiefs and the public think that judges are being assassinated as part of a political plot, the protagonist Inspector Rogas learns the truth. He is on the point of arresting the culprit but lets him go. In addition, during the investigation, Rogas has discovered the existence of a secret plot to enact a coup d'etat, but in the end he is killed by agents of the secret service. In *Equal Danger*, two plans are intertwined: the plan of the citizen seeking revenge on the judges who show no respect for the fundamental rights of the individual; and the political plan to overturn democracy and the rule of law. The vendetta of the citizen goes unpunished and is implicitly justified by the degeneration of the institutions and political morality.

The novel *Porte aperte* (*Open Doors*, 1987) is also the story of a dual vendetta. The opening episode is of the individual kind, linked to a triple murder committed by an office worker to avenge the abuses and betrayals he has suffered. The other vendetta, which is the real focus of Sciascia's reflections in this work, is a public vendetta, of society against the individual: a vendetta that is carried out in the name of the law through a farcical trial that results in a person being condemned to death (it is set during the fascist era).[56] The main character, in this case, is a judge who tries to save the defendant from the death penalty, despite the seriousness of the crime and strong pressure from politicians and public opinion. It should be remembered that two of these three works by Sciascia have been made into films (*Il contesto* and *Porte aperte*) and a made-for-television film (*Western di cose nostre*), which were greatly enjoyed by critics and the public alike.

Reflecting the widespread bewilderment in the face of the dramatic social transformations that affected Italy in the 1970s, two novels featured controversial elderly avengers reacting to the death of their offspring due to crime. Published in 1976 was the novel *Un borghese piccolo piccolo* (*An Average Little Man*) by Vincenzo Cerami, subsequently adapted into a striking film to which we will return. On the book's back cover, Italo Calvino, one of the most prominent contemporary writers in Italy, vividly noted that it is a "story of victims and at the same time of monsters." In 1980 it was the turn of the novel *Il fratello italiano* (*The Italian Brother*) by Giovanni Arpino, a bitter reflection on the vendetta as a way of fulfilling justice in a corrupt, violent, and degraded social context (it is set in the world of prostitution and drugs). The protagonists of these novels are two elderly fathers who succeed in their vendettas, despite their doubts, sufferings, and feelings of pity, passing a damning verdict on a society that is ruthless toward its weakest members, whether they be young, old, or women.

Obviously, the vendetta is also a theme of police and detective stories. With Giorgio Scerbanenco, who brought the Italian detective novel closer to the American "noir," revenge seems at times to be an unbreakable rule of the criminal world, and is thus without moral implications, as in the series titled *Milano calibro 9* (1969); other times is a tragic fate as in *I milanesi ammazzano al sabato* (*Milanese Kill on Saturdays*, 1969). Elsewhere, this genre highlights the emotional ambiguity of the thirst for vengeance in a world in which every form of moral sense and justice has disappeared. The noir by Massimo Carlotto, *L'oscura immensità della morte* (*Death's Dark Abyss*, 2004), is the story of the physical and moral decay of a successful entrepreneur (described in the novel as "a Charles Bronson-like fucking vigilante") who takes revenge on the murderers of his wife and son because he is not satisfied with the prison sentence served by one of the culprits. *Per vendetta* (*For Revenge*, 2009) by Alessandro Perissinotto tackles the search for historic truth regarding the terrible but never punished violence of the Argentine dictatorship, justifying the desire for revenge but at the same time clearly showing its absurdity.

Lastly, an explicit condemnation of the recourse to self-defense is seen in the novel by Andrea Camilleri, *Le ali della sfinge* (*The Wings of the Sphinx*, 2006), in which the killing, supposedly in self-defense, of a young thief by a shopkeeper is described as "a foolish crime committed by an idiot."

Cinema

I will try here to briefly reconstruct the way in which Italian cinema has tackled the theme of revenge and private justice.[57] American films of this genre, for example the *Death Wish* paradigm, have been successful among the public in Italy, and their stories, characters, and moral justifications are now rooted in the collective imagination. In addition, they clearly represent the main reference in production and stylistic terms for Italian films on this theme.

In general, stories of private justice and revenge have been told by Italian cinema through the lens of its most popular and characteristic genres, that is, historical, mythological, melodramas, in which revenge is framed within a tormented family or romantic relations, and of course Westerns: just think of Sergio Leone's epic masterpiece *C'era una volta il West* (*Once Upon a Time in the West*, 1968). There are also films that portray revenge in the context of common and organized crime.

Two recognizable currents are of particular interest here, although there is not the space here to discuss them in depth. The first is the practice of vendetta in Sardinia: many films set on the island, both dramas and comedies, have been inspired by the conflict between modernity and an archaic past. Films such as *Banditi a Orgosolo* (*Bandits of Orgosolo*, 1961) concern the tension between the formal law of the Italian State with its representatives the Carabinieri on the one hand, and the custom-based law of certain parts of the island in which the principle of vendetta plays a key role on the other hand. The background of these films was influenced by the studies by jurist Antonio Pigliaru,[58] in which he investigates customary law among certain pastoralist communities in Sardinia, specifically the so-called Barbagian Revenge.

The second current is the rape-revenge film,[59] which arose in the 1970s, inspired by contemporaneous American examples and includes many exploitation films, such as *L'ultimo treno della notte* (*Last Stop on the Night Train*, 1975), or, more recently, *Sono Angelica, voglio vendetta* (*Angelica Wants Revenge*, 2018). In the same subgenre, there are some narratively more complex films, for example *La sindrome di Stendhal* (*The Stendhal Syndrome*, 1996), *La sconosciuta* (*The Unknown Woman*, 2006), and others directly inspired by real events, such as *Senza movente* (*No Apparent Motive*, 1999).

The Italian vigilante film in its fullest sense arose (and disappeared) in the 1970s, the main character usually being a police inspector. Guided by the conventions of the cop film, the so-called poliziottesco genre saw a rapid rise in popularity in Italy precisely in those years.[60] Among the stylistic and production considerations that favored the rise of the cop film were the decline of the genres that had been dominant in Italian cinema in the previous decades, particularly the homemade Westerns and comedies, and the substantial fall in cinema audiences as a result of the growth of television. The cop film reprised the narrative and stylistic conventions of the Spaghetti Western, transposing them to the context, which appeared equally wild and violent, of contemporary Italian society. In addition, it used the themes and motifs of the political cinema of the 1960s, albeit with "different ideological intentions."[61] The influence of American films of the period, such as *Dirty Harry* and *Death Wish*, was considerable, but not, as we will see, sufficient to entirely annul the films' specifically Italian characteristics.

Among the external factors affecting the development of the Italian cop film, which was considered realistic and inspired by real events, was the increase in political violence and crime in Italian society. The cinema of these years, in a close but at the same time conflictual dialogue with Italian intellectuals, looked at these phenomena through its own narrative lens, contributing to the "total disintegration of the idea of the state in the popular imagination."[62] A famous example is the film that won Oscar for Best Foreign Language Film, *Indagine su un cittadino al di sopra di ogni sospetto* (*Investigation of a Citizen Above Suspicion*, 1970). The crisis of the state was also depicted as the crisis of the relationship between citizens and the institutions and officers of the law. The seminal work by Vincenzo Tomeo reflects on these themes analyzing the sudden flourishing in 1971 and 1972 of Italian legal films after decades in which the cinema rarely paid any attention to issues of justice.[63] In this vein, a significant figure is the judge who turns vigilante in the comedy *In nome del popolo italiano* (*In the Name of the Italian People*, 1971), where a prosecutor resolves to present false evidence in a trial in order to portray himself as a crusader against the corruption and immorality of Italian society

This is the cultural, thematic, and narrative background in which the themes of private justice and the crisis of the law are tackled in the films of the 1970s. Two films would provide the model for the subsequent vigilante-cop films: *Confessione di un commissario di polizia al procuratore della repubblica* (*Confessions of a Police Captain*, 1971) and *La polizia ringrazia* (*Execution Squad*, 1972). Both films depict the impotence of the police and the law in the face of the brutal power of the Mafia and growing metropolitan violence. The protagonists of both films are two "problematic" Police Inspectors, to paraphrase Tomeo: through their doubts and misadventures the possible recourse to private justice, administered by policemen themselves or by secret groups of vigilantes, is explored. The conclusion of these films is that the response to the crisis of confidence in the institutions and the temptation to seek private vengeance lies in the hard work and rigor of committed judges. Condemnation of organized vigilante groups is strong, but the ambivalence of the problem is amplified and not resolved by these narratives.

The great success of these films inspired dozens of emulators, in which the increasingly reductive and simplified exploitation of the themes went hand in hand with ever more spectacular violence and action. The "problematic" police inspector would eventually give way to the resolute avenger cop, for example, *La polizia incrimina, la legge assolve* (*High Crime*, 1973); *Roma violenta* (*Violent City*, 1975); *Il grande racket* (*The Big Racket*, 1976); *Torino violenta* (*Double Game*, 1977).

The 1970s saw a large number of police inspectors but few cases of a common man playing the role of avenger. An initial group of films can however be considered typical of the vigilante genre as described in the previous section and exemplified by *Death Wish*. These works deployed directors and actors, narrative components, and forms of representation that were typical of the Italian cop film. In 1974, three months after *Death Wish* was released in the US (and thus before its arrival in Italy!), Italian cinemas showed *Il cittadino si ribella* (*Street Law*), which enjoyed considerable success (grossing over 1.8 billion lire in the 1974–1975 season).[64] 1975 saw the release of *L'uomo della strada fa giustizia* (*The Manhunt*) and *La città sconvolta: caccia spietata ai rapitori* (*Kidnap Syndicate*) followed in 1976 by *Roma, l'altra faccia della violenza* (*Rome, the Other Face of Violence*) and in 1977 by *No alla violenza* (*Death Hunt*). Despite their differences, the plot of these films was centered on a citizen—always a man, usually middle class or perhaps a manual worker—who seeks revenge against desperate criminals who the police will not or cannot arrest. In some cases, this man receives offers of help from secret vigilante groups to carry out his revenge, yet he categorically refuses them, even denouncing these subversive groups to the police. These films are narratively and ideologically closest to the *Death Wish* model. Moreover, their structure is congruent with the narrative scheme of the vigilante film genre suggested by Peter Robson.[65]

Paraphrasing Clarens,[66] while the above-mentioned films are generic stock "vigilante films," the following films of the same period are "films about a vigilante": *Un borghese piccolo piccolo* (*An Average Little Man*, 1977), *L'arma* (*The Gun*, 1978) and *Il giocattolo* (*A Dangerous Toy*, 1979), all films lying outside the canon of the cop film. Made by top-flight directors with some of the most representative Italian actors of the period, they tackle the figure of the vigilante in decidedly more problematic, reflective, and dramatic terms.

An Average Little Man is the most significant example of the way Italian cinema has portrayed the vigilante. Based on Cerami's novel (see the previous part), it is the story of the office worker Vivaldi, close to retirement and nostalgic for the fascist era. The main objective in his life is to get his young son a job in the Ministry where he is already employed. The disruptive random event in the story is the accidental murder of his son during a robbery. As his wife is so shocked that she becomes paralyzed and loses the power of speech, Vivaldi decides to seek revenge. He prevents the arrest of his son's killer, not reporting him to the police. After having kidnapped him, his revenge consists of the full-fledged torture of the criminal, performed as a spectacle for the eyes of him and his wife, and as such it is ultimately an intimate and private act. The elderly office worker in *An Average Little Man*, now retired, is alone, his wife dead. He is the only character in these films who will apparently continue as a vigilante.

In Italy, the 1980s and 1990s saw the emergence of organized crime, the scourge of heroin, and the struggle against systemic corruption. In this context, the figure of the vigilante, whether policeman or citizen, becomes increasingly improbable, partly as a consequence of a renewed interest in the personnel of the law. In the cinema and on television there were many heroic police inspectors and judges, committed to the point of martyrdom in the struggle against the Mafia and the degeneration of politics.[67] Apart from *L'angelo con la pistola* (*Angel with a Gun*, 1992), the only film to mention for this period is *Camorra. Un complicato intrigo di donne, vicoli e delitti* (*Camorra. A Story of Streets, Women and Crime*, 1986). Here, in a rarity for Italian cinema, revenge is sought by a group of mothers against the Camorra and heroin dealers.

In recent years, private revenge is once more a topic of interest. The stories of contemporary films[68] are set in the desperate world of petty crime and violent and deprived urban areas. Two recently released films are especially interesting for our purposes. *Dogman* (2018)[69] has been compared by public and critics with *An Average Little Man*. Marcello, the main character, is a meek man in a violent world, he even admires the thug who oppresses him and seeks his approval. But after suffering yet another humiliation being badly beaten in front of the whole neighborhood, he seeks revenge just to force his tormentor to show some respect ("you have to apologize," he asks his caged victim). With *Villetta con ospiti* (*Guests in the Villa*, 2020) we are in a rich house of the small town bourgeoisie, where in the night a woman kills a Romanian boy, believing him to be a thief. But the boy was innocent, he was a guest of the woman's daughter. Moreover, the gun that killed him was illegally obtained. The woman and her family, but also a policeman, a priest, and a doctor, agree to hide the murder. Everyone in this community is morally corrupt, no one wants to face the law and lose his or her position of privilege and power. This film denounces all the risks of self-defense and the use of weapons by private citizens, drawing on the present-day Italian public debate.

To summarize, what emerges from this exploration of nearly fifty years of cinematographic production is that in Italy a solid and lasting tradition of vigilante films was not established. From a thematic and stylistic point of view, it is hard to identify a homogeneous and consistent body of work, except for the small group of films made in the mid-1970s similar to *Death Wish*. But there are some themes and motifs common to the films cited about private justice.

In Italian cinema, revenge is a male affair. With the exception of the rape-revenge film, in films centered on private justice, the main character is always a man. In contrast, the female characters are fragile and subordinate to men and they appear mostly in domestic settings.

If on one hand, these films reproduce female stereotypes, then on the other they highlight the crisis of male identity. The male protagonists endure strained conditions, in which freedom and self-determination are structurally denied by the society in which they live. The engineer in *Street Law* rebels because the symbols of his self-realization (house and money) are derided by criminals. For him, as for the other male protagonists, it is his honor that is at stake.

In the Italian films, the crisis of the individual is also the crisis of society. The Italian "giustiziere" is ambiguous. Indeed, it is no coincidence that the main characters of *An Average Little Man* and *A Dangerous Toy*, both tragic films, are played by two of the greatest Italian comic actors, respectively Alberto Sordi and Nino Manfredi. Comedy has been the main genre by which cinema has tackled the contradictions of Italian society, including issues of law and justice.[70] The main character of *An Average Little Man* has been dubbed the Italian Doctor Jekyll by critics, seeing in him the coexistence of loving family bonds and violent impulses. The film's director, Monicelli, described him as "a man with a closed mind, egotistical and absolutely without social values."[71]

But in these films, revenge is depicted neither as an instinctive action nor as the expression of a violent subculture. Despite their differences, these stories portray a general state of demoralization in the Durkheimian sense,[72] in which the individual feels and appears alienated and powerless. The everyday violence and widespread crime are the symbols of this anomic condition, where values have broken down.

The impression of a society where the juridical and moral norms are defunct, ruled by the law of the strongest, is reinforced by the fact that the officers of the law in Italian vigilante films are ineffective, corrupt, or violent themselves. The police and the judiciary are depicted as bureaucratic institutions, distant and lacking empathy toward the suffering of the victim. Indeed, the police seem to be in conflict with the citizen, who, in turn, feels a deep mistrust of the officers. This lack of trust goes so far as to preclude any investigation and trial, as with the office worker Vivaldi in *An Average Little Man*.

A final remark on the use of firearms. In Italian films, it is generally deplored, seen as useless and harmful, and leads to tragic consequences.

Television

As in some other countries, the theme of revenge has been a common feature on Italian television in popular series involving intrigue and betrayal. This includes both domestic soap operas and programs imported from the US or Latin America. Less common but still significant have been representations of the culture of honor and vendetta characteristic of certain parts of Italy, in both television documentaries and TV dramas, such as *Canne al vento* (*Reeds in the Wind*),[73] drawn from the book of the same name by the Nobel Prize–writer Grazia Deledda, and produced by RAI, the national public broadcasting company, in 1958. In these programs, killing for revenge is justified by custom but also by the situation of poverty and injustice in which protagonists find themselves, as in *Maria Zef* (RAI, 1981), on the terrible conditions of the peasantry at the beginning of the twentieth century.

Regarding the figure of the vigilante, it is quite rare, or at least so it appears, to find Italian television programs, either series or single episodes, based explicitly on the problem of private justice or self-defense. Is this due to a deliberate choice by the producers or the result of a tradition of themes and styles characteristic of Italian television dramas? In fact, it is likely to be a combination of the two.

In contrast, as with cinema, on television the vigilante has appeared in American productions, via the innumerable TV series imported and broadcast by public and private stations, of which we shall cite just a few examples. Some imported TV series have obviously been about policeman avengers, such as *The Sweeney*[74] and *Hunter*.[75] Others have been more specifically concerned with avenger figures who do not belong to the police, such as the crime drama *Cain's Hundred*[76] on a lawyer's vendetta against organized crime, and the crime drama *The Equalizer*.[77] For the television critic of "L'Unità," then the daily newspaper of the Italian Communist Party, this series was abysmal, its main character "gloomy, arrogant and a bit of a fascist," and similar verdicts regarding this type of television program were heard from many other Italian intellectuals.[78] More recently, Italian television has offered other vigilante crime dramas including *Dark Justice*,[79] *Vengeance Unlimited*,[80] and *Hand of God*.[81] However, even in Italy the most successful in terms of audience share and interest is *Dexter*.[82]

Regarding domestic Italian television series, we must inevitably consider programming that tackles the theme of the Mafia, which accounts for the bulk of Italian crime dramas.[83] Mafia-oriented dramas reproduce the most popular narrative schemes and the most widely held stereotypes linked to organized crime. For this reason, they are always about honor, betrayal, and revenge. Exemplary in this regard are crime dramas such as *L'Onore e il rispetto* (*Honor and Respect*, 2006–2017) produced by Mediaset, the largest commercial broadcaster in Italy, and high-quality internationally successful series such as *Gomorrah* (produced by Sky, 2014–).

Avengers, vigilante groups, and the problem of private justice are frequently key features of Mafia stories. One of the earliest Italian series on this theme, *Alle origini della mafia* (*Origins of the Mafia*, RAI, 1976) for which Sciascia and the English historian Eric Hobsbawm acted as consultants, looks at the above-mentioned history of the secret society of avengers known as the Beati Paoli. There are also women, playing the wives, mothers, daughters, and sisters of Mafiosi, who choose the path of do-it-yourself justice.[84]

Above all, however, in Mafia-based drama series, the figure that most resembles a true vigilante on Italian television, in search of justice at all costs, is the policeman avenger. The most popular policeman avenger was Commissario Cattani in *La Piovra* (*The Octopus*, RAI, 1984–2001). Cattani is driven by a profound sense of justice, although he often vacillates. He also has a desire for revenge, since the Mafia killed his wife and only daughter, as well as many of his colleagues and friends. Cattani is the prototype of the Italian hero, caught between the desire for justice and the thirst for revenge.[85] As always, these feelings remain unresolved and are not legitimized, given that in the end the hero is defeated and dies. This type of avenger reappears, again in the context of Mafia-based TV series, in the crime drama *Racket* (RAI, 1997), created by the same authors and directors and the same lead actor, Michele Placido, as *The Octopus*. Briefly, this is the story of an ex-policeman, who, after years fighting organized crime, retires and goes to live as a private citizen in a peaceful town far from the Mafia, where he opens a restaurant and lives quietly with his family. However, the Mafia then arrives in the town where he now works and begins to threaten the ex-policeman, his family, and other law-abiding citizens. Thus, the policeman once more finds himself struggling against his old enemies: seeking to protect his family and pursue a vendetta for his past suffering, in the end he defeats the crime gang, with the help of the police, but he is forced to flee and adopt a new identity, thereby losing contact with his family and normal life.

This ambivalence between the desire for absolute justice and revenge has been seen in other policemen in popular Italian television crime dramas over the last two decades. These include *Rocco Schiavone* (RAI, 2016–), a policeman who is impatient with official procedures and ready to seek justice on his own account in order to avenge the death of his wife. In these characters, the total dedication to the search for justice and the struggle against crime seems to be more a consequence of the thirst for vendetta rather than an unconditional commitment to the values of the rule of law. In addition, the tendency to seek private justice seems to be reinforced by the importance of family ties and friendship within the work context.[86]

However, this symbolic construction of the policeman avenger should not be seen as absolute, as in the American model represented by Dirty Harry and his television counterpart Rick Hunter. First and foremost, because on Italian television the policeman's vendetta seems to be the narrative theme that holds the series episodes together rather than the main goal of the policeman's actions; in the second place, because there is no reflection, no dialogue, and no comparison of the meaning of revenge and justice. The instinct for revenge seems to be spared public condemnation, although it is not explicitly approved of, either. In other words, these sentiments are whispered rather than stated out loud, not officially admissible but accepted in practice. Indeed, it is precisely this unresolved ambivalence with regard to revenge that helps to bring the public closer to these characters.

It is also true however that the most popular and long-lived police officers and detectives on Italian television eschew this moral ambiguity. They are not ruled by a thirst for revenge and they do not believe in private justice. Examples include *Il Maresciallo Rocca* (*Marshal Rocca*, RAI, 1996–2005), *Don Matteo* (RAI, 2000–), and *Il Commissario Montalbano* (*Inspector Montalbano*, RAI, 1999–). It is true that at times Inspector Montalbano, "probably the most ideologically progressive of the lead detectives,"[87] feels the need to take revenge, especially when investigating a particularly shocking case of murder against defenseless victims, but this impulse is always controlled in the end. In these highly successful dramas, even crimes committed by normal citizens in revenge or self-defense are condemned, although they are seen to be partly justified, and their perpetrators are sometimes acquitted. The 2006 episode "Self-Defense" of the series *Don Matteo* is about a robbery in a jewelry store: the owner appears to kill the robber in self-defense, but in the end the story is more complex than it seems, mixing heroes and villains. The killing, the purpose of which is to defend the loved ones and the livelihood of the owner from the threat posed by the robber, is punished by the law (albeit lightly) and above all is pardoned by the moral code of Don Matteo, the priest-detective. In this way, more shade than light is thrown on the notion of self-defense: it seems to lack reasonable justification yet it is condemned in a rather bland and lenient way, replicating the ambiguity of the situations in which it is used. Similar processes are at work in the episode of the legal drama *Un caso di coscienza* (*A Question of Conscience*, RAI, 2003–2013) also titled "Self-Defense," and the episode of the series Montalbano that reprises the novel *The Wings of the Sphinx* cited above.

Among the crime dramas that have specifically tackled the theme of private justice and revenge on the part of private citizens against the common criminals is *La caccia* (*The Hunt*, RAI, 2005). This is the story of a jeweler (this profession again) in a rich province of northern Italy, who tries to kill the criminal who killed his wife and son during a robbery. The drama highlights the process by which an honest citizen and family man is brutalized as he is progressively consumed by the thirst for revenge. However, replicating the dual scheme seen in some works of literature, the drama is also seen from the point of view of the original robber-murderer, who rediscovers his humanity and aspires to flee and make a new life for himself.

Since 2017 especially, there has been a renewed interest on the part of Italian television in the issue of do-it-yourself justice in all its forms. Worthy of mention here is the interesting documentary *La percezione della paura* (*The Perception of Fear*, Sky, 2017) on the use of weapons and self-defense. Then there is a large number of episodes of talk shows, entertainment programs, and investigative documentaries that have looked at self-defense and private justice. In terms of narrative strategies, these programs tend to focus first on a case from the news, which serves as a starting point for the episode as a whole. There is an interview with the victim-killer, who describes the repeated robberies that they have suffered and the state of acute insecurity in which they and their families have been living for years. The next step is the "chorus," that is, interviews with residents, who give similar accounts of being the target of robbery and violence, confirming the widespread climate of insecurity and thus the innocence of the avenger. There are calls for increasingly relaxed measures with regard to self-defense and the use of weapons by private citizens. The narrative in these programs concludes with comments by political exponents and experts, whose ideological positions are usually aligned with the afore-going interpretations of the facts; those who seek to question such positions typically do so with some embarrassment.

The quantity and frequency of attention paid to these themes obviously vary depending on the political and cultural orientation of the public targeted by the single programs. It can be observed that the talk shows of private networks and those aimed at a generally older and less well-educated audience tend to focus more insistently on the fear of crime issue and to favor the use of private justice. And yet interest in this theme has been ambivalent. It may be that television's growing willingness to engage with this issue is due to the supposedly growing number of killings and robberies, as well as cases of self-defense. However, as seen in the previous chapter, these figures have decreased in Italy in recent years.

CONCLUSION

Although the examples cited belong to different periods and genres within Italian popular culture, they share a number of recurring themes and motifs. This convergence is explained by the revenge scenario which these works are all based on.[88] But this is not the only reason: these narratives seem to reflect, and at the same time to replicate, interpretations of private justice that are rooted in Italian society.

Generally, the violence represented is not just that of crime and the criminal. Violence is a structural aspect of society, which is reflected in economic, social, and gender relations, as well as in the law itself, which is perceived as external and imposed from above. The law is depicted as being ineffective in ensuring that citizens' feelings of justice are fulfilled. The agents of the law are unable or unwilling to do justice, sometimes they are antagonistic to the victim, other times they are themselves avengers beyond the limits of the rule of law.

Sentiments of revenge seem to spring from a context of violence but also a lack of meaning, both at an individual level (the violation of identity and honor, the betrayal of trust) and a social level (major social inequalities, the absence of just retribution). Revenge is nourished by the double crisis of the law and social ties, and becomes, as a logical solution, the only mean in the hands of the victim for an attempt at recovery.

But such an attempt only rarely succeeds in Italian popular culture. This is the case of the stories from the genre of the popular novel or the TV detective story. Far more often, private justice results in a failure: there are many tragic figures, from Rigoletto to Marcello in *Dogman* whose end is defeat, insanity, or death. Revenge is almost always depicted as a solitary and meaningless act. As for Italian cinema or television, the vigilante "hero" is ultimately a loser, and perhaps this is the most striking difference with respect to the American vigilante films. This is why the protagonist of these Italian stories about private justice is rarely a figure that the public can completely identify with.

Just as in these stories the main characters are represented as both monsters and victims (reminding us of Italo Calvino's comment above), so in Italian society private justice has at times been condemned and strictly controlled, at other times accepted and tolerated. The historical and legal evidence we have tried to trace shows that there has been a certain fluidity in the transition from legal forms of individual self-defense to illegal forms of revenge. Equally, it has been difficult to draw a clear distinction between neighborhood wardens and vigilantism.

If, according to Zimring,[89] vigilantism is a matter of interpretation, it is essential for a liberal democracy that private justice is a vibrant topic of debate. Admittedly, in Italy the historical legacy of fascism and "squadrismo" should lead us not to underestimate either the slightest signs of vigilantism or the hate speech circulating in public debate and social media. Nevertheless, more problematic than vigilantism per se is the distrust toward the law and the judiciary that is widespread and that underlies the most recent self-defense reform. In this regard, the lessons that can be drawn from Italian popular culture, whose stories warn us of the excessive distance that exists between citizens and the institutions of the law, should receive the utmost consideration.

NOTES

1. Franklin E. Zimring, *The Contradictions of American Capital Punishment* (New York: Oxford University Press, 2003), 103–4.

2. Peter Robson, "Vengeance in Popular Culture," in *Oxford Encyclopedia of Crime, Media, and Popular Culture* (Oxford: Oxford University Press, December 22, 2016), https://doi.org/10.1093/acrefore/9780190264079.013.45; Stefan Machura, "The Law and Cinema Movement," in *Framing Law and Crime: An Interdisciplinary Anthology*, ed. Caroline Joan "Kay" S. Picart, Michael Hviid Jacobsen, and Cecil

Greek (Lanham, MD: Rowman & Littlefield, 2016), 25–58. For the sociological relevance of literary narratives, see Mariano Longo, *Fiction and Social Reality: Literature and Narrative as Sociological Resources* (Farnham: Ashgate, 2015).

3. Cosimo Braccesi, "Le Pattuglie Cittadine. 160 anni di storia," *Sicurezza e territorio* 10 (1993): 11–16.

4. Steven C. Hughes, *Crime, Disorder, and the Risorgimento: The Politics of Policing in Bologna* (Cambridge: Cambridge University Press, 1994), 103.

5. Max Weber, *From Max Weber: Essays in Sociology*, ed. Hans Heinrich Gerth and Charls Wright Mills (New York: Oxford University Press, 1946).

6. Mark Cooney, "Social and Legal Responses to Homicide," in *The Handbook of Homicide*, ed. Fiona Brookman, Edward R. Maguire, and Mike Maguire (Chichester, Malden, MA: Wiley/ Blackwell, 2017), 54–69.

7. Manuel Eisner, "Long-Term Historical Trends in Violent Crime," *Crime and Justice* 30 (2003): 99.

8. Dario Melossi, "Andamento economico, incarcerazione, omicidi e allarme sociale in Italia: 1863–1994," in *Storia d'Italia. Annali 12. La criminalità*, ed. Luciano Violante (Turin: Einaudi, 1997), 35–62.

9. Domenico Siciliano, "Per una denealogia del diritto alla legittima difesa: da Carrara ai Rocco," *Quaderni fiorentini per la storia del pensiero giuridico moderno* 35, no. 2 (2006): 723–847; Matteo Millan, "Sostituire l'autorità, riaffermare la sovranità. Legittima difesa, corpi armati e crisi dello Stato nell'Italia giolittiana," *Studi storici*, no. 1 (2019): 139–66, https://doi.org/10.7375/92947.

10. Matteo Millan, "In Defence of Freedom? The Practices of Armed Movements in Pre-1914 Europe: Italy, Spain and France," *European History Quarterly* 46, no. 1 (January 2016): 48–71, https://doi.org/10.1177/0265691415619614; Millan, "Sostituire l'autorità, riaffermare la sovranità. Legittima difesa, corpi armati e crisi dello Stato nell'Italia giolittiana."

11. Anthony L. Cardoza, *Agrarian Elites and Italian Fascism the Province of Bologne, 1901–1926* (Princeton: Princeton University Press, 1982); see also Matteo Millan, "The Origins," in *The Politics of Everyday Life in Fascist Italy*, ed. Joshua Arthurs, Michael Ebner, and Kate Ferris (New York: Palgrave Macmillan, 2017), 19–49; Michael R. Ebner, *Ordinary Violence in Mussolini's Italy* (New York: Cambridge University Press, 2011).

12. Cardoza, *Agrarian Elites and Italian Fascism the Province of Bologne, 1901–1926*, 295–99.

13. Martin Clark, "Italian Squadrismo and Contemporary Vigilantism," *European History Quarterly* 18, no. 1 (January 1988): 33–49, https://doi.org/10.1177/026569148801800102.

14. See Emilio Gentile, "Fascism in Power: The Totalitarian Experiment," in *Liberal and Fascist Italy: 1900–1945*, ed. Adrian Lyttelton (Oxford; New York: Oxford University Press, 2002), 139–74; Mimmo Franzinelli, *Squadristi: protagonisti e techniche della violenza fascista: 1919–1922* (Milan: A. Mondadori, 2003); Ebner, *Ordinary Violence in Mussolini's Italy*.

15. See Mario Sbriccoli, "Caratteri originari e tratti permanenti del sistema penale italiano (1860–1990)," in *Storia d'Italia. Annali, 14: Legge Diritto Giustizia*, ed.

Luciano Violante (Turin: Einaudi, 1988), 485–551; "Tainted Law? The Italian Penal Code, Fascism and Democracy," *International Journal of Law in Context* 7, no. 4 (December 2011): 423–46, https://doi.org/10.1017/S1744552311000231.

16. See Claudio Pavone, *A Civil War: A History of the Italian Resistance* (London; New York: Verso, 2013), chap. 7; Santo Peli, *La Resistenza difficile* (Milan: FrancoAngeli, 1999); Pier Paolo Portinaro, *I conti con il passato vendetta, amnistia, giustizia* (Milan: Feltrinelli, 2011), chap. 1; Andrea Martini, "Punishing the Fascists: An Intense Debate During the Italian Civil War," in *Italy and the Second World War: Alternative Perspectives*, ed. Emanuele Sica and Richard Carrier (Leiden; Boston: Brill, 2018), 249–71.

17. Gabriele Ranzato, *Il linciaggio di Carretta. Roma 1944: violenza politica e ordinaria violenza* (Milan: Il Saggiatore, 1997).

18. Lara Pucci, "Shooting Corpses: The Fosse Ardeatine in Giorni Di Gloria (1945)," *Italian Studies* 68, no. 3 (2013): 356–77.

19. Melossi, "Andamento economico, incarcerazione, omicidi e allarme sociale in italia"; Raffaella Sette, "Honneur, terrorisme et criminalité: soixante ans d'homicides en Italie (1945–2005)," in *Histoire de l'homicide en Europe: de la fin du moyen âge à nos jours*, ed. Laurent Mucchieli and Pieter Spierenburg (Paris: Découverte, 2009), 163–95.

20. Manuel Eisner, "Modernity Strikes Back? A Historical Perspective on the Latest Increase in Interpersonal Violence (1960–1990)," *International Journal of Conflict and Violence (IJCV)* 2, no. 2 (2008): 288–316.

21. Eisner, 302.

22. Guido Crainz, *Storia del miracolo italiano. Culture, identità, trasformazioni fra anni cinquanta e sessanta* (Rome: Donzelli, 2005), 99–100.

23. Dario Melossi and Rossella Selmini, "'Modernisation'of Institutions of Social and Penal Control in Italy/Europe: The 'New'Crime Prevention," in *Crime Prevention Policies in Comparative Perspective*, ed. Adam Crawford (Cullompton, Devon: Willan, 2009), 179–202; Sette, "Honneur, terrorisme et criminalité: soixante ans d'homicides en Italie (1945–2005)."

24. "Polemiche a Bologna Sul Ruolo Del Corpo 'pattuglie Cittadine,'" *Corriere Della Sera*, June 7, 1978.

25. "Continua La Polemica Sul Progetto Delle 'Pattuglie Civili Dell'ordine,'" *Corriere Della Sera*, February 8, 1974; Giancarlo Ghislanzoni, "Primavalle: Ottanta Negozianti Di Notte Diventano 'Vigilantes,'" *Corriere Della Sera*, December 23, 1974.

26. Laura Balbo and Luigi Manconi, *Razzismi, un vocabolario* (Milan: Feltrinelli, 1993), 51–52; Vincenzo Scalia, "The Context of Decentralised Policing or Local Squads? The Case of the Italian Ronde," *International Journal of Sociology and Anthropology* 4, no. 2 (2012): 38–47.

27. Gian Guido Nobili, "Ronde cittadine: una nuova strategia di sicurezza urbana?," *Autonomie locali e servizi sociali*, no. 3 (2009): 487–98, https://doi.org/10.1447/31566.

28. Jonathan Simon, *Governing through Crime: How the War on Crime Transformed American Democracy and Created a Culture of Fear* (New York: Oxford University Press, 2007).

29. Giovanni Moro, "La cittadinanza attiva e le politiche locali della sicurezza," in *Oltre le ordinanze. I sindaci e la sicurezza urbana* (Rome: Cittalia. Fondazione Anci ricerche, 2009), 181–208; Nobili, "VI. Ronde cittadine."

30. Gian Guido Nobili, "Le politiche di sicurezza urbana in Italia: lo stato dell'arte e i nodi irrisolti," *SINAPPSI* 2 (October 5, 2020): 120, https://doi.org/10.1485/2532-8549-202002-9.

31. Adolfo Ceretti and Roberto Cornelli, *Oltre la paura: cinque riflessioni su criminalità, società e politica* (Milan: Feltrinelli, 2013).

32. David Forgacs, *Italy's Margins: Social Exclusion and Nation Formation since 1861* (Cambridge: Cambridge University Press, 2014), 280–85.

33. Ana Ivasiuc, "Watching over the Neighbourhood: Vigilante Discourses and Practices in the Suburbs of Rome," *Etnofoor* 27, no. 2 (2015): 53–72.

34. Pietro Castelli Gattinara, "Forza Nuova and the Security Walks: Squadrismo and Extreme Right Vigilantism in Italy," in *Vigilantism against Migrants and Minorities*, ed. Tore Bjørgo and Miroslav Mareš (Abingdon, Oxon: Routledge, 2019), 199–212.

35. Office for Democratic Institutions and Human Rights (ODIHR), https://hatecrime.osce.org/italy.

36. ISTAT, "BES Report 2019. Equitable and Sustainable Well-Being in Italy" (Rome, 2020), 99,101,106, https://www.istat.it/it/files//2019/12/BES-2019-en.pdf.

37. ISTAT, 87.

38. CENSIS, "1° Rapporto Sulla Filiera Della Sicurezza in Italia" (Rome, 2018), 25.

39. Nando Pagnoncelli, "Un Elettore Su Due è Favorevole a Estendere La Legittima Difesa," *Corriere Della Sera*, December 18, 2018, https://www.corriere.it/politica/18_dicembre_10/elettore-due-favorevole-estendere-legittima-difesa-35feaf9e-fcbe-11e8-9879-765e1cc1d300.shtml.

40. Carmen Andreuccioli, "La Legittima Difesa: Alcuni Dati" (Servizio Studi del Senato, October 2018), https://www.senato.it/service/PDF/PDFServer/BGT/01076418.pdf.

41. Ministero della Giustizia, "Monitoraggio della giustizia penale - anni 2003 - II trimestre 2020," November 11, 2020, https://www.giustizia.it/giustizia/it/mg_2_9_13.page.

42. CENSIS, "1° Rapporto Sulla Filiera Della Sicurezza in Italia," 24.

43. Aaron Karp, "Estimating Global Civilian-HELD Firearms Numbers" (Small Arms Survey, June 2018), 4.

44. Derek Dunne, *Shakespeare, Revenge Tragedy and Early Modern Law: Vindictive Justice* (Houndmills: Palgrave Macmillan, 2016); Emily L. King, *Civil Vengeance: Literature, Culture, and Early Modern Revenge* (Ithaca: Cornell University Press, 2019).

45. Giambattista Giraldi Cinzio, *Orbeche* (1541); Vittorio Alfieri, *Filippo* (1783).

46. Scipione Maffei, *Merope* (1713), and, with the same subject, Vittorio Alfieri, *Merope* (1782).

47. See Mario A. Cattaneo, *Carlo Goldoni e Alessandro Manzoni. Illuminismo e diritto penale* (Milan: Giuffrè, 1991).

48. This is what Goldoni wrote in the preface for the reader of *La donna vendicativa* (The Vengeful Woman, 1752).

49. See Gianfranco Bettetini, Aldo Grasso, and Laura Tettamanzi, *Le mille e una volta dei Promessi sposi* (Turin: Nuova ERI, 1990); Antonella Brancaccio, *Il dilavato e graffiato schermo di Alessandro Manzoni* (Bergamo: Sestante, 2016).

50. See also Pierantonio Frare, "La via stretta. Giustizia, vendetta e perdono nei 'Promessi sposi,'" in *Giustizia e letteratura. II.*, ed. Gabrio Forti, Claudia Mazzucato, and Arianna Visconti (Milan: Vita e Pensiero, 2014), 38–54.

51. Susan Amatangelo, "'Chi Cerca Trova e Chi Seguita Vince': Seeking Revenge in Verga's Cavalleria Rusticana and Pirandello's Liolà," in *Vendetta: Essays on Honor and Revenge*, ed. Giovanna Summerfield (Newcastle upon Tyne: Cambridge Scholars Publishing, 2010), 137–55; Giuseppe Lorini and Olimpia Giuliana Loddo, "Revenge Between Legal and Social Norms in Cavalleria Rusticana," in *Law and Opera*, ed. Filippo Annunziata and Giorgio Fabio Colombo (Cham: Springer, 2018), 209–21.

52. Mariano Longo, *Emotions through Literature: Fictional Narratives, Society and the Emotional Self* (Abingdon, Oxon: Routledge, 2020), 127–35.

53. Antonio Gramsci, *Prison Notebooks. Vol. 3*, ed. Joseph A. Buttigieg (New York: Columbia University Press, 2011), 106.

54. Umberto Eco, "I Beati Paoli e l'ideologia del romanzo popolare," in *I Beati Paoli*, by Luigi Natoli, vol. I (Palermo: Flaccovio, 1986), VII–XVIII.

55. Rino Coluccello, *Challenging the Mafia Mystique. Cosa Nostra from Legitimisation to Denunciation* (Basingstoke: Palgrave, 2016), 89–117.

56. See Floriana Colao, "I processi ai 'maggiori esponenti di idee contrarie al governo nazionale' prima dell'istituzione del Tribunale speciale per la difesa dello Stato," in *Il diritto del duce. Giustizia e repressione nell'Italia fascista*, ed. Luigi Lacchè (Rome: Donzelli, 2015), 31–55.

57. This section is partly based on Ferdinando Spina, "Stories of Revenge in Italian Popular Culture: A Narrative Study of Vigilante Films," *Italian Journal of Sociology of Education* 11, no. 2 (2019): 218–52, to which one can refer for a more in-depth discussion of the topic.

58. Antonio Pigliaru, *La vendetta barbaricina come ordinamento giuridico* (Milan: Giuffrè, 1959).

59. Alexandra Heller-Nicholas, *Rape-Revenge Films: A Critical Study*, second ed. (Jefferson, NC: McFarland, 2021); Peter Robson, "Developments in Revenge, Justice and Rape in the Cinema," *International Journal for the Semiotics of Law* 34, no. 1 (2021): 69–88.

60. Peter Bondanella and Federico Pacchioni, *A History of Italian Cinema* (New York: Bloomsbury, 2017), 475–574; Roberto Curti, *Italian Crime Filmography, 1968–1980* (Jefferson, NC: McFarland, 2013); Austin Fisher, "Il Braccio Violento Della Legge: Revelation, Conspiracy and the Politics of Violence in the

Poliziottesco," *Journal of Italian Cinema & Media Studies* 2, no. 2 (June 1, 2014): 167–81, https://doi.org/10.1386/jicms.2.2.167_1.

61. Gian Piero Brunetta, *The History of Italian Cinema* (Princeton: Princeton University Press, 2009), 210; see also Alex Marlow-Mann, "Strategies of Tension: Towards a Reinterpretation of Enzo G. Castellari's The Big Racket and the Italian Crime Film," in *Popular Italian Cinema*, ed. Louis Bayman and Sergio Rigoletto (New York: Palgrave Macmillan, 2013), 133–46.

62. Gian Piero Brunetta, "Il cinema legge la società italiana," in *Storia dell'Italia repubblicana*, vol. II, t. 2° (Turin: Einaudi, 1995), 833.

63. Vincenzo Tomeo, *Il giudice sullo schermo. Magistratura e polizia nel cinema italiano* (Rome-Bari: Laterza, 1973).

64. Curti, *Italian Crime Filmography, 1968–1980*, 123.

65. Robson, "Vengeance in Popular Culture"; Peter Robson, "Beyond the Courtroom: Vigilantism, Revenge and Rape-Revenge Films in the Cinema of Justice," in *Framing Law and Crime*, ed. Caroline Joan S. Picart, Michael Hviid Jacobsen, and Cecil Greek (Lanham, MD: Rowman & Littlefield, 2016), 165–202.

66. Carlos Clarens, *Crime Movies* (New York: Norton, 1980), 322–24.

67. Ferdinando Spina, "Italy," in *A Transnational Study of Law and Justice on TV*, ed. Peter Robson and Jennifer L. Schulz (Oxford: Hart, 2016), 145–62.

68. E.g., *Tre punto sei* (*Three Point Six*, 2003); *Cemento armato* (*Concrete Romance*, 2007); *Lo chiamavano Jeeg Robot* (*They Call Me Jeeg*, 2015); *Il codice del babbuino* (*The Baboon Code*, 2018).

69. 2018 winner of the *Palme d'Or* at the Cannes festival.

70. Tomeo, *Il giudice sullo schermo*, 30.

71. Giovanni Russo, "Dietro La Faccia Del Piccolo Borghese," *Il Corriere Della Sera*, March 13, 1977.

72. Emile Durkheim, *Moral Education: A Study in the Theory and Application of the Sociology of Education* (New York: Free Press of Glencoe, 1961), 166ff.

73. *Reeds in the Wind*, RAI (Radiotelevisione italiana, the national public broadcasting company) 1958.

74. ITV, 1975.

75. NBC, 1984.

76. NBC, 1961.

77. CBS, 1985.

78. Michele Anselmi, "Detective in Tv: Il Giustiziere Battuto Da Shayne," *L'Unità*, February 1, 1988.

79. CBS, 1991.

80. ABC, 1998.

81. Amazon, 2014.

82. Showtime Networks, 2006.

83. See Milly Buonanno, *Italian TV Drama and Beyond: Stories from the Soil, Stories from the Sea* (Bristol: Intellect Books, 2012).

84. E.g., *Pupetta—Il coraggio e la passione* (*Pupetta—Courage and passion*, Mediaset, 2013).

85. Buonanno, *Italian TV Drama and Beyond*, 73.

86. Elisa Giomi, "Il 'Familismo Morale': Pubblico e Privato Nelle Rappresentazioni Della Fiction Poliziesca Italiana" (Rome: CMCS, 2010), http://eprints.luiss.it/505/1/CMCSWP_0510M.pdf.

87. Rossella Selmini, "Exploring Cultural Criminology: The Police World in Fiction," *European Journal of Criminology* 17, no. 5 (September 2020): 9, https://doi.org/10.1177/1477370820939362.

88. Carl Plantinga, *Screen Stories: Emotion and the Ethics of Engagement* (Oxford: Oxford University Press, 2018), 232ff.

89. Zimring, *The Contradictions of American Capital Punishment*, 103–4.

BIBLIOGRAPHY

Amatangelo, Susan. "'Chi Cerca Trova e Chi Seguita Vince': Seeking Revenge in Verga's Cavalleria Rusticana and Pirandello's Liolà." In *Vendetta: Essays on Honor and Revenge*, edited by Giovanna Summerfield, 137–55. Newcastle upon Tyne: Cambridge Scholars Publishing, 2010.

Andreuccioli, Carmen. "La Legittima Difesa: Alcuni Dati." Servizio Studi del Senato, October 2018. https://www.senato.it/service/PDF/PDFServer/BGT/01076418.pdf.

Anselmi, Michele. "Detective in TV: Il Giustiziere Battuto Da Shayne." *L'Unità*, February 1, 1988.

Balbo, Laura, and Luigi Manconi. *Razzismi, un vocabolario*. Milan: Feltrinelli, 1993.

Bettetini, Gianfranco, Aldo Grasso, and Laura Tettamanzi. *Le mille e una volta dei Promessi sposi*. Turin: Nuova ERI, 1990.

Bondanella, Peter, and Federico Pacchioni. *A History of Italian Cinema*. New York: Bloomsbury, 2017.

Braccesi, Cosimo. "Le Pattuglie Cittadine. 160 anni di storia." *Sicurezza e territorio* 10 (1993): 11–16.

Brancaccio, Antonella. *Il dilavato e graffiato schermo di Alessandro Manzoni*. Bergamo: Sestante, 2016.

Brunetta, Gian Piero. "Il cinema legge la società italiana." In *Storia dell'Italia repubblicana*, II, t. 2°:141–240. Turin: Einaudi, 1995.

———. *The History of Italian Cinema*. Princeton: Princeton University Press, 2009.

Buonanno, Milly. *Italian TV Drama and Beyond: Stories from the Soil, Stories from the Sea*. Bristol: Intellect Books, 2012.

Cardoza, Anthony L. *Agrarian Elites and Italian Fascism the Province of Bologne, 1901–1926*. Princeton: Princeton University Press, 1982.

Castelli Gattinara, Pietro. "Forza Nuova and the Security Walks: Squadrismo and Extreme Right Vigilantism in Italy." In *Vigilantism against Migrants and Minorities*, edited by Tore Bjørgo and Miroslav Mareš, 199–212. Abingdon, Oxon: Routledge, 2019.

Cattaneo, Mario A. *Carlo Goldoni e Alessandro Manzoni. Illuminismo e diritto penale*. Milan: Giuffrè, 1991.

CENSIS. "1° Rapporto Sulla Filiera Della Sicurezza in Italia." Rome, 2018.

Ceretti, Adolfo, and Roberto Cornelli. *Oltre la paura: cinque riflessioni su criminalità, società e politica*. Milan: Feltrinelli, 2013.
Clarens, Carlos. *Crime Movies*. New York: Norton, 1980.
Clark, Martin. "Italian Squadrismo and Contemporary Vigilantism." *European History Quarterly* 18, no. 1 (January 1988): 33–49. https://doi.org/10.1177/026569148801800102.
Colao, Floriana. "I processi ai 'maggiori esponenti di idee contrarie al governo nazionale' prima dell'istituzione del Tribunale speciale per la difesa dello Stato." In *Il diritto del duce. Giustizia e repressione nell'Italia fascista*, edited by Luigi Lacchè, 31–55. Rome: Donzelli, 2015.
Coluccello, Rino. *Challenging the Mafia Mystique: Cosa Nostra from Legitimisation to Denunciation*. Basingstoke: Palgrave, 2016.
Corriere della Sera. "Continua La Polemica Sul Progetto Delle 'Pattuglie Civili Dell'ordine,'" February 8, 1974.
Cooney, Mark. "Social and Legal Responses to Homicide." In *The Handbook of Homicide*, edited by Fiona Brookman, Edward R. Maguire, and Mike Maguire, 54–69. Chichester, Malden, MA: Wiley/ Blackwell, 2017.
Crainz, Guido. *Storia del miracolo italiano. Culture, identità, trasformazioni fra anni cinquanta e sessanta*. Rome: Donzelli, 2005.
Curti, Roberto. *Italian Crime Filmography, 1968–1980*. Jefferson, NC: McFarland, 2013.
Dunne, Derek. *Shakespeare, Revenge Tragedy and Early Modern Law: Vindictive Justice*. Houndmills: Palgrave Macmillan, 2016.
Durkheim, Emile. *Moral Education: A Study in the Theory and Application of the Sociology of Education*. New York: Free Press of Glencoe, 1961.
Ebner, Michael R. *Ordinary Violence in Mussolini's Italy*. New York: Cambridge University Press, 2011.
Eco, Umberto, and Luigi Natoli. "I Beati Paoli e l'ideologia del romanzo popolare." In *I Beati Paoli*, I:VII–XVIII. Palermo: Flaccovio, 1986.
Eisner, Manuel. "Long-Term Historical Trends in Violent Crime." *Crime and Justice* 30 (2003): 83–142.
———. "Modernity Strikes Back? A Historical Perspective on the Latest Increase in Interpersonal Violence (1960–1990)." *International Journal of Conflict and Violence (IJCV)* 2, no. 2 (2008): 288–316.
Fisher, Austin. "Il Braccio Violento Della Legge: Revelation, Conspiracy and the Politics of Violence in the Poliziottesco." *Journal of Italian Cinema & Media Studies* 2, no. 2 (June 1, 2014): 167–81. https://doi.org/10.1386/jicms.2.2.167_1.
Forgacs, David. *Italy's Margins: Social Exclusion and Nation Formation since 1861*. Cambridge: Cambridge University Press, 2014.
Franzinelli, Mimmo. *Squadristi: protagonisti e techniche della violenza fascista: 1919–1922*. Milan: Mondadori, 2003.
Frare, Pierantonio. "La via stretta. Giustizia, vendetta e perdono nei 'Promessi sposi.'" In *Giustizia e letteratura. II.*, edited by Gabrio Forti, Claudia Mazzucato, and Arianna Visconti, 38–54. Milan: Vita e Pensiero, 2014.

Gentile, Emilio. "Fascism in Power: The Totalitarian Experiment." In *Liberal and Fascist Italy: 1900–1945*, edited by Adrian Lyttelton, 139–74. Oxford: Oxford University Press, 2002.

Ghislanzoni, Giancarlo. "Primavalle: Ottanta Negozianti Di Notte Diventano 'Vigilantes.'" *Corriere Della Sera*, December 23, 1974.

Giomi, Elisa. "Il 'Familismo Morale': Pubblico e Privato Nelle Rappresentazioni Della Fiction Poliziesca Italiana." Rome: CMCS, 2010. http://eprints.luiss.it/505/1/CMCSWP_0510M.pdf.

Gramsci, Antonio. *Prison Notebooks. Vol. 3*. Edited by Joseph A Buttigieg. New York: Columbia University Press, 2011.

Heller-Nicholas, Alexandra. *Rape-Revenge Films: A Critical Study*. Second ed. Jefferson, N.C: McFarland, 2021.

Hughes, Steven C. *Crime, Disorder, and the Risorgimento: The Politics of Policing in Bologna*. Cambridge: Cambridge University Press, 1994.

ISTAT. "BES Report 2019. Equitable and Sustainable Well-Being in Italy." Rome, 2020. https://www.istat.it/it/files//2019/12/BES-2019-en.pdf.

Ivasiuc, Ana. "Watching over the Neighbourhood: Vigilante Discourses and Practices in the Suburbs of Rome." *Etnofoor* 27, no. 2 (2015): 53–72.

Karp, Aaron. "Estimating Global Civilian-HELD Firearms Numbers." Small Arms Survey, June 2018.

King, Emily L. *Civil Vengeance: Literature, Culture, and Early Modern Revenge*. Ithaca: Cornell University Press, 2019.

Longo, Mariano. *Emotions through Literature: Fictional Narratives, Society and the Emotional Self*. Abingdon, Oxon: Routledge, 2020.

———. *Fiction and Social Reality: Literature and Narrative as Sociological Resources*. Farnham: Ashgate, 2015.

Lorini, Giuseppe, and Olimpia Giuliana Loddo. "Revenge Between Legal and Social Norms in Cavalleria Rusticana." In *Law and Opera*, edited by Filippo Annunziata and Giorgio Fabio Colombo, 209–21. Cham: Springer, 2018.

Machura, Stefan. "The Law and Cinema Movement." In *Framing Law and Crime: An Interdisciplinary Anthology*, edited by Caroline Joan "Kay" S. Picart, Michael Hviid Jacobsen, and Cecil Greek, 25–58. Lanham, MD: Rowman & Littlefield, 2016.

Marlow-Mann, Alex. "Strategies of Tension: Towards a Reinterpretation of Enzo G. Castellari's The Big Racket and the Italian Crime Film." In *Popular Italian Cinema*, edited by Louis Bayman and Sergio Rigoletto, 133–46. New York: Palgrave Macmillan, 2013.

Martini, Andrea. "Punishing the Fascists: An Intense Debate During the Italian Civil War." In *Italy and the Second World War: Alternative Perspectives*, edited by Emanuele Sica and Richard Carrier, 249–71. Leiden; Boston: Brill, 2018.

Melossi, Dario. "Andamento economico, incarcerazione, omicidi e allarme sociale in Italia: 1863–1994." In *Storia d'Italia. Annali 12. La criminalità*, edited by Luciano Violante, 35–62. Turin: Einaudi, 1997.

Melossi, Dario, and Rossella Selmini. "'Modernisation'of Institutions of Social and Penal Control in Italy/Europe: The 'New'Crime Prevention." In *Crime Prevention*

Policies in Comparative Perspective, edited by Adam Crawford, 179–202. Cullompton, Devon: Willan, 2009.

Millan, Matteo. "In Defence of Freedom? The Practices of Armed Movements in Pre-1914 Europe: Italy, Spain and France." *European History Quarterly* 46, no. 1 (January 2016): 48–71. https://doi.org/10.1177/0265691415619614.

———. "Sostituire l'autorità, riaffermare la sovranità. Legittima difesa, corpi armati e crisi dello Stato nell'Italia giolittiana." *Studi storici*, no. 1 (2019): 139–66. https://doi.org/10.7375/92947.

———. "The Origins." In *The Politics of Everyday Life in Fascist Italy*, edited by Joshua Arthurs, Michael Ebner, and Kate Ferris, 19–49. New York: Palgrave Macmillan, 2017.

Moro, Giovanni. "La cittadinanza attiva e le politiche locali della sicurezza." In *Oltre le ordinanze. I sindaci e la sicurezza urbana*, 181–208. Rome: Cittalia. Fondazione Anci ricerche, 2009.

Nobili, Gian Guido. "Le politiche di sicurezza urbana in Italia: lo stato dell'arte e i nodi irrisolti." *SINAPPSI* 2 (October 5, 2020): 120. https://doi.org/10.1485/2532-8549-202002-9.

———. "Ronde cittadine: una nuova strategia di sicurezza urbana?" *Autonomie locali e servizi sociali*, no. 3 (2009): 487–98. https://doi.org/10.1447/31566.

Pagnoncelli, Nando. "Un Elettore Su Due è Favorevole a Estendere La Legittima Difesa." *Corriere Della Sera*, December 18, 2018. https://www.corriere.it/politica/18_dicembre_10/elettore-due-favorevole-estendere-legittima-difesa-35feaf9e-fcbe-11e8-9879-765e1cc1d300.shtml.

Pavone, Claudio. *A Civil War: A History of the Italian Resistance*. London; New York: Verso, 2013.

Peli, Santo. *La Resistenza difficile*. Milan: FrancoAngeli, 1999.

Pigliaru, Antonio. *La vendetta barbaricina come ordinamento giuridico*. Milan: Giuffrè, 1959.

Plantinga, Carl. *Screen Stories: Emotion and the Ethics of Engagement*. Oxford: Oxford University Press, 2018.

Corriere della Sera. "Polemiche a Bologna Sul Ruolo Del Corpo 'pattuglie Cittadine,'" June 7, 1978.

Portinaro, Pier Paolo. *I conti con il passato vendetta, amnistia, giustizia*. Milan: Feltrinelli, 2011.

Pucci, Lara. "Shooting Corpses: The Fosse Ardeatine in Giorni Di Gloria (1945)." *Italian Studies* 68, no. 3 (2013): 356–77.

Ranzato, Gabriele. *Il linciaggio di Carretta. Roma 1944: violenza politica e ordinaria violenza*. Milan: Il Saggiatore, 1997.

Robson, Peter. "Beyond the Courtroom—Vigilantism, Revenge and Rape-Revenge Films in the Cinema of Justice." In *Framing Law and Crime*, edited by Caroline Joan S. Picart, Michael Hviid Jacobsen, and Cecil Greek, 165–202. Lanham, MD: Rowman & Littlefield, 2016.

———. "Developments in Revenge, Justice and Rape in the Cinema." *International Journal for the Semiotics of Law* 34, no. 1 (2021): 69–88.

———. "Vengeance in Popular Culture." In *Oxford Encyclopedia of Crime, Media, and Popular Culture*. Oxford: Oxford University Press, December 22, 2016. https://doi.org/10.1093/acrefore/9780190264079.013.45.

Russo, Giovanni. "Dietro La Faccia Del Piccolo Borghese." *Il Corriere Della Sera*, March 13, 1977.

Sbriccoli, Mario. "Caratteri originari e tratti permanenti del sistema penale italiano (1860–1990)." In *Storia d'Italia. Annali, 14: Legge Diritto Giustizia*, edited by Luciano Violante, 485–551. Turin: Einaudi, 1988.

Scalia, Vincenzo. "The Context of Decentralised Policing or Local Squads? The Case of the Italian Ronde." *International Journal of Sociology and Anthropology* 4, no. 2 (2012): 38–47.

Selmini, Rossella. "Exploring Cultural Criminology: The Police World in Fiction." *European Journal of Criminology* 17, no. 5 (September 2020): 501–17. https://doi.org/10.1177/1477370820939362.

Sette, Raffaella. "Honneur, terrorisme et criminalité: soixante ans d'homicides en Italie (1945–2005)." In *Histoire de l'homicide en Europe: de la fin du moyen âge à nos jours*, edited by Laurent Mucchieli and Pieter Spierenburg, 163–95. Paris: Découverte, 2009.

Siciliano, Domenico. "Per una genealogia del diritto alla legittima difesa: da Carrara ai Rocco." *Quaderni fiorentini per la storia del pensiero giuridico moderno* 35, no. 2 (2006): 723–847.

Simon, Jonathan. *Governing through Crime: How the War on Crime Transformed American Democracy and Created a Culture of Fear*. New York: Oxford University Press, 2007.

Skinner, Stephen. "Tainted Law? The Italian Penal Code, Fascism and Democracy." *International Journal of Law in Context* 7, no. 4 (December 2011): 423–46. https://doi.org/10.1017/S1744552311000231.

Spina, Ferdinando. "Italy." In *A Transnational Study of Law and Justice on TV*, edited by Peter Robson and Jennifer L. Schulz, 145–62. Oxford: Hart, 2016.

———. "Stories of Revenge in Italian Popular Culture. A Narrative Study of Vigilante Films." *Italian Journal of Sociology of Education* 11, no. 2 (2019): 218–52.

Tomeo, Vincenzo. *Il giudice sullo schermo. Magistratura e polizia nel cinema italiano*. Rome-Bari: Laterza, 1973.

Weber, Max. *From Max Weber: Essays in Sociology*. Edited by Hans Heinrich Gerth and Charls Wright Mills. New York: Oxford University Press, 1946.

Zimring, Franklin E. *The Contradictions of American Capital Punishment*. New York: Oxford University Press, 2003.

Chapter 8

The Punishing Hand of Vigilante Justice in Poland

Joanna Osiejewicz

Vigilantism is an indicator of the degree of acceptance of the formal rules of social life. It also says a lot about the state of social bonds and the degree of frustration among citizens. Vigilante acts are a strong warning signal about the failure of the state, its administrative structures and agencies of formal social control. This is illustrated in Poland by historical events called *zajazd* (foray). Due to the weakness of the executive power of the First Republic of Poland, they became a de facto way for the gentry to enforce a court judgment. The forays consisted of calling on the *starosta* (county head) of the *powiat* (county) to remove the stubborn debtor by force. From the second half of the seventeenth century, arbitrary forays (without the participation of starosts) started being organized to enforce judgments through self-help. Sometimes forays were even completely illegal[1] and constituted a form of plunder. From a contemporary point of view, forays were a form of taking justice into people's own hands, carried out using force not legitimized by the state. In today's perspective, vigilantism is associated with the subjectively perceived necessary defense of arbitrary exceeding of borders, rather than with the assertion of property rights. The essence of vigilantism is to exact a penalty beyond any formalized and legally sanctioned procedures.

POLISH LITERATURE REVIEW OF THE TOPIC OF VIGILANTE JUSTICE

The only Polish scholarly publication on the subject of vigilantism is the book *Samosąd we Włodowie. Studium przypadku*[2] (*Lynching at Włodowo. Case study*) by Piotr Chlebowicz, a criminologist at the University of Warmia and Mazury in Olsztyn. This monograph takes us through a well-known event in Poland, reports the behavior of the victim and perpetrators of the lynching as well as the local policemen. It takes the reader into the realities of the life of a poor village and into the relationships of its inhabitants. It shows the ways of solving problems there. The author describes the incident hour by hour. He also points to the psychological and emotional background (fear, anxiety, frustration) of the perpetrators. He attempts to assess the activities of law enforcement officers, the prosecutor's office and the court. The book provides an in-depth and detailed description of this particular incident, adjudged by the criminal process authorities as a crime. The lynching in Włodowo is a starting point for the author's broader considerations of the phenomenon of vigilante justice. The infamous lynching was committed in July 2005, by an unidentified group of residents of the Warmian village of Włodowo on a local criminal Józef Ciechanowicz. He had been harassing them for years. It entered the annals of Polish legal history, both because of the rarity of this phenomenon and the reasons for this occurrence.

Chlebowicz rightly notes that lynching is a phenomenon that goes far beyond the sphere of criminal law. In his monograph, he presents an outline of the victim of the lynching, Józef Ciechanowicz, a depraved, repeatedly punished criminal who spent most of his life in prison. This outline was derived from the expert opinions of psychiatrists, testimonies of witnesses, and penitentiary acts. The author thoroughly analyzed the course of events in Włodowo, as well as at the Police Station in Dobre Miasto, also highlighting the days preceding the dramatic events. Besides its academic value, the book depicts how events developed. Chlebowicz provides details of the forensic expert's opinion illustrating the extensive injuries to the deceased's head.[3]. He introduces the telling remark of one of the policemen present at the place where the corpse was found: "They chopped him like a cutlet."[4] On the one hand, the author's conclusions confirm the mechanisms governing the behavior of a group of people who jointly use violence. On the other hand, they undoubtedly illustrate the scale of hatred and frustration that Ciechanowicz had aroused in the villagers.

Apart from the monograph indicated, there do not appear to be with any other academic studies on vigilantism in Poland. In this respect, only newspaper material reporting current events in the country, having the characteristics of vigilantism, are available. One can point here, for example, to a noted case of a pedophile suspected of raping a ten-year-old girl, whose neighbors surrounded the house and threatened him with death.[5]

In recent years, a problematic issue in Poland has been the vigilante punishment of drivers of incorrectly parked cars. Internet press reported about perpetrators of vigilante justice, who invented various "penalties" for leaving the car right next to or at a pedestrian crossing. The most popular of these was smearing the car's windshield with toothpaste, wrapping the car with cling film in such a way that the car was "attached" to a road sign or sticking on the windshield difficult to remove stickers with vulgar content. There were also cases of dumping garbage on the hood of a car which, improperly parked, prevented the garbage from being placed in the garbage bin. Another vigilante method was to plaster the whole car with stickers for leaving the car at a parking space reserved for a vehicle driven by a disabled person. The above acts of "justice" often gained considerable internet popularity.[6]

VIGILANTE JUSTICE IN POLAND—
PRE-DEMOCRATIC AND DEMOCRATIC EVENTS

The history of Poland has only a limited number of documented cases of vigilantism. The first of these happened on June 28, 1794, during the Kościuszko Uprising.[7] The Polish national uprising against Russia and Prussia included, among others Warsaw, Vilnius, Courland, and Great Poland. It has its roots in 1792, when several of the leading Polish magnates under the patronage of Russian Tsarina Catherine II formed a conspiracy called the Targowica confederation. The Targowica confederates, under the slogans of defending endangered freedom and the old system, stood against the Constitution of May 3 and reforms of the Great Sejm. Their supporters received military assistance from Russia. The Polish King Stanisław August Poniatowski joined the confederation and ordered the troops to lay down their arms. The direct result of the defeat was the Second Partition of Poland between Russia and Prussia, which took place in 1793.[8] Targowica was quickly recognized by a large part of Polish society as a symbol of national treason.[9]

At the behest of Russia, the Targowica confederates began to roll back the reform of the Great Sejm (Parliament). At that time, the Russians plundered Poland. This contributed significantly to the country's economic and financial collapse. The tragic rule of Targowica confederates led to widespread dissatisfaction within Polish society. In March 1794, the Kościuszko Uprising broke out. It became part of the Warsaw Uprising. From 17 to 18 April 1794, the inhabitants of Warsaw, headed by shoemaker Jan Kiliński, and the regular Polish army destroyed the Russian garrison and liberated Warsaw. After releasing the city from Russian hands, the Targowica confederates were found guilty of treason. On April 25 in Vilnius, the Criminal Court sentenced the Great Hetman[10] of Lithuania, Szymon Kossakowski, to the gallows. He was hanged in the town square. The decision to convict traitors was eagerly sought by the people of Warsaw and the so-called Polish Jacobins, proclaiming republican-libertarian slogans that had their roots in French Jacobinism. On May 9, the Provisional Temporary Council, under pressure from an outraged crowd who had invaded the town hall, issued an immediate death sentence for treason on three confederates. The Grand Hetman of the Crown Piotr Ożarowski, the Marshal of the Perpetual Council Józef Ankwicz and the Lithuanian Field Hetman Józef Zabiełła were sentenced to death. Next, the Livonian Bishop Józef Kazimierz Kossakowski was also sentenced to the gallows. He was hanged in front of the church of St. Anna in Warsaw. The death of the Targowica confederates was a result of vigilante justice. On June 28, a furious crowd broke through the gates of the prison and executed their own judgments on many of the remaining confederates. Among those hanged were the Vilnius bishop Ignacy Massalski, the Castellan of Przemyśl Prince Antoni Czetwertyński, the deputy for Turkey Karol Boscamp-Lasopolski, the chamberlain Stefan Grabowski, the crown instigator Mateusz Roguski, the Russian spy Marceli Piętka, and the criminal court Prosecutor Józef Majewski.[11]

Another historical instance of vigilante justice occurred during the 1830 Uprising in Warsaw. The November Uprising itself broke out on November 29, 1830. However, proper warfare began only after the Russian army crossed the borders of the Kingdom of Poland on February 5 and 6, 1831, under the command of Field Marshal Ivan Dybicz. Then, the regular Polish-Russian war began. General Jan Skrzynecki was the commander-in-chief. After one of the expeditions that ended in complete defeat, the public demanded that the perpetrators of the expedition's failure be punished. There was a strong rise in dissatisfaction among the Warsaw population. The reason was the deteriorating economic and living conditions of the city's residents. Also, the patriotic concern was caused by the prolonged war because it did not bring military successes.[12] Skrzynecki was afraid of being compromised. He wrote a report, in which he accused the Generals Jan Krukowiecki, Antoni Jankowski, and Józef Hurtig of preparing a plot to overthrow the commander-in-chief and hand over the capital city to the Russians. Skrzynecki ordered the arrest only of Generals Jankowski and Hurtig. He deliberately did this to divert public attention from defeat.[13]

On June 29, a double feast was celebrated—of the Church, commemorating the saints Apostles Peter and Paul and of the state—a commemoration of the outbreak of the November Uprising. On this day, orders were issued to arrest Hurtig, Jankowski, and others suspected of treason. Around 9 a.m., a crowd gathered in front of the General Hurtig's house on Świętojerska Street in Warsaw. The accused general was led out to the street. The National Guard managed to defend him. It was not until 11 a.m. that the demonstration arrived at the Castle Square, where the crowd again tried to carry out its judgment on Hurtig. However, with the help of the guards, Hurtig managed to hide in the Royal Castle.[14] At the peak of the demonstration, around noon, eight to ten thousand people gathered on the Castle Square.[15] The crowd demanded a quick and exemplary punishment of those arrested. Adam Czartoryski, the president of the national government, came to the castle. Józef Kozłowski, a member of the Patriotic Society, spoke on behalf of the gathering, demanding "court and punishment for traitors to the homeland. The Polish people are patient and go to the authorities for justice, but woe to those who would insult them. Their anger is terrible, their despair is terrible."[16] Adam Czartoryski assured those assembled that within twenty-four hours, suspects would be brought to justice and judged. A four-person delegation was selected from the crowd to determine whether the main defendants, Hurtig, Jankowski, and Bukowski, were in custody at the castle. Only after receiving confirmation from these delegates did the crowd slowly began to disperse. Around 4 p.m., the crowd that remained on the Castle Square followed the popular deputy Roman Sołtyk to pay tribute to his father, Stanisław, who was known for his patriotism.[17] That's how the June demonstrations ended. They are described as the first signal of the night of August 15.[18]

The authorities were afraid to make the final decision in the trial of those accused of treason. They could announce that the conspiracy never existed, in which case responsibility for the defeat would fall solely on the highest command. They could confirm that a secret assassination attempt was planned, but then no one would be able to prove the guilt of the accused because of the lack of evidence. In this situation, they chose the third solution, the worst possible—delay. Those accused of treason were not brought to court, not released from custody, and were not cleared of crimes against the state.[19] This delay led to a worsening of the mood of dissatisfaction and constant exasperation among the population of Warsaw.[20] This dissatisfaction was caused, first, by the failures at the front and the crossing by the Russian army of the Vistula near the Prussian border on July 17–18, which meant encircling Warsaw from the west.[21] Finally, on August 8, the Extraordinary War Court issued its judgment in the case of General Jankowski. The court stated that in the absence of evidence it could not determine the degree of guilt and decided that Jankowski would only be temporarily released from the allegation of belonging to the conspiracy. Jankowski was to remain in detention until the cases of his alleged partners were resolved. The Court's decision caused deep indignation in Warsaw.[22] On 10 August, a pamphlet by the Patriotic Society was published, in which the command and its running of the uprising were highly criticized. On August 11, the Sejm deprived General Skrzynecki's of the supreme command of the army.[23] On August 15 the Patriotic Society decided to request the removal of Skrzynecki from the army. A deputation consisting of four people was selected to present the society's demands to the national government. Surrounded by a crowd of nearly 3,000 people, the delegation went to the Presidential Palace.[24] The president of the government, Prince Adam Czartoryski, gave assurances that the authorities were in control of the situation and conducting a policy consistent with the will and interests of the nation. He promised that the government would consider the society's demands.[25] After returning to the Castle Square, the delegation called on the gathering to remain calm and separate. Despite this, the crowd began to increase and demand punishment for traitors and spies among the demonstrators. The cry went up for Jankowski and others detained at the castle. At 10 p.m., the crowd was between five and six thousand. They tried to break through the castle gate. Two hundred guards guarding the castle called a battalion of the 18th infantry regiment for help. When the guards opened the gate to let the soldiers in, the crowd took the opportunity to join the army. With a cry "Death to traitors!" people began searching the castle. Several prisoners, among them Jankowski and Hurtig, were hanged from lampposts.[26] After the executions, the crowd split up. About 600 people went to the House of Asylum and Labor with the cry "Hang the spies!" They wanted to punish those accused of espionage for Russia and former secret police agents detained before the outbreak of the November Uprising. In total, nineteen people were killed there, while another thirteen were wounded.

Then the crowd separated into two groups. The first group went to the Franciscan monastery, where around 2 a.m. they dragged out of the cell and hanged Birnbaum, a former secret police agent and Cossack Dietka, a Russian prisoner known for cruelty. At 3 a.m. the second group broke into the Inquisition House (Powder Magazine), where vigilante action was visited on three former secret police agents. One hour later, a Dominican monastery was attacked, in which Jan Hankiewicz (Secretary General of the Government Commission of Justice) stayed. After having been stabbed with bayonets, he was hanged from the lamppost in front of the building of the Commission of Justice.[27] On the morning of August 16, smaller groups of people began to gather again in some parts of the Old Town. The last few executions took place on August 16 at 12 noon.[28] In total, thirty-four people were killed during the incidents and fourteen were injured.[29] The events were spontaneous, nobody directed them.[30]

On August 16, the national government issued an appeal to the people of Warsaw. It began with the words: "A murderous night passed, a day of prudence dawned, which could reveal the truth and relieve irritated feelings."[31] The government did not openly condemn the incidents of August 15. Through this sentence, they expressed the hope that what had happened would not happen again, would in some sense be forgotten, for there was a new day when the law would triumph. The government regretted that the victims of the August night were killed not as a result of a court judgment, but as a result of the revenge of the people. They emphasized that the events of August 15 resulted from a lack of confidence in the highest authorities. They urged the city's inhabitants to remain calm, because "our 'watchword' is bravery, perseverance and agreement."[32]

A more recent example of vigilante justice occurred on September 20, 1926, shortly after Marshal Piłsudski's May 1926 coup d'état, in the village of Lipniaki in the Vilnius-Trotsky county of the Vilnius Province of the Second Republic of Poland.[33] Józef Wojniusz, a resident of this village, had been sneaking about the farms in the area for a long time clandestinely and causing them severe losses and damage. In the course of the investigation, the police identified him as the thief and, in consequence, brought him before the court. Pending the trial, however, Wojniusz was sent home under police supervision. The victims were very dissatisfied, the more so because they did not manage to get the stolen items from the thief. In relation to material harm, the victims decided to deal with Wojniusz in their own way. On September 19, 1926, a group of people seized the offender, bound him with ropes, and brought him to his home. Here, a specific examination of Wojniusz began, demanding from him the location of the stolen items. Wojniusz resisted the demands. As a result, he was beaten with fists, and then subjected to torture in the presence of his wife and son. He was beaten with wet ropes. When he fainted in pain, he was revived, and the beating continued. He was assaulted with pliers on his tongue and teeth. The harassment continued throughout the night. The next day, Wojniusz was taken to the police station in Turgiel. An investigation was initiated in this case. As a result, nine people were indicted.

The case was brought before the Vilnius District Court. Some of the accused pled guilty by stating that they were simply aiming to get recompense for their losses. Others, however, claimed that they were only there at the incident as witnesses. One of the main witnesses was Józef Wojniusz, who was currently serving a five-year prison sentence for robbing the accused. The court was unable to determine the exact roles of individuals during the incident. By finding everyone guilty of a collective act, the court sentenced each one to six months in prison, halving the sentence and suspending the remainder of the sentence.

More recently, the "Lynching at Włodow" is the media "shorthand" for the beating and assassination of Józef Ciechanowicz, nickname Ciechanek, carried out on July 1, 2005, by the inhabitants of the village Włodowo using, among other things, a shovel, clubs, and a crowbar. Józef Ciechanowicz was a criminal who had been in prison many times before. In the intervals between convictions, he extracted money from pensioners in Włodowo and Brzydów, intimidated shop staff and threatened the inhabitants.[34] According to the evidence of the residents of Włodowo, he threatened them many times.[35] On the day of the incident, he wounded his lover's daughter with a bottle (he had previously injured her with a screwdriver). He also wounded her husband with a knife and threatened to kill their son. Police officers did not respond to the telephone calls of residents and personal reporting of Marlena Winek wounded by Józef Ciechanowicz.[36] The visit of Marlena Winek and her spouse to the police station is a perfect example of how dangerous the failings of the police services can be. The files show that during the conversation at the police station it was stated that "there are worse matters, and here the whole village cannot deal with one man."[37] After returning, the spouses told the inhabitants of the village about the situation, not being sure whether it would make sense to call the police if Ciechanowicz appeared again.[38]

A detailed reconstruction of the vigilante act itself was very problematic. It was difficult to determine precisely how many people actually attacked Ciechanowicz, how many people took part in the pursuit of him, and finally, how many people were present on the spot during the beating of Ciechanowicz. It was finally established that during the incident Ciechanowicz was beaten by at least four young, strong men who additionally used dangerous tools against him. According to the forensic doctor, brain injuries occurred shortly before death, from hard, blunt or blunt-edged tools, such as a stick, club, metal tube, crowbar, spade, boots, fists, or other similar object. This was carried out many times with great force.[39] The criminal proceedings had to rely on personal testimony whose veracity was not easy for two reasons. First of all, the majority of residents were not interested in cooperating with the law enforcement agencies, whose passivity led to the vigilante action itself. Secondly, the residents of Włodowo did not understand at all why the members of their community, who defended the life and health of their loved ones, were arrested and charged with murder. They felt this was a gross injustice. The Włodowo community did not consider the vigilante justice visited on Ciechanek to be a crime, but rather a rational solution to the conflict that actually threatened the residents of Włodowo.[40]

At the trial, the prosecutor requested that three brothers accused of murdering Józef Ciechanowicz, Tomasz, Mirosław, and Krzysztof Winek, be sentenced to ten years imprisonment. For Rafał W., accused of beating the victim using a dangerous tool, the prosecutor demanded a one-year imprisonment, and for Wiesław K. and Stanisław M. accused of desecration of the corpse, a six-month imprisonment.[41] On October 23, 2007, the Olsztyn Regional Court sentenced Krzysztof, Mirosław, and Tomasz Winek to a two-year sentence—suspended for three years. Rafał W. accused of beating using a dangerous tool was sentenced to one-year imprisonment with conditional suspension of execution for three years, and Stanisław M. and Wiesław K. were sentenced to six months—with the sentence suspended for three years.[42] The prosecutor appealed in relation to the sentence and conditions. On March 27, 2008, the Białystok Court of Appeal (the court of second instance) quashed the first-instance judgment and remitted the case. The court found that the

District Court made errors of factual findings, including the place where the corpse was found and the condition of the deceased after being beaten by the accused brothers. The court also expressed doubts as to the aims of the actions of those convicted in desecrating the corpse.[43]

In July 2008, a new trial began. On January 15, 2009, the Olsztyn District Court sentenced the participants in the incident. Tomasz, Mirosław, and Krzysztof Winek were sentenced to four years of imprisonment (using extraordinary mitigation of punishment), Rafał W. was sentenced to one year of imprisonment with conditional suspension of its execution, while the others accused of the desecration of the corpse were sentenced to a six-month suspended sentence.[44] On June 19, 2009, the Court of Appeal in Białystok upheld the judgment.[45] On September 1, 2010, the Supreme Court in Warsaw finally ended the court proceedings dismissing the appeal of those convicted who requested the case to be reconsidered by the court of first instance.[46] The judgment of the Court of Appeal in Białystok remained in force.

The Prosecutor General, implementing the decision of the President of the Republic of Poland of September 16, 2009, No. PU 117–13–009, acting pursuant to the principle of 567 §2 of the Code of Criminal Procedure, initiated ex officio proceedings for pardoning the Wink brothers. By decision of the president of the Republic of Poland Lech Kaczyński of December 18, 2009, a presidential pardon was granted to the accused, with a conditional release from the rest of the sentence of imprisonment for period of ten years.[47] The case is now closed.

The murder of Józef Ciechanowicz had a strong impact on society due to its dramatic circumstances. The image, shaped mainly by the mass media, depicted the inhabitants of Włodowo as a terrorized community deprived of state protection, whose members ultimately obtain justice themselves. This case initiated a lively discussion about the level of public security and the current functioning of formal social control agencies such as the police. The narrative was used as a convenient opportunity to demonstrate the will of the authorities to fight crime. So criminal proceedings in this case were used as fuel for political disputes.

SELF-DEFENSE AND VIGILANTISM (SUBJECTIVE JUSTICE) IN THE DOMESTIC LAW

The desire to live in a just society is deeply rooted in human nature. Contemporary state punishment has a purpose. The penal code in force in Poland does not explicitly specify its purposes. This term appears only when formulating the individual prevention directive in art. 53 § 1 of the Criminal Code—"preventive and educational purposes."[48] The purposes of punishment under applicable law can be inferred from statutory sanctions, directives of judicial sentence, and the manner in which the measures of formal and legal response to the offense have been imposed. One of the main purposes of punishment—in addition to the general, the special, and the compensatory purpose—is justice.[49]

The normative basis for recognizing justice as the purpose of punishment under Polish law are sanctions laid down for individual types of crime. There is the general principle: the more serious the crime, the more severe the sanction. The punishment should, therefore, be consistent with the social sense of justice in the field of criminal sanctions for committing a criminal act, the type and amount of sanctions applied, the judicial dimension of the penalty, and the manner of its execution. The purpose understood in this way requires that the penalty be applied in proportion to the burden of crime measured by the degree of its social danger. The purpose of justice also assumes that, when imposing a total penalty, the court should not exceed the tolerance of a sense of justice. Nowadays, there is an underestimation of the justice role of penal law by associating it with revenge or retaliation.[50] Its implementation, however, plays a very important role both in addressing the mental state of the victim as a result of the crime, and in satisfying the social sense of justice. Therefore, disregarding the justice function of criminal law can have significant negative social effects.

When criminal law is properly performing its functions, criminals are punished, victims are offered justice, and justice is done, then citizens naturally accept and support the system of legal norms. When, however, there are frequent acquittals of guilty perpetrators or the imposition of disproportionately mild punishments against them, so that the victims are defenseless and alone, that is, without the support of state institutions, criminal law is perceived as unfair and society withdraws its support. When people think that the state is incapable of imposing the crimes they deserve on criminals, instead of justice, vigilante justice can emerge. This is, therefore, a phenomenon that works in opposition to state structures whose goal is to enforce the law and protect citizens. It follows from this that vigilante justice performs a function reserved for state organs in a situation where these organs do not perform the tasks assigned to them for various reasons. If the need for social order and justice is not met, there is a tendency to establish non-legal institutions to fulfill the role people expect from the law.[51] Also, penalties that are too low can lead to uncertainty in the society, or even to an increase in vigilante justice.[52] The monopoly of the state in the area of punishment aims, among other things, to exclude emotions from the criminal process.

The assessment of a crime by a victim, although important in procedural proceedings, is undoubtedly also affected by the intensity of dramatic experiences and by the personal experience. The victim may exceed the reasonable measure in retribution, which is why guilt and punishment are better ruled by an external authority.[53] This leads to the question of defense and the excess of its legally permitted boundaries. In Polish criminal law—the three Penal Codes in force in Poland in this century—the approach to self-defense and exceeding its limits has not been the subject to major changes.[54] In the Penal Code of June 6, 1997, currently in force in Poland, self-defense and crossing its borders are regulated by the provisions of Art. 25 § 1, 2 and 3. According to them:

> (§ 1) Whoever in necessary defense repels a direct illegal attack on any interest protected by law, shall not be deemed to have committed an offence. (§ 2) In the event that the limits of necessary defense have been exceeded, in particular when the perpetrator has used a means of defense disproportionate to the danger of the attack, the court may apply mitigation of the penalty and even avoid its imposition. (§ 3) The court shall reject the imposition of the punishment if exceeding the limits of necessary defense resulted from fright or emotional distress, as justified by the circumstances of the attack.[55]

The attack that allows an attacked subject the ability to defend himself by means of necessary defense can only be human behavior.[56] By its very nature, this behavior must be objectively directed either (which is the rule) to violate a good protected by law, or (which is an exception) only to expose such a good to a real danger of its violation. The attack must also be real, which means that it is not sufficient for its existence to be subjective and not based on the real state of affairs to convince the subject of the existence of the attack.[57] Motivation is important—only a subjective belief in the possibility of assault—do not therefore create a situation of self-defense necessary for a person expecting such an attack.[58] The attack must be unlawful. The unlawfulness of the attack is determined by the attacker exceeding any legal norm. The necessary defense can therefore be used not only when the perpetrator carries out an offence with his behavior, but also when he violates a provision of another area of law (civil, administrative, etc.).[59] Breaching a moral code alone does not count.[60] The attack giving rise to the possibility of repelling it by means of necessary defense must also be direct. The direct nature of the attack occurs when the perpetrator violates the property of the victim or if the violation may occur in the near future.[61] This approach then includes also the pre-attack stage. In addition, it follows that the attack does not have to be a danger to any good protected by law, and it is enough to recognize the inevitability of harm to that good. However, the requirement of a high probability of harm to any good protected by law is problematic. It is extremely difficult in a particular situation to estimate the degree of this probability. There are also no measuring tools that could be used to measure the extent to which harm to any good protected by law was likely.[62] Particularly important from the perspective of vigilante justice is also when the direct attack ends. The question arises whether this is the moment when the behavior aimed at harm to any good protected by law has ended, or the moment when the danger to that good ceased (even when the behavior which caused this danger ended earlier). The Polish Supreme Court adopts the second of the above solutions.[63]

It is fairly clear that repelling an attack must be behavior which relates to a prohibited act.[64] A person involved in any self-defense must therefore be aware of the existence of the attack and have the will to resist it. That will should only be, however, a desire to defend, not the reason for the defense actions.[65] An essential subjective element of the necessary defense means that the defender's action must stem from an awareness that he is resisting the attack and must be by way of defense. This subjective element of self-defense action allows a distinction between lawful defense activities and acts of revenge, self-trial, or lynching.

However, the analysis of the case-law of Polish courts allows one to infer that it does not fully agree on the subjective element of the defense of necessity.[66] On the one hand, the emphasis is only on the requirement that the defender be aware of the fact that there is an attack on any good protected by law. On the other hand, it is emphasized that, apart from this requirement, the condition of will to repel the attack must also be fulfilled.

VIGILANTE JUSTICE IN POPULAR LITERATURE AND FILMS

Films

The vitality of vigilante justice is indicated by its frequent use as a leitmotif of many literary and film works. Vigilantism is by its nature characterized by a certain dramaturgy: the people-crowd, for a moment, uniting around an arbitrarily chosen victim, grants itself absolute legislative, executive, and judicial power. Film has always been fascinated by the interface between crime and punishment, that is, between the act of breaking the social order and restoring it by the punishing hand of law. Various film genres were created around observing the work of various types of power apparatus operating in this space: police film, detective film, court drama. Also figures trying to evade the legal system in various ways triggered the introduction of particular film genres, such as gangster or terrorist film. A specific subgenre of films operating in this space are those about justice imposed outside the law as part of personal revenge, family vendetta, or collective lynching.

Krzysztof Krauze in *The Debt* (1999)[67] presents a portrait of an unfulfilled, still aspiring, post-communist middle class. Their dream of economic and social success shattered when they come into conflict with a dark figure from the criminal underworld, suddenly bursting into their so promising life. The action of the film takes place at the turn of 1998/1999 and is based on the real-life case of two young Warsaw businessmen, Artur Bryliński and Sławomir Sikora. In the early 1990s, they were terrorized, tortured, and intimidated by a gangster Grzegorz Gmitrzak, who had previously promised them help in guaranteeing a loan, and then forced them to pay off a nonexistent debt. On the night of March 8-9, 1994, Bryliński and Sikora, unable to find support in the Prosecutor's office and the police, placed Gmitrzak and his personal bodyguard Mariusz Kłos on trial—killing them. They were duly charged and tried. Their trial ended in November 1997. Both were sentenced to twenty-five years in prison.[68] That same month, Krzysztof Krauze and the screenwriter Jerzy Morawski visited both prisoners, collecting materials to be used to make a film that would contribute to their rehabilitation.[69] The film carefully reconstructs the course of events preceding the crime, as well as the act of murder itself.

In the film, two friends—Adam and Stefan—drop out of college to seek happiness in business. They plan to open a scooter assembly plant. However, they lack money because the bank refuses to grant a loan. At this time, businessman Gerard appears, a former neighbor of one of their friends. He offers them financial help. Unfortunately, his conditions are impossible to meet—Adam and Stefan refuse to take advantage of his offer. Then the drama begins—Gerard claims that dealing with their case incurred considerable costs. He requests a refund. The debt is getting bigger every day and the situation is getting out of control. Gerard tries to enforce a nonexistent debt by resorting to gangster methods. He uses physical and mental violence to get the money back. However, he does not write off the debt and still demands money, adding imaginary interest. As the police refuse to help Adam and Stefan, they are both desperately trying to make money to pay off the debt. Meanwhile, Gerard is still demanding his "tribute." He visits Adam's pregnant wife and as a result of this visit, she loses her child. Seeing no other way, the blackmailed friends resort to a desperate step. They lure by deceit, incapacitate and take Gerard and his bodyguard out of town. There, Gerard refers to Adam's unborn child, which causes the Adam to become very angry. As a result, he kills Gerard with a knife, and then also his bodyguard. The exhausted businessmen undress the victims and cut off their heads to make the murder look as if it is the result of a Russian mafia execution. The film caused a great stir in the media. Under the influence of public opinion, President Aleksander Kwasniewski in December 2005 provided a presidential pardon to Sikora. A few months later President Lech Kaczyński announced the pardoning of Bryliński. Bryliński was officially pardoned in December 2010 by President Bronisław Komorowski.[70]

The film *Lynch* by Krzysztof Łukaszewicz (2010)[71] refers to the events outlined above in Włodowo, where a group of local people lynched a former prisoner who persecuted one of the families and where the action was met with police indifference. The film director attempts to justify desperate people who resort to violence in defense of their loved ones. The film begins with a black screen on which two legal definitions appear in white letters: complicity in crime by negligence and self-defense. Their symmetry corresponds to the narrative construction of the film, consisting of two parallel themes. In the first, the criminal terrorizes the village—its result is the lynching. In the second, we can see the work of the police-prison-judicial machine, into which men responsible for vigilante acts end up—this thread ends with the presidential pardon that saves them from prison. The director uses film characters to persuade the viewer to sympathize with the villagers and to recognize their behavior as necessary defense. He accomplishes this intention by showing harassed wives, mothers and children. He also introduces intense, emotional music by Jarosław M. Papaj. He places the lynching in a triangle between a soulless state authority, a degenerate criminal not belonging to the society, and an idealized and harmonious rural community with a high degree of social solidarity that has the right to defend itself against danger. In the background one can see, however, a more general problem: the class nature of the state and the law. Those who are deprived of financial or social capital, whether they are decent citizens or criminals, encounter indifference or even violence in dealing with the state. This is how all the inhabitants of the village are treated in their relations with the authorities, not only when dealing with the police or prison, but even with health services.

The Lynching at Włodowo was also shown in the documentary series *Pitbull*[72] dealing with the work of Warsaw police officers in the homicide department (in later episodes of the department for combating criminal terror by the Metropolitan Police Headquarters). The Lynching at Włodowo also cropped up in the award-winning TV series *Kryminalni* about the work of policemen from the Criminal Department of the Warsaw Police Headquarters.

A sociologically interesting picture of the lynching—prevented at the last moment—can be found in Jerzy Kawalerowicz's *The Train* (1959).[73] People meet in one compartment of a night train. After the first misunderstandings, a thread of sympathy appears among them. Halfway through, militia policemen looking for a killer appear on the train. However, the identified killer escapes into the night. The passengers set off in pursuit of the criminal. Accidentally meeting with the killer unleashes the lowest instincts in people. The scene when a group of passengers suddenly off a night train, in their pajamas, chase a man suspected of murder, grabbing and throwing everything that comes to hand, turns out to be the only community action in the whole film. In this moment, a divided, passive group of passengers suddenly unites around an arbitrarily chosen victim and claim absolute power.

The theme of the fictionalized documentary film *The November Uprising 1830–1831*[74] (directed by Lucyna Smolińska, 1980) is the story of the November Uprising. The film presents the most important events from the outbreak of the uprising to its fall in October 1831. It shows the course of insurgent fighting in Warsaw and reconstructs the most important political and social events. It resembles the clashes of three main groups (conservative, liberal, and the Patriotic Society), presents the diplomatic action of the national government, and shows in brief the course of military operations from February to October 1831. It also depicts socio-political relations in the Kingdom of Poland and the attitude of European countries to the uprising. The film shows, among others, the scene of the said intrusion of the Patriotic Society's delegation into the meeting of the national government at the Governor's Palace on August 15, 1831 (the August Night). In the film, statements about vigilante justice acts are provided by a scientific consultant, Professor Jerzy Skowronek, Polish historian and, researcher into the history of Central and Eastern Europe.[75]

The motive of the August Night is also present in Aleksander Ford's film *Youth of Chopin* (1951).[76] One of the final scenes shows a public meeting of activists of the Great Emigration to Paris after the fall of the uprising. In the speech of Prince Adam Czartoryski, there are words referring to the "shameful night of August 15, when Poles were murdered by Poles."

The figure of a determined, lonely individual seeking justice is sometimes presented in the film at least as morally ambiguous, and often even positively evaluated. This type of hero can be inscribed in the iconic theme of the individual facing the whole world alone. He is usually a lonely avenger, bringing justice and establishing law with a hint of violence. The search for justice alone is justified by the harm done to the hero's loved ones, which is generally neither aided nor avenged by the helpless justice system. In the Polish cinema, the lonely avenger's schemata was followed by the director's debut of Marek Kondrat in *Father's Law* (1999).[77] The former rally driver, after the acquittal of the perpetrators of rape of his daughter, sets himself up as the fount of justice, taking revenge on the perpetrators. The film is trying to implement the typical framework developed in American cinema. However, it perfectly reflects the Polish climate of the 1990s: the widespread obsession with "security" and "crime," the fear of the middle class against the increasing brutalization of life in the Third Polish Republic, as well as the authoritarian longing for a strong individual who "will finally bring order." The action of the film takes place with a background of the new capitalist landscape of Poland. The daughter of the widowed truck driver celebrates her sixteenth birthday in a disco. Here she is brutally raped and beaten by three young men high on drugs. The girl breaks free from her torturers for a moment and throws a suitcase at them. Amphetamines ready for distribution spill out of the suitcase. The bandits, enraged by the discovery of drugs, start acting with greater cruelty. Convinced that they have beaten her to death, they decide to take her and bury her body in the forest. The perpetrators of the crime, despite evidence of guilt, remain free. The girl's father, shocked by the ineffectiveness of the police, decides to effect justice himself. In addition, he must protect his daughter, because her testimony can impact on some influential gangsters. The film provokes discussion about where the relationship between the impulse of saving one's own child and the realities of life, bills, and bloody retaliation lies.

Literature

In Polish literature, the motive of vigilante justice crops up many times. A special mention should be made of the August Night. Tadeusz Hołuj's novel *Kingdom without Land* (1964) describes, among others, the fate of soldiers of the 4th Line Infantry Regiment in Warsaw in 1819–1831 and in exile (until 1838). One of the main characters of the novel is Tomasz Wolski—a dismissed officer shot on the order of General Krukowiecki for participating in the August Night. Another participant in the local courts, Wincenty Dragoński, shot on the same day, plays a marginal role in the novel. Hołuj devoted one chapter of the novel to the August events. Echoes of the events of the night of August 15 also appear in the epilogue of Leon Przemski's story—*Gray Jacobin* (1951), which takes place in Warsaw during the November Uprising. Earlier chapters present, inter alia, the intrigues of members of the Patriotic Society, a revolutionary turmoil in the city, culminating in the August social explosion. Also, the French poet Auguste-Marseille Barthélemy devoted one of his poems to the August vigilantism—*Le seize août à Varsovie* (*16 August in Warsaw*, 1838). In the final chapters of the crime novel by Paweł Goźliński *Jul* (2010), the action of which takes place in July 1845 in Paris, the serial killer and exhibitor Colonel Koenig (a fictional character) recalls the events of the August Night as having a significant impact on his later quasi-mystical and criminal activity in exile. In the flashback of the night of August 15, 1831, there is, among others, a dramatic scene of the murder of General Jankowski.

Vigilante justice is sometimes directed against an individual who does not respect not only the legal, but also the moral rules of the community. In *Sir Michael and Colonel Wolodyjowski* of Henryk Sienkiewicz (1888), the punishment for treason is to be paid by Prince Janusz Radziwiłł. Finally, soldiers are not able to punish him, because the proud prince escapes by committing suicide. Cruel punishment for betrayal, dishonor of Ewka Nowowiejska, kidnapping of the colonel's lady and killing of Sir Nowowiejski is borne by Asia Tuhajbejowicz. He is a Tartar, who showed exceptional cruelty. The punishment imposed on him is a cruel revenge, not a just sentence. In the Young Poland's (Młoda Polska's) novel *The Peasants* (1904–1909) by Władysław Stanisław Reymont, a widow, who violates the social norms of the rural community, continuously sinning by committing adultery, is humiliated and finds herself outside the community. She leaves the village taken away on a pile of dung under a hail of stones. Justyna Bogutówna, the heroine of Zofia Nałkowska's *The Border* (1935), administers vigilante justice to her former lover by pouring acid on his face. Justice is also exacted through duels (e.g., *The Doll*, 1890, by Bolesław Prus).

Vigilante actions carried out against entire social groups, especially Jews, are the subject of the novel *A Mass for the City of Arras* (1971) by Andrzej Szczypiorski or *Mendel from Gdańsk* (1890) by Maria Konopnicka. This reached its apogee during World War II, when just being a Jew or a Roma was a ticket to death, such as in W. Szpilmann, *The Pianist* (1988; film adaptation by Roman Polański);[78] R. Ligocka, *The Girl in a Red Coat* (2000);.H. Krall, *Make It before God* (1976); and Z. Nałkowska, *Medallions* (1946). An act of punishment for bourgeois and landowners, or even revenge on the property-owning class are the revolutions described in Zygmunt Krasiński's *Non-Divine Comedy* (1835); Stanisława Przybyszewska's *The Danton Case*. (1929; famous through Andrzej Wajda's film "Danton" from 1982);[79] Stefan Żeromski's *The Spring to Come* (1924); Witold Gombrowicz's *Opérette* (1966); Witkacy's *The Shoemakers* (1948); and *Farewell to Autumn* (1927).

CONCLUSION

Vigilante justice conjures up for us very visual images: an enraged crowd, unable to be controlled for a short time by any power apparatus, eager for justice and blood is confronted with a lonely victim who, even when guilty, arouses empathy. This picture is, however, deeply disturbing. It emphasizes the original, ecstatic, collective violence. It shows that violence underlies our "civilized" institutions: the law, the political meetings, which gave rise to parliamentary bodies, the court, the criminal trial, etc. Paradoxically, the image of the lynching of the guilty person is equally tragic when it is carried out on an innocent victim. Although the "evil" actually committed has been punished in some way, it does not bring justice in any way. This calls into question all concepts: guilt, punishment, or justice. The Polish examples of vigilantism show that it involves something of a caricature of democracy:

almost always it appears as a symptom of a faulty democracy where the promise of the democratic rule of law has not been kept.

POLISH LEGAL SOURCES

Decision of the Supreme Court of October 9, 2012, III KK 153/12, LEX No. 1226707.
Judgment of the Supreme Court of March 26, 2014, II KK 321/13.
Decision of the Supreme Court of October 7, 2014, V KK 116/14, LEX No. 1532784.
Resolution of the Supreme Court of October 7, 2014, V KK 116/14.
Judgment Supreme Court of November 6, 2014, IV KK 157/14.
Decision of the Supreme Court of April 15, 2015, IV KK 409/14, OSNKW 2015, No. 9, item 78.
Resolution of the Supreme Court of April 27, 2017, IV KK 116/17, LEX No. 2284193.
Judgment of the Court of Appeal in Katowice of September 20, 2001, II AKa 299/01, LEX No. 54673.
Judgment of the Court of Appeal in Krakow of October 5, 2006, II AKa 140/06, LEX No. 227391.
Judgment of the Court of Appeal in Wrocław of December 28, 2012, II AKa 383/12, LEX No. 1254582.
Judgment of the Court of Appeal in Łódź from March 14, 2013, II AKa 12/13, LEX No. 1313341.
Judgment of the Court of Appeal in October 30, 2013, II AKa 363/13, LEX No. 1391901.
Judgment of the Court of Appeal in Łódź of December 17, 2013, II AKa 207/13.
Judgment of the Court of Appeal in Szczecin of October 23, 2014, II AKa 177/14, LEX No. 1668653.
Judgment of the Court of Appeal in Poznań of December 11, 2014, II AKa 249/14.
Judgment of the Court of Appeal in Lublin of January 26, 2015, IV K 121/14, LEX No. 2125668.
Judgment of the Court of Appeal in Wrocław of February 10, 2015, II AKa 6/15, LEX No. 1661290.
Judgment of the Court of Appeal in Warsaw of March 2, 2015, II AKa 14/15, LEX No. 1665870.
Judgment of the Court of Appeal in Krakow of July 21, 2015, II AKa 124/15.
Judgment of the Court of Appeal in Wrocław of March 8, 2017, II AKa 29/17.
Judgment of the Court of Appeal in Wrocław of March 8, 2017, II AKa 29/17.
Polish Penal Code, Journal of Laws of 1997 No. 88, item 553; unitary text Journal of Laws of 2017 item 2204 as amended.

NOTES

1. A custom commemorated in literature with the work of Adam Mickiewicz, *Pan Tadeusz, czyli ostatni zajazd na Litwie* (*Master Thaddeus, or the Last Foray in Lithuania: A Nobility's Tale of the Years 1811–1812, in Twelve Books of Verse*, Paris 1834). Armed relatives, friends, and followers pulled with a decree in hand and in the company of a janitor, they obtained (often not without bloodshed) goods that were put on the repentant, which the janitor legally traded or gave on his property. Such armed execution of the decree was called a foray.
2. Piotr Chlebowicz, *Samosąd We Włodowie: Studium Przypadku* (Olsztyn: Katedra Kryminologii i Polityki Kryminalnej. Wydział Prawa i Administracji. Uniwersytet Warmińsko-Mazurski, 2017).
3. Chlebowicz, 76.
4. Chlebowicz, 77.
5. "Kołobrzeg: Tłum chciał linczu. O krok od samosądu," Fakt24.pl, June 26, 2014, https://wiadomosci.onet.pl/szczecin/kolobrzeg-tlum-chcial-linczu-o-krok-od-samosadu/zzzjc45.
6. S. Janicki, "Dotkliwe kary za popularne samosądy na nieprawidłowo parkujących kierowcach!," *Szkoła Jazdy Sklep i Aktualności* (blog), December 27, 2018, https://www.szkola-jazdy.pl/dotkliwe-kary-za-popularne-samosady-na-nieprawidlowo-parkujacych-kierowcach/.
7. See for more Kazimierz Bartoszewicz, *Dzieje Insurekcji Kościuszkowskiej* (Wiedeń: F. Bondy, 1909).
8. The 1793 Second Partition of Poland was the second of three partitions (or partial annexations) that ended the existence of the Polish–Lithuanian Commonwealth by 1795.
9. Władysław Smoleński, *Konfederacya Targowicka* (Krakow: Skł. gł. w księg. G. Gebethnera, 1903) covers this extensively.
10. Hetman was the title of the leader of the Arm.
11. Maciej Zaremba, "Wieszanie portretów zdrajców. Jak ukarano przywódców targowicy?," Historia, May 9, 2020, https://historia.wprost.pl/10214927/wieszanie-portretow-zdrajcow-jak-ukarano-przywodcow-targowicy.html.
12. Władysław Zajewski, *Podłoże Ideologiczne i Rozwój Walk Wewnętrznych w Powstaniu Listopadowym 1830–1831* (Gdańsk, 1965), 294; Władysław Zajewski, *Walki wewnętrzne ugrupowań politycznych w powstaniu listopadowym 1830–1831*, first ed. (Gdańsk: Gdańskie Towarzystwo Naukowe, 1967), 172–73.
13. Maurycy Mochnacki, *Powstanie narodu polskiego w roku 1830 i 1831: Maurycy Mochnacki*, ed. Stefan Kieniewicz, vol. 2 (Warsaw: Panstwowy Instytut Wydawniczy, 1984), 419.
14. Tadeusz Łepkowski, *Warszawa w Powstaniu Listopadowym*, second ed. (Warsaw: Wiedza Powszechna, 1965), 175.
15. Tadeusz Łepkowski, "Tłum w Powstaniu," *Kwartalnik Historyczny: Organ Towarzystwa Historycznego* 68, no. 1 (1961): 165.
16. Tadeusz Łepkowski, *Powstanie listopadowe* (Warsaw: Panstwowe Wydawnictwo Popularno-Naukowe "Wiedza Powszechna," 1955), 53.

17. Tadeusz Łepkowski, *Polska—Narodziny Nowoczesnego Narodu, 1764–1870* (Warsaw: Państwowe Wydawn. Naukowe, 1967), 176–77.

18. Maurycy Mochnacki, "Przyczyny nocy 15 sierpnia," in *Maurycego Mochnackiego pisma rozmaite: oddzial porewolucyjny* (Paris: W Księg. polskiej, 1836), 286–307.

19. According to the law in force at the time, the crime of the state, even if it was only intended, was to be punishable by death: Maria Pasztor, "Zagadnienia Prawa Karnego w Kodeksie Stanis\lawa Augusta i Kodeksie Karzącym Królestwa Polskiego (1818)," *Kwartalnik Historii Nauki i Techniki* 40, no. 3 (1995): 110.

20. Zajewski, *Walki wewnętrzne ugrupowań politycznych w powstaniu listopadowym 1830–1831*, 306–7.

21. Tadeusz Łepkowski, "Warszawska rebelia sierpniowa 1831 r.," in *Powstanie Listopadowe: 1830–1831; dzieje wewnetrzne, militaria, Europa wobec powstania*, ed. Wladyslaw Zajewski (Warsaw: Panstw. Wydawn. Nauk., 1990), 289.

22. Zajewski, *Walki wewnętrzne ugrupowań politycznych w powstaniu listopadowym 1830–1831*, 312–13.

23. Łepkowski, "Warszawska rebelia sierpniowa 1831 r.," 289.

24. Łepkowski, 289.

25. Łepkowski, 291.

26. Łepkowski, *Powstanie listopadowe*, 56.

27. Łepkowski, *Warszawa w Powstaniu Listopadowym*, 199–201.

28. Michal Swędrowski, "Jan Krukowiecki, Opisanie Dnia 15 Sierpnia," *Meritum* 1 (2009): 265.

29. Mieczysław Weryński, "Noc 15 sierpnia, w powstaniu listopadowem," in *Ksiega pamiatkowa ku czci profesora dra Waclawa Sobieskiego:—M??langes Waclaw Sobieski.*, ed. Waclaw Sobiecki (Kraków, 1932), 335–36.

30. Łepkowski, *Warszawa w Powstaniu Listopadowym*, 205.

31. *Odezwa Rządu Narodowego do mieszkańców Warszawy*, "Kurier Polski" 1831, No. 599 (17. August), p. 2045, cited after: A. Reguła, *Prasa powstania listopadowego wobec wydarzeń czerwcowych i samosądów 15 sierpnia 1831 r.*, Historia.org, August 18, 2011, https://historia.org.pl/2011/08/18/prasa-powstania-listopadowego-wobec-wydarzen-czerwcowych-i-samosadow-15-sierpnia-1831-r/.

32. Ibid.

33. "Okrutny samosąd nad złodziejem w wiosce na Wileńszczyźnie," *ABC*, July 17, 1930, Year 5, n. 196, http://retropress.pl/abc/okrutny-samosad-nad-zlodziejem-wiosce-wilenszczyznie/.

34. Urszula Hollanek, "Krajobraz po linczu," Wprost, May 8, 2011, https://www.wprost.pl/tygodnik/243400/krajobraz-po-linczu.html.

35. Ibid.

36. Chlebowicz, *Samosąd We Włodowie*, 94.

37. Report of the interrogation of J.W., reference number act II K 96/08 District Court in Olsztyn, cited after: Chlebowicz, *Samosąd we Włodowie*, 67.

38. Testimony of K.R., reference number act II K 96/08 District Court in Olsztyn, cited after: Chlebowicz, 68.

39. Chlebowicz, 70.

40. Joanna Wojciechowska, "Lincz we Włodowie—reportaż," gazetapl, July 11, 2005, https://wyborcza.pl/7,75968,2815050.html.
41. "Nawet 10 lat chce prokurator za lincz we Włodowie," *Wprost.pl*, October 15, 2007, https://www.wprost.pl/kraj/115780/nawet-10-lat-chce-prokurator-za-lincz-we-wlodowie.html.
42. "Sąd Apelacyjny uchylił wyrok pierwszej instancji ws. linczu we Włodowie," *Gazetaprawna.pl*, March 27, 2008, https://www.gazetaprawna.pl/amp/12077,sad-apelacyjny-uchylil-wyrok-pierwszej-instancji-ws-linczu-we-wlodowie.html.
43. "Ponowny proces ws. linczu we Włodowie," *Wprost.pl*, July 15, 2008, https://www.wprost.pl/kraj/134162/ponowny-proces-ws-linczu-we-wlodowie.html.
44. "Wyrok w sprawie linczu we Włodowie," *Wprost.pl*, January 15, 2009, https://www.wprost.pl/kraj/150339/wyrok-w-sprawie-linczu-we-wlodowie.html.
45. "Mimo nowego świadka, wyrok w sprawie linczu we Włodowie utrzymany," *RMF24*, June 19, 2009, sec. documentation, https://www.rmf24.pl/fakty/polska/news-mimo-nowego-swiadka-wyrok-w-sprawie-linczu-we-wlodowie-utrzy,nId,139697.
46. "Sąd Najwyższy utrzymał wyroki za głośny lincz we Włodowie," *Gazetaprawna.pl*, September 1, 2010, https://www.gazetaprawna.pl/wiadomosci/artykuly/446992,sad-najwyzszy-utrzymal-wyroki-za-glosny-lincz-we-wlodowie.html.
47. "Prezydent ułaskawił braci skazanych za lincz we Włodowie," *Gazetaprawna.pl*, December 18, 2009, https://prawo.gazetaprawna.pl/artykuly/380382,prezydent-ulaskawil-braci-skazanych-za-lincz-we-wlodowie.html.
48. Lech Gardocki, *Prawo Karne* (Warsaw: C.H. Beck, 2005), 185.
49. Marian Cieślak, *Polskie Prawo Karne: Zarys Systemowego Ujęcia*, third ed. (Warsaw: Prawnicze PWN, 1995), 422.
50. Iwona Niewiadomska and Stanislaw Fel, "Realizacja Zasady Sprawiedliwości w Karaniu Przestępców," *Zeszyty Naukowe KUL* 59, no. 3 (2016): 62.
51. Adam Podgórecki, *Zarys socjologii prawa* (Warsaw: Państwowe Wydawn. Naukowe, 1971), 330–31.
52. Pawel Nalewajko, "Uwagi o Zależnościach Między Socjologią Prawa a Prawem Karnym," *Ruch Prawniczy, Ekonomiczny i Socjologiczny*, no. 4 (2009): 252.
53. Filip Ciepły, "O dowartościowanie retrybutywnej racjonalizacji kary," in *Hominum causa omne ius constitutum est: księga jubileuszowa ku czci profesor Alicji Grześkowiak*, ed. Antoni Dębiński et al. (Lublin: Katolicki Uniwersytet Lubelski, KUL, 2006), 236.
54. Łukasz Pohl and Konrad Burdziak, *Obraz i Analiza Wyk\ladni Sądowej Przepisów Kodeksu Karnego z 1997 r. o Obronie Koniecznej i Przekroczeniu Jej Granic* (Warsaw, 2017), 1–2; Adam Krukowski, *Obrona Konieczna Na Tle Polskiego Prawa Karnego* (Warsaw: Państwowe Wydawn. Nauk, 1965), 176ff.
55. Polish Penal Code, Journal of Laws of 1997 No. 88, item 553; unitary text Journal of Laws of 2017 item 2204 as amended.
56. Andrzej Marek, *Obrona konieczna w prawie karnym na tle teorii i orzecznictwa Sądu Najwyższego* (Warsaw: Prawnicze, 1979), 34.
57. Pawel Daniluk, in *Kodeks karny: komentarz*, ed. Ryszard Andrzej Stefanski (Warsaw: C.H. Beck, 2018), 228.

58. Decision of the Supreme Court of April 15, 2015, IV KK 409/14, OSNKW 2015, No. 9, item 78.

59. Arnold Gubiński, *Wyłączenie Bezprawności Czynu: O Okolicznościach Uchylających Społeczną Szkodliwość Czynu* (Warsaw: Uniwersytet Warszawski, 1961), 17.

60. Łukasz Pohl, "W Sprawie Wyjaśnień Oskarżonego w Polskim Postępowaniu Karnym–Odpowiedź," in *Aktualne Problemy Prawa Karnego. Księga Pamiątkowa z Okazji Jubileuszu 70. Urodzin Profesora Andrzeja Szwarca*, ed. Łukasz Pohl (Poznan: Uniwersytet Adama, 2009), 497–98.

61. Judgment of the Court of Appeal in Wrocław of March 8, 2017, II AKa 29/17.

62. Pohl and Burdziak, *Obraz i Analiza Wyk\ladni Sądowej Przepisów Kodeksu Karnego z 1997 r. o Obronie Koniecznej i Przekroczeniu Jej Granic*, 26.

63. Polish Supreme Court judgment of March 26, 2014, II KK 321/13. See also: Andrzej Zoll, ed., *Kodeks karny. Część ogólna, vol. 1, Komentarz do art. 1–116* (Warsaw: Wolters Kluwer Polska, 2012), 452; Jacek Giezek Klaczynska, Natalia, ed., *Kodeks karny. Część ogólna. Komentarz* (Warsaw: Wolters Kluwer Polska, 2012), 212.

64. Władysław Wolter, *Nauka o przestępstwie: analiza prawnicza na podstawie przepisów części ogólnej Kodeksu karnego z 1969 r*, first ed. (Warsaw: Państwowe Wydawn. Nauk, 1973), 169.

65. Marek, *Obrona konieczna w prawie karnym na tle teorii i orzecznictwa Sądu Najwyższego*, 64ff.

66. Resolution of the Supreme Court of April 27, 2017, IV KK 116/17, LEX No. 2284193; Supreme Court judgment of November 6, 2014, IV KK 157/14; Supreme Court decision of October 7, 2014, V KK 116/14, LEX No. 1532784; Supreme Court decision of October 9, 2012, III KK 153/12, LEX No. 1226707; judgment of the Court of Appeal in Wrocław of March 8, 2017, II AKa 29/17; judgment of the Court of Appeal in Wrocław of February 10, 2015, II AKa 6/15, LEX No. 1661290; judgment of the Court of Appeal in Krakow of July 21, 2015, II AKa 124/15; judgment of the Court of Appeal in Poznań of December 11, 2014, II AKa 249/14; judgment of the Court of Appeal in Szczecin of October 23, 2014, II AKa 177/14, LEX No. 1668653; judgment of the Court of Appeal in Łódź from March 14, 2013, II AKa 12/13, LEX No. 1313341; judgment of the Court of Appeal in October 30, 2013, II AKa 363/13, LEX No. 1391901; judgment of the Court of Appeal in Łódź of December 17, 2013, II AKa 207/13 judgment of the Court of Appeal in Wrocław of December 28, 2012, II AKa 383/12, LEX No. 1254582 and judgment of the Court of Appeal in Katowice of September 20, 2001, II AKa 299/01, LEX No. 54673; Resolution of the Supreme Court of October 7, 2014, V KK 116/14; judgment of the Court of Appeal in Warsaw of March 2, 2015, II AKa 14/15, LEX No. 1665870; judgment of the Court of Appeal in Krakow of October 5, 2006, II AKa 140/06, LEX No. 227391 and judgment of the Court of Appeal in Lublin of January 26, 2015, IV K 121/14, LEX No. 2125668. Analyzed in detail in: Ł. Pohl, K. Burdziak, *Obraz i analiza . . .* , op. cit., p. 47–48.

67. *The Debt (Dług)*, Krzysztof Krauze, Poland 1999, accessed February 10, 2020, https://culture.pl/en/work/the-debt-krzysztof-krauze.

68. Maciej T. Nowak, "Życie brutalniejsze niż film," *Nowa Trybuna Opolska*, August 14, 2004, https://nto.pl/zycie-brutalniejsze-niz-film/ar/4005843.

69. Tadeusz Lubelski, "Krzysztof Krauze—Młodszy Brat Kina Moralnego Niepokoju," in *Autorzy Kina Polskiego*, ed. Grażyna Stachówna, Joanna Wojnicka, and Bogusław Zmudziński, vol. 3 (Kraków: Rabid, 2007), 197–220.

70. Pawel Szaniawski, "Artur Bryliński ułaskawiony. 'Długo na to czekałem,'" *Newsweek.pl*, December 16, 2010, https://www.newsweek.pl/polska/artur-brylinski-ulaskawiony-dlugo-na-to-czekalem/1e1fj0g.

71. *Lynch (Lincz)*, Krzysztof Łukaszewicz, Poland 2010, accessed February 10, 2020, https://culture.pl/en/work/lynch-krzysztof-lukaszewicz.

72. *Pitbull* (season 3, episode 19), Patryk Vega, Poland 2008, accessed February 10, 2020, https://culture.pl/en/work/pitbull-patryk-vega.

73. *The Train (Pociąg)*, Jerzy Kawalerowicz, Poland 1959, accessed February 10, 2020, https://culture.pl/en/work/night-train-jerzy-kawalerowicz.

74. *The November Uprising. 1830–1831 (Powstanie Listopadowe. 1830–1831)*, Lucyna Smolińska, Poland 1980, accessed February 10, 2020, http://filmpolski.pl/fp/index.php?film=124078.

75. More about this figure: Tomasz Kitzwalter, ed., *Jerzy Skowronek: historyk wieku XIX* (Warsaw: DiG, 1999).

76. *Youth of Chopin (Młodość Chopina)*, Aleksander Ford, Poland 1951, accessed February 10, 2020, http://filmpolski.pl/fp/index.php?film=122506.

77. *Father's Law (Prawo ojca)*, Marek Kondrat, Polska 1999, accessed February 10, 2020, http://filmpolski.pl/fp/index.php?film=127830.

78. *The Pianist (Pianista)*, Roman Polański, France, Germany, Poland, United Kingdom 2002.

79. *Danton*, Andrzej Wajda, Polska 1982, accessed February 10, 2020, http://www.wajda.pl/en/filmy/film25.html.

BIBLIOGRAPHY

Bartoszewicz, Kazimierz. *Dzieje Insurekcji Kościuszkowskiej*. Wiedeń: F. Bondy, 1909.

Chlebowicz, Piotr. *Samosąd We Włodowie: Studium Przypadku*. Olsztyn: Katedra Kryminologii i Polityki Kryminalnej. Wydział Prawa i Administracji. Uniwersytet Warmińsko-Mazurski, 2017.

Ciepły, Filip. "O dowartościowanie retrybutywnej racjonalizacji kary." In *Hominum causa omne ius constitutum est: księga jubileuszowa ku czci profesor Alicji Grześkowiak*, edited by Antoni Dębiński, Małgorzata Gałązka, Radosław D. Halas, and Krzysztof Wiak, 231–46. Lublin: Katolicki Uniwersytet Lubelski, KUL, 2006.

Cieślak, Marian. *Polskie Prawo Karne: Zarys Systemowego Ujęcia*. third ed. Warsaw: Prawnicze PWN, 1995.

Daniluk, Pawel. In *Kodeks karny: komentarz*, edited by Ryszard Andrzej Stefanski, 220–71. Warsaw: C.H. Beck, 2018.

Gardocki, Lech. *Prawo Karne*. Warsaw: C.H. Beck, 2005.

Giezek, Jacek, Klaczynska, Natalia, ed. *Kodeks karny. Część ogólna. Komentarz.* Warsaw: Wolters Kluwer Polska, 2012.

Gubiński, Arnold. *Wyłączenie Bezprawności Czynu: O Okolicznościach Uchylających Społeczną Szkodliwość Czynu.* Warsaw: Uniwersytet Warszawski, 1961.

Hollanek, Urszula. "Krajobraz po linczu." Wprost, May 8, 2011. https://www.wprost.pl/tygodnik/243400/krajobraz-po-linczu.html.

Janicki, S. "Dotkliwe kary za popularne samosądy na nieprawidłowo parkujących kierowcach!" *Szkoła Jazdy Sklep i Aktualności* (blog), December 27, 2018. https://www.szkola-jazdy.pl/dotkliwe-kary-za-popularne-samosady-na-nieprawidlowo-parkujacych-kierowcach/.

Kitzwalter, Tomasz, ed. *Jerzy Skowronek: historyk wieku XIX.* Warsaw: DiG, 1999.

Fakt24.pl. "Kołobrzeg: Tłum chciał linczu. O krok od samosądu," June 26, 2014. https://wiadomosci.onet.pl/szczecin/kolobrzeg-tlum-chcial-linczu-o-krok-od-samosadu/zzjc45.

Krukowski, Adam. *Obrona Konieczna Na Tle Polskiego Prawa Karnego.* Warsaw: Państwowe Wydawn. Nauk, 1965.

Łepkowski, Tadeusz. *Polska—Narodziny Nowoczesnego Narodu, 1764–1870.* Warsaw: Państwowe Wydawn. Naukowe, 1967.

———. *Powstanie listopadowe.* Warsaw: Panstwowe Wydawnictwo Popularno-Naukowe "Wiedza Powszechna," 1955.

———. "Tłum w Powstaniu." *Kwartalnik Historyczny: Organ Towarzystwa Historycznego* 68, no. 1 (1961): 153–75.

———. *Warszawa w Powstaniu Listopadowym.* second ed. Warsaw: Wiedza Powszechna, 1965.

———. "Warszawska rebelia sierpniowa 1831 r." In *Powstanie Listopadowe: 1830–1831; dzieje wewnetrzne, militaria, Europa wobec powstania,* edited by Wladyslaw Zajewski, 227–34. Warsaw: Panstw. Wydawn. Nauk., 1990.

Lubelski, Tadeusz. "Krzysztof Krauze—Młodszy Brat Kina Moralnego Niepokoju." In *Autorzy Kina Polskiego,* edited by Grażyna Stachówna, Joanna Wojnicka, and Bogusław Zmudziński, 3:197–220. Kraków: Rabid, 2007.

Marek, Andrzej. *Obrona konieczna w prawie karnym na tle teorii i orzecznictwa Sądu Najwyższego.* Warsaw: Prawnicze, 1979.

RMF24. "Mimo nowego świadka, wyrok w sprawie linczu we Włodowie utrzymany," June 19, 2009, sec. documentation. https://www.rmf24.pl/fakty/polska/news-mimo-nowego-swiadka-wyrok-w-sprawie-linczu-we-wlodowie-utrzy,nId,139697.

Mochnacki, Maurycy. *Powstanie narodu polskiego w roku 1830 i 1831: Maurycy Mochnacki.* Edited by Stefan Kieniewicz. Vol. 2. Warsaw: Panstwowy Instytut Wydawniczy, 1984.

———. "Przyczyny nocy 15 sierpnia." In *Maurycego Mochnackiego pisma rozmaite: oddzial porewolucyjny.*, 286–307. Paris: W Księg. polskiej, 1836.

Nalewajko, Pawel. "Uwagi o Zależnościach Między Socjologią Prawa a Prawem Karnym." *Ruch Prawniczy, Ekonomiczny i Socjologiczny,* no. 4 (2009): 245–56.

Wprost.pl. "Nawet 10 lat chce prokurator za lincz we Włodowie," October 15, 2007. https://www.wprost.pl/kraj/115780/nawet-10-lat-chce-prokurator-za-lincz-we-wlodowie.html.

Niewiadomska, Iwona, and Stanislaw Fel. "Realizacja Zasady Sprawiedliwości w Karaniu Przestępców." *Zeszyty Naukowe KUL* 59, no. 3 (2016): 59–75.
Nowak, Maciej T. "Życie brutalniejsze niż film." *Nowa Trybuna Opolska*, August 14, 2004. https://nto.pl/zycie-brutalniejsze-niz-film/ar/4005843.
ABC. "Okrutny samosąd nad złodziejem w wiosce na Wileńszczyźnie." July 17, 1930, Year 5, n. 196 edition, sec. ABC. http://retropress.pl/abc/okrutny-samosad-nad-zlodziejem-wiosce-wilenszczyznie/.
Pasztor, Maria. "Zagadnienia Prawa Karnego w Kodeksie Stanislawa Augusta i Kodeksie Karzącym Królestwa Polskiego (1818)." *Kwartalnik Historii Nauki i Techniki* 40, no. 3 (1995): 105–14.
Podgórecki, Adam. *Zarys socjologii prawa*. Warsaw: Państwowe Wydawn. Naukowe, 1971.
Pohl, Łukasz. "W Sprawie Wyjaśnień Oskarżonego w Polskim Postępowaniu Karnym–Odpowiedź." In *Aktualne Problemy Prawa Karnego. Księga Pamiątkowa z Okazji Jubileuszu 70. Urodzin Profesora Andrzeja Szwarca*, edited by Łukasz Pohl. Poznan: Uniwersytet Adama, 2009.
Pohl, Łukasz, and Konrad Burdziak. *Obraz i Analiza Wyk\ladni Sądowej Przepisów Kodeksu Karnego z 1997 r. o Obronie Koniecznej i Przekroczeniu Jej Granic*. Warsaw, 2017.
Wprost.pl. "Ponowny proces ws. linczu we Włodowie," July 15, 2008. https://www.wprost.pl/kraj/134162/ponowny-proces-ws-linczu-we-wlodowie.html.
Gazetaprawna.pl. "Prezydent ułaskawił braci skazanych za lincz we Włodowie," December 18, 2009. https://prawo.gazetaprawna.pl/artykuly/380382,prezydent-ulaskawil-braci-skazanych-za-lincz-we-wlodowie.html.
Gazetaprawna.pl. "Sąd Najwyższy utrzymał wyroki za głośny lincz we Włodowie," September 1, 2010. https://www.gazetaprawna.pl/wiadomosci/artykuly/446992,sad-najwyzszy-utrzymal-wyroki-za-glosny-lincz-we-wlodowie.html.
Smoleński, Władysław. *Konfederacya Targowicka*. Kraków: Skł. gł. w księg. G. Gebethnera, 1903.
Swędrowski, Michal. "Jan Krukowiecki, Opisanie Dnia 15 Sierpnia." *Meritum* 1 (2009): 247–68.
Szaniawski, Pawel. "Artur Bryliński ułaskawiony. 'Długo na to czekałem.'" *Newsweek.pl*, December 16, 2010. https://www.newsweek.pl/polska/artur-brylinski-ulaskawiony-dlugo-na-to-czekalem/1e1fj0g.
Weryński, Mieczysław. "Noc 15 sierpnia, w powstaniu listopadowem." In *Księga pamiatkowa ku czci profesora dra Waclawa Sobieskiego:—M??langes Waclaw Sobieski.*, edited by Waclaw Sobiecki, 304–55. Kraków, 1932.
Wojciechowska, Joanna. "Lincz we Włodowie—reportaż." gazetapl, July 11, 2005. https://wyborcza.pl/7,75968,2815050.html.
Wolter, Władysław. *Nauka o przestępstwie: analiza prawnicza na podstawie przepisów części ogólnej Kodeksu karnego z 1969 r.* first ed. Warsaw: Państwowe Wydawn. Nauk, 1973.
Wprost.pl. "Wyrok w sprawie linczu we Włodowie," January 15, 2009. https://www.wprost.pl/kraj/150339/wyrok-w-sprawie-linczu-we-wlodowie.html.

Zajewski, Władysław. *Podłoże Ideologiczne i Rozwój Walk Wewnętrznych w Powstaniu Listopadowym 1830–1831*. Gdańsk, 1965.

———. *Walki wewnętrzne ugrupowań politycznych w powstaniu listopadowym 1830–1831*. first ed. Gdańsk: Gdańskie Towarzystwo Naukowe, 1967.

Zaremba, Maciej. "Wieszanie portretów zdrajców. Jak ukarano przywódców targowicy?" Historia, May 9, 2020. https://historia.wprost.pl/10214927/wieszanie-portretow-zdrajcow-jak-ukarano-przywodcow-targowicy.html.

Zoll, Andrzej, ed. *Kodeks karny. Część ogólna, vol. 1, Komentarz do art. 1–116*. Warsaw: Wolters Kluwer Polska, 2012.

Chapter 9

Margins Without Justice
Revenge In João Canijo's Portuguese Cinema

Júlia Garraio

Is it appropriate to talk about vigilante justice in contemporary Portuguese culture and society? The imaginaries of contemporary national audiences tend to associate it with influential American comics and cinema, as the phenomenon is marginal in Portuguese cultural productions. Violence, namely in (political) extra-judicial situations and in plots about revenge, permeates Portuguese literature and cinema's engagement with themes such as national history and identity, colonialism and its legacies, racism, economic inequalities and social exploitation, misogyny and gender-based violence; nonetheless, violent acts that could be brought in connection with vigilante justice do not tend to be articulated as such. Neither is the concept vigilantism a common referential point in debates about the present-day social-political realities in Portugal. The majority of the population would most probably argue that no such thing exists in the country. Indeed, most acts of extrajudicial violence perpetrated in the decades of Portugal as a democracy and EU member[1] do not seem to fit in Eduardo Moncada's definition of vigilantism: the collective use or threat of extra-legal violence in response to an alleged criminal act, and hence a violation of a particular order and a system of rules that govern behavior (both by the target of vigilantism and by vigilantism itself).[2] There is, however, a myriad of crimes involving a conjunction of revenge impulses, enacting of a sense of punishment and pursuit of self-interest which fit into broader definitions of vigilantism as acts of "autonomous citizenship"[3] and self-help: "the handling of a grievance by unilateral aggression"[4]; "acts taken by individuals who are attempting to enact their own rule of law or sense of morality, in essence taking the law into their own hands."[5]

THE FILMS OF JOÃO CANIJO IN CONTEXT

Portuguese filmmaker João Canijo has repeatedly and consistently structured the plots of his films around murders which, in most cases, fit into the understanding of vigilantism "as a planned criminal act, carried out by a private citizen in response to (the perceived threat of) a crime committed by a private citizen, targeting the (alleged) perpetrator of that crime."[6] *Filha da mãe*[7] (Lovely Child, 1989) culminates with Júlia murdering her husband, who had abandoned her twenty years earlier and, is currently involved sexually with her (their?) daughter. In *Sapatos Pretos* (*Black Shoes*, 1998), Dalila plans to escape her abusive husband in a small provincial town by murdering him. In *Ganhar a Vida* (*Get a Life*, 2001), the Portuguese immigrant Cidália tries to pin responsibility on someone for the death of her son, a drug dealer in the Paris suburbs who had been killed apparently by the French police. In *Noite Escura* (*In the Darkness of Night*, 2004), Celeste, who runs a brothel with her husband, kills him when he hands their youngest daughter to a Russian Mafia band as a way of meeting a debt. In *Mal Nascida* (*Misbegotten*, 2007), Lúcia and Augusto murder their mother and stepfather in a remote village in the Portuguese hinterland, as revenge for the murder of their father. *Sangue do meu Sangue* (*Blood of my Blood*, 2011) culminates with Joca shooting Telmo, a dealer, when he is raping his aunt, Ivete, as payment for a debt.

The first film in this selection dates from 1989, barely three years after Portugal joined the EEC, while the last coincides with the Euro-crisis and the implementation of austerity measures which provoked a deep recession and substantial human suffering in the country ever since. The years in between (especially the 1990s) were experienced and celebrated as a time of economic growth, modernization, improvement in health, education and public services, and positive attitudes toward European integration. Canijo's plots depict, however, a social fabric that looks disconnected from any celebration of the political-economic accomplishments pursued by contemporary Portuguese democracy and its embracing of the European project. All these plots refer to the social margins and peripheries of Portuguese society. Canijo stands not alone: Portuguese cinema has been active in making visible socio-economic exclusion in Portuguese society.[8] Films about the Lisbon suburbs contributed to rendering visible the poverty, discrimination, racism, and violence framing the daily lives of the racialized communities in the deprived suburbs of the capital and in exposing the need to address the legacies of the country's colonial past when examining the deep social inequalities within Portuguese contemporary society.[9] The topic is also present in Canijo's cinema (see Joca's black girlfriend and friends in *Sangue do meu Sangue*). However, with Canijo it never occupies the central position which we find in the acclaimed cinema of filmmakers such as Pedro Costa. In Canijo's cinema, ethnicity and race are perceived as one of the forms of exclusion in the Portuguese social fabric, and not used as the main prism of the narrative. In that sense, Canijo explores inequality and exclusion in the tradition of the engaged approach of the authors of Portuguese neo-realism, who shed light on the realities of the deprived regions beyond the capital and exposed the deep inequality and social reproduction (i.e., the maintenance and continuation of existing social relations and the role of birth as the key determiner for social status) that frame all levels and locations in Portuguese society.

In Canijo's cinema, however, those on the margins and peripheries do not necessarily embody poverty and deprivation nor marginality and/or criminality. Although these phenomena tend to be present on the peripheries depicted by Canijo, the margins in his films are defined above all by a social fabric marked by loose connections among the individual, the larger community, and the official institutions of the nation state. For those on the margins, the values shared by the community come down to football, popular Catholicism, and entertainment music, shown as emblematic expressions of what has been coined by Michael Billig as "banal nationalism."[10] These cultural phenomena and their rituals are signified in the films as forms of social alienation without capacity to forge trust among the community members nor an effective sense of belonging. When Canijo's characters are faced with what they perceive as threat, injustice and/or crime, they do not seek assistance/justice from the community nor from the State institutions (the very few attempts to seek assistance from the collective like in *Ganhar a Vida* fail); rather, they take the affair into their own hands and kill those they consider responsible for their suffering through acts of extra-judicial violence which ultimately never challenge the status quo.

Canijo's cinema with its tense plots about violence, incest, and crime within the nuclear family is usually praised as a counternarrative to the celebration of the "good Portuguese people"—an enduring legacy of the dictatorship—in tandem with a clear examination of the so-called atavism pervading Portuguese national identity, in other words, the tendency to uncritically reproduce morals and attitudes from the previous generations.[11] Drawing on this line of research, I propose an analysis of the motive of revenge as a device that explores how this resistance to social change is framed not by an excess of any sense of national belonging but by loose bonds among "the Portuguese people," thus questioning the very existence of the community as a cohesive unity. I argue that, as cinema which addresses deep social and economic disruptions and inequalities in Portuguese society, and the lack of trust of the individual in the macro-structure (the community and the State), Canijo's films expose social structures that underpin the outbreaks of vigilantism: a disconnection between the individual and the state's institutions. In that sense, Canijo's characters reclaim the Latin origin of the word "vigilant": alertly watchful, especially to avoid danger. My examination is informed by research about the pervasive social reproduction in Portugal and the role of the state apparatus as a traditional guarantor of the privileges of a small economic elite.[12] My argument is that Canijo chose the private-intimate sphere of the social-geographic margins of Portuguese society for the setting of his plots precisely to explore the Portuguese "imagined community" as a fragmentary, fragile, and deceptive cultural construction. I argue that Canijo's films expose, on one hand, how revenge among the deprived sectors in Portuguese society is framed by a lack of trust in the social order and the state institutions and, on the other, how this form of vigilantism ultimately fails to deliver effective and broad social change.

The chapter is structured in four parts. I begin with a contextualizing section consisting of a brief overview of the types of political and extrajudicial violence in democratic Portugal. Then I include a section examining how the films of the *corpus* enact revenge as a form of female agency which fails to improve the characters' situation. Since Canijo's cinema is practically unknown to an international audience, the films of the *corpus* will be covered in detail. The following section argues that the sense of the tragic pervading the lives of the protagonists is framed by their relation with the state institutions and the community. The final section discusses the contribution of Canijo's cinema to reflect on some challenges faced by Portuguese democracy.

A BRIEF SURVEY OF POLITICAL AND EXTRA-JUDICIAL VIOLENCE IN CONTEMPORARY PORTUGAL

Traditionally, the centralized state based in Lisbon promoted an ideal of Portugueseness deeply entangled in colonial themes and imaginaries, which assumed the metropole as the source of a well-defined national culture and identity that could be exported to the colonies. Post-dictatorship Portugal negotiated the role of the country—now reduced to the territory of the former metropole—in world politics without questioning its existence as a well-defined social and territorial unity. Despite the sometimes-loud left–right wing rivalries, post-dictatorship Portuguese politics denote a tendency for consensus on key issues such as liberal democracy, European integration, military transatlantic alliance, and the need to improve the economic and material living conditions of the population. Portugal has one of the lowest crime rates in Europe and has not witnessed substantial political violence in the last few decades[13] nor internal ethnic rivalries, tensions, and movements.[14] The lack of deep fractures among the major political parties, alongside the low rates of criminality, contributed to the perception of the country as a "quiet place," where the authority of the state and its militarized forces is not challenged by expressions of vigilantism.

The forces challenging the authority of state have been actually marginal in the democratic period. The far-left organization FP25 de Abril (1980–1987), labeled as a terrorist group, was a marginal movement which never posed an effective threat to the state. Until recently, the far right remained a marginal, irrelevant political actor. The National Renewal Party (PNR—Partido Nacional Renovador), founded in 2000 inspired by developments in other European countries, was the first initiative that was able to organize nationalist Eurocentric racist far-right sectors around a political party, but it was unsuccessful in Parliamentary terms.[15] Its attempts to construct an image of respectability were to a certain extent hampered by the criminal activities of some of its members. Consider Mário Machado, the most influential far-right activist in Portugal. Machado, who was the founder of the Portuguese section of the white supremacist group Hammerskins, has been involved in many other far-right national organizations. He was convicted on several occasions of criminal activities involving extortion, kidnapping, assault, and illegal possession of a weapon. He was also convicted for involvement in the murder of Alcino Monteiro in 1995, a crime with racial motivations, and more recently, in 2007, he was one of the targets of a large-scale police operation on the criminal activities and racial discrimination promoted by far-right groups.

Machado's biography also hints at connections between far-right activism and some football gangs. More broadly, and not necessarily in connection with far-right initiatives, football events and football gangs have been associated on several occasions with acts of collective violence. For instance, media reporting of the attacks by football gangs and supporters, as the famous invasion of the Sporting facilities in 2017,[16] gave national visibility to a climate of hooliganism that is present in some football events.

In recent years, reports by Homeland Security have signaled the increasing presence and reorganization of far-right activities in the country.[17] Several scholars have argued that the distrust in democratic institutions among large numbers of citizens may be creating a reservoir of supporters of nondemocratic illiberal movements.[18] Nonetheless, violence by far-right groups continues to be perceived by the broader society as being confined to narrow sectors of the Portuguese society and/or being foremost an issue of criminal gangs. The presence of the far right is undergoing significant changes though. Chega, a populist party founded by dissidents from the center-right party PSD in April 2019, gave Parliamentary representation to the far-right when it elected one MP in the October 2019 legislative elections. Despite the revelation that the party's ranks include individuals convicted of criminal activity and racist violence (i.e., members of former far-right groups involved in crime), Chega has been increasing its popularity ever since with a discourse that claims to "combat criminals."

Chega has been capitalizing on the racialization of crime that is anchored in pervasive Portuguese imaginaries that associate Roma communities with theft and public disorder and Blacks with urban violence. Gang violence in urban areas, especially when it involves racialized communities, is indeed a favorite topic for the sensationalist press and TV channels, which has been fueling moral panic and rejection of ethnic minorities.[19] Violence associated with racialized communities is often used to overlook police violence against racialized youth and violent crimes targeting Blacks.[20] Anti-racist movements, journalists, and scholars have denounced acts of violence against racialized minorities as a structural problem in Portuguese society deeply embedded in the colonial legacies of the country.[21] The media coverage of the 1996 expulsion of Roma families by the local population of Oleiros, Vila Verde (a rural area in northern Portugal), gave visibility to the deep racism, marginalization, segregation, and hostility experienced by Roma communities in the country.[22] The murder of Alcino Monteiro in 1995, the kidnap and torture of black activists in the police station of Alfragide (Lisbon metropolitan area) in 2015,[23] and more recently the lynching of Luís Giovani Rodrigues, a student from Cape Verde, in Bragança in December 2019 and the murder of Bruno Candé, a black actor, by a war veteran in Lisbon in July 2020 gave media visibility to the extent of racist hate crimes in the country, and fueled ongoing debates about racism.

A brief survey of the acts of extra-judicial violence in the country must include inevitably the thriving sector of private security firms. Police investigations of private security companies related to violence, abuse, extortion, and tax evasion[24] and media coverage of some episodes of violence by security staff in nightclubs showed the need for further regulation of this thriving private sector. Law n°46/2019 was implemented precisely to clarify and regulate the exercise of private security activities and self-protection.[25] Services provided by accredited security companies in this area are envisaged by Portuguese law as a possible complement to the work of public forces. The changes introduced by the law were aimed at improving the qualifications and professionalism of the employees of the security firms on the understanding that this would help in preventing situations of abuse. Nonetheless, an extensive work of investigative journalism by the independent information site *Fumaça* revealed that this flourishing business, which employs about 45,000 people (more than the police forces) as service providers for state institutions and private companies, operates as an invisible sector based on labor precarity, corporate bullying, ineffective trade unions, and illegal labor practices.[26]

In order to grasp an understanding of insecurity, violence, and crime among large sectors of Portuguese society we have to take into account forms of violence involving "ordinary people"[27] perpetrated by individuals often acting alone against their family members and/or acquaintances: acquaintance murder, crimes in the context of domestic violence, pedophilia, disputes between neighbors, rivalries among family members (sometimes involving inheritance), conflicts at the workplace or in the context of small (and sometimes illicit) business and affairs. Such stories make for lurid headlines especially in the context of sensationalist journalism, where they occupy a large space in the media. As we will see, the plots of Canijo's films are structured by murders involving precisely the forms of violence taking place in the private sphere. It is these films which the chapter now examines.

FEMALE AGENCY, REVENGE AND POWERLESSNESS IN CANIJO'S FILMS

Filha da Mãe (1989)

The first film of the corpus, *Filha da Mãe*, a loose adaptation of the myths of Clytemnestra and Electra,[28] introduces recurrent themes of Canijo's cinematography: the tense mother/daughter relationship, incest, revenge killing. After spending twenty years in Brazil, Álvaro returns to Lisbon as a successful painter. As he tries to reconnect with his former wife, Júlia, a theater actress and soap opera celebrity, he meets Maria, who might be his daughter (Júlia was pregnant when he abandoned her). Maria is a rebel, who hates her mother and Gigi, Júlia's scrounger lover, and who spends her time with her boyfriend Adriano, a small-time thief and drug dealer, and some rock musicians. The unpremeditated killing of a porter seems to arouse a taste for blood in Maria, who afterward brings about the destruction of all those around her: she orchestrates that the inefficient police arrest Adriano for the murder, she finally seduces Álvaro and she discloses this to her mother, Júlia, who then kills her ex-husband.

The film introduces a major trademark of Canijo's cinema: a counter-image of the celebrated myth of the "good Portuguese people" that claimed that the Portuguese were humble, honest, virtuous, hard-working, obedient, and peaceful. The social fabric depicted in the film reflects an urban modernity that contrasts with the ideal of rural and traditional society that was propagated as the Portuguese way of life during the dictatorship. The plot introduces characters who embody a certain degree of marginality (actors, musicians, thieves, drugs-dealers, gigolos). Instead of protective fathers and family providers, the film depicts weak and easily manipulated men. Instead of good housewives, caring mothers and obedient daughters, the plot places in the foreground sexualized independent women as agents of their destiny: Maria is a manipulative tomboy whose changing clothes reflect her experiencing gender roles; Júlia is a single mother and the provider for her daughter and younger lover. Their apparent compliance with the traditional attributes of femininity (beauty, seduction) emerge as strategies to achieve their aims and/or means of sexual gratification.

Sapatos Pretos (1998)

While *Filha da Mãe* is a "coming of age" drama about urban characters from the affluent middle classes, Canijo's next film, *Sapatos Pretos*, introduces major changes in the filmmaker's cinematography: plots about women who rebel against the patriarchal order; characters from lower middle and lower classes from the geographical peripheries of the country whose motivations and agency in crime are framed by economic hardships; careful use of the camera work (e.g., night filming, light and shadow effects, framing) that produces desolate dark depictions of the social fabric, the Portuguese family, and the different time frames reflected in the landscapes depicted.[29] While in *Filha da Mãe* modernity is embodied by characters who do not comply with the traditional family and professions associated with respectability—in that sense, the film is complicit in the perception of Lisbon as a place for "looser morals" and as a gateway for Western forms of socialization and consumption—*Sapatos Pretos* introduces a different approach to the tension between tradition and modernity. It inscribes it inside the traditional patriarchal family from small-town and rural areas, that is, in the spaces that were traditionally perceived as "typically Portuguese." Furthermore, while *Filha da Mãe* suggests the protagonist's empowerment through crime, the following films depict the outcome of crime with powerlessness, as the characters fail to liberate themselves and the status quo remains unchallenged. As we will see, these films signify the act of revenge as inability to achieve social change and individual improvement.

Sapatos Pretos' plot takes us to Sines, a coastal town in the Alentejo, the region that comprises much of southern Portugal. The deep social inequality, widespread poverty, and underdevelopment that characterized the Alentejo's recent history made this rural area a spot for tensions between landowners and rural workers during the dictatorship. It is also the region where the Communist party has had its major impact. Sines, a village whose economy relied on fishing, the cork industry, and some tourism until the late 1960s, underwent major changes after 1971 with the construction of the large port development complex and the petrochemical industry (1978). The Port of Sines is the main on the Atlantic seaport of Portugal and the main gateway to the energy supply of the country, while the petrochemical complex is one of the largest in Europe. The settings of the beginning of the film—the couple Dalila and Marcolino attend a traditional trade fair in a dry open-air ground and on their way home drive by the petrochemical complex—show the tensions between rurality/tradition and modernity/industrialization that frame the social interactions and the family drama at the center of the plot.

Dalila is a woman in her mid-thirties who shares the condition of many women in a country plagued by domestic violence. Her abusive husband Marcolino treats her and her belongings as his property: he regularly beats and rapes her, and he hocks their jewelry (purchased with her family's money). She rejects her fate and uses her trips to Lisbon for medical treatment for an alleged breast cancer to radically change her looks. The dark-haired housewife becomes a platinum blond wearing colorful miniskirts, makeup, and high heels, and hence becoming a target of lust among the local men and gossip among the women. *Sapatos Pretos* radically deconstructs the idealization of family life that was a trademark during the dictatorship: Dalila's home is filmed as a dark and claustrophobic place, a setting of hidden (sexual) violence, degradation, oppression, unhappiness, and (male) alcoholism, that contrasts with the sun outdoors and the colorful clothes and self-confidence that Dalila exhibits outside. Drawing on research about the pervasiveness of domestic violence in Portugal,[30] Daniel Ribas argues that the film enacts the tensions resulting from the traditional idealization of the family as refuge and the reality of its persisting violence mimicking authoritarian structures.[31]

Disgusted by her husband and determined to make the best of her sexual attractiveness, Dalila considers divorce. However, when her well-off mother threatens to disinherit her (she considers divorce to be a social shame), she orchestrates a plan: she manipulates Pompeu, her younger lover, a penniless driver who, like the most destitute in the country, wanted to emigrate to improve his life, and convinces him to engage a hit-man to murder Marcolino. Her plans for freedom apparently succeed when her unreliable lover is arrested for the crime. However, a detail (the black shoes of the title) puts her at the mercy of the lustful police inspector, thus making her liberation culminate in powerlessness. Her sexualized body becomes once again a sexual object at the disposal of a man who can reclaim the role of being her owner/protector (now not through the bonds of marriage but through blackmail). Certainly, the contrast between the humiliating rapes and the sexual empowerment she experiences when having sex with her lover suggest how successfully she reclaimed her body as a source of agency and fulfillment. However, a closer look at the basis of her empowerment hints at its precariousness.

Dalila's empowerment is concomitant with the adoption of a lifestyle associated with consumerism and urban attitudes which is propagated by Hollywood cinema and magazines, that is, her emancipation as a woman operates through the codes of American capitalism. The parallel between her new looks and the petrochemical complex are suggested throughout the film: both stand out and look alien in the desolate, dry rural landscape; both involve patterns of Americanized consumption and the global economy, coexisting with conservative morals and traditions. Dalila's empowerment depends on money to afford her expensive clothes, which reinforces her dependency on (those who own) the money. Furthermore, her empowerment is deeply associated with the commodification of her body (see how her lover, just like her husband, is obsessed with the risk of her losing her breast as a side effect of the cancer surgery). Therefore, the plot not only shows that the crime of revenge leaves the status quo unchallenged, but also suggests that Dalila's empowerment as a woman operated precisely through the enactment of the values that anchor the very status quo.

Ganhar a Vida (2001)

At the center of this adaptation of the myth of Antigone[32] there is, once again, a woman in conflict with her conservative community. However, while *Sapatos Pretos* depicted a Portuguese traditional provincial landscape under the influence of a spreading modernity, *Ganhar a Vida* brings us to a cosmopolitan space of modernity (Paris) that is also a hotspot of tradition. France was a major destination for Portuguese emigrants in the second half of the twentieth century (especially in the 1960s and early 1970s). Portuguese nationals tended to take unqualified low paid jobs: men as construction workers and taxi drivers, women as cleaning personnel. They were known as a "silent community,"[33] a reference to the widespread perception that the Portuguese were a docile working-force. However, Canijo offers a desolate depiction of the community that contrasts with their positive traditional images both in France (the "unproblematic" community) and in Portugal (the well-off emigrant). The film also deconstructs the celebration of the Schengen space[34] as an achievement for the well-being and fully integration of the Portuguese living in EU countries. Canijo films the French suburbs as a desolate dark and grey landscape made of concrete and claustrophobic noisy apartments, and depicts the daily lives of the Portuguese emigrants as consisting of hard work, poverty, subordination, segregation, and confinement. The film suggests that the "silent community" is actually a façade for a reality of violence in the private sphere (domestic violence and sexism), connivance with illicit economic structures (see the tactical agreement between Portuguese small business owners and the gangs), and a second-generation that embodies the habits, attitudes, and identity tensions of the second-generation Blacks and Arabs with whom they share the streets.

It is precisely events involving the second-generation that create a rupture in the community. Cidália's son is killed during a police raid on local gangs. With the support of some Portuguese women, Cidália organizes a petition and a demonstration demanding accountability from the police. Her actions embody a demand for full citizenship in French society, as her speech at a community party emblematically expresses: "We live here, we don't live anywhere else. We are here in what is ours. Our children were born in France, they speak French, this is the land where they were born and this is the land that we chose for them growing up." This stance puts her on a path of confrontation with her own community which assumes that "non-citizenship" is the best strategy for survival. An elderly friend of her father had warned her precisely not to go ahead with the petition because "we are not in what is ours. . . . I'm here for 40 years and what is needed is keeping a low profile." Tensions exacerbate as the increasing police surveillance and violence in the neighborhood is followed by the gangs' reprisals against Portuguese business and results in arson of her apartment. Abandoned by her husband after confessing adultery, stigmatized by her community, disconnected from the French majority society, and devastated by the truth (her son's killer was her own alleged lover), she commits suicide in the center of Paris.

Cidalia is the only character in the corpus of this chapter who does not seek justice at her own hand. She engages in a dialogue with the police and organizes civic actions aiming for social change, because her objective is preventing the occurrence of such incidents in the future. However, the French police regard the whole affair as just another "bad-publicity" incident and respond with more violence. The Portuguese community puts up with the status quo and just wants her to put an end to the protests. Her quest for justice fails not only because of a macro-structure that foments the socio-economic segregation of the immigrant communities, but also because of the conservative cultural background of the Portuguese diaspora which stigmatizes any action and form of solidarity aimed at social change. The end credits, consisting of footage of the communities' festivities and a Portuguese emigration song with the refrain "in this coming to France *chaqu'un* looks for his/herself," reinforce the lack of solidarity and public engagement among the Portuguese community, in other words, the social attitudes which doomed Cidália's quest for the empowerment of the community.

Noite Escura (2004)

Noite Escura, a loose adaptation of the Greek tragedies *Iphigenia in Aulis* (Euripides) and *Agamemnon* (Aeschylus),[35] explores further perspectives on the social margins, the geographic peripheries, and the harsh realities of transnational migration. The setting is a brothel in the Portuguese countryside near the Spanish border, which is depicted as a hotspot of sexual trafficking, illicit activities, and murder, where men from respectable society come to enjoy a few hours with young women. Nelson, the brothel owner, is given a few hours to deliver his youngest daughter, Sónia, to a Russian Mafia gang to cover a debt. Sónia has enjoyed a protected life so far: she never worked as a prostitute (like her mother Celeste) nor as a cleaner and manager of the brothel (like her older sister Carla), nor was she a victim of incest (like her sister). Celeste wants to offer her (and herself) a way out of that world and hopes that Sónia's participation in a TV contest will be her first step as professional singer, hence paving the way for social mobility to a life of respectability. However, in a film that follows so closely the codes of the tragedy (unity of space, action, and time) and the very concept of the tragic (the characters have to choose between alternatives that mean suffering and probable death), the characters cannot escape their destiny. While Sónia and Celeste joyfully plan the girl's participation in the TV show, Olga, an Eastern European girl who had been lured and trafficked by the Russian Mafia that wants Sónia, recounts in the background her ordeal when she was repeatedly raped by dozens of men until her will was broken and she was turned into an obedient sexualized body. Throughout the film, Sónia resembles more and more the Eastern European girls in the brothel: she dyes her hair blond; she takes the necklace of Irka, the murdered trafficked prostitute. All these ominous signs indicate that she is condemned to the world of prostitution, not as a profiteer (as she has lived so far) but as the most deprived and abused in this economy: young girls who are trafficked to foreign countries by transnational mafia gangs (Sónia will be taken to Spain) to became cannon fodder in a brutal and profitable business.

In these lawless margins where the state seems to be absent (police protection is not even envisaged by the characters), all efforts by the family members fail. Powerless to challenge the Russian Mafia who have just shot Carla and taken Sónia, Celeste kills the one she holds responsible: her husband Nelson. Taking revenge at her own hand is filmed as an act of failure (her helpless regard signals her impotence and loneliness). Her actions do not change Sónia's fate nor the status quo, as the section with the end credits signals: inside the brothel, clients and prostitutes continue to dance and engage in the sexual trafficking as if that were a regular evening.

Mal Nascida (2007)

Mal Nascida also uses the codes of the tragedy—the film is a loose adaptation of the myths of Clytemnestra and Electra[36]—to explore the failure of individual empowerment through revenge. The plot is set in a social-geographic Portuguese periphery: a family of impoverished emigrants who return to their deprived rural village in the mountains to open a restaurant and do some farming. Life in France is remembered as a time of misery: Adelaide, the mother, used to work sixteen hours a day cleaning offices and private homes; her first husband used to rape their oldest daughter, who died following an abortion. The family is haunted by the murder of the father at the hands of Evaristo, Adelaide's second husband, and Lúcia's obsession with taking revenge for her father's death. The camera work contrasts the filth, poverty, ugliness, moral degradation, and misery of the family's home and village with the colors, joyful music, and dreams of success and consumerism advertised in the popular shows broadcast by the ever-present TV: soap operas, football matches, Eurovision song contest; the popular show *Who Wants to Be a Millionaire*. The plot depicts an ancestral world punctuated by irruptions of modernity (TVs, cars, EU agricultural subsidies) which were not concomitant with the effective implementation of a system of justice and accountability for all citizens. The rape and death of the older sister, just like the killing of her father, remain unpunished and it is up to those close to them to take the affair into their own hand and act as revengers.

The plot reinforces Canijo's depiction of the family as a site of violence, (sexual) abuse, and oppression. While, in the previous films, incest occurred within families of the "non-conservative" and/or "non-respectability" spheres (artists, divorced couples, individuals involved in illicit businesses), *Mal Nascida* depicts incest in a traditional Catholic family of farmers whose home is furnished with religious objects. Sex and violence emerge as key elements structuring the family bonds and hierarchies. Women are abused through (sexual) violence, but their agency in sex also works as a strategy of empowerment (Lúcia's self-confidence after having sex with her brother empowers her to confront her stepfather) and as a way of using men to perform their revenge. It was Evaristo's passion for Adelaide which made him kill her first husband, just like it was Augusto's sexual involvement with his sister that led him to the killing of his stepfather and his mother. Women's cold-bloodedness as masterminds of crime contrasts with the discomfort and awe experienced by men.

However, women's agency and ability to have men as the tools of their revenge do not offer them a way out of the cycle of violence. Augusto had tried to demote Lúcia from revenge arguing that "The fact that they [*Adelaide and Evaristo*] are imprisoned/stuck here is as if they were already dead." The camera work suggests indeed that revenge is no liberating act. In the final sequence, the restaurant door framing the killer siblings is filmed in a way that reminds us of prison bars, just like Adelaide and Evaristo had been filmed before. Killing their father's killers leaves Lúcia and Augusto haunted and doomed just like the killing of the pedophile husband had left Adelaide and Evaristo.

Sangue do Meu Sangue (2011)

Sangue do meu Sangue is set in Bairro Padre da Cruz, a large social housing neighborhood in Lisbon, when the European sovereign debt crisis was beginning to unfold in Portugal. Márcia, a hard-working single mother with two children (Cláudia and Joca), shares a tiny house with her sister Ivete. Márcia's hopes rest with her daughter Cláudia, who succeeded in going to nursing school, an enormous achievement in that social milieu. Márcia hopes that her future degree and marrying César, a neighbor who works as security in a supermarket, will afford her the possible social mobility that poor whites can aspire to: respectability and the professional stability of the public sector. However Cláudia is keeping secret an affair with Beto, a married doctor and her teacher at the nursing school, who affords her commodities unthinkable for her class (cars, five-star hotels). Márcia successfully puts an end to this relationship, sparing Cláudia from the truth that Beto is actually her father. Unlike the protagonists of the previous films, Márcia acts as a reinforcer of the status quo, as someone who "knows her place" and leads Cláudia back to the path that democracy made possible for the hard-working children of the poor: using the opportunities of the public school (get an education) and the national health service (abortion of unwanted pregnancies) and climb a small step in the social ladder.

While Cláudia embodies the possibility of upward social mobility, Joca experiences the other path of impoverished urban whites: further descent of the social ladder, which in the social geography of Lisbon means merging with racially diverse poorer communities. When Ivete discusses with Márcia how the incoming housing resettlement in the neighborhood will affect the different family members, her remark "So Joca moves to the cages among the Blacks and the Gypsies and that's it?!" signals precisely Joca's future.[37] Joca got involved from early age in petty crime and, as a minor, spent some time in a reformatory. His close family ties are with his aunt Ivete. While the escalating tension might suggest a bloody ending for the triangle Márcia/Cláudia/Beto (Márcia had asserted that she would kill Beto if he did not put an end to the affair with Cláudia), it is the Ivete/Joca bond that ends in tragedy. When Joca's life is threatened by Telmo, a white boss in the drugs traffic, Ivete visits him to hand him her savings. What follows is a humiliating rape that culminates with Joca shooting the rapist. Revenge is though filmed as helplessness (see how Joca and Ivete embrace each other). Considering Joca's past and involvement in the drugs traffic, the killing of Telmo will definitely put him on a path to incarceration and marginality—at the lowest social ladder in Portuguese society.

Sangue do meu Sangue is the film of the *corpus* that makes more thorough use of a camera work that consists of the constant framing of the characters in oppressive degraded narrow spaces (walls, doors, and windows that suggest the effect of prison bars) and the inclusion on screen of different pairs/groups of characters engaged in conversation. These techniques convey the smallness of the family's home and produce a sense of a constant lack of privacy, which hinders the family members in creating their own subjectivities. The work with sound—the overlapping of the different dialogues on screen; the intrusion of the noise of off-camera screams representing what is going on in the neighbors' houses (wrangles, fights, loud music)—reinforces that sense of claustrophobia. These techniques add intensity to the sense of the tragic pervading the plot, suggesting the enclosure of the characters and the impossibility of escaping the frames of their social landscape and the forces operating there. The community and its habitat are not experienced as a refuge; on the contrary, they are experienced as destructive forces. Desperate acts to take control of one's destiny, like Joca's, do not empower the characters and bring their liberation; on the contrary, they push them even deeper in their helplessness and tragic fate.

THE STATE: INEFFICIENCY, CORRUPTION, AND/OR ABSENCE

A closer look at the plots of the six films of the *corpus* identifies a dense net of thematic connections, intersections, and overlapping lines of action that results in the cinematographic production of a geography of the Portuguese social fabric anchored in its peripheries. While *Filha da Mãe* has as one of its main characters a glamorous actress of the increasing popular TV soap operas, *Sapatos Pretos* fictionalizes the life of a woman in the province who reclaims for herself the glamour, romance, and sexual pleasure that she watches on the soap operas. While her ill-fated young lover dreams of social empowerment through emigration, *Ganhar a Vida* depicts the reality of Portuguese emigration in France as the perpetuation of social subordination, precariousness, and traditional Portuguese cultural practices. *Noite Escura* looks at other angles of migration: sexual trafficking and transnational crime in Portugal as an immigration country. *Mal Nascida* revisits the theme of incest by fictionalizing the miserable existence of Portuguese emigrants in France who return to their home village (the path undertaken by Cidália's husband in *Ganhar a Vida*). *Sangue do Meu Sangue* focuses on an emblematic deprived neighborhood in Lisbon to develop themes and aesthetics from the previous films.

The cohesion among the films is largely sustained by the recurring themes of revenge, degrading family life, and lack of a civic community.[38] Entangled in oppressive and violent families and communities that offer no support, the individual resorts to crime to improve his/her situation and/or to punish those he/she considers responsible for his/her misery. Dalila in *Sapatos Pretos* is emblematic of this pattern: tied by the laws of marriage, she sees in murder the possibility of winning on all fronts without having to endure the stigma and the financial quarrels of a divorcee.

Dalila's decision only makes sense if we consider how the state is depicted by Canijo as being unable to provide justice because its institutions, values, and representatives are associated with inefficiency, corruption, and/or violence. In *Filha da Mãe* the police officers are caricatures of incompetence who fall into the protagonist's trap. In *Sapatos Pretos* the police inspector cunningly identifies the mastermind of the murder, but uses this information for his own sexual gratification, thus misusing his status as a representative of the state for the exercise of corruption and the perpetuation of patriarchy. In *Ganhar a Vida* the French police do not provide security and protection for the immigrant communities, and act as forces of violence and surveillance whose actions provoke more insecurity and fear in the multicultural suburbs. Media attention on the suburbs ends up by fueling the escalation of communitarian tensions and police violence. *Noite Escura* depicts a brutal milieu of transnational crime and sexual exploitation over which the state apparently has no control (nor interest). In *Mal Nascida* the state representatives are associated with corruption. We can also observe the doctor from the National Health Service who is willing to receive money to issue a medical certificate to send Lúcia to a psychiatric public hospital where patients are mistreated; and the doctor and the police officers who issue false documents regarding the causes of death of Augusto's partner. In *Sangue do meu Sangue* the state is present, on one hand, as an (inefficient) agent of control and punishment: Joca's previous incarceration in the reformatory did not succeed in "putting him on the right track"; Telmo leads a gang of traffickers and threatens the inhabitants of the neighborhood apparently unchallenged by the police. On the other hand, the state is present in the neighborhood as a promoter of social programs (access to health care and birth control, public education, housing resettlement), which are depicted as basic services and opportunities that can help the condition of the inhabitants (or at least of some of them like Cláudia). Nonetheless, these initiatives are experienced by the characters as programs to manage poverty and, in the case of house resettlement, of segregating it, rather than as social empowerment, that is, they are not depicted as initiatives with the involvement of the community nor as promoters of a stronger social cohesion between the community and the state.

The forms of social identification operate, just like in the other films of the *corpus*, through cultural practices associated with expressions of "banal nationalism"[39]: football, entertaining music, popular Catholicism, and TV (soap operas and sensationalist news). TV shows and football matches function as joyful and colorful counterpoints to the misery of the characters, thus reinforcing the sense of alienation as the major trademark of their lives. We can see, for instance, how César, Cláudia's thick boyfriend, who has a low-paid job as security in a suburban supermarket, likes wearing T-shirts of international football icon, sex symbol, and millionaire Cristiano Ronaldo. The alienation framing the lives of the deprived is stressed by the ever present TV. While Beto's rich and educated family watches a national news channel (SIC Notícias) that broadcasts about the unfolding financial crisis, the inhabitants of the deprived neighborhood (who, as part of the lower classes, would be hard hit by the crisis in the following years) watch entertainment (music, soap operas, football matches), and sensationalist news (e.g., the recovery of an image of the Virgin in the floods of Madeira), totally indifferent to the processes of political decision-making that determine their lives.

The depiction of the state and the community are of the greatest relevance to grasp the sense of the tragic that pervades Canijo's cinema. Even the films that are not adaptations of Greek tragedies like *Sapatos Pretos* are structured by elements of the tragedy such as the recurrent use of tragic irony (see, for instance, Pompeu's lustful first words to glamorous Dalila: "You are an assassin"). *Sapatos Pretos* and the subsequent films enact the basic structure of the tragedy that determines that the protagonists are doomed by major forces framing their existence: the social context (the absences and shortcomings of the state as a justice enforcer) and the cultural subtext (the atavism pervading the community). In that sense, Canijo enacts a sense of the tragic that Schurmans[40] identified in some contemporary writers of the Global South: the roots of the tragedy do not lie in the will of gods but in the socioeconomic milieu that pushes the protagonists to pursue paths that inevitably fail (and destroy them).

FINAL REMARKS: DISAFFECTION AND THE STATUS QUO

The perception of Portugal as a fully consolidated democratic regime contrasts with the decreasing electoral turnout (from 8% abstention in 1975 to 51% in 2019) and a significant lack of interest in democratic institutions among large sectors of the population.[41] Though the Euro-crisis may have contributed to the eroding of the confidence in democracy,[42] the disconnection between large sectors of the society and its state institutions has deeper roots in the Portuguese social fabric which result from specific historical processes: lack of democratic traditions; the long-standing grip on the state's institutions by an elite; the pervasive tendency for social reproduction; the lack of and/or deficient literacy among large sectors. According to Pedro Magalhães,[43] the feelings of estrangement and distance from politics among significant sectors of Portuguese society (reluctance to engage in political action altogether) exemplify what Mariano Torcal and José Ramón Montero defined as political disaffection: a "subjective feeling of powerlessness, cynicism and lack of confidence in the political process, politicians and democratic institutions, but with no questioning of the political regime."[44] Magalhães argues that in Portugal these "feelings of estrangement from politics tend to breed political passivity and acquiescence."[45]

Canijo's accurate depictions of the margins of Portuguese society[46] can be understood as cinematographic approaches through fiction to that precise cultural disaffection. His depictions of the peripheries conjure up self-made-(wo)men in a lumpen sense: those who do not invest in the community, who are indifferent to the state, from whose institutions they do not expect much, and who count only on their bare bodies and cunning to survive and thrive. His plots are basically about communities pervaded by violence in the private sphere resulting from entrenched authoritarian patriarchal structures that contribute to the traditional submission of women in Portuguese society. As such, his films are counter-narratives not only to the propaganda of the dictatorship about the "good Portuguese people" and its celebration of rural life, family values, and Catholic identity, but also to the success story of Portuguese democracy and European integration as paths to prosperity and collective decision-making. The killing by revenge and/or as punishment occurs in contexts where the community offers neither refuge nor protection and the state is not perceived as an enforcer of justice. Nationality is not experienced as a collective destiny and political decision-making but as shared cultural traits and entertainment practices which do not foster empowerment or political participation; on the contrary, they contribute to alienation and the perpetuation of the status quo. The path to tragedy is entrenched in the protagonist's lack of belief in the community and the state's institutions and the assumption that issues like self-protection, empowerment, and justice cannot be addressed and overcome collectively. Hence, Canijo's characters embody extreme forms of individualism (and loneliness), whose most radical expression culminates in the exercise of autonomous citizenship in the form of killing those they hold responsible for their misery. In that sense, they perform acts of vigilantism to make justice at their own hand and/or develop strategies of self-defense. The adoption of the conventions of tragedy reinforces, on one hand, the association of the act of vigilantism with loneliness and, on the other, the ineffectiveness of these acts in promoting social justice and change.

The *corpus* of the films for this chapter fictionalizes realities marked by tensions between modernity and tradition pervading Portuguese social peripheries in the decades following European integration. The *corpus* ends in 2011 and ever since major changes have operated in the country resulting from the financial crisis. 2019 saw a parliamentary far-right emergence with an "anti-system" propaganda[47] and a discourse anchored in the creation of moral panic around crime and security. While surveys suggest that the majority of Portuguese people consider that democratization brought improvements especially in housing, health care, education, and living standards, lower percentages of respondents believe that "crime, safety, corruption and unemployment levels have improved since democratization."[48] It is too early to know if the illiberal political forces will succeed in appealing to the disaffected citizens who have been contributing to records in abstention from formal politics. Likewise, it is too early to know if the situation observed by Magalhães regarding lower levels of disaffection among the younger generations will contribute to a greater identification between Portuguese citizens and their democratic institutions, more political engagement and participation, more unconventional civic activism, and the improvement in the quality of democracy and communitarian institutions.

Research undertaken within the project "DeCodeM (De)Coding Masculinities: Towards an enhanced understanding of media's role in shaping perceptions of masculinities in Portugal," which is supported by the Foundation for Science and Technology (Portugal) under Grant PTDC/COM-CSS/31740/2017

ACKNOWLEDGMENTS:

I would like to thank the ICA (Instituto do Cinema e do Audiovisual) and Sérgio Dias Branco for their support in providing me with materials.

NOTES

1. In 1974, a military coup, known as the Carnation Revolution, overthrew the right-wing dictatorship (1926–1974). After some initial social turmoil, the promulgation of the 1976 constitution paved the way for a stable Parliamentary democracy. In 1986, Portugal joined the European Economic Community (later EU).

2. Eduardo Moncada, "Varieties of Vigilantism: Conceptual Discord, Meaning and Strategies," *Global Crime* 18, no. 4 (2017): 6.

3. Les Johnston, "What Is Vigilantism?," *The British Journal of Criminology* 36, no. 2 (1996): 220–36.

4. Donald J. Black, *The Social Structure of Right and Wrong*, Rev. ed (San Diego: Academic Press, 1998), xxiv.

5. Jacob Vander Ende, "Vigilantism," in *The Encyclopedia of Criminology and Criminal Justice*, ed. Jay S. Albanese (Hoboken, NJ: Wiley Blackwell, 2014), doi: 10.1002/9781118517383.wbeccj347.

6. Nicole E. Haas, Jan W. de Keijser, and Gerben J. N. Bruinsma, "Public Support for Vigilantism: An Experimental Study," *Journal of Experimental Criminology* 8, no. 4 (2012): 226.

7. The title consists of a wordplay. It literally means "the daughter of the mother." This expression can be used to insinuate that the daughter's character resembles her mother's; it is also the feminine form of the insult "son of a bitch."

8. See, among many others, *Uma Abelha na Chuva* (1971) by Fernando Lopes, *Os Mutantes* (1998) by Teresa Villaverde, *Duas Mulheres* (2009) by João Mário Grilo, *Raiva* (2018) by Sérgio Tréfaut, and Pedro Neves's documentaries.

9. The most emblematic examples include Pedro Costa's acclaimed trilogy of Fontainhas (*Ossos*, 1997; *No Quarto da Vanda*, 2000; *Juventude em Marcha*, 2006) and successful commercial productions supported by private TV channels such as Leonel Vieira's *Zona Jota* (1998).

10. Michael Billig, *Banal Nationalism* (London; Thousand Oaks, CA: Sage, 1995).

11. Daniel Ribas, *Uma dramaturgia da violência: os filmes de João Canijo* (Lisbon: Imprensa de História Contemporânea, 2019), http://library.oapen.org/handle/20.500.12657/24951.

12. Fernando Rosas et al., eds., *Os Donos de Portugal: Cem Anos de Poder Económico (1910–2010)* (Porto: Edições Afrontamento, 2010).

13. The Global Peace Index ranks Portugal among the most peaceful places in the globe. In its first edition (2008), Portugal was on the tenth place. The situation deteriorated in the following years until 2013, when it was ranked in seventeenth place. Since then the situation has been improving. In 2019 it was in third place (after Iceland and New Zealand) and in 2020 in fourth place having been "overtaken" by Denmark.

14. In the regions of Madeira and the Azores there is certainly a strong sense of regional identity which, however, has not fostered effective separatist political agendas, but rather focuses on action and moves for more political autonomy from the central government.

15. José Mourão Da Costa, "O Partido Nacional Renovador: A Nova Extrema-Direita Na Democracia Portuguesa," *Análise Social*, 2011, 765–87; Riccardo Marchi, "The Extreme Right in 21st-Century Portugal: The Partido Nacional Renovador," in *Right-Wing Extremism in Europe: Country Analyses, Counter-Strategies and Labor-Market Oriented Exit Strategies*, ed. Ralf Melzer, Sebastian Serafin, and Friedrich-Ebert-Stiftung (Berlin: Friedrich-Ebert-Stiftung, Forum Berlin, 2013), 133–55.

16. In May 2018, over forty supporters invaded the Sporting Clube de Portugal facilities in Alcochete (Lisbon) and injured several players and members of the technical team as a "punishment" for the bad results of the football club.

17. The annual report on home security (Relatório Anual de Segurança Interna) is available at: https://www.portugal.gov.pt/download-ficheiros/ficheiro.aspx?v =19cabc8c-e3f1-4cb2-a491-a10c8a3e4bf0. The Home Security Office identified 2017 as a key moment in the reorganization of the far-right groups in Portugal. The 2017 report is available at: https://www.portugal.gov.pt/download-ficheiros/ficheiro .aspx?v=9f0d7743-7d45-40f3-8cf2-e448600f3af6.

18. Tiago Fernandes, ed., *Cultura Política e Democracia* (Lisboa: Fundação Francisco Manuel dos Santos, 2019), 12.

19. As the documentary "Era uma vez um arrastão" (Diana Andringa, 2005) convincingly argues, this pattern does not only appear in sensationalist media. In June 2005 there were minor incidents involving some youths at a beach on the outskirts of Lisbon. The opening news that evening reported an *arrastão* involving hundreds of black boys. The concept *arrastão* (steaming) was imported from Brazilian Portuguese, where it refers to a robbery performed by a gang or a large group of people on beaches. Although the police denied the allegations, the narrative about the "insecurity and terror" posed by gangs of black boys from the suburbs pervaded the media coverage of the events.

20. Otávio Raposo et al., "Negro Drama. Racismo, Segregação e Violência Policial Nas Periferias de Lisboa," *Revista Crítica de Ciências Sociais*, no. 119 (2019): 5–28.

21. Joana Gorjão Henriques, *Racismo Em Português: O Lado Esquecido Do Colonialismo*, 1a edição (Lisboa: Tinta da China, 2016); Silvia Rodríguez Maeso, "O Estado de Negação e o Presente-Futuro Do Antirracismo: Discursos Oficiais Sobre Racismo,'Multirracialidade'e Pobreza Em Portugal (1985–2016)," *Revista Direito e Práxis* 10 (2019): 2033–67.

22. Araújo 2019; Maeso 2015; Silva and Silva 2002; Marta Araújo, "À Procura Do 'Sujeito Racista': A Segregação Da População Cigana Como Caso Paradigmático," *Cadernos Do Lepaarq (Dossiê 'Comunidades Quilombolas, Negras, Ciganas e Indígenas Na América Latina: Racismos Institucional e Epistemológico')* 16, no. 31 (2019): 147–62; Silvia Rodríguez Maeso, "'Civilising' the Roma? The Depoliticisation of (Anti-) Racism within the Politics of Integration," *Identities* 22, no. 1 (2015): 53–70; Manuel Carlos Silva and Susana Silva, "Práticas e Representações Sociais Face Aos Ciganos. O Caso de Oleiros, Vila Verde," *Antropológicas*, no. 6 (2002): 57–86.

23. This incident triggered an intense public debate about racism within the police force. As *Publico*'s investigative journalism showed, for the local population of these neighborhoods, racial violence by the police is pervasive. See, for instance, Joana Gorjão Henriques, "Queixas de violência policial na Cova da Moura: uma história antiga," Público, July 14, 2017, https://www.publico.pt/2017/07/14/sociedade/noticia /queixas-de-violencia-policial-na-cova-da-moura-uma-historia-antiga-1779028.

24. For example, Rute Coelho, "A queda dos três grupos de segurança privada que dominavam a noite," *Diário de Notícias*, December 31, 2016, https://www.dn.pt

/sociedade/-a-queda-dos-tres-grupos-de-seguranca-privada-que-dominavam-a-noite-no-pais-5579033.html.

25. The law is available at https://dre.pt/home/-/dre/122996202/details/maximized.

26. "Segurança Privada: Exército de Precários," *Fumaça* (blog), January 14, 2021, https://fumaca.pt/seguranca-privada-exercito-precarios/.

27. I use this problematic concept in its daily usage as a reference to anonymous people who are perceived as being part of the "imagined community."

28. Nuno Simões Rodrigues, "As Clitemnestras portuguesas de João Canijo," in *Clitemnestra o la desgracia de ser mujer en un mundo de hombres: homenaje de las Universidades de Valencia, Foggia, Bari y Coimbra a los Profesores Doctores Doña Aurora López López y Don Andrés Pociña Pérez*, ed. Francesco De Martino, Aurora López López, and Andrés Pociña Pérez (Bari: Levante, 2017).

29. Ribas, *Uma dramaturgia da violência?*, 132, 189ff, 205ff, 267.

30. Cláudia Casimiro, "Tensões, Tiranias e Violência Familiar: Da Invisibilidade à Denúncia," in *História Da Vida Privada Em Portugal: Os Nossos Dias*, ed. Ana Nunes Almeida (Lisbon: Temas e Debates, 2011), 112–40.

31. Ribas, *Uma dramaturgia da violência?*, 88.

32. Nuno Simões Rodrigues, "'Like a Ghost of Antigone': Ganhar a Vida (Get a Life), by João Canijo," in *Portrayals of Antigone in Portugal*, ed. Carlos Morais, Lorna Hardwick, and Maria de Fátima Silva (Leiden: Brill, 2017), 239–50.

33. Manuel Dias Vaz, ed., *La Communauté Silencieuse: Histoire de l'immigration Portugaise En France* (Bordeaux: Elytis, 2014).

34. The Schengen Area covers the twenty-six European countries which have abolished border controls and passports from Austria to Switzerland—most are EU states—https://ec.europa.eu/home-affairs.

35. Nuno Simões Rodrigues, "Uma Ifigénia portuguesa: noite escura de João Canijo," in *A receção dos clássicos em Portugal e no Brasil*, ed. M. F. S. Silva and M. G. M. Augusto (Coimbra: Imprensa da Universidade de Coimbra, 2016); Rodrigues, "As Clitemnestras portuguesas de João Canijo."

36. Rodrigues, "As Clitemnestras portuguesas de João Canijo."

37. There is a wordplay with "gaiolas" [cages]: it refers to buildings with small overcrowded apartments but it can be used as well as a reference to prison.

38. Ribas, 262. The recurring actors reinforce the sense of cohesion in Canijo's cinema. For instance, actress Rita Blanco has leading roles in *Filha da Mãe*, *Ganhar a Vida*, *Noite Escura*, and *Sangue do Meu Sangue*.

39. Billig, *Banal Nationalism*.

40. Fabrice Schurmans, *O Trágico Do Estado Pós-Colonial: Pius Ngandu Nkashama, Sony Labou Tansi, Pepetela* (Coimbra: Almedina: CES, 2014).

41. Edalina Rodrigues Sanches and Ekaterina Gorbunova, "Portuguese Citizens' Support for Democracy: 40 Years after the Carnation Revolution," *South European Society and Politics* 21, no. 2 (2016): 211–26.

42. Fernandes, *Cultura Política e Democracia*.

43. Pedro C. Magalhães, "Disaffected Democrats: Political Attitudes and Political Action in Portugal," *West European Politics* 28, no. 5 (2005): 973–91.

44. Mariano Torcal and José R. Montero, eds., *Political Disaffection in Contemporary Democracies: Social Capital, Institutions and Politics* (London; New York: Routledge, 2006), 6.

45. Magalhães, "Disaffected Democrats," 976.

46. Canijo is well known for his method of making a cinema that reproduces faithfully the sociocultural milieus that his films refer to, resulting from his efforts to let the cinema be influenced by reality. This method consists of careful research work about the social sectors and landscapes represented (hence Canijo's long observation stays in these spaces in order to prepare scripts and camera work), the adoption of techniques of the documentary (and introduction of real footage) and the obligation of his actors to live for a certain period of time in these spaces (and hence being able to adopt the right accent, gestures, dressing habits, etc.).

47. A closer look at the party's program exposes the fallacy of the "anti-system" discourse. It does not challenge the neoliberal order and international financial institutions. Investigative journalism pointed out at the close contacts between the party leaders and the members of the economic elite (see Miguel Carvalho, "Os empresários e as redes que embalam André Ventura," Visão, July 22, 2020, https://visao.sapo.pt/atualidade/politica/2020-07-22-os-empresarios-e-as-redes-que-embalam-andre-ventura/).

48. Marina Costa Lobo, António Costa Pinto, and Pedro C. Magalhães, "Portuguese Democratisation 40 Years on: Its Meaning and Enduring Legacies," *South European Society and Politics* 21, no. 2 (2016): 163–80.

BIBLIOGRAPHY

Araújo, Marta. "À Procura Do 'Sujeito Racista': A Segregação Da População Cigana Como Caso Paradigmático." *Cadernos Do Lepaarq (Dossiê 'Comunidades Quilombolas, Negras, Ciganas e Indígenas Na América Latina: Racismos Institucional e Epistemológico')* 16, no. 31 (2019): 147–62.

Billig, Michael. *Banal Nationalism*. London; Thousand Oaks, CA: Sage, 1995.

Black, Donald J. *The Social Structure of Right and Wrong*. Rev. ed. San Diego: Academic Press, 1998.

Carvalho, Miguel. "Os empresários e as redes que embalam André Ventura." Visão, July 22, 2020. https://visao.sapo.pt/atualidade/politica/2020-07-22-os-empresarios-e-as-redes-que-embalam-andre-ventura/.

Casimiro, Cláudia. "Tensões, Tiranias e Violência Familiar: Da Invisibilidade à Denúncia." In *História Da Vida Privada Em Portugal: Os Nossos Dias*, edited by Ana Nunes Almeida, 112–40. Lisbon: Temas e Debates, 2011.

Coelho, Rute. "A queda dos três grupos de segurança privada que dominavam a noite." *Diário de Notícias*, December 31, 2016. https://www.dn.pt/sociedade/-a-queda-dos-tres-grupos-de-seguranca-privada-que-dominavam-a-noite-no-pais-5579033.html.

Costa Lobo, Marina, António Costa Pinto, and Pedro C. Magalhães. "Portuguese Democratisation 40 Years on: Its Meaning and Enduring Legacies." *South European Society and Politics* 21, no. 2 (2016): 163–80.

Da Costa, José Mourão. "O Partido Nacional Renovador: A Nova Extrema-Direita Na Democracia Portuguesa." *Análise Social*, 2011, 765–87.

Fernandes, Tiago, ed. *Cultura Política e Democracia*. Lisboa: Fundação Francisco Manuel dos Santos, 2019.

Haas, Nicole E., Jan W. de Keijser, and Gerben JN Bruinsma. "Public Support for Vigilantism: An Experimental Study." *Journal of Experimental Criminology* 8, no. 4 (2012): 387–413.

Henriques, Joana Gorjão. "Queixas de violência policial na Cova da Moura: uma história antiga." Público, July 14, 2017. https://www.publico.pt/2017/07/14/sociedade/noticia/queixas-de-violencia-policial-na-cova-da-moura-uma-historia-antiga-1779028.

———. *Racismo Em Português: O Lado Esquecido Do Colonialismo*. 1a edição. Lisboa: Tinta da China, 2016.

Johnston, Les. "What Is Vigilantism?" *The British Journal of Criminology* 36, no. 2 (1996): 220–36.

Maeso, Silvia Rodríguez. "'Civilising' the Roma? The Depoliticisation of (Anti-)Racism within the Politics of Integration." *Identities* 22, no. 1 (2015): 53–70.

———. "O Estado de Negação e o Presente-Futuro Do Antirracismo: Discursos Oficiais Sobre Racismo,'Multirracialidade'e Pobreza Em Portugal (1985–2016)." *Revista Direito e Práxis* 10 (2019): 2033–67.

Magalhães, Pedro C. "Disaffected Democrats: Political Attitudes and Political Action in Portugal." *West European Politics* 28, no. 5 (2005): 973–91.

Marchi, Riccardo. "The Extreme Right in 21st-Century Portugal: The Partido Nacional Renovador." In *Right-Wing Extremism in Europe: Country Analyses, Counter-Strategies and Labor-Market Oriented Exit Strategies*, edited by Ralf Melzer, Sebastian Serafin, and Friedrich-Ebert-Stiftung, 133–55. Berlin: Friedrich-Ebert-Stiftung, Forum Berlin, 2013.

Moncada, Eduardo. "Varieties of Vigilantism: Conceptual Discord, Meaning and Strategies." *Global Crime* 18, no. 4 (2017): 403–23.

Raposo, Otávio, Ana Rita Alves, Pedro Varela, and Cristina Roldão. "Negro Drama. Racismo, Segregação e Violência Policial Nas Periferias de Lisboa." *Revista Crítica de Ciências Sociais*, no. 119 (2019): 5–28.

Ribas, Daniel. *Uma dramaturgia da violência: os filmes de João Canijo*. Lisbon: Imprensa de História Contemporânea, 2019. http://library.oapen.org/handle/20.500.12657/24951.

Rodrigues, Nuno Simões. "As Clitemnestras portuguesas de João Canijo." In *Clitemnestra o la desgracia de ser mujer en un mundo de hombres: homenaje de las Universidades de Valencia, Foggia, Bari y Coimbra a los Profesores Doctores Doña Aurora López López y Don Andrés Pociña Pérez*, edited by Francesco De Martino, Aurora López López, and Andrés Pociña Pérez. Bari: Levante, 2017.

———. "'Like a Ghost of Antigone': Ganhar a Vida (Get a Life), by João Canijo." In *Portrayals of Antigone in Portugal*, edited by Carlos Morais, Lorna Hardwick, and Maria de Fátima Silva, 239–50. Leiden: Brill, 2017.

———. "Uma Ifigénia portuguesa: noite escura de João Canijo." In *A receção dos clássicos em Portugal e no Brasil*, edited by M. F. S. Silva and M. G. M. Augusto. Coimbra: Imprensa da Universidade de Coimbra, 2016.

Rosas, Fernando, Francisco Louçã, Luís Fazenda, Jorge Costa, and Cecília Honório, eds. *Os Donos de Portugal: Cem Anos de Poder Económico (1910–2010)*. Porto: Edições Afrontamento, 2010.

Sanches, Edalina Rodrigues, and Ekaterina Gorbunova. "Portuguese Citizens' Support for Democracy: 40 Years after the Carnation Revolution." *South European Society and Politics* 21, no. 2 (2016): 211–26.

Schurmans, Fabrice. *O Trágico Do Estado Pós-Colonial: Pius Ngandu Nkashama, Sony Labou Tansi, Pepetela*. Coimbra: Almedina: CES, 2014.

Fumaça. "Segurança Privada: Exército de Precários," January 14, 2021. https://fumaca.pt/seguranca-privada-exercito-precarios/.

Silva, Manuel Carlos, and Susana Silva. "Práticas e representações sociais face aos ciganos. O caso de Oleiros, Vila Verde." *Antropológicas*, no. 6 (2002): 57–86.

Torcal, Mariano, and José R. Montero, eds. *Political Disaffection in Contemporary Democracies: Social Capital, Institutions and Politics*. London; New York: Routledge, 2006.

Vander Ende, Jacob. "Vigilantism." In *The Encyclopedia of Criminology and Criminal Justice*, edited by Jay S. Albanese. Hoboken, NJ: Wiley Blackwell, 2014. doi: 10.1002/9781118517383.wbeccj347.

Vaz, Manuel Dias, ed. *La Communauté Silencieuse: Histoire de l'immigration Portugaise En France*. Bordeaux: Elytis, 2014.

PART III

A South American Perspective

Chapter 10

"You Said Perpetual!"
Approaches to Vigilantism in Argentine Culture

Sebastian Viqueira

The most important scene in the film *El secreto de sus ojos* (*The Secret in Their Eyes*, 2009), the second Argentine film to win an Oscar, finds Ricardo Morales—whose wife had been raped and murdered at the beginning of the film—telling Benjamín Esposito, a former employee of the court which had investigated the crime thirty years before: "You said perpetual." His serenely and strictly pronounced words represent Morales' attempt to justify his revenge for the rape and murder of his wife. The way in which the core debate within this historic Argentine film is expressed offers a starting point to characterize the features from which vigilantism could be framed within Argentinian legal culture. We are looking at citizens who feel that the law has not fulfilled its promises and decide to assume punitive powers, even resorting to physical violence.

Justice by their own hand, lynching and revenge, among others, are actions associated with the idea of vigilantism. In this chapter we understand vigilantism as the practices of ordinary people who ignore state legal institutions and seek to punish other citizens for criminal acts or on suspicion that they have committed them.

These practices are generally linked to a lack of trust in the administration of justice, the police, or other institutions and a perception, in many cases unfounded, of insufficient punishment for the crime. This chapter will look at vigilantism in the context of modern-day Argentina. This exploratory study will be carried out establishing the connections between these practices and the law, the mass media, the popular culture, the feeling of insecurity, the notion of "pedagogy of cruelty," and the political dimension of vigilante practices. The recent Argentine context—especially the last two decades—will be the focus, including cases or examples linked to the democratic process initiated in 1983, as well as previous aspects of Argentinian history.

WHAT DO WE MEAN BY VIGILANTISM IN ARGENTINA?

Looking at the general context in Argentina and the legal culture in which vigilante actions there are carried out, it is worth mentioning that there is a crisis of legitimacy of the state, a perception of its absence in criminal matters, as well as a quite punitive legal culture.[1]

In this context, the influence of the mass media is an aspect that cannot be overlooked. Apart from the growing presence of police stories in the media, there is an appeal to stereotypes, such as the figure of the *neighbor* who reacts to the crime committed by the *criminal, moto chorro*,[2] or *pibe chorro*[3] expressions that work as stigmas that usually apply to people from the most deprived groups of Argentine society. When acts of violence occur, the media usually tends to reinforce the idea of state inactivity, lack of punishment of minors,[4] and the *garantismo* of judges in the country.[5]

We can also observe a process of privatization and commercialization of security exemplified in the growth of private security services. In 2018, the number of private guards was already higher than the number of police officers.[6] Moreover, there has been an expansion of the network of surveillance cameras, the presence of community alarms in different neighborhoods, and the growth of gated neighborhoods with restricted access and protected perimeters.

In addition, Argentina has had a long history of violence and permanent interruptions to the rule of law, as it has happened in the rest of Latin America/South America. The armed forces and the security, federal, and provincial forces have been repeatedly tried for serious violations of human rights, even during the period of democracy and the rule of law. In addition, our country has been characterized by high and chronic levels of non-compliance with the law. In this context, it is not surprising that, as Kaufman claims, "the configuration of collective violence phenomena as a representation of 'Justice by their own hand' has appeared in Latin America as a recurrent event, as recorded both in the media and in the academic and institutional writings."[7]

In this sense, Caravaca proposes the link between violence and social order to address lynchings in the region as follows: "We maintain that revisiting the problem of violence in our region gives our work an urgency and is an alarm call: if we consider that to think about violence is to think about the constitutive nucleus of the social order, we must gamble on building an analytical view that privileges the density, both theoretical and in meaning, that the term violence involves."[8]

FEATURES OF THE ARGENTINIAN SITUATION

Focusing on the specific features of vigilantism in Argentina requires a theoretical position and a brief comparison with the rest of the countries in Latin America. As Johnston remarks, the conceptualization of vigilantism has been linked to discussions that restrict and expand the universe of cases that could be included in the concept of vigilantism.[9] As stated in the introduction, this analysis will consider a broad conception of vigilantism which aims at making an approach oriented to future research that assesses vigilante actions and helps to deepen theoretical aspects.

Furthermore the occurrence of events, their characteristics, and the presence of vigilantism in Argentina presents significant differences from the rest of Latin America/South America. In countries such as Mexico[10] and Brazil,[11] for example, there is extensive academic scholarship related to vigilantism and a presence of vigilante organizations with stability, resources, and organization, as it is in the case of community policy and self-defense bodies (*autodefensas*) in Mexico and death squads in Brazil.

These differences have caused an apparent neglect in the analysis of these phenomena by Argentinian social scientists. Although there are reactions to acts of lynching and violence by social organizations, we could not find a significant amount of academic scholarship that seeks to understand the meaning of these actions. In general, we have noted formal disapproval of such behavior.

On the contrary, this chapter adopts the perspective proposed by Caracava who argues: "the construction of the theme is considered as a sociopolitical problem along with the proliferation of multiple voices and speeches, which convert the so-called lynching phenomenon into a fertile vector to think about the social conflict in Argentina today. We face an often diffuse network in which (in) security coexists as a social problem, the speeches of harsher penalties and 'justice at their own hand,' the construction of a social subject of the 'dangerous,' and the debates and political projects around changes in the Criminal Procedure Code."[12]

WHY DO ARGENTINIAN VIGILANTES ACT?

As stated above, understanding the meaning of vigilante actions requires a departure from moral and normative perspectives. This chapter will focus on this issue through the link between vigilante actions and the following features:

1. Criminal selectivity and trigger events
2. Sense of social action and pedagogy of cruelty
3. Spatial environment
4. Feeling of insecurity
5. Political participation

It is clear that this approach is not exclusive of others, but it aims to represent a possible way to understand the meaning of vigilante acts in Argentina.

Criminal Selectivity and Trigger Events

Not all crimes (for example white collar crimes) result in vigilante actions. Generally the crimes that most frequently result in vigilante actions are sexual abuse and murder of infants, femicide, daylight robberies on the streets, and cases of excessive police reactions. In addition there is actual or imagined involvement of members of the forces of law and order in overlooking certain crimes. The actions taken in response to these events include homicides, injuries, sexual abuse and harassment, attacks on police personnel, and destruction or arson of homes and public offices.

We might think that, behind this kind of behavior, there is an attempt to consolidate and specify the scope of what is allowed and forbidden, as Emile Durkheim pointed out. It could also be considered that we are facing revenge against the property (usually the destruction and setting fire to a house) and the body of the suspect that seeks to send messages and warnings to others who are willing to commit crimes and even to the official justice administration to make it harder to apply penalties.

The selection noted above is not limited by the type of crimes but also to those who commit them and their victims. In relation to those who commit them, we find social representations in which the crime is carried out by a person outside the intimate circle of the victim, who arrive from outside and commit assault. Young people from marginal sectors tend to be the most common victims of resulting vigilante actions. In a certain way, the vigilantes *catch* the habitual clients of the penal system.

There are also certain people who deserve more attention from the vigilantes such as children and young people from the middle and upper classes. In this sense, there are similarities with Butler's view. Taking into account the deaths from attacks and bombings of the United States in the Middle East, he claims that there are "lives that deserve mourning" and others that do not.[13]

Sense of Social Action and Pedagogy of Cruelty

Unlike common sense thinking, in this chapter we understand that vigilante actions are not irrational practices or meaningless. They embody, in Weberian terms, a value-oriented rationality (although in many cases they are expressed violently), which are motivated (although not necessarily planned) and that seek to cause consequences that may exceed the context in which they are executed. In the media, vigilante actions, particularly the most violent ones, are usually described as actions that disrupt a peaceful community. Contrary to this standard pattern, those who carry out vigilante actions do not arrive at them completely spontaneously but have gone through developing violent devices and justifying ideas as occurs with other violent actions.

One issue that deserves a rigorous approach is the relationship between vigilantism and gender. The vast majority presence of heterosexual men in acts of vigilantism in Argentina could be addressed following the notion of a "pedagogy of cruelty" by Segato, who explains in rather apocalyptic tones:

> I call all acts and practices that teach, accustom and program subjects to transmute the living and their vitality into things, pedagogies of cruelty.
>
> When I speak of pedagogy of cruelty I mean something very precise, such as the capture of something that flowed errant and unpredictable, such as life, to install there the inertia and sterility of the thing, measurable, sellable, affordable and obsolescent, as it is convenient for consumption in this apocalyptic phase of capital. The sexual assault and sexual exploitation of women are today acts of prey and consumption of the body that constitute the most precise language with which the objectification of life is expressed. Those who are left do not go to cemeteries, they go to landfills. The repetition of violence produces a normalization effect of a landscape of cruelty and, with this, promotes in people low thresholds of empathy indispensable for predatory business. Habitual cruelty is directly proportional to forms of narcissistic and consumerist joy, and to the isolation of citizens through their desensitization to the suffering of others. A historical project directed by the goal of the link as the realization of happiness mutates towards a historical project directed by the goal of things as a form of satisfaction. Pedagogy of cruelty is, then, what accustoms us to this dissection of the living and the vital, and seems to be the inescapable path of modernity, its ultimate destiny.[14]

Segato's point of view allows us to think that, even in brutal and apparently irrational lynching acts which are not preceded by a previous organization, there are a number of elements transmitted in the socialization process that have become natural and can manifest themselves daily in overlapping ways. Those elements, under certain conditions, abruptly display all their violence.

This series of predispositions to act as a vigilante becomes evident when we ask ourselves about the role of women and other genders in violent acts. The answer, in general, is they appear as victims of acts of violence and cruelty. In this way, the link between gender / sexual violence and vigilante actions is not diminished by the fact that the former are usually triggers of the latter. In cases of aberrant crimes, vigilante actions sometimes include sexual assault and even rape.[15] Furthermore, it is possible to hear requests to convicts to visit sexual violence on those accused of these crimes. Many of these requests are even presented in humorous and sarcastic ways. A recent case of a group of young rugby players accused of murdering another young man in the city of Villa Gesell included this type of exhortation and even videos of prisoners offering to attack the rugby players.[16]

Another link between sexual abuse and the more violent acts of vigilantism could be found in the justifications given by those who commit them. They seek to discipline others by applying corporal punishment. It is an art of unbearable sensations, according to Foucault, which tries to reestablish a social hierarchy that the vigilante considers altered.[17]

Spatial Environment

The relationship between vigilantism and the spatial environment in which it occurs involves the delimitation of dangerous areas and safe areas or the generation of feelings of insecurity that do not recognize safe areas. This places citizens in states of alert and permanent fear.

From this perspective, lynching or other acts of vigilantism can be approached as attempts to reaffirm local sovereignty and the sense of belonging to a certain territory. This is especially relevant for other regional examples such as Mexico and the self-defense groups, but also for the Argentinian situation in which organizations of residents of a certain area build levels of social solidarity around preventive and reactive actions against crime. That is the case of those posters placed in April 2019 in the Escalante neighborhood Santa Fe City that says, *"'Low life' in this area we dont call the police. If we catch you you will get a bullet"*[18] and which are similar to those that can be observed in different areas of Argentinian cities.

As Santillán states, there is a link between lynching and social inequality.[19] Following a left realist perspective, both crime victims and regular clients of the criminal system come from the most vulnerable sectors of society. The privatization of security, the inequality in access to these services for the majority of society and the selectivity of criminal punishment generate conditions that mean both ends of vigilant acts—the one who carries them out and the one who suffers them—come from disadvantaged sectors of society. The aforementioned perspective has a political function as it fragments the ties of the popular classes, diminishing their revolutionary potential. This view is particularly pertinent to address phenomena such the case of the Escalante neighborhood in Santa Fe shown above.

Also, focusing on the dynamics of the escalation of violence in urban vigilante acts, the contributions proposed by the French sociologist Mauger are valuable for this approach, although he focuses on the problem of the Parisian suburbs. In his work "The revolt of the French suburbs,"[20] he argues that the sequence of triggering violence, particularly urban ones, seems immutable: the death of a young man from the suburbs, perceived with or without foundation as a direct consequence of a police *excess* causes the initial outbreak. It is in this movement that the victim is transformed into a martyr who must be avenged through multiple operations and reprisals. At this point, he claims, emotion, solidarity, and rumors generate a rapid escalation of violence. The feeling of injustice is in this determining scheme in the "moral economy of the crowds." In the same sense, he understands the "revolt" not only as a manifestation, but also as other forms of "street emotion" that can be defined as "collective takeovers of public spaces."[21]

The increase in crime rates or the feeling of insecurity in certain areas may also function as decisive factors in gentrification processes that make the original population of that place move to more outlying areas while more favored sectors take over.

Feeling of Insecurity

Argentinians' fear of being a victim of a crime would not seem to respond completely to objective data or subjective experiences. According to the Latino barometer report (2018), while 69.3 percent of respondents stated that they had not been the victim of a crime in the last twelve months, 42.8 percent said that all or almost all the time they had been worried about suffering such an action.[22] This data makes it necessary to analyze the emotional bond of Argentinians with crime. This is possibly one of the central dimensions we need to consider to understand the acts of vigilantism in our country.

In this sense, Kessler, in relation to the notion of feeling of insecurity, argues:[23] "In recent studies it has been proposed to differentiate between an 'experiential fear,' linked to threats that are actually suffered, and 'expressive fear,' concentrating on rather a diffuse fear, a social criticism or a political discontent." Now, what is insecurity, according to Argentinian respondents?

It does not refer to all violent crimes, it excludes those that are linked to organized crime, which would only affect their partners and may include actions that do not involve the violation of the law, such as the fear caused by the presence of some of youth groups on the street without violating any rule. Its particular feature is the randomness of danger. It could be defined as any threat to physical integrity, rather than to property, which seems to be able to fall upon anyone. Randomness is based on the perception of the increase in actions and it is projected both in space and in the plurality of figures of the fearsome.

The increase in the sense of insecurity affects the quality of life, favors support for the most punitive policies, contributes to the de-legitimization of criminal justice, promotes consensus around actions "on their own," and dissemination of weapons. The data we have about Buenos Aires does not show a rise in punitive attitudes despite the increase in concern. In the survey held in Buenos Aires, the concern for crime reached 70 percent of those interviewed, but the measures to combat the insecurity that had more support were social: consolidate education and fight unemployment; they were followed by the legal ones: to fight police corruption and make the laws be enforced and punitive approaches only came in last place such as more severe punishments and the application of the death penalty. Alejandra Otamendi (2009), in the analysis of a national survey, notes an element of support for a minimum state, the predilection of punitive measures and quick solution to crime, compared to another associated with a broader definition of the role of the state, which supports social measures as a solution to crime and conceives accordingly that the solution will be slower.[24]

As we will see when describing cases in which violent vigilante actions were deployed, the situation of extreme fear appears in the testimonies of those who took part in them. Fear, frustration, a sense of vulnerability, indignation, and the feeling of being abandoned are examples of feelings of large sectors of the Argentine population and that represent the intersubjective platform which generates favorable conditions for the deployment of vigilante actions.

Political Participation

As Sozzo indicates,[25] governments are faced with a situation in which the issue of insecurity is something that cannot be questioned and, in that sense, is "depoliticized." Despite their violent characteristics and modest cost, vigilante acts have a profound political dimension and can be understood as an attempt to participate in the community. This is reflected in the reported actions of a young man who participated in acts of vigilantism during the police strike in Cordoba in 2013 who said: "I felt like an actor in some way."

His words represent the passage from a passive stage characterized by fear to an active dimension in which violence is applied to criminal gangs. These actions also portray a political message of a moral character that seeks to dissuade others from committing crimes. The same person whose testimony is reproduced at the beginning of this paragraph claimed that punishing the alleged criminals was like when "one beats his dog for pissing on the carpet so it doesn't do it again" and then he adds that while doing so he thought, "Look what you did, look what you force me to do."

The political message is extended to the state authorities in search of greater severity or to expand participation in punitive policies. Paradoxically, one of the interviewees of that documentary acknowledges that, despite the fact that they arrested and locked up the suspects and even beat them, their acts were much less cruel than those that the police then applied, which, in his words, consisted of shooting at close range the bosses of the criminal gangs.

As signaled at the beginning of this section, an in-depth exploration of these dimensions goes beyond the objectives of the present work and would require further empirical research, as well as an analysis of cases that allow deepening the links of those in the development of vigilante actions. As part of that exploratory objective, the following section will look at cases that have had wider public repercussions in Argentina.

Data and Cases of Wide Public Impact

As stated in the introduction, the production and access to firm data on this issue is complex in Argentina. Existing investigations are isolated and the data is limited both in the period and area covered. No systematic data was found nationwide. In this sense, Caravaca indicates that the number of studies at the regional level contrasts with a shortage at the local level.[26] Among the few examples mentioned by this author, it is worth mentioning the one by González, Ladeuix, and Ferreyra, who argue that in the period from 1997 to 2008, no less than ninety cases of lynching and punitive collective actions in the country took place. It is estimated that more lynchings have occurred in the province of Buenos Aires, and particularly, in the metropolitan area.[27]

Due to the scarcity of "hard" data, we will resort to the description of relevant cases in recent Argentine history which had public repercussions but which are not exclusive of a wider scope that would emerge from a detailed study. When selecting the cases, the following parameters were taken into account:

- Individual acts of revenge or justice by a criminal act: the cases of engineer Horacio Aníbal Santos, Doctor Villar Cataldo, and the so-called Samurai Cordobes were selected.

- Acts of collective lynching: the David Moreira case was selected.
- Vigilantism when general coexistence rules are broken: the police strike of 2013.

Acts of Revenge or Justice at Their Own Hand at an Individual Level

In this section we discuss the actions taken by a person who has suffered a criminal act. The framing of this behavior as legitimate defense (not recognized in Argentinian law as we will see later) will depend on aspects such as the proportionality between the first crime and the reaction, the moment in which it is exercised, and other circumstantial factors. In the selected cases we note that the Argentine law is usually soft in the application of criminal sanctions to these individual vigilantes. Also, culturally, they tend to generate high levels of popularity and empathy. These cases are known by the name of the *avenger*, while lynchings focus on the name of the victim. In the third type, by way of contrast, attention is placed on the general context rather than on victims and offenders.

Engineer Santos

A paradigmatic case in Argentina was what was done by engineer Horacio Aníbal Santos, who on June 16, 1990, murdered two people who had stolen the audio equipment from his vehicle. The case had great public impact and it could be said that it marked a milestone in terms of the general debate on *self-administered* justice in a democracy as well as the limits of self-defense. Santos received a lesser penalty and, after many years of judicial process, had to compensate the families of the victims.

Doctor Villar Cataldo

On August 26, 2016, one of the cases with the most attention in the media was that of Doctor Lino Villar Cataldo who murdered Ricardo Krabrel while he tried to rob him when he left his home. The Villar Cataldo case once again brought into public discussion issues related to the harshness of sentences, the supposed *garantismo* of judges, the need to lower the age of criminal liability of minors, the possession of firearms, and ultimately, the legitimacy of the exercise of violence by citizens. The case had a novel prosecution since it was the first of these cases to be tried by a jury, who declared him not guilty of manslaughter. The popularity of Villar Cataldo led the later Minister of Security, Patricia Bulrich, defender of tough policies, to receive him in her office.

The apparent lack of harshness in the punishment of such individuals changes when the number of participants increases. In the Córdoba Province in 2019 there was a trial by jury in which three people were convicted of the lynching of Gabriel Fernández in the city of Capilla del Monte. Fernandez was accused on social media by his ex-partner of having abused her daughter. Faced with this complaint, the complainant's brother and father lynched Fernandez. All three were convicted while Fernandez's case for abuse was closed at first and later on reopened. The case led to a discussion of the complaints made through social media and the consequences that could be triggered.

The Samurai Cordobes

A case of great notoriety occurred in Córdoba in 2015. A metalworker resisted an attempted robbery using a Japanese katana sword. The action caused serious injuries to three people and there was wide coverage in the media. Criminal charges were dismissed because he was deemed to have a legitimate defense. As in the previous cases, his behavior aroused not only empathy across broad sectors of the Córdoba population but also it involved humorous elements. Unlike the case of Santos and Villar Cataldo, the samurai never claimed his actions; he said that his life turned into a nightmare afterward and that he had only tried to defend himself.

Acts of Collective Lynching

Unlike what happens in individual acts of vigilantism, the cases in which there is more than one person involved with another with an evident inequality of force awakens further debates in Argentinian society and in the mass media. The Administration of Justice, on the other hand, seems to have a greater propensity to severely punish this type of behavior. Another element here is the "copycat" effect they have in society as a whole. Once there is a case of lynching with public repercussion, it is possible to witness several others in different parts of the country for a period of time, as we shall see.

David Moreira Case

David Moreira, an eighteen-year-old boy, was murdered in Rosario on March 25, 2014, after snatching a wallet from a pregnant woman. His case had wide coverage in the media and unleashed widespread social debates as well as a wave of lynchings throughout the country.

The violence against Moreira even provoked the reaction of Pope Francis who sent a letter to two humanist Argentinians residing in Sweden and who posted it on the social network Facebook: "The scene hurt me.

Fuenteovejuna,[28] I said. I felt the kicks in the soul. He was not a Martian, he was a boy of our people; he is truly a criminal. And I remembered Jesus. What would he say if he were a referee there? Who is without sin to cast the first stone? What failed? 'Everything hurt, the body of the kid hurt, the heart of the kickers hurt, I thought that we made that boy, he grew up among us, he educated himself among us, what failed? The worst thing that can happen to us is to forget the scene. And may the Lord give us the grace to be able to cry . . . cry for the delinquent boy, cry also for us.'"[29]

Pope Francis's words represent a typical approach to these types of cases, consisting of treating them as a great social failure. This represents both failure attributed to education (official and family) by young people initiated into crime and institutional failure due to the perception of a lack of channeling of violence through state institutions.

Vigilantism When General Social Rules Are Broken

We include under this section the context in which, for many reasons such as a police strike or violence unleashed by drug trafficking, the state is unable to control crime or social violence and part of the population has organized themselves to prevent and punish crime and / or to unleash the most violent aspects of their personality as marked above by introducing the notion of the learned culture of cruelty.

The Police Strike of 2013

The dawn of December 3, 2013, there was a strike of members of the police of the province of Córdoba—and other provinces. This was the final consequence of several months of wage claims and a conflict that included the detention of the drug division from that province, raids in police headquarters, and suicides of police officers suspected of being linked to drug trafficking.

In the case of Córdoba, the result of the political confrontation between the provincial government—by José Manuel De la Sota—and the national government—commanded by Cristina Fernández de Kirchner—the federal forces did not provide immediate assistance to the province, leaving it without security forces capable of controlling the territory.

The absence of police control in the streets of the province and especially in the capital, produced a series of criminal acts such as looting of businesses. This led to a final total of three people killed while nationally eighteen people were killed (not officially confirmed), hundreds of wounded and economic losses which, according to a report of the Argentine Confederation of the Company, was Argentine pesos $568,450,000.[30] Also, 1,900 businesses were affected by the looting.

To face the looting, barricades and groups organized acts of vigilantism. One of the most emblematic places was in the neighborhood of Nueva Córdoba where many university students from different parts of the country live. It is estimated that there was a population of 37,000 people in that neighborhood at the time of the event. Those at the barricades, mostly young male university students, began to arrest anyone considered suspicious. Riding a motorcycle, residing in peripheral neighborhoods, wearing certain clothing, or having a particular skin color were enough to stop a person and, in many cases, subject them to lynching.

This hunting of human beings was captured in a documentary directed by Natalia Ferreyra and produced by members of the Faculty of Information Sciences of the National University of Córdoba. It was titled *The Hour of the Wolf*.[31] Through cell phone images from residents of the neighborhood and testimonies of participants in acts of vigilantism, the films tries to reconstruct the meaning of such actions. They included physical violence, barricades, and vehicle and document control mechanisms of citizens trying to move around that area of the city.

The documentary included the testimony of a young law student who went to the aid of a person who had been brutally beaten. Despite the different attitudes between the group of vigilantes and the young man who rescued the victim, they all considered that their actions were socially transcendent and expressed the need they felt to do something outstanding in their lives. He underlined the desire to have a decisive participation in collective matters. This represents an interesting aspect on which to focus when we consider that we face young men, heterosexuals, with access to higher education and belonging to middle and upper classes of society who have open formal and informal channels of citizen participation.

In the first scene of the documentary, a close-up shot focuses on the interviewee and the interviewer reads a post on Facebook that he wrote days after the events:

> Last night was the first time in my life that I felt I was going to be killed. Locked up behind the blinds of the business without being able to see what was happening outside and with TV as the only connection with the outside, I began to feel panic. I got the information: they are stealing three blocks from your store. Two. Half a block. And I got tired of waiting till the end. I got tired of waiting for the horde. I got tired of feeling scared. The body can only tolerate that sensation only for a definite time. After that it becomes something else. I was cornered. Without escape. Knowing that if they had entered, it would have been the end. And with that feeling of "they are going to kill me" still throbbing in my chest, I decided to stop waiting for them to come, and I went out to look for them. Today there are those who judge you, they judge behind a camera, they judge from their house which has not been attacked; that doesn't help, that makes you

feel more alone, that generates more anger, more resentment. Why do you have to help the thugs? Why do you have to understand them, tolerate them? And who helps me? Who tolerates me and understands me? Yesterday I understood that if you are alone you can still do something. They make you believe that you have to swallow anger and indignation if something happens, if something happens to you. It is not like that, you are also alive, you can make yourself heard, you can also send a message, you can also say that not everything is acceptable. You can say it is enough. The time to start rebuilding is now but last night there was no room for that, last night it was to kill or die, last night, with everything that happened in the middle of the chaos in the middle of the action there was no time to wonder if someone who throws you to the floor and kicks you reads Marcel Marceau or Levinas. There was no time to quote Sartre; yesterday there was no place for humanism, yesterday the thing was primitive, yesterday was Darwin to the fifth power, survival. We were pawns of a political movement. They sacrificed all of us, they shit on people like you and me; those above and those below. And they come to ask me to respect, to sacrifice myself? Today intellectuals, judge you behind the cameras. It must be because the only things that remain intact are the libraries, because you know what? the other one to be taken care of cannot care less what books tell you to do when the hour of the wolf arrives.[32]

The richness of this testimony allows us to delineate some features mentioned in this chapter; the feeling of unbearable fear, loneliness, and misunderstanding, the need to do something to survive and the perception of abandonment by the state and the absence of laws that regulate coexistence. Such perceptions could be understood as the final corollary of the internalization of the neoliberal way of life and that provide a fertile context for the deployment of vigilante violence. The perception of lack of state and law mentioned by the vigilantes and through which they justify their actions, highlights the need to investigate the way in which the Argentinian state law deals with acts of vigilantism.

WHAT DOES THE ARGENTINIAN STATE LAW SAY?

The current Argentinian penal code does not punish vigilantism as an autonomous crime. However, we can find a variety of facts that are associated with vigilantism, such as injuries and homicides after arguments or attacks, misuse of weapons,[33] the simple possession of weapons,[34] aggravated homicide by premeditated conspiracy of two or more people, as well as behavior tolerated by the legal system such as legitimate defense or violent emotion.

In this sense, article 4, subsection 6 establishes that those who act in self-defense will not be punished, provided that the following circumstances are satisfied:

a. Illegitimate aggression;
b. Rational need of the means used to prevent or repel it;
c. Absence of provocation on the part of the defending party.

It will be understood that these circumstances apply in relation to anyone who during the night resists the climbing or breaking of fences, walls or entrances of his house, or occupied apartment or its outbuildings, whatever the damage caused to the aggressor.

This is also the case in relation to anyone who finds a stranger inside his home, provided there is resistance.

Paragraph 7 of that article determines that it is not a crime to act in defense of the person or rights of another, provided that circumstances (a) and (b) of the preceding paragraph apply. Where there has been provocation by the victim, that the third party was not involved in this.

Finally, article 35 sets a penalty—corresponding to that of the crime committed—in case the limits imposed for self-defense had been exceeded.

A common framework for the behaviors that occur in this legal situation is that of injury or homicide in a fight or assault regulated by articles 95 and 96.[35] This criminal law operates where it is not possible to determine who caused the injuries or the homicide in which case everyone is held liable. Where it is possible to identify who committed the act, the simple or aggravated injuries or homicide rule is applied.

Legal Partner Approach: Between *Garantismo* and Punitivism

As part of popular views on the law, those who legitimize the actions of vigilantism direct their criticism toward certain currents within the law, prominent personalities within it and salient social movements in the recent history of Argentina. Such is the case of legalism, Dr. Raúl Eugenio Zafaroni and the Human Rights movement.

Under the so-called *garantismo*, they describe the alleged extreme attachment to the constitutional guarantees of due process by Argentinian judges. This presumption has become a distinctive aspect of the external legal culture of our country despite the fact that the increase in experiences of trials by juries do not show significant differences between the decisions of judges and ordinary citizens in terms of punishment, as Bergoglio points out.[36]

In this sense, the idea of *garantismo* is usually associated with the movement for human rights which has had a very important impact in Argentina when it comes to prosecuting and punishing the perpetrators of crimes against humanity from the military dictatorship of 1976 to 1983 and to work for the proper operation of constitutional guarantees during the democratic process.

Finally, the legal figure who has embodied this idea of legalism the most is the former Judge of the Supreme Court Dr. Raúl Eugenio Zafaroni. Going beyond the specific field of law in which he had a strong influence with a minimalist view of criminal law, adherence to his ideas has become a social division in Argentina. For some groups, Zafaroni represents the figure of the *defender* judge of the *criminals* and aggressor of the *good citizens*.

Gargarella[37] argues that both criminal minimalism and punitivism are elitist ways of conceiving criminal law striving for democratic mechanisms with citizen participation in the definition and application of penalties. Accordingly, the expansion of the jury trial in different Argentine provinces could be read as a process of democratization in the application of penalties. We could also think that it is a mechanism used by the administration of justice to legitimize and control citizen participation in this field, as was argued in Bergoglio, Gastiazoro, and Viqueira.[38]

As we can see, Argentina is immersed in a situation of strong tensions between law operators, the general public, and the mass media. The ways in which popular culture is expressed, the mass media and the cultural industry will be addressed in the next section.

VIGILANTISM IN THE PRESS AND POPULAR CULTURE

The apparent lack of attention on the part of the academy and the absence of consolidated data on the phenomenon at national level contrasts with the interest in popular culture, the mass media, and the cultural industry. Cultural and audiovisual production in Argentina, as in a number of other regions, have paid special attention to acts of vigilantism. This chapter includes cultural productions that reflect acts of revenge, justice by their own hand, and lynching that, among others, have been part of the central themes of films and television series. It should be noted that the cultural industry in Argentina shows the legal system as inefficient, slow, and corrupt. This reinforces the low levels of positive image that the administration of justice and other institutions such as the police and politicians have in our country. In addition to this, the mass media have built and reinforced a criminal stereotype that functions as a true stigma for broad sectors of the population.

One aspect that must be taken into account is the level of cultural penetration of the American film and TV industry in the country that causes, for example, many people not to watch Argentinian films because they find them boring. The social representations of vigilante justice in Argentina are possibly more related to those exhibited in American films and series. Unlike what could happen in the Hollywood films, the option of taking the law directly in the hands of citizens is not always shown in Argentine cinema as something that works. Even with positive results, in several films, series, and novels the consequences of such *success* often leave negative consequences for the vigilantes themselves.

Another characteristic of the cultural dimension of vigilantism in Argentina, particularly in the cultural industry, is that part of the revenge or act of justice that is carried out intends to reveal a truth that only the avenger knows and which is not visible to the rest of society, who see the avenger as a respectable person. Finally, the stories have a moralizing closing message in which justice, despite everything, ends up triumphing.

In this section, we briefly describe some cultural productions that have dealt with this issue, and make comparisons that help us approach the main characteristics that vigilantism has in Argentine culture. Finally, we reflect on the approach to the news in the mass media.

Movies and TV Series

Fair Revenge, Thirst for Justice and Unfulfilled Promises of the Law: **El Secreto De Sus Ojos (2009)**

El secreto de sus ojos, as mentioned, was the second Argentine film to win an Oscar (in addition to other national and international distinctions) after *The Official History* (1985).[39] *El secreto* begins with the rape and death of Liliana Colotto and recounts the search for justice by her husband Ricardo Morales who is helped by Benjamín Esposito, Pablo Sandoval, and Dr. Irene Menéndez-Hastings—members of the court investigating the case. Despite being caught and sentenced, Morales only spends a few years in prison and he is later released during the time of the military government to become part of a repressive group.[40] Some years later, Esposito tries to write a novel about the case and those times. When he looks for Morales, he discovers that he had finally taken revenge for his wife's crime. When he is discovered, Morales pronounces the phrase that gives title to this article. The film exposes the idea of fair revenge in the face of flagrant injustice. It also shows the disappointment of an ordinary citizen for the lack of fulfillment of the promises of justice that the law carries. As in the other Argentine film that won the Oscar, the story is situated in the context of the last Argentine military dictatorship between 1976 and 1983 and it expresses the brutality of that time that included aberrant crimes such as the forced disappearance of people, the theft of children (issue dealt in the film *The Official History*), and the operation of paramilitary forces to assassinate political dissidents.

Punish and Moralize: 4x4 (2019)

This recent film, inspired by a case that occurred in the city of Córdoba, narrates the story of a doctor who suffered repeated robberies, and who introduces a series of technological devices in his truck to catch anyone who would steal it. The film takes place mostly in the suffocating cabin of the vehicle where the thief is a victim of inhuman punishments, such as extreme heat and cold, lack of food and drink. The film is not totally relaxed with acts of vigilantism and shows how the attempt to punish and moralize the offender represents a way to transform oneself into an immoral and brutal person.

As in the case of *El Secreto de sus ojos*, revenge is shown as a planned act unlike what happens in the news of the mass media in which it is shown as the result of unbearable emotions such as anger, fear, and tiredness.

The Explosion of People on the Edge: Relatos Salvajes (Wild Tales, 2014)

The film shows six stories of revenge and justice by their own hand for different offenses: an engineer who is tired of the arbitrariness of the authorities and an unjust social order so he blows up a traffic office; a frustrated musician who crashes a plane boarded by people who are responsible for bullying him; a woman who exposes her future husband at the wedding party for an infidelity; a driver who fights a pitched battle for his dignity taunted by another driver; and a cook who has nothing to lose and who poisons a usurer and corrupt politician. All the stories, as the title of the film indicates, present revenge as a desperate and irrational act driven by fatigue from unbearable living conditions. They also exhibit these acts of vigilantism as actions that are not to be valued but which turn out to be the final result of intolerable situations and feelings.

Justice without Violence: Los Simuladores (The Pretenders, 2002–2003)

In this television series a group of paid avengers exact justice through ingenious and deceptive techniques. The peculiarity of it is that their acts of vigilantism are operated without the use of physical violence. In addition, these avengers only deal with noble cases and part of the final payment for their services is paid by the person who committed the crime or reprehensible act that they try to deal with.

News

The presence of police news has increased in Argentina in both television and the written media. The permanent bombardment of news about crimes, particularly exceptional instances, leads to increasing levels of sensitivity and fear. In this sense, their influence on the social production of fear and its consequences is central. Although the message that is transmitted includes critical segments with vigilante practices, it generally involves the construction of *non-citizen* inhabitants as *other* to be fought by the *neighbors* or the *good citizens*.

The media draw a clear boundary between the world of crime and everyday life and between criminals and *honest* citizens even when the latter are involved in acts of vigilantism punished by law.

FINAL THOUGHTS

The breadth of practices that could be classified as *vigilantism* covers a wide range that always makes it difficult to specify and delimit the object of investigation. This, which could be considered a disadvantage, distances the study of these phenomena from essentialist perspectives, enriching both theoretical and empirical sources used for their approach. Likewise, as mentioned above, the situation in Argentina presents differences in relation to what happens in the rest of the region both at the level of practice and cultural representations.

However, it would seem that we face a growth of acts of revenge, lynching, justice by individuals or in groups. This situation is part of an increase in the demand for greater punishment and distrust in institutions, particularly the administration of justice. In addition, it occurs in a context of privatization of security (private guards, cameras, alarms, etc.) and disciplinary means (violent reactions outside the state) and a strengthening of the feeling of insecurity against crime.

Argentina, as in the case of the rest of Latin/South America, has a long history of violence by the state as well as a general tendency to breach the rules. Also, in the last four decades, the state has abandoned its roles at all levels. Despite this, the budgets for security and administration of justice grow in relative terms. Incarceration levels, meanwhile, show significant growth rates as the 2018 annual report by the Nation's Prison Procuration demonstrates. Finally, criminal rates, particularly homicide rates, are not significantly high in relation to the regional context according to *Latinobarómetro*.[41]

The mass media, particularly news and newspapers, have collaborated in reinforcing negative images of the rule of law and its institutions. In addition, they contribute to the construction of otherness through speeches in which the vigilante acts are shown as being carried out by honest neighbors who are tired of insecurity and victims such as delinquent kids, motorcycle thieves, or people belonging to impoverished groups.

The law in Argentina, beyond the formal level, exercises tolerance toward certain forms of vigilantism, particularly those preceded by aggression against the victim and exercised individually. It would appear to be less tolerant with those collectively exercised in cases of crimes against property without risks to the victim (robberies through street muggings). In the case of breach of general patterns of social or legal order the reactions in the Argentine context resemble what happens in other countries of the region. More violent and cruel reactions, relative levels of organization and mechanisms of moral justification of the actions undertaken appear.

The gender and vigilantism connection is an aspect to be explored with some care. The apparent dominance of heterosexual men involved in the active exercise of these actions and the propensity to use physical violence against a crime, fear or presumption of suffering is a feature. The general framework in which vigilantism takes place in Argentina is linked not only to a concrete and real experience as a victim of crimes, but also to the feelings of insecurity caused, partially, by the message of the mass media. Finally, it would be relevant to expand systematic studies on this phenomenon in the country that, even from a critical perspective, provide a certain moral and normative look in order to understand the meaning of vigilante actions.

NOTES

1. Maria Inés Bergoglio, Maria Eugenia Gastiazoro, and Sebastian Viqueira, eds., *En El Estrado. La Consolidación de Las Estrategias Participativas En La Justicia Penal* (Córdoba, Argentina: Editorial Advocatus, 2019).
2. Thief who rides a motorcycle.
3. Young thief.
4. In Argentina the legal age to be convicted of a crime is eighteen years old.
5. Under the so-called guarantee, they describe the alleged extreme attachment to the constitutional guarantees of due process by Argentine judges. See *Las razones del garantismo* (https://www.aadproc.org.ar/institucional/opinion/118-las-razones-del-garantismo)
6. According to the newspaper *Clarin* (one of the most popular in Argentina), "In the country the 'army' of private security has 250,000 men and women. Almost 70 percent are in the capital and in Buenos Aires Province. In those same jurisdictions metropolitan police and Province police forces amount to 115,000 officials. See "Los

Vigiladores Privados Ya Son Un 'Ejército' Pero Casi La Mitad Está En Negro," *Clarin.com*, October 11, 2018, https://www.clarin.com/policiales/vigiladores-privados-ejercito-mitad-negro_0_6fEGsr3xK.html.

7. "la configuración de fenómenos de violencia colectiva como representación de la 'Justicia por mano propia' ha aparecido en América Latina como un evento reiterado, tal como se registra tanto en los medios de comunicación como en las escrituras académicas e institucionales" (Alejandro Kaufman, "Genealogías de La Violencia Colectiva," *Pensamiento de Los Confines* 18 (July 2006): 113).

8. "sostenemos que revisitar la problemática de las violencias en nuestra región dota a nuestros trabajos de una urgencia y un alerta: si concebimos que pensar las violencias es pensar el núcleo constitutivo del orden social, debemos apostar a construir una mirada analítica que privilegie la densidad, tanto teórica como de sentido, que involucra el término violencia" (Evangelina Caravaca, "De Qué Hablamos Cuando Hablamos de Linchamientos. Una Sociología de La Actualidad," *Question/Cuestión* 1, no. 42 (2014): 37).

9. Les Johnston, "What Is Vigilantism?," *The British Journal of Criminology* 36, no. 2 (1996): 220–36.

10. See Ana Georgina Aldaba Guzmán, "La Policía Comunitaria de La Costa Chica Del Estado de Guerrero: Modelo de Seguridad Frente a La Crisis Del Estado Mexicano" (XVI Congreso nacional y VI latinoamericano de sociología jurídica "Latinoamérica entre disensos y consensos, nuevos abordajes en sociología jurídica," Santiago del Estero, Argentina, 2015), http://www.sasju.org.ar/interfaz/blog_nivel_3/123/archivos/com-4---aldaba-guzman.pdf.

11. See Bruno Teixeira Bahia, "Entre o Vigilantismo e o Empreendedorismo Violento" (Universidade Federal da Bahia. Faculdade de Filosofia e Ciências Humanas. Mestrado em Ciências Sociais, 2015), https://repositorio.ufba.br/ri/handle/ri/19021.

12. "se considera la construcción del tema como problema político-social junto a la proliferación de múltiples voces y discursos, que convierten al llamado fenómeno de los linchamientos en un vector fértil para pensar el conflicto social de la Argentina actual. Nos enfrentamos a un entramado, muchas veces difuso, en el cual conviven la (in)seguridad como problema social, los discursos de mano dura y 'justicia por mano propia,' la construcción de un sujeto social de los 'peligrosos,' y los debates y proyectos políticos en torno a los cambios en el Código Procesal Penal" (Caravaca, "De Qué Hablamos Cuando Hablamos de Linchamientos. Una Sociología de La Actualidad").

13. Judith Butler, *Vida precaria: el poder del duelo y la violencia* (Buenos Aires: Paidós, 2006).

14. "Llamo pedagogías de la crueldad a todos los actos y prácticas que enseñan, habitúan y programan a los sujetos a transmutar lo vivo y su vitalidad en cosas.

Cuando hablo de una pedagogía de la crueldad me refiero a algo muy preciso, como es la captura de algo que fluía errante e imprevisible, como es la vida, para instalar allí la inercia y la esterilidad de la cosa, mensurable, vendible, comprable y obsolescente, como conviene al consumo en esta fase apocalíptica del capital. El ataque sexual y la explotación sexual de las mujeres son hoy actos de rapiña y consumición del cuerpo que constituyen el lenguaje más preciso con que la cosificación de la vida se expresa. Sus deyectos no van a cementerios, van a basurales. La repetición de la violencia produce un efecto de normalización de un paisaje de crueldad y, con esto, promueve en la gente los bajos umbrales de empatía indispensables para la empresa predadora. La crueldad habitual es directamente proporcional a formas de gozo narcisístico y consumista, y al aislamiento de los ciudadanos mediante su desensibilización al sufrimiento de los otros. Un proyecto histórico dirigido por la meta del vínculo como realización de la felicidad muta hacia un proyecto histórico dirigido por la meta de las cosas como forma de satisfacción.

La pedagogía de la crueldad es, entonces, la que nos habitúa a esa disecación de lo vivo y lo vital, y parece ser el camino inescapable de la modernidad, su último destino" (Rita Laura Segato, *Contra-Pedagogías de La Crueldad* (Buenos Aires: Prometeo Libros, 2018), 11–12).

15. In a lynching case in Cordoba during 2017, punishment included sexual assault. See "'Me apuñalaron en la zona del ano,' habló el hombre linchado por falsa denuncia de su ex | Vía Córdoba," Vía País, November 5, 2019, https://viapais.com.ar/cordoba/1390125-me-apunalaron-en-la-zona-del-ano-hablo-el-hombre-linchado-por-falsa-denuncia-de-su-ex/.

16. See "'Estamos esperando a los rugbiers': el video de los presos que desafían a los acusados de matar a Fernando Báez Sosa," Infobae, January 24, 2020, https://www.infobae.com/sociedad/policiales/2020/01/25/estamos-esperando-a-los-rugbiers-el-video-de-los-presos-que-desafian-a-los-acusados-de-matar-a-fernando-baez-sosa/.

17. Michel Foucault, *Discipline and Punish: The Birth of the Prison*, trans. Alan Sheridan (New York: Vintage Books, 1977).

18. "El fuerte mensaje de vecinos de un barrio por la inseguridad," Uno Santa Fe, December 26, 2019, https://www.unosantafe.com.ar/santa-fe/el-fuerte-mensaje-vecinos-un-barrio-santafesino-la-inseguridad-n2552650.html.

19. Alfredo Santillán, "Linchamientos urbanos. 'Ajusticiamiento popular' en tiempos de la seguridad ciudadana," *Íconos—Revista de Ciencias Sociales* 0, no. 31 (2008): 57, https://doi.org/10.17141/iconos.31.2008.268.

20. Gérard Mauger, *La Revuelta de los suburbios franceses: una sociología de la actualidad* (Buenos Aires: Antropofagia, 2007).

21. "secuencia de desencadenamiento de las violencias, particularmente las urbanas, parece inmutable: la muerte de un joven de los suburbios, percibida con o sin fundamento como consecuencia directa de una 'exceso' policial, provoca el estallido inicial. Es en este movimiento en el cual la víctima es transformada en un mártir que debe ser vengado mediante múltiples operaciones y represalias. En este punto, para el autor, la emoción, la solidaridad y los rumores generan una rápida escalada de violencia. El sentimiento de injusticia es en este esquema determinante en la 'economía moral de las multitudes.' En un mismo sentido, entiende la 'revuelta,' en tanto manifestación pero también como otras formas de 'emotividad callejera' que pueden ser definidas como 'tomas de posesión colectivas de espacios públicos'" (Caravaca, "De Qué Hablamos Cuando Hablamos de Linchamientos. Una Sociología de La Actualidad," 35).

22. See Corporación Latinobarómetro: http://www.latinobarometro.org/latOnline.jsp.

23. Gabriel Kessler, "Algunas Hipótesis Sobre La Extensión Del Sentimiento de Inseguridad En América Latina," *Cuadernos de Antropología Social*, no. 37 (2013): 25–42.

24. See Kessler, 29ff: "En los últimos trabajos se ha propuesto diferenciar entre un 'miedo experiencial,' ligado a amenazas que efectivamente se sufren, y 'miedo expresivo,' concentrando más bien un temor difuso, una crítica social o un descontento político (Farrall et al., 2009). Ahora bien, ¿qué es la inseguridad, según los entrevistados argentinos? No se refiere a todos los delitos violentos, se excluyen los que se vinculan con el crimen organizado, que sólo afectarían a sus copartícipes y puede incluir acciones que no suponen la infracción de la ley, como el temor que ocasiona, en algunos, la presencia de grupos de jóvenes en la calle sin violar norma alguna. Su rasgo particular es la aleatoriedad del peligro. Podría definirse como toda amenaza a la integridad física, más que a los bienes, que parecería poder abatirse sobre cualquiera. La aleatoriedad se fundamenta en la percepción del incremento de hechos y se proyecta tanto en el espacio como en la pluralidad de figuras de lo temible. [. . .] El incremento de la sensación de inseguridad afecta la calidad de vida, favorece el apoyo a las políticas más punitivas, contribuye a la deslegitimación de la justicia penal, promueve el consenso en torno a las acciones 'por mano propia' y a la difusión del armamentismo (Hale, 1996). [. . .] Los datos que tenemos sobre Buenos Aires no muestran una extensión de las actitudes punitivas a pesar del incremento de la preocupación. En la encuesta de la ciudad de Buenos Aires, la preocupación por el delito alcanzaba a un 70% de los entrevistados, pero las medidas para combatir la inseguridad que más apoyo tenían eran las sociales: consolidar la educación y luchar contra el desempleo; les seguían las legales: combatir la corrupción policial y hacer que las leyes se cumplan y recién en último lugar se ubicaban las punitivas: castigos más severos y la aplicación de la pena de muerte. Alejandra Otamendi (2009), en el análisis de una encuesta nacional, distingue un polo de apoyo a un Estado mínimo, la predilección de medidas punitivas y de solución rápida al delito, frente a otro asociado con una definición más amplia del rol del Estado, que apoya medidas sociales como solución al delito y concibe en consecuencia que la solución será más lenta."

25. Máximo Sozzo, "Gobierno local y prevención del delito en la Argentina," *URVIO. Revista Latinoamericana de Estudios de Seguridad*, no. 6 (2009): 58–73, https://doi.org/10.17141/urvio.6.2009.1104.

26. Caravaca, "De Qué Hablamos Cuando Hablamos de Linchamientos. Una Sociología de La Actualidad."

27. Leandro Ignacio Gonzáles, Juan Iván Ladeuix, and Gabriela Ferreyra, "Acciones Colectivas de Violencia Punitiva En La Argentina Reciente," *Bajo El Volcán* 10, no. 16 (2011): 165–93.

28. *Fuenteovejuna* is a play by Lope de Vega 1619 based on real events in Fuenteovejuna in Castille, where a cruel tirano was killed and when a magistrate from the king arrived the response of the village was "Fuenteovejuna did it."

29. "Me dolió la escena. Fuenteovejuna, me dije. Sentía las patadas en el alma. No era un marciano, era un muchacho de nuestro pueblo; es verdad un delincuente. Y me acordé de Jesús ¿Qué diría si estuviera de árbitro allí? El que esté sin pecado que dé la primera patada ¿Qué falló?. Me dolía todo, me dolía el cuerpo del pibe, me dolía el

corazón de los que pateaban. Pensé que a ese chico lo hicimos nosotros, creció entre nosotros, se educó entre nosotros. ¿Qué cosa falló? Lo peor que nos puede pasar es olvidarnos de la escena. Y que el Señor nos dé la gracia de poder llorar . . . llorar por el muchacho delincuente, llorar también por nosotros."

30. American dollars at the rate of exchange at the time US$ 91.685.483.

31. See https://www.youtube.com/watch?v=oxrqyhuyXis.

32. "Anoche fue la primera vez en mi vida que sentí que me iban a matar. Encerrado tras las persianas del negocio sin poder ver lo que pasaba afuera y con la tele como única conexión con el exterior, comencé a sentir pánico. Me llegaban los datos: están robando a tres cuadras de tu local. A dos. A una y media. Y me harté de esperar el final. Me cansé de esperar a la horda. Me cansé de sentir miedo. El cuerpo solo puede tolerar esa sensación solo un tiempo definido. Después de eso se transforma en otra cosa. Estaba acorralado. Sin escapatoria. Sabiendo que si entraban, era el fin. Y con esa angustia de 'me van a matar' todavía palpitándome en el pecho, decidí dejar de esperar a que vinieran, y salí a buscarlos yo. Hoy están los que te juzgan, juzgan detrás de una cámara, juzgan desde su casa no perpetrada; eso tampoco ayuda, eso te hace sentir más solo, eso genera más ira, más rencor. ¿Por qué hay que ayudar al maleante? ¿Por qué hay que comprenderlo, tolerarlo? Y a mí ¿Quién me ayuda? ¿Quién me tolera y me comprende? Ayer entendí que si estas solo todavía podes hacer algo. Te hacen creer que te tenes que comer la bronca y la indignación si pasa algo, si te pasa algo. No es así, vos también estas vivo, vos podes hacerte escuchar, también podes enviar un mensaje, también podes decir que no todo vale. Podes decir basta. El momento para comenzar a reconstruir es ahora pero anoche no hubo margen para eso, anoche era morir o matar, anoche, con todo lo que paso en medio del caos en el medio de la acción no había tiempo para preguntarse si aquel que te tira al piso y te patotea leyó a Marcel Marceau o a Levinas. No había tiempo a citar a Sartre; ayer no hubo lugar para el humanismo, ayer la cosa fue primitiva, ayer era Darwin a la quinta potencia, la supervivencia. Fuimos peones de una movida política. Nos sacrificaron a todos, se cagaron en la gente como vos y como yo; los de arriba y los de abajo. ¿Y me vienen a pedir a mí que respete, que me sacrifique? Hoy la rama intelectual te juzga detrás de las cámaras. Debe ser porque lo único que quedo intacto son las librerías, porque ¿saben qué?, el otro al que hay que cuidar le importa tres pitos lo que los libros te dicen que hay que hacer cuando llega la hora del lobo."

33. Arms abuse Art. 104: The person who fires a firearm at a person without injuring him will be given one to three years in prison.

This penalty shall apply even if an injury is incurred to which a lesser penalty corresponds, provided that a more serious crime is not committed.

Assault with any weapon will be given imprisonment of fifteen days to six months, even where no injury is caused.

34. Art. 189bis(2): "The simple possession of firearms for civil use, without due legal authorization, will be punished with imprisonment of 6 (SIX) months to 2 (TWO) years and a fine of THOUSAND PESOS ($ 1,000) to TEN THOUSAND PESOS ($ 10,000).

If the weapons are of war, the penalty will be TWO (2) to SIX (6) years in prison.

The carrying of civilian firearms, without proper legal authorization, will be punished with imprisonment of ONE (1) year to FOUR (4) years.

If the weapons are of war, the penalty shall be THREE (3) years and SIX (6) months to EIGHT (8) years and SIX (6) months of imprisonment or imprisonment.

If the bearer of the weapons to which the two preceding paragraphs refer is authorized holder of the weapon in question, the corresponding criminal scale shall be reduced by one third of the minimum and maximum.

The same reduction envisaged in the previous paragraph may be practiced when, due to the circumstances of the act and the personal conditions of the author, the lack of intention to use the weapons carried for illicit purposes is evident.

In the two preceding cases, special disqualification will also be imposed for double the time of the sentence.

Anyone who records a criminal record for a criminal offence against persons or with the use of weapons, or who is enjoying a release or exemption from previous imprisonment and carrying a firearm of any caliber, shall be subject to a a prison sentence of FOUR (4) a TEN (10) years."

Art. 189bis(3): "The collection of firearms, parts or ammunition thereof, or the possession of instruments to produce them, without proper authorization, shall be subject to imprisonment from FOUR (4) to TEN (10) years. Anyone who makes the illegal manufacture of firearms a habitual activity will attract a penalty of imprisonment or imprisonment from FIVE (5) to TEN (10) years. (4) It will be subject to sentence of imprisonment of ONE (1) year to SIX (6) years who will deliver a firearm, by any title, to whom he will not accredit his status as a legitimate user. The penalty shall be THREE (3) years and SIX (6) months to TEN (10) years in prison if the weapon were delivered to a minor of EIGHTEEN (18) years. If the author is guilty of the repeat offence of 1 provision of firearms, the penalty shall be FOUR (4) to FIFTEEN (15) years of imprisonment. If the culprit of any of the behaviors contemplated in the three preceding paragraphs has authorization for the sale of firearms, it will be imposed, in addition, absolute and perpetual special disqualification, and a fine of TEN THOUSAND PESOS ($ 10,000). (5) It will be subject to imprisonment of THREE (3) to EIGHT (8) years and special disqualification for double the time of the sentence which, having the proper legal authorization to manufacture weapons, omits its number or engraving in accordance with the current regulations, or I will assign TWO (2) or more identical numbers or engraved weapons. The same penalty shall be incurred by the person who adulterates or removes the number or engraving of a firearm."

35. Homicide or injury in an assault Art. 95: "When in a quarrel or assault involving more than two persons, death or injury results from those determined in articles 90 and 91, without stating who caused them, all authors shall be considered those who exercised violence on the person of the offended person and imprisonment or imprisonment will be applied for two to six years in case of death and one to four in case of injury."

Art. 96: "If the injuries were those provided for in article 89, the applicable penalty shall be four to one hundred and twenty days in prison."

36. Maria Inés Bergoglio, ed., *Subiendo al estrado: la experiencia cordobesa del juicio por jurado* (Córdoba, Argentina: Editorial Advocatus, 2010).

37. Roberto Gargarella, *Castigar al Prójimo: Por Una Refundación Democrática Del Derecho Penal* (Buenos Aires: Siglo Veintiuno Editores, 2016); see also Roberto Gargarella, "Igualitarismo vs Garantismo," *Revista Pensamiento Penal*, June 12, 2017, http://revista.pensamientopenal.org/doctrina/45400-igualitarismo-vs-garantismo .http://www.pensamientopenal.com.ar/system/files/2017/06/doctrina45400.pdf

38. Bergoglio, Maria Inés, Gastiazoro, and Viqueira, *En El Estrado. La Consolidación de Las Estrategias Participativas En La Justicia Penal*.

39. Film that shows the illegal appropriation of a child who was the daughter of two persons kidnapped and killed during the military dictatorship from 1976 to 1983.

40. Paramilitaries groups in charge to kidnap, disappear, and murder people persecuted by the military government.

41. Corporación Latinobarómetro, "Informe 2018," 2018, http://www.latinobarometro.org/latOnline.jsp.

BIBLIOGRAPHY

Aldaba Guzmán, Ana Georgina. "La Polícia Comunitaria de La Costa Chica Del Estado de Guerrero: Modelo de Seguridad Frente a La Crisis Del Estado Mexicano" (XVI Congreso nacional y VI latinoamerica de sociología jurídica "Latinoamérica entre disensos y consensos, nuevos abordajes en sociología jurídica," Santiago del Estero, Argentina), 2015. http://www.sasju.org.ar/interfaz/blog_nivel_3/123/archivos/com-4---aldaba-guzman.pdf.

Bergoglio, Maria Inés, ed. *Subiendo al estrado: la experiencia cordobesa del juicio por jurado*. Córdoba, Argentina: Editorial Advocatus, 2010.

Bergoglio, Maria Inés, Maria Eugenia Gastiazoro, and Sebastian Viqueira, eds. *En El Estrado. La Consolidación de Las Estrategias Participativas En La Justicia Penal*. Córdoba, Argentina: Editorial Advocatus, 2019.

Butler, Judith. *Vida precaria: el poder del duelo y la violencia*. Buenos Aires: Paidós, 2006.

Caravaca, Evangelina. "De Qué Hablamos Cuando Hablamos de Linchamientos. Una Sociología de La Actualidad." *Question/Cuestión* 1, no. 42 (2014): 29–41.

Corporación Latinobarómetro. "Informe 2018," 2018. http://www.latinobarometro.org/latOnline.jsp.

Uno Santa Fe. "El fuerte mensaje de vecinos de un barrio por la inseguridad," December 26, 2019. https://www.unosantafe.com.ar/santa-fe/el-fuerte-mensaje-vecinos-un-barrio-santafesino-la-inseguridad-n2552650.html.

Infobae. "'Estamos esperando a los rugbiers': el video de los presos que desafían a los acusados de matar a Fernando Báez Sosa," January 24, 2020. https://www.infobae.com/sociedad/policiales/2020/01/25/estamos-esperando-a-los-rugbiers-el-video-de-los-presos-que-desafian-a-los-acusados-de-matar-a-fernando-baez-sosa/.

Foucault, Michel. *Discipline and Punish: The Birth of the Prison*. Translated by Alan Sheridan. New York: Vintage Books, 1977.

Gargarella, Roberto. *Castigar al Prójimo: Por Una Refundación Democrática Del Derecho Penal*. Buenos Aires: Siglo Veintiuno Editores, 2016.

———. "Igualitarismo vs Garantismo." *Revista Pensamiento Penal*, June 12, 2017. http://revista.pensamientopenal.org/doctrina/45400-igualitarismo-vs-garantismo.

Gonzáles, Leandro Ignacio, Juan Iván Ladeuix, and Gabriela Ferreyra. "Acciones Colectivas de Violencia Punitiva En La Argentina Reciente." *Bajo El Volcán* 10, no. 16 (2011): 165–93.

Johnston, Les. "What Is Vigilantism?" *The British Journal of Criminology* 36, no. 2 (1996): 220–36.

Kaufman, Alejandro. "Genealogías de La Violencia Colectiva." *Pensamiento de Los Confines* 18 (July 2006).

Kessler, Gabriel. "Algunas Hipótesis Sobre La Extensión Del Sentimiento de Inseguridad En América Latina." *Cuadernos de Antropología Social*, no. 37 (2013): 25–42.

Clarin.com. "Los Vigiladores Privados Ya Son Un 'Ejército' Pero Casi La Mitad Está En Negro," October 11, 2018. https://www.clarin.com/policiales/vigiladores-privados-ejercito-mitad-negro_0_6fEGsr3xK.html.

Mauger, Gérard. *La Revuelta de los suburbios franceses: una sociología de la actualidad*. Buenos Aires: Antropofagia, 2007.

Vía País. "'Me apuñalaron en la zona del ano,' habló el hombre linchado por falsa denuncia de su ex | Vía Córdoba," November 5, 2019. https://viapais.com.ar/cordoba/1390125-me-apunalaron-en-la-zona-del-ano-hablo-el-hombre-linchado-por-falsa-denuncia-de-su-ex/.

Santillán, Alfredo. "Linchamientos urbanos. 'Ajusticiamiento popular' en tiempos de la seguridad ciudadana." *Íconos—Revista de Ciencias Sociales* 0, no. 31 (2008): 57. https://doi.org/10.17141/iconos.31.2008.268.

Segato, Rita Laura. *Contra-Pedagogías de La Crueldad*. Buenos Aires: Prometeo Libros, 2018.

Sozzo, Máximo. "Gobierno local y prevención del delito en la Argentina." *URVIO. Revista Latinoamericana de Estudios de Seguridad*, no. 6 (2009): 58–73. https://doi.org/10.17141/urvio.6.2009.1104.

Teixeira Bahia, Bruno. "Entre o Vigilantismo e o Empreendedorismo Violento." Universidade Federal da Bahia. Faculdade de Filosofia e Ciências Humanas. Mestrado em Ciências Sociais, 2015. https://repositorio.ufba.br/ri/handle/ri/19021.

Chapter 11

Vigilante Justice and the Rule of Death

The Existential Threat to the state and its People in Brazil

Pedro Fortes

The purpose of this chapter is to examine the existential threat posed by professional killers and their informal justice in Brazil. Traditions of private justice vary according to the geographical location, the legal culture, institutional design, and the particular context. Particularly in the case of Brazil, there is a conflict of narratives, discourses, and ideas about the killing of criminal suspects. On one hand, there are popular narratives that endorse the possibility of extrajudicial executions—symbolized by the expression repeated by part of the population and certain politicians that "a good bandit is a dead bandit" (*"bandido bom é bandido morto"*).[1] On the other hand, human rights discourse emerged as a powerful source for protection of criminal guarantees and limitations on authoritarianism after the enactment of the democratic constitution in 1988.[2] In the case of these killings, the opinions of lay people become decisive for the final outcome, because criminal juries have the task of processing and judging cases of murder and they are influenced by factors not directly related to the evidence of the case, such as the profile of the defendant and the passage of time since the violent death.[3] Therefore, even if the Brazilian Constitution states that death penalties may not be imposed, jurors may acquit vigilantes based on the perspective that private justice, extrajudicial executions, and an informal application of the death penalty are justifiable. In this context, there is not only an existential threat to the individual victims potentially murdered by vigilantes, but also to the justice system and the rule of law.

In terms of methodology, this chapter is empirical and interpretative. Following the pattern established by the editors of this collection, a typology of vigilantes emerged from the literature review of academic articles. Empirical observation of data and representations of vigilante justice revealed patterns of killings, providing a context for anyone concerned with the existential threat posed by extrajudicial executions to the rule of law. Additionally, positive law, potential legislative reforms, and the context of vigilante justice are discussed, especially if law provides tacit support for actions outside the formal state. Furthermore, literature, films and television provide extensive examples of vigilantism.

A TYPOLOGY OF VIGILANTISM: HIRED KILLER, DEATH SQUAD, ORGANIZED CRIME, AND MILITIA

The literature review on vigilantism in Brazilian academia provides a variety of different ideal types of informal justice providers. Operating as functional equivalents of formal judicial institutions, their intent to provide informal justice is found in the killing of criminal suspects, extrajudicial executions, or informal death penalties. There are different types of killers in both academic and fictional literature. First, there is the hired killer (*"matador de aluguel"*), normally someone hired specifically for particular services with the mission of killing one defined target. Second, there is the death squad (*"grupo de extermínio"*), typically constituted by a group of people whose work is somehow related to the provision of private or public security and who exterminate criminal suspects through the coordinated action of its members. Third, members of organized crime (*"crime organizado"*) constitute a group of criminal offenders, whose illegal activity is related to the domination of an area and provide reasons for killing. Fourth, there is the militia member (*"miliciano"*), normally someone who provides hired security services to an area abandoned by the state and dominated by a group of local residents who patrol the area, enforce an informal code of criminal norms, and charge a fee from individuals and business to maintain their operations.

The hired killer (*"matador de aluguel"*) originated from the rural areas of Brazil, especially from the northeast region of the country.[4] Originally, the gunman (*"pistoleiro"*) was an important player in local politics, functioning as an armed arm for powerful landowners, so that they could exercise political pressure over voters, workers, and political rivals.[5] Traditionally, the political structure of these rural areas consisted of the personal rule of individuals who accumulated land and capital, mobilizing a number of gunmen according to their wealth. In this context, killing an opponent became a technique for problem solving, especially to eliminate political opposition, risk of strikes, and even romantic competition. In parts of the country, these powerful landowners received informally the title of colonel (*"coronel"*), an important military ranking that demonstrated their local power, even if often they had no formal role in the military and their status actually derived from the informal armed group made up of his own gunmen.[6] Historically, farmers counted on their henchmen (*"capangas"*) to exercise their power through violence.[7] Nowadays, however, killers are no longer salaried workers, but rather mercenaries hired on demand to commit specific homicides.[8] Typically, there is a mastermind (*"mandante"*), who decides that an opponent should be killed. Someone may function as the intermediate (*"intermediário"*), that is, the individual responsible for the liaison between the mastermind and the killer.[9] Additionally, an important collaboration comes from the motorcycle driver (*"piloto da motocicleta"*) who drives the killer to the crime scene, as a co-author who positions the gunman next to the target so that he may shoot and kill the victim.[10] Someone may also support the killer as a protector (*"protetor"*), offering help to the killer after the homicide.[11] Finally, the hired gun (*"matador de aluguel"*) carries out the killing.[12]

The death squad (*"grupo de extermínio"*) originated inside the military police in urban areas of the southeast region of the country in the 1960s.[13] Initially, a group of military police officers created an informal association named *Escuderie Le Coq* after a murdered police officer called Milton Le Coq and they established a routine of killing criminal suspects as part of an ideology of social cleansing, that is the large scale removal of members of society who were considered undesirable.[14] Their targets were not the most sophisticated or dangerous criminals, but rather the ones that disturbed everyday life and public order, like drug addicts, petty robbers, and homeless children living on the streets.[15] The act of killing criminal suspects may take place during the professional activity of the police or during the off-duty period. When police officers execute a criminal suspect while on duty, there is an informal protocol to qualify their killing as self-defense.[16] In most of these cases, criminal suspects are taken to the emergency department of a hospital, even if they were severely shot and were clearly dead.[17] By rescuing the dead criminal suspects, police officers remove the body from the crime scene and prevent the forensic experts examining the dynamics of the shooting and the version given by those who carried out the shooting.[18] Moreover, the narrative provided by the police officers repeats itself, as part of the legitimate self-defense story that states that they were only responding to an unjustified attack started by the criminal suspect and they ended up killing him.[19] At the police station, the local chief police officer register these cases as a File of Resistance to Imprisonment (*"Auto de Resistência à Prisão"*), liberating the killers without any consequence, so that they may return immediately to patrol the streets again.[20] Some police officers even carry artifacts in their police car that may be use as false evidence to incriminate the criminal suspect—an act known as "planting evidence" at the crime scene. The planted evidence may be illegal drugs, a stolen cell phone, and sometimes an unregistered gun to suggest that the criminal suspect was armed and dangerous.[21] Additionally, death squads may also operate off-duty, when police officers decide to return to a particular place to exterminate a particular target, such as children living on the streets, prostitutes, drug addicts, and members of a given community, for instance.

Organized crime ("*crime organizado*") originates from the development of organizations, networks, or groups who make the exercise of violence part of their regular activities.[22] These organizations depend on the existence of their own illegal markets, in which a commodity—lottery, drugs, arms, or protection—is exploited economically in association with their violent action.[23] Particularly in Brazil's largest cities, organized crime grew exponentially in the less urbanized areas, expanding their power in the slums ("*favelas*") and suburbs. Historically, the "red command" ("*Comando Vermelho*") developed into a large criminal organization responsible for the drug trade in Rio de Janeiro and formed a new narco-culture during the period of the military dictatorial regime in Brazil.[24] Nowadays, these criminals replicate the structure of business corporations, establishing a legal department responsible for coordinating defense attorneys, a financial department which manages their funds, and a revenue collector who charges, receives, and registers their monetary resources.[25] In the slums, the drug lords established their own informal justice system, taking decisions on house evictions, individual disputes, and also enforcing their own parallel criminal code.[26] As a result, nowadays organized crime controls land law, civil justice, and criminal law enforcement and functions like a parallel state.[27] Importantly, previously the Residents' Association performed this role by keeping a record of letters of house possession transfers and mediating dispute settlements.[28] Violent social relations of organized crime members are shaped by a warlike culture typical of the confrontation between armed groups and their informal mechanisms for vigilante justice occupy a space abandoned by the official state and its formal justice system.[29] Additionally, organized crime emerged also through mafia-like organizations that exploited illegal gambling through an animal lottery developed during the period of the early republic in Brazil (1889–1930).[30] The bosses of the so-called Animal game ("*Jogo do Bicho*") are named "*bicheiros*" and their economic power turned them into leading sponsors of carnival and providers of bribes to the police.[31] Their political domination corresponds also to the geographical area of their places for gambling and their corrupting power guarantees the continuity of their illegal activity in the streets dominated by them.[32] The most powerful *bicheiros* become the patron or president of a samba school—a strategy to consolidate their social prestige and to legitimate their status, even if their main business remains a criminal offence.[33] In parallel with their support of a genuine form of popular art, their power depends also on their violent means and the capacity to mobilize gunmen to protect their lives and eventually also kill their opponents.[34]

Finally, the militia member (*"miliciano"*) corresponds with the member of a private paramilitary organization created by individual residents of favelas to resist the invasion of drug lords.[35] Historically, residents of a slum in Rio de Janeiro established the first militia (*"milícia"*) formed by police officers, firemen, and security guards, who patrolled the area and prohibited drug trafficking and consumption there.[36] Importantly, even if some of the members of a militia may professionally work within the state official police force, their paramilitary activity operates at the margins of the official law on their own behalf and for their own benefit.[37] Militia members exercise political control over a territory, where they provide security for residents under the threat of violence if individual families do not contribute with the payment of a fee for the militia.[38] In the twenty-first century, militias expanded their paramilitary activities geographically and came into conflict with rival drug lords and organized criminals for the control of the slums.[39] Their expansion involved also the operation of services inside the slums, with militia members charging fees for provision of illegal transportation services (unlicensed motorcycle taxis and minivans), illegal cable television (unlicensed content in violation of copyright), illegal Internet, gas, and water distribution.[40] Interestingly, Alexandre Werneck considers the militia member to be a combination of the characteristics of the drug lord, the corrupt police officer, and the hired killer—like drug lords, their force is used to form economic monopolies; like the death squads, their killing is targeted toward extermination; like the hired killers, their power transforms into capital through charging for their violence.[41]

THE RULE OF DEATH: INFORMAL DISPUTE RESOLUTION, DEATH PENALTY, AND PLURALITY OF FORCE

The empirical experience of contemporary Brazil involves a divided state, in which the central areas of cities and wealthy neighborhoods are shaped by the rule of law, constitutional rights, and political freedoms, but the peripheral areas are subject to the exercise of violent power by hired killers, death squads, organized crime, and militias. Personally, I had direct contact with this reality as a public prosecutor in the state of Rio de Janeiro and professionally worked with investigations, procedures, and jury trials related to homicides. Based on the methodology of participant observation (albeit retrospectively),[42] I immediately reflect on this experience and made mental notes about it when presented with the research question proposed by the editors of this collection on places with a tradition of vengeance and private justice in contrast to places where the rule of law is more effective. When I worked in the county of Itaguaí located 65 kilometers from the center of Rio de Janeiro, there was a tradition of violent crimes among politicians and killing seemed to be a method for informal dispute resolution. However, this strategy generated a vicious cycle of homicides among politicians and regularly local politicians were shot. Moreover, this city also experienced a large number of murders with characteristics of extrajudicial execution, in which police officers decided to kill criminal suspects instead of arresting them—a practice analogous to an informal conviction with the death penalty. Finally, many cases of homicides were simply not properly investigated, because the potential witnesses feared the power of criminal organizations, local colonels, death squads, and militia members. In contrast to the rule of law, constitutional rights, and political freedoms, the experience in the suburbs and slums requires the development of new political concepts tailored to the context of vigilante justice. The *rule of death* implies that individuals do not consider the positive law as a rationale for actions, but are rather impacted and have their conduct governed by fear of death. Instead of constitutional rights typical of the liberal democratic state, individuals suffer the imposition of *unconstitutional duties* through unjust orders back by death threats. Political freedoms are replaced by the exercise of violent power and *authoritarian restrictions*.

In terms of practical examples that may clarify these points, I would like to initially describe cases from my professional experience in Itaguaí between 2002 and 2004 involving hired killers, colonels, death squads, organized crime, and militias. First, there was one case of a politically motivated homicide of a former deputy mayor appointed as a special investigator for a corruption scandal in the municipal hospital. Two hired killers murdered this local politician on the exact day on which he was due to start to investigate the embezzlement and fraud at the accounting department of the hospital. As the evidence demonstrated that the hospital accountant hired these killers, this homicide attempted to interrupt the investigation and to pose an existential threat to anyone who would consider searching for evidence of corruption. Particularly in this case, however, the investigation was assigned to the Special Division for Homicide Investigation (*"Delegacia de Homicídios"*) and investigators from the state capital beyond local politics found the necessary evidence to convict the killers and the contractor. Second, landowners attempted to kill members of the Landless Workers Movement ("*Movimento dos Trabalhadores Sem Terra*") who occupied a camp inside a farm by setting fire to their tents and shooting at the political leaders, including a political aide from the Labor Party (*"Partido dos Trabalhadores"*) who supported the land invaders.[43] The defendant conducted himself as a typical colonel, entering the camp with a group of henchmen and exercising brute force to restore his authority over his occupied land. Third, military police officers investigated the murder of a colleague and decided to kill a criminal suspect by taking him away from his house and shooting him in the nearby street alleging self-defense and presenting a gun as evidence that the suspect was armed, dangerous, and attempted to kill them before being killed. However, evidence revealed the victim was shot in his back and his head—a typical sign of an extrajudicial execution. Fourth, a leader of a militia who controlled the activity of illegal transportation and was a military police officer decided to kill the thief who entered his apartment and stole his electronic devices while this militia member was at the beach on holiday. After an initial investigation and the identification of a suspect, he informed all his drivers working in his illegal transportation business that they should inform him if they found the thief. After learning that the thief was playing football, three militia members came onto the football field in the middle of a game and shot the suspect in the legs, handcuffed him, and brought him to the trunk of a car. As the car left the area of the football field, the driver lost control and hit a wall, damaging the front wheels. As the car had to be abandoned, the militia members finished killing the thief and escaped from the crime scene, but the police managed to establish their identity due to the car's ownership. All these cases provide examples of killings motivated by sentiments of vengeance, but also as crude exercises of violent power and attempts to impose the rule of death, unconstitutional duties, and authoritarian restrictions on the people.

These local cases are a relatively small sample of a large body of tens of thousands of killings committed annually in contemporary Brazil. A recent project from the Center for Studies on Violence (*"Núcleo de Estudos da Violência"*) of the University of São Paulo and the Brazilian Forum for Public Security established the monitor of violence and monitors the quantitative data and statistical evidence related to killings. According to their data, Brazil registered 59,103 violent deaths in 2017, 51,589 violent deaths in 2018, and 41,635 violent deaths in 2019.[44] Even if the total number of deaths remained a very large one, it was the lowest since the beginning of the monitoring in 2007. Explanations for this reduction come from a variety of factors. First, a reconfiguration of the drug market with new alliances and less conflicts involving competitors in a highly lucrative activity in which disputes are normally solved through killings has a significant impact on the growth or reduction of annual violence in Brazil.[45] Another factor involves the capacity of the states to monitor and control the conduct of the bosses of organized crime in prison, especially because the political authorities developed a strategy to transfer them to federal prisons and to impose a Differentiated Disciplinary Regime ("*Regime Disciplinar Diferenciado*") for the heads of criminal organizations who order violent crimes and killings in the streets.[46] Moreover, the political leadership of newly elected governors who prioritized public security also impacted the reduction of homicides, especially because of the consistent adoption of public policies on violence control and reduction based on intelligence, criminological analysis, evidence-based decisions, and integration between public security and social policies.[47]

In contrast to the reduction in the total number of violent deaths, statistical evidence shows that the number of killings committed by the police remains high.[48] According to their data, the police killed 5,716 individuals in 2018 and 5,804 individuals in 2019.[49] These numbers correspond to the official violent deaths committed by police officers on duty and registered as a killing committed in self defense as a consequence of resistance to arrest. Corresponding to around 10–15 percent of the total number of killings, statistical evidence reveals the highly lethal nature of the Brazilian police. Importantly, however, most of these cases are never properly investigated as a homicide, killers are immediately liberated based on their own version of the facts, and their narratives of self defense are self-legitimating grounds for the future closing of the case without any criminal charges. In practice, police officers exercise control over the crime scene by rescuing even dead criminal suspects, over the registration of deaths by claiming that they killed in self-defense, and over the investigation by threatening witnesses who may testify against them in court. Even if the Brazilian Constitution prohibits the general application of the death penalty, these killings in fact amount to an informal death penalty in many cases—as an extrajudicial execution may be functionally equivalent to the death penalty in which violent police officers function as investigators, accusers, judges, and executioners at once. In summary, police officers decide that a criminal suspect should be killed without a fair trial and the guarantees of due process of law, applying the sentence of the street-level court ("*Tribunal de Rua*") through an extrajudicial execution. According to research conducted by the International Human Rights Clinic of Harvard Law School, this extreme exercise of violent power by the police is the basis of their economic power.[50] Their informal license to kill facilitates not only the extraction of bribes, but also the purchase of private security services.[51] In the end, tolerance of police violence stimulates the development of the paramilitary groups that benefit from their license to kill to make a profit from illegal activities, to eliminate rivals, and even threaten the authorities in charge of investigating their crimes.[52] Not surprisingly, police officers may also be responsible for killings as hired gunmen, participants in death squads, and members of militia. This high level of the lethal nature of the Brazilian police only partially shows their participation in violent deaths, since victims from death squads, militias, and hired killers are not included in this data.

In the end, a serious problem exists with the high number of killers and of powerful groups that may exercise brutal violent force. In contrast to Max Weber's well-known definition of the state as the entity entitled to a monopoly in the use of legitimate power,[53] there are various groups in rural and urban areas who may kill individuals with a low probability of punishment. Statistical evidence reveals that the vast majority of investigations of homicides do not reveal the identity of the killer, nor show who is guilty. From the small number of successful investigations, a significant number of cases will not lead to a conviction of the defendant. Because of the extremely low enforcement of the criminal law against killers, there are various groups who exercise violent power over different areas dominated by them in parallel to the exercise of state power. Vigilante justice emerges in this context as another example of normative pluralism in the sense that a new set of informal rules are developed in communities under the rule of death by drug lords, militias, death squads, *bicheiros*, and colonels with their henchmen.[54] On the one hand, this situation poses an existential threat to the state and its citizens, resulting from the plurality of force and the complex combination of formal and informal rules of conduct resulting from the fusion of state law with vigilante justice that disciplines killings within particular geographical areas.[55] On the other hand, vigilante justice coexists with the justice system, the official police force, and all formal institutions of the modern state because this social phenomenon somehow accommodates itself within socio-legal spaces in urban peripheries and rural areas through interactions with positive law and its loopholes. The criminal justice system could filter episodes of police violence.[56] The next section examines exactly this relationship between the law of the state and of the parallel state.

BETWEEN THE LAW OF THE STATE AND OF THE PARALLEL STATE: AN EXISTENTIAL THREAT

The law of the state regarding violent deaths partially explains the emergence of a parallel state. The point of departure for our analysis is not only the black letter law of the criminal code and criminal procedure, but also the law in action and the realist perspective from the institutional experience related to these killings. The Brazilian criminal code defines the crime of homicide as "killing someone" and establishes a minimum sanction of six years for simple homicide (Article 121, *caput*, of the Criminal Code). There are some special characteristics that may give the act of killing the character of a qualified homicide and a minimum sanction of twelve years in prison (Article 121, § 2o, of the Criminal Code). Examining these special elements, some characteristics are directly related to the types of vigilante justice found in Brazil and described above in section 2. The hired killer, for instance, kills someone as a result of the promise of payment or a reward. Death squads normally resort to an ambush or any other means that make defense by the victim more difficult or even impossible. Finally, members of organized crime and militias often commit their killings to secure execution, impunity, and advantage in relation to other crimes.

Importantly, the Brazilian Constitution states that a jury has jurisdiction over cases of intentional crimes against life, including intentional homicides (Article 5o, XXXVIII, of the Brazilian Constitution). Because juries are responsible for cases of homicide, these cases are shaped by the fact that the final decision is taken by a group of seven lay jurors. According to the Criminal Procedure Code, a criminal indictment requires an oral hearing of around one hour and a half, which is followed by an oral defense of up to one hour and a half (Article 477). After these initial debates, the prosecution may decide to argue for another additional hour in *treplica*, which is followed by a final oral argumentation of the defense for a similar period of time. The criminal judge supervises the case, but the decision over guilt is taken by individuals selected through a combination of case management and luck. The criminal judge requests a list with names of potential jurors from state authorities, private associations, clubs, schools, universities, unions, public offices, and other community centers (Article 425). Based on these lists, the criminal judge conducts a lottery to select the twenty-five jurors selected for particular seasons of jury trials (Article 433). Therefore, citizens are responsible for judging criminal defendants accused of murder.

Interestingly, there are very few legal rules regulating the debates between the criminal prosecutor and the defense attorney. The parties cannot refer to the justifications made by the criminal judge to admit the case for trial or to the decision related to handcuffing, because these arguments based on the technical authority of the criminal judge should not be used to influence the decision-making process of the lay judges (Article 478, I). Likewise, the Criminal Procedure Code prohibits the parties from making reference to the decision to exercise the right to remain silent in the defendant's testimony (Article 478, II). Moreover, there is also a prohibition of surprising the other party, as the legislation prohibits the provision of any document or the exhibition of any object that had not been shared with the legal opponent at least three days before the beginning of the jury trial (Article 479). On the other hand, there are no precise guidelines or instructions on how to proceed with the structure of the oral debate, analyzing comprehensively the evidence, and demonstrating the guilt of the defendant through an analytical presentation of the facts of the case and the applicable law. In contrast to the U.S. criminal jury trials, there are no equivalent precise formal rules of evidence that need to be strictly followed by the representatives of the parties.[57] The lack of strict discursive rules provides extreme freedom for lawyers to frame their defenses and to develop strategies to persuade the lay jurors to acquit the defendant. As Ana Schritzmaier puts it in her ethnographical study of the Brazilian jury trial, depending on how the violent deaths are contextualized, imagined, and reconstructed, the individual power of killing someone may be considered legitimate or illegitimate.[58] These jury trials contribute to the social image of death emerging as an instrument for regulation of the exercise of force to commit violent death within society.[59] Therefore, popular culture decisively shapes the context of decisions on all cases of violent death, including those episodes of vigilante justice.

Aline Duvoisin and Thais Leobeth consider that the semiotics of legal discourse within the Brazilian jury trials corresponds to the authoritarian exercise of power found in fascist regimes.[60] Their opinion is based on the observation that criminal defendants do not feel comfortable, speak in a low voice with limited language level, and have unequal power in comparison with professional lawyers.[61] However, their analysis seems superficial and misses the point that criminal defendants are technically defended by one of these professional lawyers, whose arguments may succeed in securing an acquittal. In contrast to the criminal judge, lay jurors do not need to provide justification for their decisions and actually respond to questions related to facts of a case with simple "yes" or "no" answers in ballots that are put in a box and counted to reach the final verdict of a murder trial. In this context, the jury trial may even be considered more democratic than judicial decision-making, as the opinion of the lay juror is influenced by common sense, public opinion, and popular culture. Because of this particular institutional design, defense attorneys may invoke various strategies, arguments, and analysis in support of their clients in the oral debates. A detailed semiotics of legal discourse in the Brazilian jury would examine the arguments that lawyers use in these oral debates and identify the more successful ones to understand argumentative clusters and the production of meaning for the legal audience.[62] In the cases of violent deaths, arguments of defense attorneys include also argumentative clusters involving the endorsement of vigilante justice. Experienced lawyers may reverse the dynamics of the trial by accusing the victim of being a criminal and somehow stating that the killing committed by the defendant is legitimate and benefits the community. Discourses accusing the victims explore the sentiments of jurors with characteristics of a case, suggesting that the victim was a criminal suspect who could even have committed a crime against them or their family members, had he not been killed. Defense attorneys may actually praise the role of death squads in promoting social cleansing and the role of militias in establishing social order. Their discursive freedom allows them to engage with the jurors in an exercise of social imagination of death in which the law of the parallel state may emerge as a justification for killing. The expression "a good bandit is a bad bandit" ("*bandido bom é bandido morto*") symbolizes this ideology against human rights and the rhetoric that defense attorneys may adopt in these oral debates to advocate in favor of vigilante justice. Paradoxically, the semiotics of legal discourse within Brazilian jury trials may reveal that authoritarian messages actually result from its democratic institutional design and the extreme freedom that defense attorneys have to defend their clients, including the possibility of praising vigilante justice and laws of the parallel state.

Importantly, however, this discourse of justification of violent death does not work for all types of vigilantism. Defense attorneys may attempt to justify killings of criminals committed by hired gunmen, death squads, and militia members, but this line of the defense does not work for criminal defendants who are part of organized crime. Therefore, even if a drug lord kills one of his rivals as part of a dispute for control of a geographical area for drug trade, defense attorneys are not able to justify the killing based on the fact that the victim was a criminal. The reversal of the dynamics of a trial in this case is impossible, because both victim and defendant share the same condition of being part of organized crime. On the other hand, if the killer belongs to a death squad or a militia and the victim belongs to organized crime, jurors may eventually be open to the ideological discourse of social cleansing and the justification of killing criminals for the benefit of their community. Within organized crime, there are also divisions established by law in society. For instance, if drug trafficking is deemed to be a heinous crime according to the Brazilian legislation (Heinous Crime Act of 1990), the bosses of the "*Animal Game*" are offenders of illegal lottery games, which are deemed to be misdemeanors according to the Brazilian legislation (Misdemeanors Act of 1940). Therefore, their social status is much different from the drug lords, as these "*bicheiros*" are often patrons of samba schools, normally do not hide from the police, and manage to develop their parallel illegal activities without the same burdens as the drug lords. In common, however, their power is based on their capacity of exercising violent force and their impunity is normally based on one informal law of the Parallel state, which is the "*law of silence*."[63] In practice, investigations of killings committed by bosses of organized crime have no witnesses, because individuals are not willing to risk their lives to testify against them. Therefore, homicides committed inside geographical areas controlled by drug commands—like the Red Command, the Third Command, or the First Command of the capital—are almost never successfully investigated, because there are simply no witnesses. In these slums, a large number of residents have never been involved with drug trafficking or any other illegal activity, but they live under a situation of existential death threat. If they decide to present themselves as witnesses of a homicide in a jury trial, these individuals will be murdered. In the end, criminal defendants related to organized crime rely less on the complicity of their lay jurors and more on the fear of the potential witnesses. Therefore, investigations of homicides committed by members of organized crime normally depend on the testimony of police officers in combination with information provided anonymously through the hotlines of crime watchers ("*Disque Denúncia*") which allows witnesses to share their evidence without risking their lives. On the other hand, however, anonymous information may not be sufficient for a criminal conviction without strong complementary evidence that confirms its content.[64]

In terms of the prosecution, the discursive freedom is much more limited than the defense attorneys.' As the defender of society, public prosecutors must develop their indictment based on the evidence of the case, describing the circumstances of the violent death, analyzing the conduct of the criminal defendant, and explaining to the lay jurors how they should reach their decision. In cases of vigilantism, however, there is the additional challenge of deconstructing these legitimating discourses of justification of killings of criminals and accusations of victims. Therefore, the argument on the indictment cannot simply be limited to the facts of a case, but should also discuss the existential threat to the state that is posed by vigilante justice. The monopoly of the legitimate exercise of power is an essential feature of the modern state for the preservation of human freedom. If lay jurors break this monopolistic authority of the state and authorize others to exercise violent force in parallel with official state authorities, then authoritarian rule emerges in geographical areas controlled by these powerful groups that are licensed to kill. Once a colonel, a militia member, and a death squad are free to kill someone, their authority may overcome state authority in practice. Consequently, the state loses control over parts of its territory and population and positive law's capacity to provide reasons for action may also become compromised.[65] The modern origins of this argument may be found in Thomas Hobbes' *Leviathan* and his insight that the fear of violent death provides social justification for the establishment of the modern state.[66] On the contrary, approval of violent death erodes the authority of the state, leading to the emergence of a plurality of authoritarian force.

However, legislative reforms put even more pressure on the democratic rule of law, as recently elected governments support more flexible laws to legitimate violent death and killings of criminals in contemporary Brazil. In addition to the traditional legal formula that protects those who moderately use the necessary means to respond to an unjustified attack (Article 25 of the Criminal Code), criminal law now considers also as self-defense the act of a security agent that repeals aggression or risk of aggression to a hostage during the commission of a crime (Article 25-A of the Criminal Code introduced by the Law n. 13,964 of 2019). According to this new standard, moderation is not necessary and risk of aggression may be sufficient legitimation for lethal police action. This new legislation is aligned with the political discourse of Wilson Witzel, a former federal judge who got elected governor of Rio de Janeiro on a platform of being extremely tough on crime. Defending the use of drones and trained snipers for patrolling, in his opinion the police should always target the head of armed criminal suspects and shoot.[67] Moreover, President Jair Bolsonaro supports the enactment of a new type of self-defense in the Brazilian Criminal Code, which would authorize any use of violent force against trespassers of rural and urban property—"we would like an absolute guarantee that inside your house you are allowed to do anything against an invader."[68] Contemporary political discourse echoes the ideology of vigilante justice. The next section examines the images of vigilante justice in popular culture.

IMAGES OF VIGILANTE JUSTICE IN POPULAR CULTURE

Popular legal culture refers to all knowledge on law, lawyers, and the legal system that people may have.[69] On the other hand, the rule of law also shapes our experience of meaning.[70] In the case of images of popular culture in television, film, and literature, our experiential learning results from the typical combination of realism and fiction that art produces and cultivates in our perception as reflections and distortions on the law in society. In the semiotic process of meaning making, an image is a *signifier* that generates potential *signified* meanings as it circulates through a process of *signification*.[71] Importantly, the process of decoding meaning by the response of a spectator depends on a series of emotional and rational connections with the text that are relatively independent from the meaning encoded by its creator and varies according to class, race, gender, politics, experience, mood, time, and place.[72] Even if filmmakers take sides and are politically engaged in protecting vulnerable minority rights, the audience may respond differently.[73] In this context, images of vigilante justice in Brazilian popular culture reproduce the typology of vigilantism, describing killings committed by hired killers, death squads, organized crime, and militias. Popular culture reflects law with distortions, but also with realism.[74] In addition to the images found in film and literature, there are also iconic cases of violent death reported on television news that shape the public debate on vigilant justice. In terms of televisual justice, these real stories reported in the news also receive a story-telling treatment typical of "infotainment" and audiences may follow some investigations, procedures, imprisonment, and trials as a sort of television series with a realist human drama.[75]

One of the major real life cases discussed nowadays in Brazilian public opinion consists of the assassination of municipal representative Marielle Franco, who was killed in an ambush on March 14, 2018. A black lesbian woman born in a poor violent slum who studied sociology and had a master's degree in public policy, Marielle Franco became a powerful iconic symbol for progressive leftist politics after being murdered. Two former policemen are accused of committing this homicide. Moreover, the police are investigating the theory that another politician hired these gunners to kill a political opponent and the question of "who ordered Marielle Franco's murder?" remains an open one.[76] Importantly, as a human rights activist, she condemned instances of police violence in the Brazilian slums and perhaps there is a connection with death squads, organized crime, or militias. In terms of well-known cases of murders committed by death squads, there are some landmark episodes of slaughter ("*chacina*"), which involve the assassination of a large number of victims, such as the massacres committed in Candelária with eight adolescents executed in 1993, in Vigário Geral with twenty-one victims killed in 1993, and with twenty-nine individuals dead in Nova Iguaçu and Queimados in 2005. Military police officers were investigated and accused of carrying out violent murders in all these cases. These crimes had the common characteristics of being executions in the middle of the night of individuals whom these police officers hated and decided to eliminate from society. A recent police operation against drug trafficking resulted in twenty-eight deaths at the slum of Jacarezinho in May 2021. Another important case was the massacre of Carandiru, in which the military police invaded a penitentiary in São Paulo to restore its internal order and shot to death 111 prisoners in 1992.

Extensive examples of vigilante justice involving organized crime include the executions of rivals by the bosses of the "animal game," but also death sentences carried out on the orders of the drug lords. The murder of investigative journalist Tim Lopes reveals the internal proceedings of the street-level courts of drug lords and their vigilante justice. An award-winning investigative reporter, Tim Lopes had publicized many secrets of the drug trade in the slums with the support of hidden cameras that he used to register the activities of organized crime. On June 2, 2002 while trying to capture images of drugs and guns inside a slum, drug dealers noticed the light of the hidden camera, captured the journalist, and took Tim Lopes in a car to drug lord Crazy Elijah ("*Elias Maluco*"). After confirming that Tim Lopes had authored the news report on a drug sale that harmed their illegal business in the previous year, the drug lord sentenced him to an exemplary violent death. With a ninja sword Crazy Elijah cut off the hands, arms, and legs of the victim, while the journalist was still alive. The execution was completed through the method of the "*microwave*," that is, the body parts of the journalists were put inside rubber tires and were burned at high temperature, so that the identification of the victim by the police would be especially difficult. Crazy Elijah was arrested three months later for this homicide and subsequently he and eight members of his criminal organization were charged with and convicted of this murder. In the same month of the imprisonment of Crazy Elijah, the boss of the Red Command ("*Comando Vermelho*"), Fernandinho Beira-Mar also conducted an informal trial that resulted in the violent death of five individuals on September 11, 2002. Inside the maximal security penitentiary of Bangu 1, Fernandinho Beira-Mar bribed a security agent to get the keys and guns that allowed him to capture and execute the leader of the rival criminal organization Eraldo Medeiros, known as "*Uê*" and four of his associates who were also in the same penitentiary. Revenge was the motive for the murder, as *Uê* had left the Red Command in 1994 to found his own criminal organization and was considered a traitor. Fernandinho Beira-Mar was sentenced to 120 years in prison for these murders. However, the convictions of Crazy Elijah and Fernandinho Beira-Mar are exceptions and most murders committed by drug lords are not properly investigated, nor effectively punished. The same is also true of murders committed by militia members.

The type of vigilantism found in real life and on the television news has also inspired fictional narratives in literature and cinema. Rubem Fonseca, the great master of detective short stories and novels in Brazilian literature, wrote powerful stories of hired killers. In contrast with reality, Fonseca's fictional gunmen are sophisticated, well read, and reflect philosophically on social issues. A former police commissioner with a law degree from the National Law School, Rubem Fonseca revolutionized Brazilian literature with a direct style, street language and realist narratives of violent crimes. In his 2009 novel *The Seminarian*, his hired gunman was the "*specialist*"—a highly efficient killer—who received packages with the services and the description of his "*customers*"—the victims of his executions.[77] After performing his role for a long time without guilt and with the precision of always shooting his victims in the head, the character decided to retire to enjoy his passion for cinema, poetry, wine, women, and football. The naturalistic narrative shocks, especially because the task of killing is described as a mere job that requires professional planning and efficient performance. Inspired by Rubem Fonseca, many other authors also explored narratives of violent crime. Among them, Patrícia Melo wrote *The Killer*—the story of young car salesman who transformed himself into a gunman after dyeing his hair blond as a result of a lost bet.[78] After committing his first killing in his neighborhood instead of moral condemnation and police persecution, the killer received praise from the community and support from the local authorities. Consequently, the killer became a hired gunman and carried out his vigilante justice backed by local businesses and politicians. The narrative is humorous, ironic, and counterintuitive, especially because of the everyday language, moral relativism, and contradictory personalities of the characters. This story was adapted into a screenplay by Rubem Fonseca and became the film *The Man of the Year* in 2003.

There are also interesting books on death squads, notably the documentary produced by investigative journalist Caco Barcellos on the killings committed by the lethal special unit of the military police of the state of São Paulo called *Rota 66: The Police Who Kill*.[79] After five years of interviews and documentary analysis, the book shows that this police unit was a death squad responsible for extermination and killings of thousands of people. Based on empirical data, this book revealed their method for killing, their collective consciousness, and their incentives for the exercise of violent force. This same logic was behind the massacre of Carandiru, which became part of Brazilian literature through the book *Carandiru Station*—the memories of Drauzio Varella, a medical doctor who worked as a volunteer for thirteen years inside the prison of Carandiru and captured the human comedy and dramas behind the lives of many of the 111 victims of the slaughter.[80] The story revealed vulnerable individuals behind bars and provided a shocking intimate narrative of how disproportionate the decision of the military police was to invade the penitentiary and shoot to kill unarmed prisoners and became the film *Carandiru* in 2003. Another tragic story of a killing committed by the police was described in the documentary film *Bus 174*—the kidnapping of a bus in Rio de Janeiro that led to the murder of one of the hostages accidentally shot by a sniper and the criminal suspect who kept the bus under violent control for four hours on June 12, 2000. After the murder of the hostage Geisa Firmo Gonçalves was broadcast live on television around 6:55 p.m., military police officers immobilized the suspect Sandro do Nascimento, put him in a patrol car, and killed him by asphyxiation. The documentary investigated the problematic childhood of Sandro do Nascimento, as an orphan living on the streets after witnessing the murder of his own mother at the age of eight and surviving the massacre of Candelária at the age of fifteen, suggesting that he was also a victim of social exclusion and failed state policies. This story was also told in the film *Final Stop 174* in 2008.

Interestingly, some authors responsible for renowned works on hired killers and death squads also decided to write about organized crime. For instance, Patrícia Melo wrote the fictional novel *Hell* on the life of a member of a criminal organization specializing in drug trafficking, revealing disputes with the police and rival gangs, betrayals and revenge murders, and the marginal life of someone totally involved with criminal activities.[81] Likewise, Caco Barcelos produced another impressive piece of investigative journalism in his book titled *Abused: The Owner of Dona Marta Slum*—a portrait of the drug lord Marcinho VP, his biographical information, leadership in the community and of the criminal organization, and the internal operations of the drug trade, including its informal justice system and their dispute resolution mechanisms.[82] However, the best example of vigilante justice involving drug traffickers came in the book *City of God* written by Paulo Lins.[83] Based on empirical data collected for eight years about the slum City of God, the book described different stories of the social transformation and the evolution of criminal activities from petty crimes in the 1960s to the emergence of organized crime and drug trafficking in the 1990s. This story became one the most important Brazilian films in 2002 with a plot that explored the violent use of force by the drug lord "*Little Dice/Little Zé*" and how internal wars for political control of geographical areas shaped killings, violent deaths, and revenge murders.

Images of vigilante justice committed by militias have been rarer in the cinema, because the political domination of geographical areas by urban militias is a more recent phenomenon. However, the sequel of the 2007 blockbuster *Elite Squad* titled *Elite Squad 2: The Enemy Within* in 2010 provided a rare picture of the militia phenomenon in contemporary cinema. In the first film, the spectator followed the challenges of the elite squad BOPE—Battalion for Special Police Operations—of the Military Police of Rio de Janeiro in providing security for the Pope's visit to Rio de Janeiro, when he stayed in an area dominated by drug lords of the Turano slum. Even if the movie Director José Padilha considered this film to be critical of police violence, Brazilian audiences often considered the police officers to be heroes in their war against drug traffickers. In the second film, however, the viewer followed the new challenges of public safety in Rio de Janeiro with the growth of militias formed by corrupt police officers who replaced drug lords in the control of some geographical areas directly leading illegal activities and charging fees to the local residents. The existential threat posed by the militia to the state seemed to be even greater than the one posed by drug lords, as the militia member may benefit from the role of police officer in obstructing investigations of their crimes, eliminate potential threats, and remain unpunished from their violent action against the communities they dominate. This movie had an audience of eleven million in Brazil alone, reaching the position of the most watched movie in Brazilian cinemas of all time. These stories were influenced by real facts reported by former Public Safety Secretary Luiz Eduardo Soares and former member of BOPE Rodrigo Pimentel.[84]

CONCLUSION

The existential threat to the state by vigilante justice is also influenced by the logic of political disputes based on conflicts between enemies and cooperation between friends.[85] The notion that "a good bandit is a dead bandit" finds an echo among right-wing conservative politicians. For instance, during his political career President Jair Bolsonaro traditionally supported violent action directly carried out by the police on criminal suspects. In contrast, left-wing progressive politicians voice their criticisms against human rights violations, extrajudicial executions committed by the police, and violence against the people in poor rural and urban communities. In their political dialogue, former President Lula and former presidential candidate Fernando Haddad referred to President Jair Bolsonaro as a militia member or *"miliciano"*—because of the alleged close links of members of the Bolsonaro family with military police officers accused of being involved with local militias in Rio de Janeiro. On the other hand, President Bolsonaro was the victim of a homicide attempt during his presidential campaign, as a former member of a socialist party stabbed him during a rally in Juiz de Fora on September 6, 2018. Even if the police concluded that the criminal Adélio Bispo de Oliveira acted alone and was not a *hired killer*, Bolsonaro repeatedly states that he would like to know who ordered his murder, insisting that his political opponents wanted him dead. Therefore, this typology of vigilante justice appears also at the apex of the Brazilian political debate, indicating that these images are extremely powerful in the country's political imagination.

In this context, however, the real threat to the state may emerge through the polarization of political disputes and the radicalization that the logic of enemy/friend may bring into politics with potential negative consequences to the democratic rule of law and the respect for institutional rules of the game. For the Brazilian people, these negative consequences may include the rule of death, unconstitutional duties, and authoritarian restrictions. More than just images in television, literature, and cinema, the type of vigilante justice and the social image of violent death shape the popular experience of the law of the state and of the parallel state.

NOTES

1. Simone Maria Rocha and Ângela Cristina Salgueiro Marques, "'Bandido Bom é Bandido Morto': Violência Policial, Tortura e Execuções Em Tropa de Elite," *Galáxia*, no. 19 (2010): 90–104.

2. Ignacio Cano, "Direitos Para Os Bandidos?: Direitos Humanos e Criminalidade No Brasil," in *Desafios Aos Direitos Humanos No Brasil Contemporâneo*, ed. Biorn Maybury-Lewis and Sonia Ranincheski (Brasilia: Verbena Editora, 2011), 33–46.

3. Igor Tadeu Silva Viana Stemler, Gabriela Moreira de Azevedo Soares, and Maria Tereza Aina Sadez, "Tribunal Do Júri: Condenações e Absolvições," *Revista CNJ* 2 (2017): 2–11.

4. César Barreira, "Matadores de Aluguel: Códigos e Mediações Na Rota de Uma Pesquisa," *Revista de Ciência Sociais* 37, no. 1 (2006): 41–52.

5. Ibid., 42.

6. Victor Nunes Leal, *Coronelismo, Enxada e Voto: O Município e o Regime Representativo No Brasil* (São Paulo: Editora Companhia das Letras, 2012).

7. César Barreira, *Crimes Por Encomenda: Violência e Pistolagem No Cenário Brasileiro* (Rio de Janeiro: Relume Dumará, 1998).

8. Ricardo Henrique Arruda de Paula, "Matadores: A Construção Social e Simbólica de Identidades Violentas," *Dilemas-Revista de Estudos de Conflito e Controle Social* 3, no. 9 (2010): 61–89.

9. Ibid., 62.

10. Ibid.

11. Ibid.

12. Ibid.

13. Tatiana Merlino, "Em Cada Batalhão Da PM Tem Um Grupo de Extermínio," *Caros Amigos*, 2012, 10–13.

14. Ibid., 12.

15. Umberto Guaspari Sudbrack, "O Extermínio de Meninos de Rua No Brasil," *São Paulo Em Perspectiva* 18, no. 1 (2004): 22–30.

16. Pedro Fortes, "O Direito à Vida," *O Globo*, May 25, 2006.

17. Ibid.

18. Ibid.

19. Ibid.

20. Ibid.

21. Merlino, "Em Cada Batalhão Da PM Tem Um Grupo de Extermínio," 10.

22. Michel Misse, "Crime organizado e crime comum no Rio de Janeiro: diferenças e afinidades," *Revista de Sociologia e Política* 19 (October 2011): 13–25, https://doi.org/10.1590/S0104-44782011000300003.

23. Ibid.

24. Ben Penglase, "The Bastard Child of the Dictatorship: The Comando Vermelho and the Birth of 'Narco-Culture' in Rio de Janeiro," *Luso-Brazilian Review* 45, no. 1 (June 1, 2008): 118–45, https://doi.org/10.1353/lbr.0.0001.

25. Jose Divanilson Junior Cavalcanti and Lúcia Dídia Lima Soares, "Crime organizado: uma nova luta pelo dominio da territorialidade," *Revista de Sociologia, Antropologia e Cultura Jurídica* 2, no. 1 (October 31, 2016), https://doi.org/10.26668/IndexLawJournals/2526-0251/2016.v2i1.382.

26. Eliane Botelho Junqueira and José Augusto de Souza Rodrigues, "Pasárgada revisitada," October 1992, 13–14.

27. Junqueira and Rodrigues, 14–15.

28. Boaventura De Sousa Santos, "The Law of the Oppressed: The Construction and Reproduction of Legality in Pasargada," *Law & Society Review* 12 (1977): 5.

29. Alba Zaluar, "Juventude violenta: processos, retrocessos e novos percursos," *Dados* 55, no. 2 (2012): 327–65, https://doi.org/10.1590/S0011-52582012000200003.

30. Amy Chazkel, "Beyond Law and Order: The Origins of the Jogo Do Bicho in Republican Rio de Janeiro*," *Journal of Latin American Studies* 39, no. 3 (August 2007): 535–65, https://doi.org/10.1017/S0022216X07002830.

31. Tania Fischer and Jair Nascimento Santos, "O 'Capo' no jogo do bicho—uma oranização Paratodos," *Organizações & Sociedade* 2, no. 3 (1994).

32. Michel Misse, "Crime organizado e crime comum no Rio de Janeiro: diferenças e afinidades," *Revista de Sociologia e Política* 19 (October 2011): 13–25, https://doi.org/10.1590/S0104-44782011000300003.

33. Ibid.

34. Ibid.

35. Alba Zaluar and Isabel Siqueira Conceição, "Favelas sob o controle das Milícias no Rio de Janeiro," *São Paulo em Perspectiva* 21, no. 2 (2007): 13.

36. Ibid.

37. Luiz Kleber Rodrigues Farias, "Territorialização e Segregação Urbana: as milícias e a conformação de estruturas de oportunidades," *Revista Intratextos* 1, no. 0 (April 17, 2010): 47–53, https://doi.org/10.12957/intratextos.2010.408.

38. Ibid.

39. Alexandre Werneck, "O ornitorrinco de criminalização: A construção social moral do miliciano a partir dos personagens da 'violência urbana' do Rio de Janeiro," *Dilemas—Revista de Estudos de Conflito e Controle Social* 8, no. 3 (July 1, 2015): 429–54.

40. Werneck, 434.

41. Werneck, 441.

42. Pedro Fortes, "How Socio-Legal Norms Emerge within Complex Networks: Law and (In)Formality at Ipanema Beach," *FIU Law Review* 10 (2014): 183.

43. On the Landless Workers Movement, see: George Meszaros, "Taking the Land into Their Hands: The Landless Workers' Movement and the Brazilian state," *Journal of Law and Society* 27, no. 4 (2000): 517–41, https://doi.org/10.1111/1467-6478.00166; George Mészáros, *Social Movements, Law, and the Politics of Land Reform: Lessons from Brazil* (Abingdon, Oxon: Routledge, 2013).

44. "Número de Assassinatos Cai 19% No Brasil Em 2019 e é o Menor Da Série Histórica | Monitor Da Violência | G1," *Globo.Com*, February 14, 2020, https://g1.globo.com/monitor-da-violencia/noticia/2020/02/14/numero-de-assassinatos-cai-19percent-no-brasil-em-2019-e-e-o-menor-da-serie-historica.ghtml. (checked in 20.05.2020).

45. Ibid.

46. Ibid.

47. Ibid.

48. On the mathematical turn in law, see Pedro Fortes, "How Legal Indicators Influence a Justice System and Judicial Behavior: The Brazilian National Council of

Justice and 'Justice in Numbers,'" *The Journal of Legal Pluralism and Unofficial Law* 47, no. 1 (Gennaio 2015): 39–55, https://doi.org/10.1080/07329113.2014.994356.

49. "Número de pessoas mortas pela polícia cresce no Brasil em 2019; assassinatos de policiais caem pela metade," *Globo.com*, April 16, 2020, https://g1.globo.com/monitor-da-violencia/noticia/2020/04/16/numero-de-pessoas-mortas-pela-policia-cresce-no-brasil-em-2019-assassinatos-de-policiais-caem-pela-metade.ghtml.

50. Fernando Ribeiro Delgado, Raquel Elias Ferreira Dodge, and Sandra Carvalho, "Corrupção, Crime Organizado e Violência Institucional Em Maio de 2006" (Relatório da International Human Rights Clinic, 2011), http://www.global.org.br/wp-content/uploads/2011/05/SaoPaulosobAchaque_JusticaGlobal_2011.pdf.

51. Ibid.

52. Bruno Paes Manso, "Novo recorde de letalidade mostra dificuldade dos estados em controlar suas polícias," *Globo.com*, April 16, 2020, https://g1.globo.com/monitor-da-violencia/noticia/2020/04/16/novo-recorde-de-letalidade-mostra-dificuldade-dos-estados-em-controlar-suas-policias.ghtml.

53. Max Weber, *Economy and Society: An Outline of Interpretive Sociology*, ed. Guenther Roth and Claus Wittich (Berkeley: University of California Press, 1978), 54.

54. William Twining, "Normative and Legal Pluralism: A Global Perspective," *Duke Journal of Comparative & International Law* 20 (2010, 2009): 473; Pedro Fortes, "An Explorer of Legal Borderlands: A Review of William Twining's Jurist in Context, a Memoir," *REI-Revista Estudos Institucionais* 5, no. 2 (2019): 777–90.

55. Pedro Fortes, "Pluripoiesis of Law and the Kaleidoscope of Legal Cultures," in *Law, Legal Culture and Society: Mirrored Identities of the Legal Order*, ed. Alberto Febbrajo (Abingdon, Oxon: Routledge, 2018).

56. Pedro Fortes, "Human Rights and Remains: A Policy Proposal to Prevent Human Rights Violations in Brazil," in *Law and Policy in Latin America: Transforming Courts, Institutions, and Rights*, ed. Larissa Boratti, Andrés Palacios Lleras, and Tom Gerald Daly (London: Palgrave Macmillan, 2017), 257–72, https://doi.org/10.1057/978-1-137-56694-2_15; Pedro Fortes, "Direito e Restos Humanos: uma hipótese para o enfrentamento jurídico-penal da tortura no Brasil," *Revista De Estudos Empíricos Em Direito* 1, no. 1 (January 25, 2014), https://doi.org/10.19092/reed.v1i1.7.

57. George Fisher, *Evidence*, third ed. (New York: Foundation Press, 2013).

58. Ana Lúcia Pastore Schritzmeyer, "Controlando o poder de matar: uma leitura antropológica do Tribunal do Júri—ritual lúdico e teatralizado" (text, Universidade de São Paulo, 2002), https://doi.org/10.11606/T.8.2002.tde-31082007-095427.

59. Ibid.

60. Aline Duvoisin and Thaís Leobeth, "Marcas do fascismo nas traduções e tensionamentos da Semiosfera do Tribunal do Júri," *Estudos Semióticos* 14, no. 3 (December 19, 2018): 98–111, https://doi.org/10.11606/issn.1980-4016.esse.2018.137736.

61. Ibid.

62. Duncan Kennedy, "A Semiotics of Legal Argument," *Syracuse Law Review* 42 (1991): 75.

63. Andrey Borges de Mendonça, "A Colaboração premiada e a nova Lei do Crime Organizado (Lei 12.850/2013)," *Custos Legis* 4 (2013): 38; Luiz Antonio Machado da Silva and Márcia Pereira Leite, "Violência, crime e polícia: o que os favelados dizem quando falam desses temas?," *Sociedade e Estado* 22 (December 2007): 545–91, https://doi.org/10.1590/S0102-69922007000300004.

64. Thadeu Augimeri de Goes Lima and Florestan Rodrigo do Prado, "DELAÇÃO ANÔNIMA, PERSECUÇÃO CRIMINAL E CONSTITUIÇÃO: BUSCANDO O NECESSÁRIO EQUILÍBRIO ENTRE OS DIREITOS FUNDAMENTAIS E A REPRESSÃO PENAL EFICAZ," *Argumenta Journal Law*, no. 20 (August 18, 2014): 109–26, https://doi.org/10.35356/argumenta.v0i20.306.

65. On the classical general theory of the state about territory and population as essential concepts, see Georg Jellinek, *Teoría General del Estado* (Buenos Aires: Editorial Albatros, 1973).

66. Thomas Hobbes, *Leviathan*, ed. Richard Tuck (Cambridge: Cambridge University Press, 1996).

67. "Wilson Witzel: 'A polícia vai mirar na cabecinha e . . . fogo,'" VEJA, January 1, 2018, https://veja.abril.com.br/politica/wilson-witzel-a-policia-vai-mirar-na-cabecinha-e-fogo/.

68. "Bolsonaro anuncia PL para ampliar legítima defesa contra invasões de casas," VEJA, December 26, 2019, https://veja.abril.com.br/brasil/bolsonaro-anuncia-pl-para-ampliar-legitima-defesa-contra-invasoes-de-casas/.

69. Michael Asimow and Shannon Mader, *Law and Popular Culture: A Course Book* (New York: Peter Lang, 2007), 4.

70. Asimow and Mader, 5.

71. Asimow and Mader, 9.

72. Asimow and Mader, 11–12.

73. Pedro Fortes, "Affirmative Cinema: When Film-Makers Defend Minorities," in *Law and Popular Culture: International Perspectives*, ed. Michael Asimow, Kathryn Brown, and David Papke (Newcastle upon Tyne: Cambridge Scholars Publishing, 2014), 269–84; Pedro Fortes, "Lights, Camera, and Affirmative Action: Does Hollywood Protect Minorities?," *Journal of the Oxford Centre for Socio-Legal Studies*, no. Special Issue (2017); Pedro Fortes and Michael Asimow, "Law, Popular Culture, and Classical Culture: Representations of Underdogs in Arts and Media," *Journal of the Oxford Centre for Socio-Legal Studies*, no. Special Issue (2017): 1, https://joxcsls.files.wordpress.com/2017/07/intro_changed.pdf.

74. Lawrence M. Friedman, "Law, Lawyers, and Popular Culture," *Yale Law Journal* 98, no. 8 (1989): 1579–1606; Fortes and Asimow, "Law, Popular Culture, and Classical Culture: Representations of Underdogs in Arts and Media," 5; Pedro Fortes, "O Expositor da Cultura Jurídica e da História do Direito: Pioneirismo e Impacto de Lawrence Friedman," *Passagens: Revista Internacional de História Política e Cultura Jurídica*, February 3, 2019, 24–40, https://doi.org/10.15175/1984-2503-2019111002.

75. Pedro Fortes and Germano Schwartz, "Dramas of Televisual Justice," in *Ethnicity, Gender, and Diversity: Law and Justice on TV*, ed. Peter Robson and Jennifer L. Schulz (Lanham, MD: Lexington Books, 2018), 23–44.

76. David Miranda, "Who Ordered Marielle Franco's Murder?," *The Guardian*, March 14, 2019, https://www.theguardian.com/commentisfree/2019/mar/14/marielle-franco-murder-brazil.

77. Rubem Fonseca, *O Seminarista* (Rio de Janeiro: Agir, 2009).

78. Patricia Melo, *O Matador* (São Paulo: Companhia das Letras, 1995).

79. Caco Barcellos, *Rota 66* (São Paulo: Record, 2003).

80. Drauzio Varella, *Estação Carandiru* (São Paulo: Companhia das Letras, 1999).

81. Patrícia Melo, *Inferno* (São Paulo: Companhia das Letras, 2000).

82. Caco Barcellos, *Abusado: O Dono Do Morro Dona Marta* (Rio de Janeiro: Editora Record, 2003).

83. Paulo Lins, *Cidade de Deus* (São Paulo: Companhia das Letras, 1997).

84. Luiz Eduardo Soares, André Batista, and Rodrigo Pimentel, *Elite Da Tropa* (Rio de Janeiro: Objetiva, 2006).

85. Carl Schmitt, *The Concept of the Political* (Chicago: University of Chicago Press, 2007).

BIBLIOGRAPHY

Asimow, Michael, and Shannon Mader. *Law and Popular Culture: A Course Book*. New York: Peter Lang, 2007.

Barcellos, Caco. *Abusado: O Dono Do Morro Dona Marta*. Rio de Janeiro: Editora Record, 2003.

———. *Rota 66*. São Paulo: Record, 2003.

Barreira, César. *Crimes Por Encomenda: Violência e Pistolagem No Cenário Brasileiro*. Rio de Janeiro: Relume Dumará, 1998.

———. "Matadores de Aluguel: Códigos e Mediações Na Rota de Uma Pesquisa." *Revista de Ciência Sociais* 37, no. 1 (2006): 41–52.

VEJA. "Bolsonaro anuncia PL para ampliar legítima defesa contra invasões de casas," December 26, 2019. https://veja.abril.com.br/brasil/bolsonaro-anuncia-pl-para-ampliar-legitima-defesa-contra-invasoes-de-casas/.

Cano, Ignacio. "Direitos Para Os Bandidos?: Direitos Humanos e Criminalidade No Brasil." In *Desafios Aos Direitos Humanos No Brasil Contemporâneo*, edited by Biorn Maybury-Lewis and Sonia Ranincheski, 33–46. Brasilia: Verbena Editora, 2011.

Cavalcanti, Jose Divanilson Junior, and Lúcia Dídia Lima Soares. "Crime organizado: uma nova luta pelo dominio da territorialidade." *Revista de Sociologia, Antropologia e Cultura Jurídica* 2, no. 1 (October 31, 2016). https://doi.org/10.26668/IndexLawJournals/2526-0251/2016.v2i1.382.

Chazkel, Amy. "Beyond Law and Order: The Origins of the Jogo Do Bicho in Republican Rio de Janeiro*." *Journal of Latin American Studies* 39, no. 3 (August 2007): 535–65. https://doi.org/10.1017/S0022216X07002830.

De Sousa Santos, Boaventura. "The Law of the Oppressed: The Construction and Reproduction of Legality in Pasargada." *Law & Society Review* 12 (1977): 5.

Delgado, Fernando Ribeiro, Raquel Elias Ferreira Dodge, and Sandra Carvalho. "Corrupção, Crime Organizado e Violência Institucional Em Maio de 2006." Relatório da International Human Rights Clinic, 2011. http://www.global.org.br/wp-content/uploads/2011/05/SaoPaulosobAchaque_JusticaGlobal_2011.pdf.

Duvoisin, Aline, and Thaís Leobeth. "Marcas do fascismo nas traduções e tensionamentos da Semiosfera do Tribunal do Júri." *Estudos Semióticos* 14, no. 3 (December 19, 2018): 98–111. https://doi.org/10.11606/issn.1980-4016.esse.2018.137736.

Farias, Luiz Kleber Rodrigues. "Territorialização e Segregação Urbana: as milícias e a conformação de estruturas de oportunidades." *Revista Intratextos* 1, no. 0 (April 17, 2010): 47–53. https://doi.org/10.12957/intratextos.2010.408.

Fischer, Tania, and Jair Nascimento Santos. "O 'Capo' no jogo do bicho—uma oranização Paratodos." *Organizações & Sociedade* 2, no. 3 (1994).

Fisher, George. *Evidence*. Third ed. New York: Foundation Press, 2013.

Fonseca, Rubem. *O Seminarista*. Rio de Janeiro: Agir, 2009.

Fortes, Pedro. "Affirmative Cinema: When Film-Makers Defend Minorities." In *Law and Popular Culture: International Perspectives*, edited by Michael Asimow, Kathryn Brown, and David Papke, 269–84. Newcastle upon Tyne: Cambridge Scholars Publishing, 2014.

———. "An Explorer of Legal Borderlands: A Review of William Twining's Jurist in Context, a Memoir." *REI-Revista Estudos Institucionais* 5, no. 2 (2019): 777–90.

———. "Direito e Restos Humanos: uma hipótese para o enfrentamento jurídico-penal da tortura no Brasil." *Revista De Estudos Empíricos Em Direito* 1, no. 1 (January 25, 2014). https://doi.org/10.19092/reed.v1i1.7.

———. "How Legal Indicators Influence a Justice System and Judicial Behavior: The Brazilian National Council of Justice and 'Justice in Numbers.'" *The Journal of Legal Pluralism and Unofficial Law* 47, no. 1 (Gennaio 2015): 39–55. https://doi.org/10.1080/07329113.2014.994356.

———. "How Socio-Legal Norms Emerge within Complex Networks: Law and (In) Formality at Ipanema Beach." *FIU Law Review* 10 (2014): 183.

———. "Human Rights and Remains: A Policy Proposal to Prevent Human Rights Violations in Brazil." In *Law and Policy in Latin America: Transforming Courts, Institutions, and Rights*, edited by Larissa Boratti, Andrés Palacios Lleras, and Tom Gerald Daly, 257–72. London: Palgrave Macmillan, 2017. https://doi.org/10.1057/978-1-137-56694-2_15.

———. "Lights, Camera, and Affirmative Action: Does Hollywood Protect Minorities?" *Journal of the Oxford Centre for Socio-Legal Studies*, no. Special Issue (2017).

———. "O Direito à Vida." *O Globo*, May 25, 2006.

———. "O Expositor da Cultura Jurídica e da História do Direito: Pioneirismo e Impacto de Lawrence Friedman." *Passagens: Revista Internacional de História Política e Cultura Jurídica*, February 3, 2019, 24–40. https://doi.org/10.15175/1984-2503-2019111002.

———. "Pluripoiesis of Law and the Kaleidoscope of Legal Cultures." In *Law, Legal Culture and Society: Mirrored Identities of the Legal Order*, edited by Alberto Febbrajo. Abingdon, Oxon: Routledge, 2018.

Fortes, Pedro, and Michael Asimow. "Law, Popular Culture, and Classical Culture: Representations of Underdogs in Arts and Media." *Journal of the Oxford Centre for Socio-Legal Studies*, no. Special Issue (2017). https://joxcsls.files.wordpress.com/2017/07/intro_changed.pdf.

Fortes, Pedro, and Germano Schwartz. "Dramas of Televisual Justice." In *Ethnicity, Gender, and Diversity: Law and Justice on TV*, edited by Peter Robson and Jennifer L. Schulz, 23–44. Lanham, MD: Lexington Books, 2018.

Friedman, Lawrence M. "Law, Lawyers, and Popular Culture." *Yale Law Journal* 98, no. 8 (1989): 1579–1606.

Hobbes, Thomas. *Leviathan*. Edited by Richard Tuck. Cambridge: Cambridge University Press, 1996.

Jellinek, Georg. *Teoría General del Estado*. Buenos Aires: Editorial Albatros, 1973.

Junqueira, Eliane Botelho, and José Augusto de Souza Rodrigues. "Pasárgada revisitada," October 1992.

Kennedy, Duncan. "A Semiotics of Legal Argument." *Syracuse Law Review* 42 (1991): 75.

Leal, Victor Nunes. *Coronelismo, Enxada e Voto: O Município e o Regime Representativo No Brasil*. São Paulo: Editora Companhia das Letras, 2012.

Lima, Thadeu Augimeri de Goes, and Florestan Rodrigo do Prado. "DELAÇÃO ANÔNIMA, PERSECUÇÃO CRIMINAL E CONSTITUIÇÃO: BUSCANDO O NECESSÁRIO EQUILÍBRIO ENTRE OS DIREITOS FUNDAMENTAIS E A REPRESSÃO PENAL EFICAZ." *Argumenta Journal Law*, no. 20 (August 18, 2014): 109–26. https://doi.org/10.35356/argumenta.v0i20.306.

Lins, Paulo. *Cidade de Deus*. São Paulo: Companhia das Letras, 1997.

Melo, Patrícia. *Inferno*. São Paulo: Companhia das Letras, 2000.

Melo, Patricia. *O Matador*. São Paulo: Companhia das Letras, 1995.

Mendonça, Andrey Borges de. "A Colaboração premiada e a nova Lei do Crime Organizado (Lei 12.850/2013)." *Custos Legis* 4 (2013): 38.

Merlino, Tatiana. "Em Cada Batalhão Da PM Tem Um Grupo de Extermínio." *Caros Amigos*, 2012, 10–13.

Mészáros, George. *Social Movements, Law, and the Politics of Land Reform: Lessons from Brazil*. Abingdon, Oxon: Routledge, 2013.

Meszaros, George. "Taking the Land into Their Hands: The Landless Workers' Movement and the Brazilian State." *Journal of Law and Society* 27, no. 4 (2000): 517–41. https://doi.org/10.1111/1467-6478.00166.

Miranda, David. "Who Ordered Marielle Franco's Murder?" *The Guardian*, March 14, 2019. https://www.theguardian.com/commentisfree/2019/mar/14/marielle-franco-murder-brazil.

Misse, Michel. "Crime organizado e crime comum no Rio de Janeiro: diferenças e afinidades." *Revista de Sociologia e Política* 19 (October 2011): 13–25. https://doi.org/10.1590/S0104-44782011000300003.

Globo.com. "Número de Assassinatos Cai 19% No Brasil Em 2019 e é o Menor Da Série Histórica | Monitor Da Violência | G1," February 14, 2020. https://g1.globo.com/monitor-da-violencia/noticia/2020/02/14/numero-de-assassinatos-cai-19percent-no-brasil-em-2019-e-e-o-menor-da-serie-historica.ghtml.

Globo.com. "Número de pessoas mortas pela polícia cresce no Brasil em 2019; assassinatos de policiais caem pela metade," April 16, 2020. https://g1.globo.com/monitor-da-violencia/noticia/2020/04/16/numero-de-pessoas-mortas-pela-policia-cresce-no-brasil-em-2019-assassinatos-de-policiais-caem-pela-metade.ghtml.

Paes Manso, Bruno. "Novo recorde de letalidade mostra dificuldade dos estados em controlar suas polícias." *Globo.com*, April 16, 2020. https://g1.globo.com/monitor-da-violencia/noticia/2020/04/16/novo-recorde-de-letalidade-mostra-dificuldade-dos-estados-em-controlar-suas-policias.ghtml.

Paula, Ricardo Henrique Arruda de. "Matadores: A Construção Social e Simbólica de Identidades Violentas." *Dilemas-Revista de Estudos de Conflito e Controle Social* 3, no. 9 (2010): 61–89.

Penglase, Ben. "The Bastard Child of the Dictatorship: The Comando Vermelho and the Birth of 'Narco-Culture' in Rio de Janeiro." *Luso-Brazilian Review* 45, no. 1 (June 1, 2008): 118–45. https://doi.org/10.1353/lbr.0.0001.

Rocha, Simone Maria, and Ângela Cristina Salgueiro Marques. "'Bandido Bom é Bandido Morto': Violência Policial, Tortura e Execuções Em Tropa de Elite." *Galáxia*, no. 19 (2010): 90–104.

Schmitt, Carl. *The Concept of the Political*. Chicago: University of Chicago Press, 2007.

Schritzmeyer, Ana Lúcia Pastore. "Controlando o poder de matar: uma leitura antropológica do Tribunal do Júri—ritual lúdico e teatralizado." Text, Universidade de São Paulo, 2002. https://doi.org/10.11606/T.8.2002.tde-31082007-095427.

Silva, Luiz Antonio Machado da, and Márcia Pereira Leite. "Violência, crime e polícia: o que os favelados dizem quando falam desses temas?" *Sociedade e Estado* 22 (December 2007): 545–91. https://doi.org/10.1590/S0102-69922007000300004.

Soares, Luiz Eduardo, André Batista, and Rodrigo Pimentel. *Elite Da Tropa*. Rio de Janeiro: Objetiva, 2006.

Stemler, Igor Tadeu Silva Viana, Gabriela Moreira de Azevedo Soares, and Maria Tereza Aina Sadez. "Tribunal Do Júri: Condenações e Absolvições." *Revista CNJ* 2 (2017): 2–11.

Sudbrack, Umberto Guaspari. "O Extermínio de Meninos de Rua No Brasil." *São Paulo Em Perspectiva* 18, no. 1 (2004): 22–30.

Twining, William. "Normative and Legal Pluralism: A Global Perspective." *Duke Journal of Comparative & International Law* 20 (2010 2009): 473.

Varella, Drauzio. *Estação Carandiru*. São Paulo: Companhia das Letras, 1999.

Weber, Max. *Economy and Society: An Outline of Interpretive Sociology*. Edited by Guenther Roth and Claus Wittich. Berkeley: University of California Press, 1978.

Werneck, Alexandre. "O ornitorrinco de criminalização: A construção social moral do miliciano a partir dos personagens da 'violência urbana' do Rio de Janeiro." *Dilemas—Revista de Estudos de Conflito e Controle Social* 8, no. 3 (July 1, 2015): 429–54.

VEJA. "Wilson Witzel: 'A polícia vai mirar na cabecinha e . . . fogo,'" January 1, 2018. https://veja.abril.com.br/politica/wilson-witzel-a-policia-vai-mirar-na-cabecinha-e-fogo/.
Zaluar, Alba. "Juventude violenta: processos, retrocessos e novos percursos." *Dados* 55, no. 2 (2012): 327–65. https://doi.org/10.1590/S0011-52582012000200003.
Zaluar, Alba, and Isabel Siqueira Conceição. "Favelas sob o controle das Milícias no Rio de Janeiro." *São Paulo em Perspectiva* 21, no. 2 (2007): 13.

Filmography

#

12 Angry Men (1957)
4x4 (2019)

A

A Bee in the Rain (1972)
A Civil Action (1998)
A Dangerous Toy (1979)
A Regular Woman (2019)
A Vigilante (2018)
Against the Wall (2004)
Age of Uprising: The Legend of Michael Kohlhaas (2013)
Airplane! (1980)
An Average Little Man (1976)
Anatomy of a Murder (1959)
Angel with a Gun (1992)
Angelica Wants Revenge (2018)
Annas Mutter (1984)

B

Bad Day for the Cut (2017)
Bandits of Orgosolo (1961)
Barry Lyndon (1975)
Beverly Hills Cop (1984)
Beverly Hills Cop II (1987)
Black Shoes (1998)

Blazing Saddles (1974)
Blood of My Blood (2011)
Bones (1997)
Braveheart (1995)
Bus 174 (2002)

C

Camorra (A Story of Streets, Women and Crime) (1986)
Carandiru (2003)
City of God (2002)
Coffy (1973)
Cold Pursuit (2019)
Colossal Youth (2006)
Concrete Romance (2007)
Confessions of a Police Captain (1971)
Crocodile Dundee (1986)

D

Danton (1982)
Das tote Mädchen vom Bodensee [The Dead Girl from Lake Constance] (2010)
Dead Man's Shoes (2004)
Death Hunt (1977)
Death Sentence (2007)
Der Fall Bachmeier—Keine Zeit Für Tränen [The Bachmeier case—No Time for Tears] (1984)

Dirty Harry (1971)
Dirty Weekend (1993)
Dogman (2018)
Dominion (2018)
Double Game (1977)
Dr Syn Alias the Scarecrow (1963)

E

Elite Squad (2007)
Elite Squad 2: The Enemy Within (2010)
Erin Brockovich (2000)
Execution Squad (1972)

Eye for an Eye (1996)

F

Falling Down (1993)
Father's Law (1999)
Foxy Brown (1974)
Fury (1936)

G

Get a Life (2001)
Get Carter (1975)
Gideon's Day (aka Gideon of Scotland Yard) (1958)
Gran Torino (2008)
Guests in the Villa (2020)

H

Hang 'Em High (1968)
Harry Brown (2009)
High Crime (1973)
High Plains Drifter (1973)
Hostage (2005)

I

Incident at Restigouche (1984)
In the Bedroom (2001)
In the Darkness of the Night (2004)
In the Name of the Italian People (1971)
In Vanda's Room (2000)
Investigation of a Citizen above Suspicion (1970)
It's a Long Road (1998)

J

Joe (1970)
Joker (2019)

K

Kalinka (2016)
Kalinkas Letzte Reise [Kalinka's Last Journey] (2006)
Kidnap Syndicate (1975)
Kind Hearts and Coronets (1949)
Kohlhaas Oder Die Verhältnismäßigkeit Der Mittel [Kohlhaas or the Proportionality of Means] (2012)

L

Last Stop 174 (2008)
Last Stop on the Night Train (1975)
Law Abiding Citizen (2009)
Lethal Weapon (1987)
Lovely Child (1989)
Lynch (2010)

M

Mad Max (1979)
Magnum Force (1973)
Michael Kohlhaas (2013)
Misbegotten (2007)
Mystic River (2003)

N

Ned Kelly (1970)
Ned Kelly (2003)
Nîpawistamâsowin: We Will Stand Up (2017)
No Apparent Motive (1999)

O

Once Upon a Time in the West (1968)
Outlaw (2007)

P

Peppermint (2018)
Plunkett and Macleane (1998)

Promising Young Woman (2020)

R

Rage (2018)
Reckless Kelly (1993)
Request for a Song (1980)
Rhymes for Young Ghouls (2013)
Robert the Bruce (2019)
Robin Hood (1922)
Robin Hood: Prince of Thieves (1991)
Robin Hood (2010)
Robin Hood (2018)
Rob Roy (1995)
Rob Roy: the Highland Rogue (1953)
Rome, the Other Face of Violence (1976)

S

Seeking Justice (2011)
Shame (1988)
Shichinin no samurai [The Seven Samurai] (1954)
Snowtown (2011)
Straw Dogs (1971)
Street Law (1974)
Sudden Impact (1983)
Sweet Country (2017)

T

Taxi Driver (1976)
Ten Dead Men (2007)
The Accused (1988)
The Adventures of Robin Hood (1938)
The Baboon Code (2018)
The Big Racket (1976)
The Birth of a Nation (1915)
The Brave One (2007)
The Cars That Ate Paris (1974)
The Collini Case (2019)
The Dead Pool (1988)
The Debt (1999)

The Enemy Within (2013)
The Enforcer (1976)
The Equalizer (2014)
The Equalizer 2 (2018)
The Fourth Angel (2001)
The Girl from Millelire Street (1980)
The Gun (1978)
The Highwayman (1951)
The Limey (1999)
The Magnificent Seven (1960)
The Manhunt (1975)
The Molly Maguires (1970)
The Mutants (1998)
The Naked Gun: From the Files of Police Squad! (1988)
The November Uprising. 1830–1831 (1980)
The Official Story (1985)
The Other Me (2016)
The Ox-Bow Incident (1942)
The Pianist (2002)
The Secret in Their Eyes (2009)
The Star Chamber (1983)
The Stendhal Syndrome (1996)
The Story of the Kelly Gang (1906)
The Sun Shines Bright (1953)
The Train (1959)
The Unknown Woman (2006)
The Verdict (1982)
The Wicked Lady (1945)
The Young Philadelphians (1959)
They Call Me Jeeg (2015)
They Won't Forget (1937)
Three Point Six (2003)
To Kill a Mockingbird (1962)
Two Women (2009)

U

Unforgiven (1992)

V

Vendetta (2013)

Vigilante (2009)
Violent City (1975)

W

Wake in Fright (1971)
Walk among the Tombstones (2014)
Wild Tales (2014)
Wolf Creek (2005)

Y

Young Mr. Lincoln (1939)
Youth of Chopin (1951)

Z

Zona J (1998)

List of TV Movies and Series

'Die Großen Kriminalfälle.' Die Rache Der Marianne Bachmeier ['The Great Criminal Cases.' The Revenge of Marianne Bachmeier] (2006)

A

Alarm For Cobra 11 (1996–)

C

Cain's Hundred (1961)
Cleverman (2016–2017)
Crime Scene Cleaner (2011–2018)

D

Dark Justice (1991–1993)
Dexter (2006–2021)
Dixon of Dock Green (1955–1976)
Don Matteo (2000–)

G

Gideon's Way (1964–1966)
Gomorrah (2014–2021)
Gunrush (2009)

H

Hand of God (2014–2017)
Hunter (1984)

I

Il maresciallo Rocca [Marshal Rocca] (1996–2005)
Inspector Montalbano (1999–)

K

Kryminalni [Criminals] (2004–)

L

L'onore e il rispetto [Honor and Respect] (2006–2017)
La caccia [The Hunt] (2005)
Los Simuladores [The Pretenders] (2002–2003)

M

Maria Zef (1981)

O

Origins of the Mafia (1976)

P

Pitbull (2005–2008)
Pretenders (2002–2004)
Pupetta—Il coraggio e la passione [Pupetta—Courage and passion] (2013)

R

Racket (1997)
Reeds in the Wind (1958)
Rocco Schiavone (2016–)
Rota 66: The Police Who Kill (2003)

T

Tatort [Crime Scene] (1970–)
The Adventures of Robin Hood (1955–1960)
The Equalizer (1985)
The Four Just Men (1959–1960)

The Octopus (1984–2001)
The Persuaders! (1971–1972)
The Professionals (1977–1983)
The Saint (1962–1969)
The Secret River (2015)
The Shield (2002–2008)
The Sweeney (1975)
The Tölz Cop (1996–)
Ti Psyhi Tha Paradoseis Mori? [What Soul Will You Deliver?] (2000)

U

Un caso di coscienza [A question of conscience] (2003–2013)
Unterleuten. Das zerrissene Dorf [Unterleuten. The Torn Village] (2020)

V

Vendetta (1999–)
Vengeance Unlimited (1998)

W

William Tell (1958–1959)

Index

4x4, 284
16 August in Warsaw, 228

aboriginal title, 114
According to the Evidence, 54, 55
The Accused, 5
AchtNacht, 141, 147, 148
A Civil Action, 5
adjudicative phase. *See* vigilante film: trial phase
Adventures of Martin Cash, 81
Africa, 160
Agatha Christie Theatre Company, 53
Airplane, 6
Akın, Fatih, 146
Albania, 167, 168, 178
alcohol, 91, 109, 119–120, 165, 166, 247
Alibi for a Judge, 54
A Mass for the City of Arras, 229
American criminal procedure, 27, 34–35; criminal procedure compromise, 34; impact on viewers, 34
American popular culture: impact in Britain, 56–58; lifestyle, influence of, 248; political message of vigilante movies, 33, 43–45, 46; private vigilantism in the movies, 32, 46; TV series, 82, 197; vigilante movies, 32–33, 46; vigilante movies and their influence, 1–2, 191, 192, 201, 227, 239, 283
American vigilantism, 27–45; forms of vigilantism, 28–29; history of vigilantism, 28–29; Ku Klux Klan, 28; lynching, 28; police vigilantism, 35–36, 40–41, 43–44; popular culture (*see* American popular culture); public sector vigilantism, 35; San Francisco vigilantism (*see* San Francisco)
An Inspector Calls, 53
Anatomy of a Murder, 5
And Then There Were None, 53
Andringa, Diana, 259n19
anti-pedophile groups and activities. *See* pedophiles
Argentina, 18, 20, 267–293; and American popular culture, 283; feeling of insecurity, 267, 270, 272–274; interruptions in the rule of law, 286; legal culture, 267–269, 281; movies on revenge and vigilantism, 283–285; privatization of security, 268, 273, 285; punitivism, 281–282; self-defense laws, 280–281; vigilantism in, 275–280

Aristotle, 163
Australia, 14, 29, 58, 79–104; community, 88–90, 92, 94–95; frontier zones, 82, 87, 89, 92–93, 95; laws on vigilantism, 83–84; vigilantism in, 82–83. *See also* convictism; indigenous Australians
Australian Gothic, 14, 85–87, 89
Australian popular culture: cars and motorbikes in popular culture, 85, 86–87, 89; colonial narratives, 79–82, 86, 91, 93–94; violence in popular culture, 87–88, 90, 92–95. *See also* Australian Gothic
An Average Little Man (movie), 194–196
An Average Little Man (novel), 190

Bachmeier, Marianne, 138, 145
Bacon, Sir Francis, 3
Bamberski, André, 138–139, 145
banal nationalism, 241, 255–256
Bancroft, Hubert, 31
Barcellos, Caco, 311–312
Barnaby, Jeff, 108, 118, 129n42
Battle of Stanhope, 52
Beccaria, Cesare, 187
Beckford v R [1988] AC 130, 64
Belsatzar, 144–145
The Betrothed, 187–188
Beverly Hills Cop, 8
Beverly Hills Cop 2, 8
bicheiros, 298–299, 303, 306
The Birth of a Nation, 32
Blazing Saddles, 6
blockades. *See* Canada: political protest
bogan, 89
Bolsonaro, Jair, 308, 313
Boudicca, 51
Bourdieu, Pierre, 161, 173, 178
The Brave One, 7, 10, 11, 19, 59, 60
Brazil, 18, 246, 269, 295–322; police violence, 297–298, 299, 300, 302, 309, 311, 312; vigilante justice and the Criminal Code, 303–308; vigilante justice in popular culture, 308–312; vigilantism in, 299–303. *See also* death squad; drug lords; hired killer
Britain, 13, 14, 51–78; Criminal Justice and Immigration Act 2008, 64; Criminal Law (Defence and the Dwelling Act) 2011, 66; firearms certificates, criteria to obtain, 63; impact of American cinema, 56–58; self-defense laws, 62–66; self-defense, limited right to, 63–65; shotgun licence, 63; theater, 52–54; vigilantism in, 52, 60. *See also* British cinema; British TV; folk heroes
British cinema, 56–60; British production tests, 56–58; financial value, 56–57; gun violence, limited, 60; vigilante themes in, 58–60
British TV, 60–62; funding, 61; revenge themes, 62; viewing patterns, 61
Bronson, Charles, 7, 191
Brown, Richard Maxwell, 30
Bürgerwehr. *See* militia
Bus 174, 311
bushrangers, 80–81

Callahan, Harry. See *Dirty Harry*
Calvino, Italo, 191, 201
Camilleri, Andrea, 191
Camorra. A Story of Streets, Women and Crime, 195
Canada, 14–15, 63, 105–132; colonization, 105–106, 114–116, 118–120, 123–124, 127n27, 129n41; courts, 107, 108–115, 123–124; jurisdiction, 107–108, 114–117, 118–119, 129n46; police, 105, 109, 111–112, 116, 120; political protest, 107, 108, 113, 115, 117; rule of law, 107, 112–113, 116–117, 121, 124; sentencing, 110–113; social media and vigilantism, 109–110, 112–113, 126n11–12; sovereignty, claim to,

113–114, 118–119, 128n39. *See also* Indigenous Canadians
Candé, Bruno, 244
Canijo, João, 17, 240–242, 245–255, 256–257, 261n46
Captain Swing, 52
Carandiru, massacre of, 309, 311
cars, 86–7, 89, 284
The Cars That Ate Paris, 85, 86–7
Catharina von Georgien, 143
Catholicism, 188, 241, 251, 255, 256
Cecil, Henry, 54–55
Cerami, Vincezo, 190, 194
charivari, 160
Chega, 243–244, 261n47
children, 14, 61, 91, 93, 120, 171, 226, 252, 271; death of, 108–110, 111, 113, 123; homeless children, 297–298; online abuse of, 67; removal of children by their families, 118–119; sexual assaults on, 138; theft of, 284. *See also* pedophiles
Chlebowicz, Piotr, 214
Christie, Agatha, 53–54
Ciechanowicz, Józef, 214, 219–220
citizenship, 82, 158, 239, 249
Citizens Patrols Corps in Bologna, 182, 184
City of God, 312
civil disobedience. *See* Canada: political protest
clans, 115, 159
Cleverman, 14, 91–4
Coffy, 7, 10, 11
Colette, 56
Confessions of a Police Captain, 193
convictism, 80–82, 91
Coriolanus, 53
corporal punishment, 160
corruption, 42, 158, 194, 298, 300; of the law, 18, 29, 85, 160, 187, 196, 254, 282; moral corruption, 90, 191, 195. *See also* police: corruption
Costa, Pedro, 241, 258n9
Crete, 162, 163, 172

Crocodile Dundee, 87

A Dangerous Toy, 194, 196
Dante Alighieri, 186
Danton, 229
The Danton Case, 229
Dead Man's Shoes, 58, 60
The Dead Pool, 43
Death Sentence, 7, 9, 10, 11, 19
death squad, 40, 44, 296, 297, 302–303, 304, 308
Death Wish (1974), 7, 8, 10, 11, 33, 58, 59, 60, 191, 192, 193, 194, 195
Death Wish (2018), 11
The Debt, 225–226
Deledda, Grazia, 189, 196
Delgamuukw, 114, 127n31
democracy: anti-democratic forces, 140, 190; confidence in, 17, 185, 255–256; democratic deficit, 12–13, 229–230; and penality, 282; vigilantism and the defence of, 137, 146–147; vigilantism and popular culture, 20, 202
Der Besuch der alten Dame, 145
Der Bulle von Tölz, 146
Der Fall Collini, 145, 148
Der Tatortreiniger, 146–147
deterrence, 84, 112
Dexter, 62, 197
Die Füße im Feuer, 144
Dirty Harry and its sequels, 8, 13, 36–43, 192, 198; conservative ideology, 44–45; *Dirty Harry*, 36–40; Harry Callahan, 37–44; messages to viewers, 36, 43–45
Dirty Weekend, 55, 58
Disque Denúncia, 307
dissent, 106, 108, 112, 124
The Divine Comedy, 186
divine judgement, 143–145
doctrine of discovery, 105
Dogman, 195, 201
The Doll, 229
Dominion, 84

Don Matteo, 199
Donna and the Fatman, 55
drug dealers, 32, 59, 184, 245, 252, 254, 278
drug lords, 299, 301, 306–307, 309–310, 311–312
drugs, 31, 112, 118, 120–121, 191, 228, 297
Durkheim, Émile, 196, 270
Dürrenmatt, Friedrich, 145

Eastwood, Clint, 32, 36, 44
The Elephant to Hollywood, 59
Elite Squad, 312
El secreto de sus ojos, 283–284
Emilia Galotti, 143
The Enforcer, 41–42
The Equalizer, 7, 9, 10, 11
The Equalizer 2, 7, 9, 11
Erin Brockovich, 5
Eteros Ego (My Other Self), 169
Execution Squad, 193
extrajudicial executions, 295, 302, 308
An Eye for an Eye (1981), 11
Eye for an Eye (1995), 7, 9, 10, 11

Falling Down, 8
Farewell to Autumn, 229
far-right politics, 1, 15, 243–244, 257, 259n17, 261n47. *See also* Chega; fascism
fascism, 16, 183, 190, 197, 201, 305
The Fatal Shore, 80, 82
Father's Law, 227–228
female sexuality, 245–248, 250, 251, 253
femicide, 164, 270
feud, 92, 159, 170, 182, 184
firearms: deploring of, 196; glorification of, 40; homicide deaths, 63; ownership, 63, 142, 176–177n49, 186, 290–291n34
Fitzek, Sebastian, 141, 147
Five Little Pigs, 53
folk heroes, 51, 80

Fonseca, Rubem, 310–311
football, 241, 243, 255, 259n23
Foucault, Michel, 272
The Four Just Men, 62
The Fourth Angel, 58, 59
Foxy Brown, 32
Francis (pope), 277–278
Franco, Marielle, 309
Fraser, Eliza, 81, 91
Fury, 33

gang, 9, 31, 41, 59, 62, 85, 168, 243, 249, 275
Gangster Squad, 45
garantismo, 281–282
Garland, David, 7
Gegen die Wand, 146
genocide, 106, 113, 120, 123
German popular culture: condemnation of vigilantism, 146; honor killing jn movies, 146; revenge in literature, 142–145; social media and vigilantism, 147
Germany, 15, 19, 20, 135–155; firearms, 142; right to resistance, 137, 146–147; self-administered justice, 135–137; self-administered justice, examples of, 138–139; self-defense laws, 135–137; vigilantism, 139–142. *See also* German popular culture
Get Carter, 58
Giannaris, Konstantinos, 167
The Girl in a Red Coat, 229
Gladue Reports, 111–112, 126n19
Glendower, Owen, 51
Go Back for Murder, 53
Goetz, Bernhard, 8
Gogou, Katerina, 165
Goldoni, Carlo, 187
Gomorrah, 197
"A good bandit is a dead bandit," 295, 306, 313
Gramsci, Antonio, 188
Gran Torino, 7, 11, 47n18

Greece, 16, 19, 20, 157–180; culture of honor, 161–173; family vendetta, 159, 162–164, 168–172; junta regime, 164, 165, 171; vigilantism in the Common Penal Code, 176n49. *See also* Greek popular culture
Greek popular culture: police violence in movies: 164, 167–168; vigilantism in cinema, 164–170; vigilantism in television, 170–172
Grilo, João Mário, 258n8
Gryphius, Andreas, 143
Guests in the Villa, 195
gun possession for a lawful object, 65
The Gun, 194
guns. *See* firearms

Hamlet, 53
Hang 'Em High, 32
Harry Brown, 58, 59
Hays Code, 7
Heine, Heinrich, 144
Hereward the Wake, 51
Hexham Riot, 52
High Plains Drifter, 32
hired killer, 18, 296, 302–303, 304, 308, 313
Homer, 162
honor, 16, 141, 146, 161–173, 189, 196, 197, 201, 229

I Beati Paoli, 189
The Iliad, 162–163, 167
incest, 86, 240, 245, 250–253
Indian Act (Canada), 114, 118, 120, 129n45
Indigenous Australians: Myall Creek Massacre, 82; vigilantism against, 81–83, 91–95
Indigenous Canadians: Canadian law, 106, 115, 125n2; denial of indigenous legal orders, 106; legal orders, 107, 117, 118, 119, 121, 124, 125n2; offenders (*see* Gladue Reports)

inequalities, 91, 165, 188, 201, 239–242, 246, 272–273
injunctions, 115, 127n28
Inspector Montalbano, 199
intergenerational trauma, 119, 121–123
internet vigilantism, 67, 140–141, 147, 148, 152n, 159, 175, 179. *See also* social media
In the Bedroom, 32
Ireland, 51, 57, 66; self-defense, limited right of, 66; self-defense laws, 66
Isle of Dogs, 56
Itaguaí, 300–301
Italian Mafia, 184, 189, 190, 193, 195; revenge against the Mafia, 198; Mafia TV series, 197–198
Italian popular culture: ambivalence toward private justice, 193, 196, 198–201; and American popular culture, 192, 197, 198, 201; condemnation of vigilantism, 193, 195; distrust towards law, 187–188, 196; male hero, 195; police vigilantism, 193, 194, 198; private justice in literature and theatre, 186–192; self-defense in Italian TV programs, 199–200; vigilante movies, 192–196
Italy, 4, 7, 16, 20, 145, 181–211; family, importance of, 198; fear of crime, 184–185, 199, 200; firearms, 186; judiciary, 184, 190, 196; homicide rate, 182, 183, 184, 185; self-defense laws, 182, 183, 184, 185, 186. *See also* fascism; Italian Mafia; Italian popular culture; squadrismo

Joe, 8
Joker, 8
judiciary, 28, 29, 184, 185, 190, 196, 201
Jul, 228
jury trials, 64, 276, 277, 282, 300–301, 304–307

katzenmusik, 160
Kelly, Ned, 80–81
Kersey, Paul. See *Death Wish*
Kick-Ass, 56
Kiliński, Jan, 215
Kind Hearts and Coronets, 60
Kingdom without Land, 228
Kleist, Heinrich von, 143, 148
Koemtzis, Nikos, 164, 165
Kościuszko Uprising, 215

L.A. Confidential, 45
larrikins, 87, 89
The Last Dwarf Geese, 166
Law Abiding Citizen, 7, 9, 10, 11
law and film movement, 5
"law of silence," 306–307
Leere Herzen, 140
Leone, Sergio, 192
Lessing, Gotthold Ephraim, 143
Lethal Weapon, 8
local neighborhood patrols, 28, 83, 158, 184, 296, 299
Lopes, Fernando, 258n8
Lopes, Tim, 309
Los Simuladores, 284–285
Luddites, 52
Lula (Luiz Inacio Lula da Silva), 313
Lynch, 226
lynching: attempted lynchings in contemporary Italy, 186; in contemporary Argentina, 275, 277; of David Moreira, 277; of Donato Carretta, 183; of Gabriel Fernández, 277; of Luís Giovani Rodrigues, 244; and social inequality, 273; at Włodowo, 213–214, 219–221. See also American popular culture: vigilante movies; American vigilantism

Machado, Mário, 243
machismo, 164
Mad Max, 85, 87
The Magnificent Seven, 5

Magnum Force, 40–41
Make It before God, 229
The Manhunt, 194
Mani, 162, 163, 170, 172
manslaughter, 64, 66, 137, 139
Manzoni, Alessandro, 187–188
Marcus Aurelius, 3
Marlowe, Christopher, 52
Marshal Rocca, 199
Martin, Tony, 65
Mascagni, Pietro, 188
masculinity, 85, 87, 88, 142, 161, 169, 173, 195, 276
Medallions, 229
Melo, Patrícia, 310–311
Mendel from Gdańsk, 229
The Merchant of Venice, 53
methodological approach, 20n4, 164, 173, 181, 241, 296, 300
Mexico, 12, 18, 269, 272
Meyer, Conrad Ferdinand, 144
Michael Kohlhaas, 143–144, 148
militia, 1, 135, 137, 139–141, 297–299, 301, 312
The Molly Maguires, 19
Monteiro, Alcino, 244
motorbikes, 85, 87
Mystic River, 32n18

Naked Gun, 6
neoliberalism, 160, 261, 280
Neves, Pedro, 258n8
Nibelungenlied, 142
Night Falls on Manhattan, 34
night of August 15, 217–219, 227, 228
Non-Divine Comedy, 229
November Uprising, 216–218, 227
The November Uprising, 1830–1831, 227

obligation to retreat, position on, 64–66
The Octopus, 198
The Odyssey, 162, 163
O Ehthros Mou (The Enemy Within), 168

Ola Einai Dromos (Everything Is a Road), 166
Omiros (The Hostage), 167
Opérette, 229
organized crime, 19, 158, 184, 192, 194, 197, 198, 274, 296, 298–299, 304, 308. *See also* Italian Mafia; Russian Mafia
Othello, 53
Outlaw, 58, 59
Overstall, Richard, 116
The Ox-Bow Incident, 32

Paraggelia, 164, 165, 170
parking, 214–215
patriarchy, 161, 166, 168, 169, 171, 172, 246, 254, 256
The Peasants, 229
pedagogy of cruelty, 268, 270–271
pedophiles, 67, 87, 89, 90, 138, 214, 270
Peppermint, 7, 9, 10, 11
The Persuaders, 62
The Pianist, 229
Pigliaru, Antonio, 192
pipelines, 108, 114–115, 117, 124, 127n27
Pirandello, Luigi, 188, 189
Pitbull, 226
Poland, 16–17, 19, 20, 213–239; necessary defense, 223–224; presidential pardon, 221, 226; purpose of punishment in Criminal Code, 221–222; self-defense laws, 221–224, 226; vigilante actions against Jews, 229; vigilante justice events, 215–221; vigilantism in literature, 228–229; vigilantism in movies, 224–228. *See also* lynching at Włodowo; night of August 15; November Uprising; Warsaw Uprising
police: 2013 strike and vigilantism, 278–280; corruption, 45, 59, 60, 167, 254, 274, 299, 312; failures of, 55, 140, 190, 194, 220, 228, 254; refusal of police action, 194, 250, 272; and vigilantism, 193, 194, 198. *See also* American vigilantism: public sector vigilantism; police violence
police violence: controlled under the rule of law, 34, 35; in films, 36, 45, 167–168, 249, 311, 312; killings committed by, 302, 309; on racial or ethnic basis, 35, 244, 254, 259n23. *See also* death squad; police
Portrait of a Judge, 55
Portugal, 17, 19, 20, 239–263; Blacks, 244, 252, 259n19–23; colonialism, 239–244; community, 241, 242, 248–249, 254, 255, 256; crime, racialization of, 244; criminality, rates of, 243; democracy, 239, 240, 242, 243, 255–256, 257, 257n1; dictatorship, 241, 245, 246, 256, 257n1; European integration of, 239, 240, 242, 256–257, 257n1; family in popular culture, 246–247, 250–253, 254; police violence, 244, 249, 254, 259n23; Portuguese emigration, 247, 248–249, 251, 253; social policies, 240, 252, 254–255; tensions between tradition and modernity, 245–247, 248, 257. *See also* Chega
"Pote tha Kanei Ksasteria," 163, 171
preemptive strike, 64
private security, 244–245, 268, 273, 285, 302
Promising Young Woman, 7, 11
Proud Boys, 1

rape revenge film, 12, 17, 58, 71n, 87, 192, 195
rape in vigilante film: as a means of revenge, 110, 272; and patriarchy, 168–169; to prevent a rape, 36, 120; revenge for, 32, 42, 56, 58, 172, 228, 252, 267, 283; victims of, 33, 85, 90, 168, 169, 247
reasonable force defence, 64, 65, 66

Rebetiko, 164, 166, 178n54
Red, 11
Red Bandits of Mawddwy, 51
refugees, 83, 140–141, 168
Relatos Salvajes, 284
residential school, 118–120, 122–123
retreat. *See* obligation to retreat
Revenge, 7
Reynolds, Henry, 81–82, 93
Rhymes for Young Ghouls, 108, 118–124
right-wing politics, 169, 313; and vigilantism, 141, 148, 184–185
right-wing extremism. *See* far-right politics
Rigoletto, 188, 201
Rebecca Riots, 52
religion. *See* Catholicism
Robert the Bruce, 51
Robin Hood, 4, 52, 81; films, 5, 21n16
Rob Roy, 51
Rocco Schiavone, 198
Rodrigues, Luís Giovani, 244
Roma, 185, 229, 244, 252
Rome, the Other Face of Violence, 194
Ronaldo, Cristiano, 255
ronde. *See* local neighborhood patrols
rough music, 160
Royal Canadian Mounted Police (RCMP). *See* Canada: police
Royal Commission on Aboriginal Peoples (RCAP), 105
rule of death, 299–303, 313
Russian Mafia, 250
Rustic Chivalry, 188
R v. Suter, 107–112, 120, 123, 125n7
R v. Vollrath, 107–108, 111–113, 120, 123

San Francisco: 1851 committee, 29, 30–31; 1856 committee, 29–31; assessment of vigilantism in, 30–31; depiction in *Dirty Harry* movies, 38, 44; Chinatown squad, 31, 35; vigilantism, 29–31
samosud, 160

Sardinia, 182, 189, 192; *Bandits of Orgosolo*, 192; Barbagian Revenge, 192
Schirach, Ferdinand von, 145
Sciascia, Leonardo, 189–190, 197
Scotland, 51, 62, 66; self-defense, limited right of, 65; self-defense laws, 65–66
The Secret River, 91
Seeking Justice, 7, 11, 19
Selbstjustiz. *See* Germany: self-administered justice
Settled Out of Court, 54
The Seven Samurai, 5
Shakespeare, William, 52–53
Shame, 14, 85–88
The Shield, 47n16
The Shoemakers, 229
The Siege at Trencher's Farm, 55
Sir Michael and Colonel Wolodyjowski, 228–229
Snowtown, 14, 88–90
social media, 20, 67, 147, 201, 277; support to vigilante justice, 109–110, 112–113, 126n11–12; and vigilante groups, 83. *See also* internet vigilantism
Solo: A Star Wars Story, 56
The Spring to Come, 229
squadrismo, 16, 183, 185, 201
stand-your-ground law, 14, 28, 68, 83
The Star Chamber, 34
Straw Dogs, 55
Street Law, 194, 195
Sudden Impact, 7, 42
The Sun Shines Bright, 33
Sweet Country, 81

Targowica, 215–216
Tassios, Pavlos, 164
Taxi Driver, 8, 33
The Tempest, 53
terra nullius, 105
terrorism, 42, 140–141, 184, 243
They Won't Forget, 33, 33n20

Ti Psihi Tha Paradoseis Mori?, 171–172
Titus Andonicus, 53
To Kill a Mockingbird, 5, 33
Tomeo, Vincenzo, 193
tragedy (dramatic composition), 163, 170, 250, 255, 257; revenge tragedy, 187
The Train, 226–227
Tréfaut, Sérgio, 258n8
trespass law, 64, 66, 84, 116
Truth and Reconciliation Commission (TRC), 105, 113
Tsafoulias, Sotiris, 169
Tsemperopoulos, Yorgos, 168
Tsifteteli, 165
The Unexpected Guest, 53–54
The Unforgiven, 32

United Irishmen, 51
United Kingdom. *See* Britain
United States, 6, 13, 27–50, 57, 63, 158, 271, 305. *See also* American criminal procedure; American popular culture; American television series; American vigilantism; San Francisco; stand-your-ground law
U.S. *See* United States
Unterleuten, 148

Varella, Drauzio, 311
Veggos, Thanassis, 167
Vendetta, 58, 60
Verdi, Giuseppe, 188
The Verdict, 5
Verga, Giuseppe, 188
Vieira, Leonel, 258n9
A Vigilante, 7, 11, 59, 60
vigilante: bystander vigilante, 108,113; justice vigilante, 4, 5, 19; power vigilante, 4, 14, 19, 151n21, 183
vigilante films: final film scene, 10–11; Hollywood template, 6–12; justice system malfunctioning, 6, 184; narrative trope, 8, 194; and social critique, 19; trial phase, 9
vigilantism: civic centric explanation of, 160; criminal selectivity and, 270, 273; definition of, 3–4, 79–80; 239, devolutionist perspective of, 160; evolutionist perspective of, 160; and the failure of the state, 222; "new vigilantism," 67; racial or ethnic motivations of, 158, 161, 185, 244; reactive, 82–83, 87–88, 95; state centric explanation of, 160; transvigilantism, 83, 91, 93–94; trigger events of, 270, 272–273, 277; typology of, 158, 296, 308. *See also* vigilante; vigilantism against immigrants
vigilantism against immigrants: Australia, 83; Germany, 140–142; Greece, 167–168; Italy, 185, 195; Portugal, 244
Villaverde, Teresa, 258n8
violence against women, 164–165, 239, 247–248, 251, 256
Voulgaris, Pantelis, 166

Wake in Fright, 85
Wallace, William, 51
Waltzing Matilda, 79, 94
Ward, Russell, 80, 82
Warsaw Uprising, 215–216
Weber, Max, 182, 270, 303
Western (genre), 5, 32, 85, 190, 192
Wet'suwet'en, 114–117, 134
Williams, Gordon, 55
William Tell, 62
Witness for the Prosecution, 53
Wojniusz, Józef, 219
Wolf Creek, 87
The Wolf and the Mushroom, 121, 123

Young Mr. Lincoln, 33, 34
The Young Philadelphians, 5
Youth of Chopin, 227

Zahavi, Helen, 55–56
zajazd (foray), 213

Zeh, Juli, 140, 147–148
Zeibekiko, 164

About the Editors and Contributors

Peter Robson has an LLB from St. Andrews University and a PhD from Strathclyde University. He is a solicitor, sits as a judge in H.M. Courts and Tribunals Service dealing with disability issues, and is professor of social welfare law at the University of Strathclyde School of Law. He has written on law, film, and television in journals and edited collections including coediting *Law and Film* (with Stefan Machura) in 2001. His most recent film work (with Steve Greenfield and Guy Osborn) *Film and the Law: The Cinema of Justice*, was published in 2010 and updates the influential first edition. He is coeditor, with Jessica Silbey, of *Law and Justice on the Small Screen* (2012), with Jennifer L. Schulz, of *A Transnational Study of Law and Justice on TV* (2016) and *Ethnicity, Gender, and Diversity: Law and Justice on TV* (2018). He has also published essays on law and theater, women lawyers on TV, law in modern popular fiction, British lawyers on TV, vengeance in popular culture and revenge, and justice and rape on the cinema screen.

Ferdinando Spina, PhD, is associate professor of Sociology of Law at the University of Salento, where he teaches courses on the sociology of law, sociology of crime, crime and media. He is the author of several publications, including the book *Il doppio codice: Diritto e tecnologie della comunicazione* (*The Double Code: Law and Media Technology*, 2012). He has recently published essays on law and justice on Italian television, crime films, and revenge and vigilantism in Italian popular culture. He has been visiting scholar at the International Institute for the Sociology of Law in Oñati, visiting researcher at Coventry University, and Jinan University (Guangzhou). He has been on the Executive Board of the Research Committee on Sociology of Law of the Italian Sociological Association (2011–2018).

* * *

Michael Asimow is Dean's Executive Professor, Santa Clara Law School, and Professor of Law Emeritus, UCLA Law School. He was visiting professor of law at Stanford Law School from 2010–2019. Michael is co-author of *Real to Reel: Truth and Trickery in Courtroom Movies* (2021) (with Paul Bergman), a book about the courtroom movies of the past and present. He is also co-author of *Law and Popular Culture: A Course Book* (2020) (with Jessica Silbey), a teaching book for graduate and undergraduate classes that study the intersection of law and pop culture. He has published many articles about law and popular culture, including "Bad Lawyers in the Movies" *Nova L. Rev.* (2000) 24:533 (2000), "When the Lawyer Knows the Client Is Guilty: Client Confessions in Legal Ethics, Popular Culture, and Literature," *So. Calif. Interdiscip. L. Rev.* (2009) 18:229, and "Jewish Lawyers in Popular Culture" (forthcoming). Michael also co-authored a course book on administrative law, *State and Federal Administrative Law* (5th ed. 2020) (with Ron Levin), as well as *California Practice Guide: Administrative Law* (2021). He has written numerous articles on state and federal administrative law as well as comparative administrative law, including "Five Models of Administrative Adjudication" (2015) *Amer. J. Comparative L.* 63:3. He is a consultant to the Administrative Conference of the United States. His email address is asimow@law.ucla.edu and his website address is michaelasimow.com.

Pedro Fortes is a visting professor of law at the Doctoral Programme of the National Law School at the Federal University of Rio de Janeiro (PPGD/UFRJ) and a public prosecutor at the Attorney General's Office of Rio de Janeiro, Brazil. He holds a DPhil (Oxford), a JSM (Stanford), a LLM (Harvard), a MBE (COPPE), a LLB (UFRJ), and a BA (PUC-Rio). Recipient of three teaching awards, he has taught complex litigation, constitutional law, and criminal law and procedure. His research interests include law and development, law and popular culture, and law and technology. Between 2012 and 2017, he was the editor-in-chief of the FGV Law School series (Cadernos FGV Direito Rio) and edited two books on law, legal education, and popular culture. Additionally, he edited the special issue of the *Journal of the Oxford Centre for Social Legal Studies* on law and popular culture in 2017, together with coeditor Michael Asimow. In this field, he coined the expression "symbolic affirmative action" and discusses the theme of (un)equal representation in "Affirmative Cinema: When Film-Makers Defend Minorities" in Michael Asimow et al., *Law and Popular Culture: International Perspectives* (2014), "Lights, Camera, Affirmative Action: Does Hollywood Protect Minorities?" (JOxCSLS, Special Issue 2017). He has been visiting professor at the WB NUJS (Kolkata), visiting scholar at the Goethe Universität (Frankfurt), and visiting researcher at the MPI (Hamburg and Frankfurt). Fortes currently chairs the WG Law and Development at the RCSL, the CRN Law and Development at the LSA, and the stream Exploring Legal Borderlands at the SLSA.

Júlia Garraio is researcher at the Center for Social Studies of the University of Coimbra, integrating the research group Humanities, Migrations and Peace Studies. She is a researcher of the project DECODEM(De)Coding Masculinities: Towards an enhanced understanding of media's role in shaping perceptions of masculinities in Portugal. She is co-founder of the international research group SVAC-Sexual Violence in Armed Conflict (https://warandgender.net/about/). She integrates the International Editorial Board of the *European Journal of Women's Studies* (https://journals.sagepub.com/editorial-board/EJW). She has published extensively about narratives and the politics of representing sexual violence in literature and the media. She has conducted research in the area of German literature and culture, namely about the cultural memories of the rape of German women and girls in the context of World War II. Her work examines how women's experiences in wartime were appropriated by gendered national scripts and how writers and artists engaged with those scripts. She has conducted research about other contexts of sexual violence: Portuguese colonialism and its legacies, Angolan wars, the 2011 war in Libya, contemporary migrations. Her current research interests include sexual violence, masculinities, feminisms, nationalism, comparative literature, and media.

Rebecca Johnson is professor of law, and associate director of the Indigenous Legal Research Unit at the University of Victoria, Canada. Her research and teaching engage with criminal law, business associations, legal theory and law and film. Before that, she clerked for Madame Justice Claire L'Heureux-Dubé at the Supreme Court of Canada, and completed her LLM and SJD at the University of Michigan. The work there resulted in her award-winning book, *Taxing Choices: the Intersection of Class, Gender, Parenthood and the Law*. A pioneer in Canadian law-and-film scholarship, she has written on such topics as same-sex family formation, colonialism, dissent, mothers and babies in prison, cinematic violence, the Western, affect and emotion, and Inuit cinema. She co-edited a special issue of the *Canadian Journal of Women and the Law* on "Law, Film and Feminism," and has a blog dedicated to the same.

Nickos Myrtou is a specialized teaching personnel and a PhD candidate in the Department of Communication and Media Studies of the National and Kapodistrian University of Athens where he teaches television and radio production as well as documentary production. While his curriculum focuses mainly on technical aspects of audio-visual production, his research interests and publications also incorporate content, story-telling, and tropes analysis. He holds a BA and MA degree from the same department and has worked in number of research projects, most notably on the H2020 iMedia Cities. As a member of the department's Audiovisual Media Laboratory, he oversees student productions and research on new technologies and practices. His MA thesis explores the new medium for documentarians and how the basic schools of documentary have transcended in the age of Internet while his PhD examines the transformative extent of digital media on archives and documentaries. He is a guest lecturer on the yearly project "Dialogue of Civilizations: Greece: Then and Now—The Greek Media" of Northeastern University. Also, as a videographer and editor, he was worked in several short films and documentaries. He edited the book *Television Production, Video Montage, Technology: Art, and Technique* and has authored articles for major technical publications about montage techniques and post-production.

Joanna Osiejewicz is associate professor and head of Department of International Legal Communication, Faculty of Applied Linguistics, University of Warsaw. She received PhD in applied linguistics from University of Warsaw in 2010, PhD in law from Lazarsky University in 2013, and habilitation in Law from University of Gdańsk in 2018. Her research interests are: legal communication, global governance, fragmentation of law, harmonization of law, transnational law, application of international law and European Union law. Vice-Rector's Proxy for International Cooperation at the University of Warsaw (2020–2024), seconded to Management Committee of the 4EU+ Alliance. Board Member of University of Warsaw Foundation. Creator and editor-in-chief of *Journal of International Legal Communication* (Publisher: University of Warsaw). Sworn translator and interpreter for German in Poland. Attorney-at-law at the Bar Association in Warsaw.

Lili Pâquet specializes in writing studies, rhetoric, and literary criticism, with particular interest in contemporary forms of authorship. Her book, *Crime Fiction from a Professional Eye*, examines the crime novels of women who have previously worked in the criminal justice system as lawyers, forensic experts, and detectives. Her current research focuses on digital literatures, and interdisciplinary climate change rhetorics. Before joining the staff at UNE, Lili completed a PhD at the University of Sydney and lectured in the Writing Department there.

Stamatis Poulakidakos is assistant professor at the Department of Communication and Digital Media of the University of Western Macedonia. He holds a BA and a PhD from the Department of Communication and Media Studies (NKUA), and an MA degree in new media, information, and society from London School of Economics (LSE). He has taken part in many research projects and has participated in various Greek and international conferences. He has authored the book *Propaganda and Public Discourse: The*

Presentation of the MoU by the Greek Media. In addition, he has published several papers on issues having to do with political communication, propaganda, social media and the public sphere, political advertisements, protests, and other media-related issues.

Franziska Stürmer, PhD, is currently working as post-doc at Julius-Maximilians-Universität Würzburg, Germany. She received her PhD in 2014 with a study on Thomas Mann's "Doktor Faustus" and has since done research on law in popular media and on transcultural identity in contemporary literature. Stürmer's recent publications on law and media include: Recht Populär: Populärkulturelle Rechtsdarstellungen in aktuellen Texten und Medien, Nomos (with Patrick Meier, 2016); "Love and Other Flights—Legal Subtexts and the Law as a Strategy of Reader Guidance in Bernhard Schlink's Liebesfluchten" (also with Patrick Meier; *Law and Literature* 2(28): 255–75); "Germany: Diversity on its Way," in: Peter Robson/Jennifer Schulz (ed.): *Ethnicity, Gender and Diversity: Law and Justice on TV*. Since 2021, Stürmer is also head of the editorial management of the yearbook "Jahrbuch für Kulinaristik" and the book series "Wissenschaftsforum Kulinaristik."

Sebastian Viqueira, is lawyer, master in sociology and assistant professor of Sociology of Law, Law and Social Sciences School, National University of Córdoba, Argentina. Researcher at the Centre of Social and Legal Studies at the same university. He has worked on Lay Participacion and Juries, Legal professions and Legal Culture. He recently published, with other researchers, the book *En el estrado. La consolidación de las estrategias participativas en la justicia penal* (Inside Courts. The consolidation of participatory strategies in penal justice).

www.ingramcontent.com/pod-product-compliance
Lightning Source LLC
Chambersburg PA
CBHW021341300426
44114CB00012B/1026